Living with Children 5-10

Living with Children 5-10

A Parent's Guide

The Open University in association with the Health Education Council

The Open University Press
Milton Keynes

Produced by
Harper & Row Ltd.
28 Tavistock Street,
London, WC2E 7PN.

Managing Editor: Michael Forster
Production Editor: Martin Creese
Design/Art direction: Richard Dewing and Nigel Soper, Millions Design, London
Editor: Denise Winn

Open University Course Team: Monica Darlington, Nick Farnes, Roger Harrison, Jane Rosoman, Pam Shakespeare, Jane Wolfson

Academic Co-ordinator for Community Education: Nick Farnes

Consultants: Nick Balmforth, Len Bloom, Richard Bourne, Mike Dick, Jane Dobbin, Rosalind Draper, Patrick Easen, Jane Farnes, Gill Feeley, Ronny Flynn, Elizabeth Grugeon, Jenny Lewis, Janet Maybin, Robert Rapoport, Florence Robinson, Jessie Shakespeare, Martyn Shakespeare, Tim Steward, Judith Ward, Barbara Webb, Richard White, Graham Williams

External Assessor: Professor Hazel Francis, Institute of Education, University of London

Course Team Secretaries: Lin Dell, Corrine Dowle

The course was produced in association with the Health Education Council and the Open University would like to express its gratitude to them. The Open University would also like to acknowledge the value of collaboration with the Scottish Health Education group.

British Library Cataloguing in Publications Data
Open University Childhood 5-10 Course Team
Living with Children 5-10 – A Parent's Guide

Living with children 5–10
1. Children-Management
649'.124 HQ769

ISBN 0 335 100090

Phototypeset by Oliver Burridge & Co. Ltd., Crawley
Printed and bound by New Interlitho S.P.A., Milan

Contents

What is this book about? viii

A community education course from the Open University ix

1 **The developing child** 1
Physical change, physical growth 2
Drawing, painting and writing 6
Understanding the physical world 10
Understanding other points of view 18
Learning right from wrong 26

2 **A child's world** 32
A daily diary 34
Let's play 38
Your child's temperament 40
Boys and girls 44
Friends 46
In a world of their own 50
Toys 54
Children's folklore 56
Fashions and fads 58
Standing on their own two feet 60

3 **Family patterns** 64
Family life 66

	Families are...	70
	Family roles	74
	Family work	78
	Working mothers	82
	House rules	86
	Pocket money	90
4	**Family feelings**	92
	Inside the family	94
	Strictly for the family?	98
	Children's fights	100
	Facing ups and downs	106
	Words matter	110
	Family tension	112
	Family break-up	116
	Family change	120
5	**Learning the basics**	124
	How schools are organised	126
	Learning at school	128
	Talking	130
	Learning to read	134
	Reading at home	138
	Writing and spelling	142
	Maths at school	148
	Maths at home	152

6 **Getting on with school** 156
A new school 158
Fitting in 164
Trouble with other children 172
Making progress 176
Approaching the school 182
Getting involved with the school 184

7 **Out and about** 188
People... 190
...Places 196
Something different 200
Outdoor risks and hazards 204
Adventures and trouble 210
Mum, can I join a club? 212

8 **Getting involved** 220
A caring society 222
Finding care for children 226
Action! setting up a playscheme 230
Planning to play 238
Branching out 240
Self-help schemes 244

List of organisations 248
Further reading 250

What is this book about?

You will find that the chapters in this book fall into four sections, each of two chapters.

The first two chapters **The developing child** and **A child's world** deal with the way in which your child grows and changes during the years between five and ten, and give you some insight into the way children feel about, and react to, the world about them.

The next two chapters, **Family patterns** and **Family feelings** focus on your family and what is going on there. You'll be looking at the work your family does – both jobs around the house and what happens when mothers go out to work – and at pocket money and house rules. Children's fights, family tension and break-up are also dealt with. If you decide you want to make some changes you'll find some suggestions here.

School is the subject of chapters five and six. **Learning the basics** looks at what is taught to children in primary and middle schools and **Getting on with school** looks at choosing a school and helping your child to get on well once he's there.

Chapters seven **Out and about** and eight **Getting involved** look at what happens to your child when he wants to go out into the community and find new friends and new opportunities. How can you help him? And could you help yourself at the same time?

This course deals with boys and girls equally, so don't worry when we say 'he does this' or 'she does that' – unless it is made clear otherwise, just apply what is said to your own child, whichever sex. We've also talked of 'your child' though many parents will have more than one child in the five-to-ten age group. It is up to you whether you repeat the activities for each child, or just do them with the child you think most suitable.

Don't expect that you are going to get easy straightforward answers to all your questions. Every child in every family is different so all their answers will be different too. And as you well know from your experience as a parent, easy answers are in short supply anyway! But we hope that you will enjoy working through this book with your child – and that you will be able to draw from it whatever fits your needs and those of your child.

A community education course from the Open University

This book has been written as part of an Open University course called *Childhood 5–10*.

Childhood 5–10 is an Open University community education course which deals with the practical concerns of everyday life. It has been produced by the Open University in association with the Health Education Council.

Childhood 5–10 is a learn-at-home course. There are no classes, no teachers and no set hours. You can study where and when you like and you work through the materials in whatever order you choose. To give you a rough idea of how much work is involved we estimate that if you were to study the course over eight weeks you would need to spend about five to six hours a week on it. However, you can spread the work out over a longer period because there is plenty of time allowed to complete the assignments after the broadcasts finish. (See below.)

What's in the course?

This book – *Living with Children 5–10: a parent's guide* – is the course book and forms the core of the course.

Four television programmes – which have been especially made for this course. The programmes follow themes dealt with in this book. To find out when these programmes are broadcast, look in the *Radio Times* from October to December and again in January to March each year. Registered students are sent a broadcast calendar and Broadcast Notes about the programmes.

TV1 Play: Children spend much of their day involved in play activities. What do you as a parent think is acceptable play?

TV2 Family Matters: All families are bound to have disagreements. How can you prevent them where possible or deal with them when they arise?

TV3 Getting used to School: Going to school is a child's first big step out of the home. What sort of things go on in a modern primary classroom and why is school such a different experience from home?

TV4 Self-help projects: Working together with other people can be effective and it can be fun. How do self-help schemes operate and what's it like to be involved in one?

A resource pack which contains the following things:

Television notes – which help you to get more out of watching the television programmes.

A cassette tape and notes – which use real examples to examine issues like how parents can help their children to develop language and reading skills, and how they can get a fair deal from professionals like teachers and doctors.

A course guide – which explains how all the parts of the course are related. It suggests various ways to follow the course, and helps you choose the study plan which best suits you. It also explains schemes to help students contact each other and form a group. Of course, you might like to form your own group by persuading some of your friends to join at the same time as you. (The course is specially designed to help you learn on your own but you may find it helpful to share your learning, your experiences and problems with other students.)

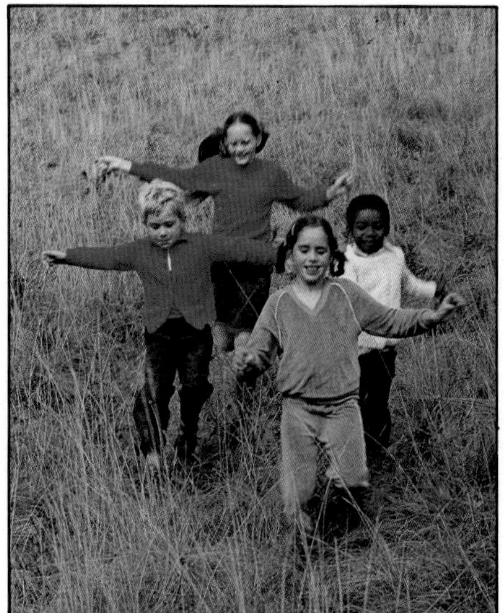

Assignment booklet – this contains four quiz-style assignments to check your understanding of the course. If you complete them satisfactorily, you will be sent a letter of Course Completion.

The resource pack also contains a selection of leaflets and other material.

Other community education courses

The community education courses from the Open University deal with the practical concerns of everyday life. They're written for anyone who wants to make his or her life better. All the courses are presented in an easy-to-read style which helps you get to the root of matters that concern you. They help you decide whether you need to make changes in your life and to weigh up what's best for you.

Courses for parents

This book is part of the third of three courses for parents. The first two are called *The First Years of Life* and *The Pre-School Child* and deal with pregnancy and childbirth, right through the toddling stage up till the time your child is ready to start school.

Courses for consumers

There are two courses for consumers, *Consumer Decisions*, which helps you decide the best ways of managing and spending your money, and *Energy in the Home*, to help you save on your fuel bills. There's a course to help school governors called *Governing Schools*, and another called *Health Choices* to help you assess your lifestyle and decide whether to change it in any way.

If you want more details of any of these courses or wish to sign on for *Childhood 5–10* write to:
A.S.C.O., The Open University,
PO Box 76, Milton Keynes MK7 6AN.

Living with Children 5-10

The developing child

Parents will know from experience how dramatic are the changes that occur in their children between birth and five years of age.

The big physical changes that take place between five and ten may not be quite so obvious, but exist nonetheless. Children grow taller, their shape changes and they acquire and develop new physical skills. These skills vary between big, whole-body movements like jumping and skipping and the closely-controlled movements of the hand necessary for drawing and writing.

Children's thinking changes in important ways during these years, but how do you find out what's going on? You can play special games with your child to see how his understanding of the physical world and of other people's views is changing: such games are included in this chapter.

It's better to do things with him and see for yourself how he is developing than to read about other children and compare him with them. Don't worry about whether he is keeping pace.

All children go through different stages at different speeds (you'll certainly have noticed this if you have brought up more than one child) and the only person that it's fair to compare your child with is himself. What does he do now that he didn't used to do? Development is not a race, and each child sets his own pace.

The understanding and insight you gain from working through these games with your child and repeating them some time later will enable you to see and overcome some of the difficulties your child faces as he learns about the world and about people.

You can help by providing plenty of opportunities for learning and by explaining things to him. It takes a lot of living for his abilities and understanding to develop.

1

Physical changes, physical growth

The bigger your child's body grows, the more he dares to use it.

We can think of physical growth as taking place in three main stages: infancy, childhood and adolescence. The change from infancy to childhood occurs before five and the change to adolescence usually occurs after ten. Both these stages involve very noticeable physical changes.

While the changes that occur during the middle years, five to ten, are not quite so dramatic, there is still a lot that is going on. Your child is not simply growing taller and heavier. He is learning to use the physical skills that go together with getting bigger and stronger. Skills like running, jumping and hopping that involve the whole body and large movements.

Physical growth and physical skills are therefore closely related. But children develop at different rates and there are no hard and fast rules about how tall or how skilled a six-year-old should be, although of course there are general guidelines which help us tell, on average, that everything is going all right.

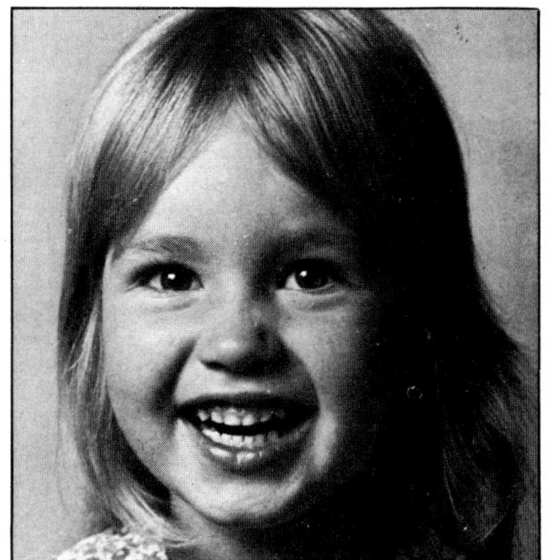

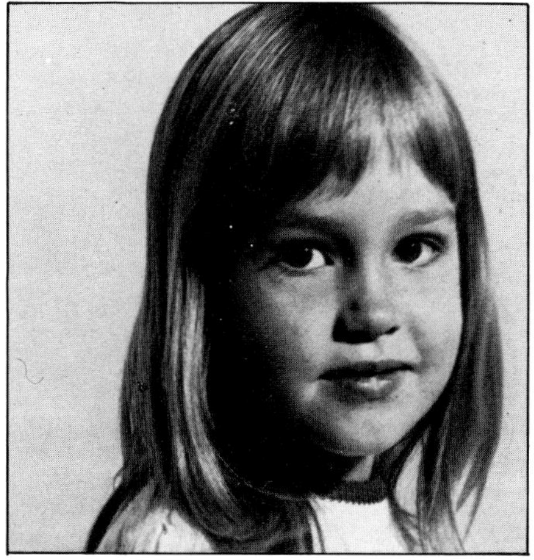

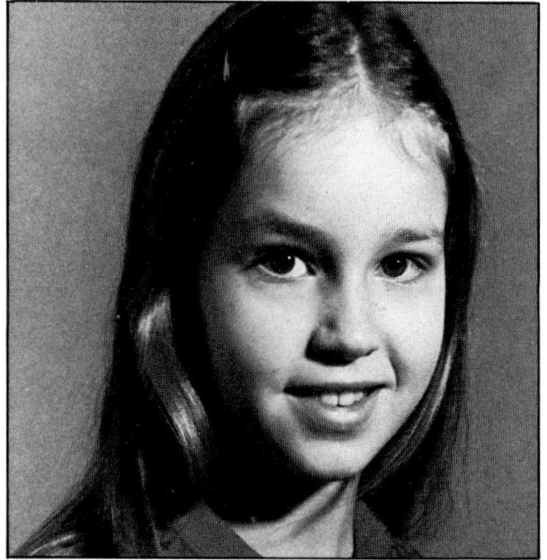

Growth

Look at these photos of Laura. In the first, she is five years old. In the last she is ten years old. See the difference. A five-year-old still has a chubby baby face. Then her jaw and chin lengthen. Head and eyes seem extra big in children because rapid growth of these parts occurs early. By the age of eight, a child's head is ninety per cent of its adult size.

It isn't just the parts of the body that we can see which are growing. Parts inside are growing too. The heart, lungs and digestive organs all keep pace to cope with the increasing demands made upon them.

Weight and height

Growth in all parts of the body results in increasing weight and height. It's very difficult to say what is the right height and weight for any child. There is an enormous variation. You can only say that if a six-year-old is taller than most six-year-olds he should also be heavier. And a child of six who is heavier than most should also be taller.

Bearing that in mind, you can see that it is pointless to worry just because your child is smaller/taller than the rest of his classmates. His eventual height is not necessarily governed by the height he is at any one age. Some growth-rates slow down, whilst others speed up.

Boys of between five and ten tend to be a little bit taller and heavier than girls of the same age. Also, your child at five is likely to be bigger than his grandfather or her grandmother was at the same age. Better food and housing and fewer infectious illnesses have all led to more rapid growth.

The height and weight tables shown opposite are the average heights and weights for children in Great Britain. You might like to see where your child fits in on the chart. But remember that these are only averages and there is no need to worry if your child is slightly above or below.

Puberty

Puberty is the time when boys and girls start to grow very fast again. Their sexual organs are starting to mature. For girls this means the start of menstruation (periods), the development of breasts, hips and pubic hair. Boys' shoulders broaden, sex organs develop rapidly and hair appears around the genitals and on the face.

Huge changes also take place in their feelings as a result of this new fast growth. They have to adjust to their new sexual identity. They may also be a bit clumsy for a while when they are getting used to their new sizes. But this is just the start of their preparation for adulthood.

Some children start this rapid growth at nine or ten years old. But puberty can occur at any time between nine and sixteen years. Girls tend to reach puberty earlier than boys. But when the boys do start growing, they grow much faster than girls. They quickly become taller and heavier, but this normally happens when they are well past ten.

Physical skills

There are no such clearly defined stages during the physical growth of a child between five and ten. But there are stages in the development of their physical skills, such as playing ball, bicycle riding and skipping.

It is fairly easy to notice changes in these areas of development. For example, when your child first rides a bicycle alone, or climbs to the top of a tree. Children will develop different skills at different times. However, the learning and improving of skills usually follows a path that is the same for all children. So riding a bike safely comes *after* being wobbly on it but *before* riding with no hands, or doing tricks. Also, skills need practice. If your ten-year-old has never ridden a bike before, you wouldn't expect her to learn straight away.

Boys			Girls		
	Average height	**Average weight**		**Average height**	**Average weight**
5 years	108.0 cm	18.5 kg	5 years	107.5 cm	17.5 kg
6 years	114.3 cm	20.5 kg	6 years	113.7 cm	19.5 kg
7 years	120.0 cm	22.5 kg	7 years	119.4 cm	21.5 kg
8 years	125.6 cm	24.5 kg	8 years	124.8 cm	24.0 kg
9 years	131.0 cm	27.0 kg	9 years	130.0 cm	26.5 kg
10 years	136.3 cm	29.5 kg	10 years	135.2 cm	29.5 kg

Remember height and weight go together! Any worries about growth and height and weight should be mentioned to your child's school doctor or your own family doctor.

	1	2	3
Ball catching	Can catch a football using hands instead of arms ☐	Can catch a ball thrown at different angles ☐	Can catch a tennis ball thrown against the wall ☐
Bicycle riding	Rides using pedals but with stabilisers ☐	Can ride without stabilisers ☐	Can ride with 'no hands' ☐
Skipping	Beginning to try to skip with a rope ☐	Can skip with rope ☐	Can skip forwards and backwards ☐
Running	Runs well, with arms and legs working smoothly together ☐	Can run and jump over and around obstacles ☐	Can run and jump smoothly without stopping in between ☐
Jumping	Can jump on the spot. Can jump off low things like a stair ☐	Can jump over a stick a few inches off the ground ☐	Can jump in the air with legs curled under ☐
Activities involving rhythm	Can move to music. Can beat out a simple rhythm ☐	Can change movements to match the music: fast or slow, quiet or noisy ☐	Can run quickly round the room to a rhythm and can combine movements ☐

During the early school years, most children master or have mastered basic skills like running, climbing, hopping and balancing. They then develop these skills by finding new ways of using them.

Look at this table and tick column 1, 2, or 3, according to your child's skill in each of the activities listed.

The column with the most ticks gives you an idea of which stage your child has reached for a number of skills in this area of development.

Remember that children differ considerably in their rate of development and you should not worry about children of the same age who are at a different stage from your child. It is more useful to compare the ticks you have today with those your child gets in a year's time.

Ages and stages

No ages are given in the chart, as children's skills vary a great deal. In general, a five-year-old can usually run, climb, dance and jump. He can just about skip. He can throw a ball and catch it sometimes. He is good at using a scooter and can ride a two wheeler with stabilisers. He can build with boxes and planks. Most of your ticks will be in the first column for five-year-olds.

The six-year-old usually enjoys climbing and swinging by his arms and hanging by his knees. He has learnt to somersault. He can skip with a rope quite well. He can use climbing ropes. He's beginning to use a bat and ball. He's getting better at throwing and catching.

The seven-year-old can walk along narrow planks. He uses a bat and ball fairly well and gets more rhythm into his dancing as well as other actions like trampolining and gymnastics. Six and seven-year-olds will usually have most ticks in the second column.

The eight to ten-year-olds begin to enjoy more complicated activities like hopscotch, conkers and skipping games. They can get quite good at juggling. They can take part in longer hiking expeditions and climbing hills. And they may have considerable skill at swimming. They will score most in the third column.

At which stages do you think Susan is likely to be on the chart? Put ticks for her in the table below after you have read the following paragraph.

Susan is eight. Last Saturday she rode her bicycle along the estate footpath to her friend Joan's house, in the next road. They played at throwing a ball against a wall, practised skipping backwards and pretended to be horses by jumping cardboard boxes put out for the dustmen. After tea, they watched a pop show on TV and danced about to the noisiest records.

		1	2	3
A	Ball catching	☐	☐	☐
B	Bicycle riding	☐	☐	☐
C	Skipping	☐	☐	☐
D	Running	☐	☐	☐
E	Jumping	☐	☐	☐
F	Rhythm	☐	☐	☐
Total				

Answer: A(3); B(2); C(3); D(3); E(3); F(2). There are no ticks in column 1; 2 in column 2; 4 in column 3. Susan is mainly at stage 3 in the development of her larger movement skill.

Exercise

For children, exercise and play are much the same thing, especially if they like joining in games in the playground or gym at school. Most children get enough exercise every day from ordinary activities such as running, jumping and bike riding. But some forms of exercise, such as swimming, cycling, trampolining, involve special skills.

What benefit can your child get from exercise? Instead of the three Rs, it's the three Ss.

○ Suppleness	–	having easy-moving joints.
○ Stamina	–	being able to keep action up for a long time.
○ Strength	–	making muscles work. Although there's little evidence that exercise in children speeds up the growth of their muscles, it certainly helps them learn to use them.

Some activities such as swimming and cycling, help with all the three Ss.

But the most important benefit children get from exercise is co-ordination. This is the ability, while using the three Ss, to get different parts of their minds and bodies working together on the same action. A seven-year-old can make his body work for him better than a five-year-old can. He is better co-ordinated. So it's co-ordination that increases as he moves through the stages of achieving movement skills.

You can encourage your child's co-ordination skills best by finding time to watch and play with him. Then you can admire his determination to succeed and, of course, congratulate his success when it occurs.

Being sarcastic or unkind about his first clumsy attempts at a skill, such as juggling, won't help at all. If he thinks that you feel he can't do it, why should he try? Not noticing what he can do well also kills enthusiasm. But the worst approach of all is to nag him to practise his football or bike riding. This will simply make him react against doing it, as it will become for him a chore instead of a pleasure.

Remember: you can't do it for him, but you can notice what he can do for himself. Using skills all together isn't easy when so many are developing at once. It takes lots of practice and lots of enthusiasm too.

Drawing, painting and writing

Drawing and writing are not just skills.

They are a child's way of expressing what he is learning.

As well as being able to perform skills that involve the whole body, like running and jumping, the five to ten-year-old child gains control over much finer, more precise movements, like those of fingers and thumbs. He starts to use them in drawing, painting and writing.

Drawing and painting

Like the development of movement skills, the skills of drawing and painting usually progress through fairly clear stages. In this area of development it is not the activity itself but the results that show us most about how children develop. The drawings and paintings of children can be grouped into three main stages which are illustrated here. You can look at your child's drawing and estimate which stage he has reached.

Stage 1

By five years old, a child will probably be drawing people with big heads and narrow hairpin or looped bodies, like these

Soon houses and trees and other similar everyday sights appear in his work

Notice the strips for sky and earth, with nothing in between. As one child said when asked why, 'Well, you can wave your arms about and feel there's nothing'

Stage 2

Now you can see the child's ideas of perspective. He knows cars have four wheels and tables have four legs, so they all have to go in the picture. He also knows that houses go straight up from the ground – so look what happens on a hill!

Stage 3

Gradually he gets better at representing the world realistically on paper. He can draw a model from life or use his imagination and his new perspective skill to create an exciting scene

Identifying which stage children have reached in their drawings and paintings requires judgement. Looking at your child's pictures over a period of time will give you insight into how his skill develops. Remember, not all children develop at the same rate; some do not even like drawing and painting, while others show remarkable talent.

Write down which stage your child has reached □.

What's the problem?

The problem with drawing is that real objects have three dimensions–breadth, width and height. But paper has only two dimensions – up or down, and across. So we have to *learn* how to draw pictures.

First, a child must be aware of details if he is going to try and draw them.

Second, he must learn to draw only what he can actually see, from one place. In other words, having noticed that all cars have four wheels, he still needs to realise that from one side you can only see two of them at once.

As the child gets older, he starts to look at his finished work and say it's not right; it doesn't look like the real thing. That's when he learns about perspective, and realistic drawing. Being aware of how things look from different angles is a skill that develops gradually through experience and encouragement. You can see this when older children enjoy games involving identification of familiar objects seen from strange angles.

They also like trick drawings:

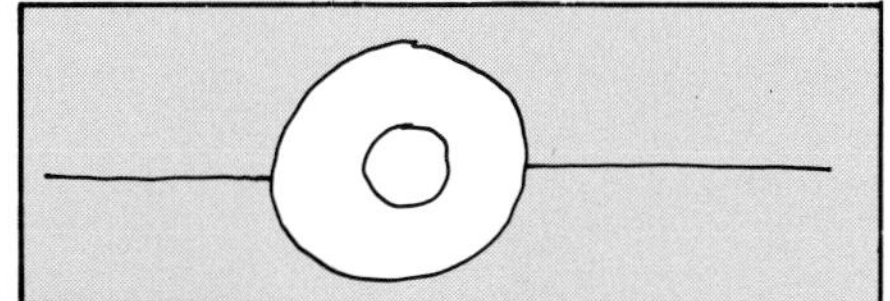

QUESTION: What's this?
ANSWER: A cowboy on a bicycle, seen from above.

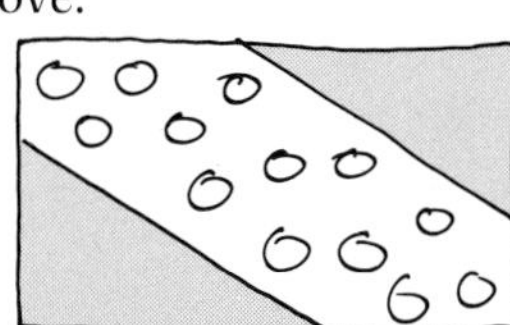

QUESTION: What's this?
ANSWER: A giraffe walking past a window.

What does a child get out of drawing?

A five or six-year-old can talk fluently, but this doesn't mean he's good at finding words for everything he might want to say. And he probably can't express himself much in writing yet.

Drawing and painting are his picture language. With his pictures, he can talk to other people, and he can talk to himself. Watch a child this age making a picture. He becomes totally absorbed in it and may talk to the people he's drawn. He may even pretend he is in the world he has created on the paper. At this stage children often change their minds about what it is their picture is showing.

When it's finished, it's forgotten. If someone admires it later and asks what it is called, the child may come up with yet a different title.

Pictures are exercise for the imagination, just as skipping is exercise for the body. Talking to ourselves is a uniquely human habit and it's not your child's first sign of madness if he talks as he draws. It shows the beginning of his ability to think about what he's doing.

So, from drawing and painting your child has opportunities for practising these things.

Self-expression

○ He can use picture language to show his feelings.

○ He can use his imagination.

○ He can talk to himself about what's going on.

○ He can learn to give titles to pictures – joining words and pictures together.

Fine skills

○ He can use hand and eye in co-ordination.

○ He can learn how colours mix.

○ He can make patterns.

○ He can fit pictures into a given space.

○ He can enjoy concentrating.

○ He can sharpen observation skills.

How can you help?

DO:

○ provide as much space and materials for painting and drawing as you can manage.

○ show an interest in his efforts. Saying everything is 'lovely' in the same tone of voice isn't as good as 'I do like that big tree in the corner'.

○ remember that older children can become highly skilled at various arts and crafts as well as painting. These are often taught in schools. Children take a great pride in learning skills. Everyone has a talent for some activity and when this is recognised, a child's self-confidence can improve greatly.

DON'T:

○ worry if he isn't interested in the picture afterwards, or even colours it over. It's the process of doing it that matters.

○ make a habit of suggesting what he should draw, even if he does ask. Say 'something you like' or 'whatever you feel like drawing'. It's his imagination you're trying to exercise, not yours!

○ expect a young child to sit and copy real objects. He may, of course, draw pictures of what he sees around him, but you don't have to collect up things for him to draw.

○ use colouring books, except as a short-term measure to keep children quiet – they don't help his imagination.

○ criticise the work. It's so easy to say 'but the arms are much too long', or 'the sky's not like that'. A child who is ready to draw realistically will know this and ask for help. If you help a child before you're asked, he'll be confused by trying to draw what you want rather than how he feels.

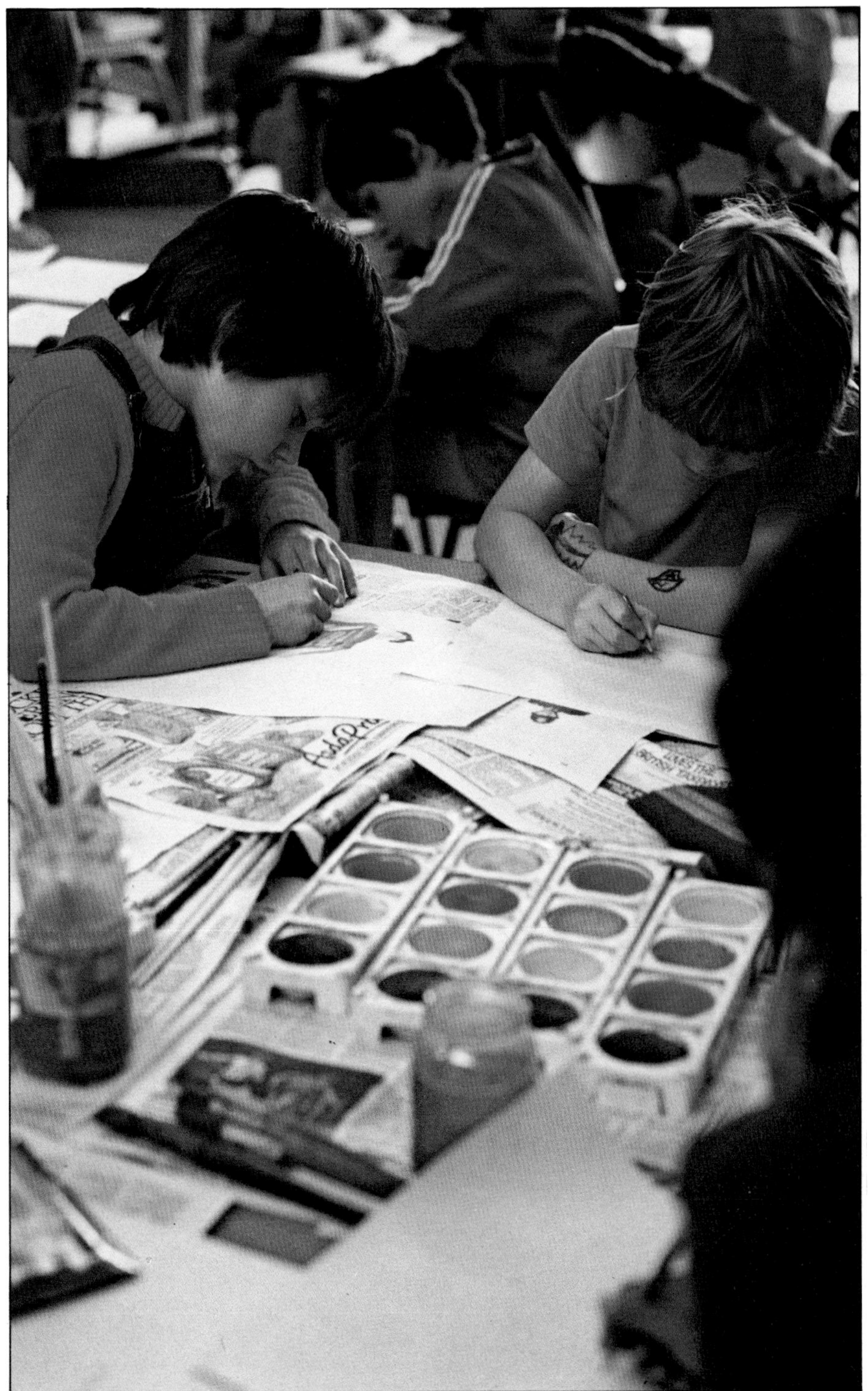

Writing

Like drawing and painting, writing requires co-ordination of the fingers, hand and arm. This skill develops gradually through stages. On the right are some examples of children's writing at different stages:

Stage 1 is mainly concerned with acquiring sufficient skill to write and to copy words. In Stage 2, children can begin to express themselves and they can give more attention to what they want to say. By Stage 3, the main effort is in creating meaning and communicating.

At which stage is your child's writing? ☐

Writing is a skill which, in its early stages, is far behind a child's ability to think and express himself. Only gradually does the fine co-ordination required in writing enable the child to put his thoughts on paper.

Co-ordination and thinking

Movement skills mainly require physical co-ordination. Drawing and writing skills not only require co-ordination but are also related to the development of thinking skills. In other words, co-ordination *and* thinking are developing together in these activities. The more encouragement you give your child, the more confident he will be about expressing the new ideas that come into his head.

Stage 1

Before five, children will be doing patterns like this

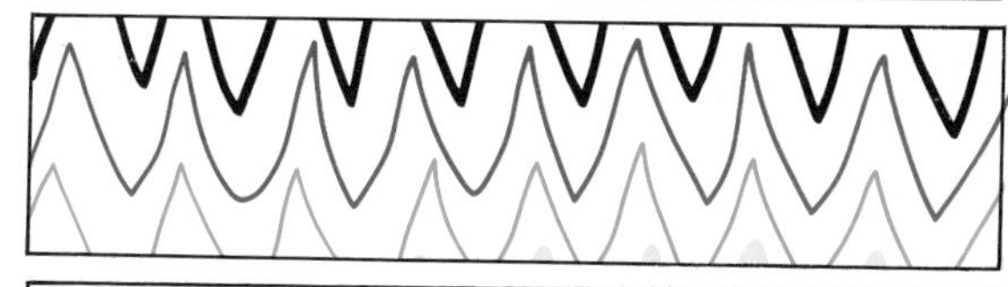

Later they will be able to write their name on their own, but will mostly be copying other peoples' writing

RoBeRt RYan

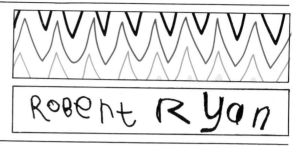

Stage 2

Children will be writing a few sentences without help. They may still be using a mixture of large and small letters and words

Later they will be able to write stories but could still have trouble in setting out the writing neatly

Darlington. Thursday 1st Febuary

The Mountain

Once upon a time there lived a boy called Tom and he was set upon going to look for Fame and Fortune. Well, pretty soon he heard about a mountain which many men had gone up but never come back! and he decided to go up there. And he did. One fine day he went off, looking for the mountain.

Stage 3

Children begin to develop an individual writing style and writing is joined up

To a mouse with a cockatoo's tail.
He'd invented it himself,
Using glue from the shelf,
By crossing an elephant and a quail.
In the middle of the day,
He went for some hay,
And ate it, in a pond with his cat.
Of course, the cat spat,
And sat on his hat,

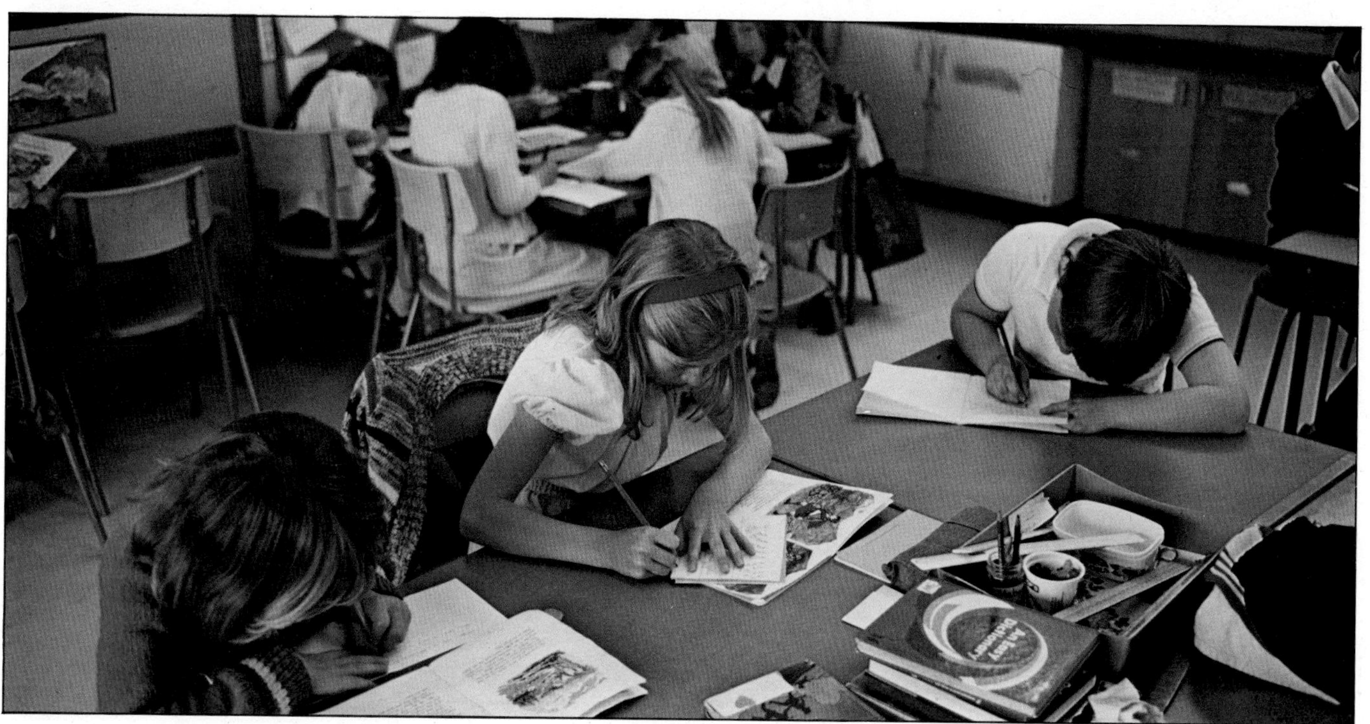

Understanding the physical world

Children don't see the world as adults see it. Here we help you take a child's eye view.

Children's understanding of the physical world about them is based on how they think about objects – their size and shape. In infancy, children learn that an object continues to be there even when they stop looking at it. But only gradually do they learn that mugs of different shapes may hold the same amount of water.

It is relatively easy to see changes in children's growth and movement, drawing and writing. But because it is less easy to see how children understand the physical world we often don't realise that they think in different ways from us.

Games

To help us understand how children think about the physical world, we can use special games. The games we give here are based on those used by researchers studying child development. The games have been designed so that children of different ages will give different answers. The answers they give help show us how they think.

The youngest children in the five-to-ten age group will normally give Stage 1 answers, and the oldest Stage 3 answers. Stage 2 answers are given when the child's thinking is moving from Stage 1 to Stage 3, and he is still unsure, sometimes giving Stage 1 and sometimes Stage 3 answers.

Each game differs in the demands it makes on a child's thinking which means that one child will probably be at different stages in different games. Some schools provide opportunities for children to play games of this kind and your child may be familiar with them. However, this should not affect the results.

If your child is at the top of the five-to-ten age range, he may think that the games are silly because he is at Stage 3 for all of them. Try them on a younger child if you can. The answers will help you understand some of the things he does and thinks in everyday life and how he gradually gets better able to cope.

Sweets for you and me

Every five-year-old knows what more means . . . or does she? When you ask if she wants more of her favourite pudding, there's no problem. You understand each other. But try some of these games with your child and see how misunderstanding can happen.

Spread out two rows of sweets (or you could use buttons, cakes or apples). There should be the same number in each row, and each one should be lined up opposite one in the other row (see picture).

○ Ask *'Have we got the same?'*

○ Let your child count out each row so that she agrees that her row and yours are the same.

Now let her watch you spread out your row (see picture).

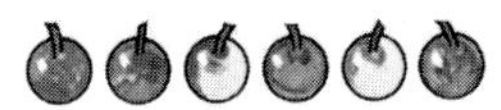

○ Ask again, *'Have we got the same?'*

○ If she says *'No'*, ask, *'Who has got more?'*

○ If she's not sure, ask her to count them again – or go back to the first

arrangement and then expand her row and ask the question again.

It's sometimes quite interesting to get a child to talk about how she came to give her particular answer, especially with children at Stage 2 or 3. Below are some examples of what children at the different stages said.

Helen, age 6 *Stage 1*
Two rows of sweets are spread out in front of Helen, both rows equal.

Parent: *'Have we got the same?'*

Helen: (counts both rows) *'Yes.'*

Parent spreads out his row.

Parent: *'Have we got the same now?'*

Helen: *'No.'*

Parent: *'Who's got more?'*

Helen: *'You.'*

Ben, age 7 *Stage 2*
Same arrangement as before.

Parent: *'Have we got the same?'*

Ben: (counts both rows) *'Yes.'*

Parent spreads out his row.

Parent: *'Have we got the same now?'*

Ben: *'No, you've got more.'*

Parent: *'I see, now count how many I've got.'*

Ben: *'Six.'*

Parent: *'And now count your row.'*

Ben: *'I've got six.'*

Parent: *'Have we got the same?'*

Ben: *'Well . . . no, you've still got more.'*

Parent: spreads Ben's row out more than his own. *'Have we got the same now?'*

Ben: *'Well, I've got more.'*

Ben counts each row and looks very puzzled.

Ben: *'We've both got six though.'*

Sophie, age 8 *Stage 3*
Same arrangement as before.

Parent: *'Have we got the same?'*

Sophie: (counts them) *'Yes.'*

Parent spreads out his row.

Parent: *'Have we got the same now?'*

Sophie: *'Yes.'*

Parent: *'How do you know?'*

Sophie: *'Because you've only just moved them out. . . you didn't take any away or add any on.'*

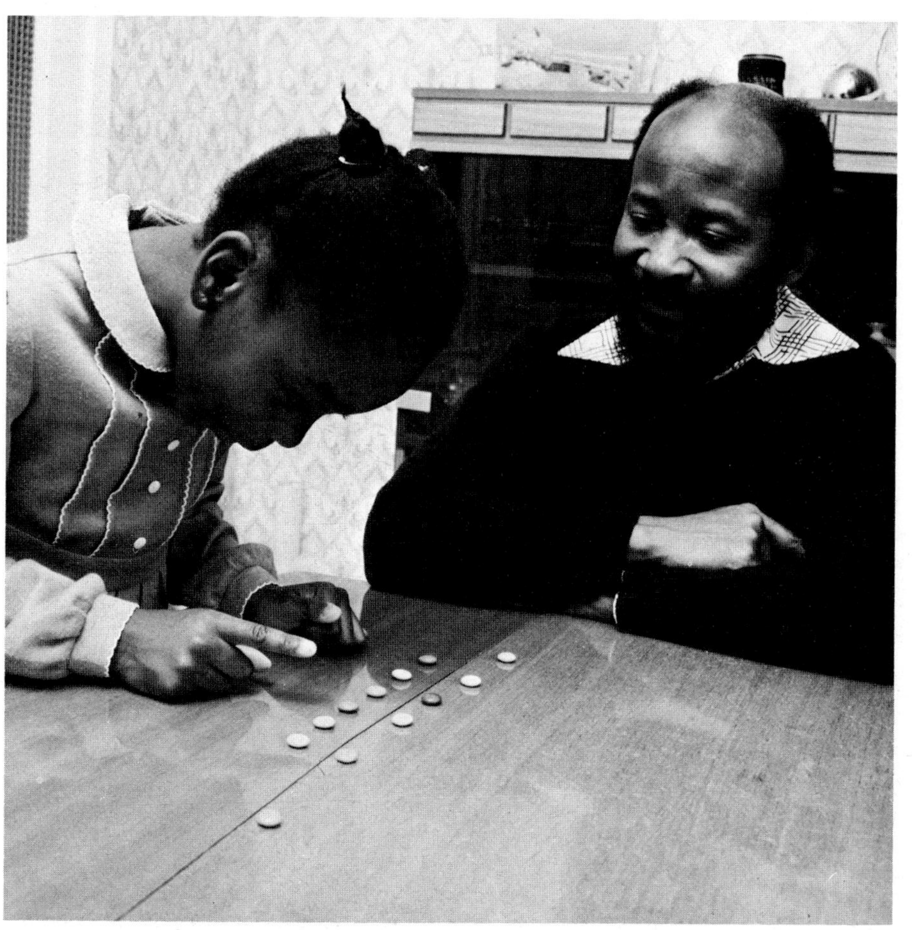

Younger children will say that your row (the longer) has more, whereas older children will always get the answer right and even think it is silly to ask the question. Before they understand they usually pass through a middle stage where they may agree the number is the same, but the longer row is still 'more'.

		Your child
Stage 1	Longer is more	☐
Stage 2	Unsure	☐
Stage 3	Always the same	☐

Why is this?
Children have learnt that longer rows of things usually have more things in them than shorter rows. At Stage 1 they use this clue and ignore the fact that no sweets have been added or taken away. Their answer is based on what they see and to them it looks as if there are more. They may admit that

the number will be the same if the sweets are put back to how they were before. Even if they know that there are the same number they might use 'more' to mean 'more length', thus misunderstanding your question. At Stage 3, they understand the words the same way as you do, and *know* that the number of things cannot have changed because nothing was added or taken away.

Which straw is the longer?

The row of sweets got longer by being extended at both ends. But what happens if we have two straws that cannot be stretched? Take two straws of the same length and put them on a table in front of your child, like this.

○ Say, *'Are these straws the same length?'*

○ Move one straw along a bit. Make sure your child sees you move it.

○ Ask, *'Are these straws the same length?'*

○ If he says *'no'*, ask him: *'Which one is longer?'*

You might like to ask a few questions of your own to get the child to talk about how he sees things. Children's answers fall into three stages again. Here are some sample replies:

Susie, age 5 *Stage 1*
Two straws are put in front of Susie, as first shown.

Parent: *'Are these straws the same length?'*

Susie: *'Yes.'*

Parent moves one straw along a bit: *'Are they the same length now?'*

Susie: *'No.'*

Parent: *'Which one is longer?'*

Susie: *'That one,'* pointing to the straw the parent has moved.

Parent puts the straw back as before: *'Are they the same length now?'*

Susie: *'Yes.'*

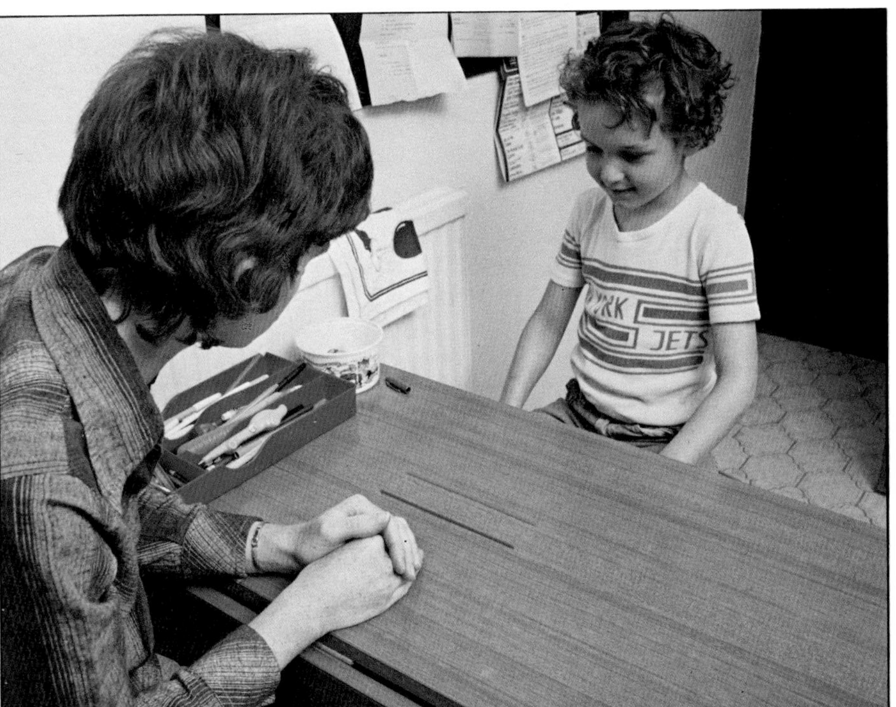

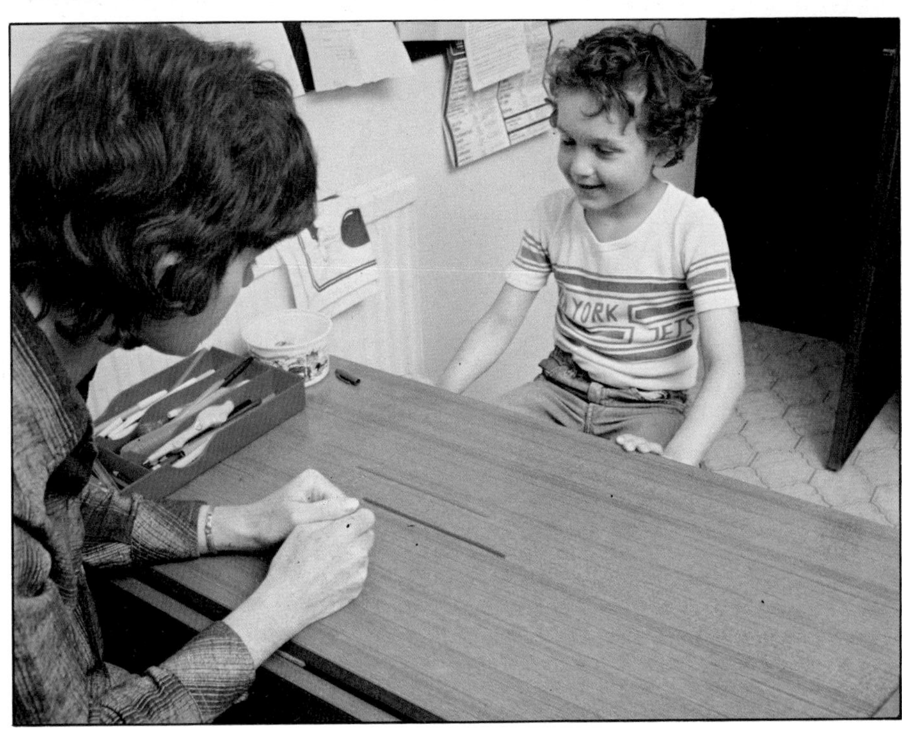

Karen, age 7 *Stage 2*
Two straws are put in front of Karen as first shown.

Parent: *'Are these straws the same length?'*
Karen: *'Yes.'*

Parent moves one straw along a bit: *'Are they the same length now?'*

Karen: *'No, that one's longer,'* pointing to the straw the parent has moved.

Parent: *'Why is that one longer?'*

Karen: *'Because you moved it along.'*

Parent: *'Does it just look longer or is it really longer?'*

Karen: *'No.'*

Parent: *'It just looks longer does it?'*

Karen: *'Yes.'*

Andrew, age 9 *Stage 3*
Two straws are put in front of Andrew as first shown.

Parent: *'Are these straws the same length?'*

Andrew: *'Yes.'*

Parent moves one along a bit: *'Are they the same length now?'*

Andrew: *'Yes, of course – just because you've moved them – it doesn't change their length.'*

At Stage 1, children will say that one straw is longer. At Stage 3 they know that this cannot happen and the straws stay the same length. Stage 2 children are unsure, they may say one straw is longer and agree that if the straws were to be put back together as in the first picture, they are the same length. Children at Stage 1 know that the straws have not been changed, but one end appears longer when moved (as in the second picture), so they ignore the fact that the other end has become shorter by the same amount.

At which stage is your child? ☐

Out to grass

If the children say length changes when the arrangement confuses them, what about area? If you cut up a piece of paper, do you have more paper?

Take two identical pieces of rectangular paper or card (green, if possible). Place both of these on the table and tell your child to pretend that they are two big fields of grass for cows to eat.

○ Ask: *'Have the cows in this field as much to eat as the cows in this field?'* (Point to each piece of paper.)

Now, in front of the child, cut one piece of paper into several different pieces. Spread them out on the table.

○ Ask: *'Now there are a lot of little fields. Have the cows in the little fields got the same, more, or less to eat than the cows in this field?'* (Point to large piece of paper.)

The younger child at Stage 1 says that there is more grass in the little fields. Because there are more pieces, he ignores the fact that the area remains the same, and you didn't add or take any away. At Stage 3, he realises this and always says the cows have got the same amount of grass to eat. Stage 2 children are unsure.

Which stage is your child at in this game? ☐

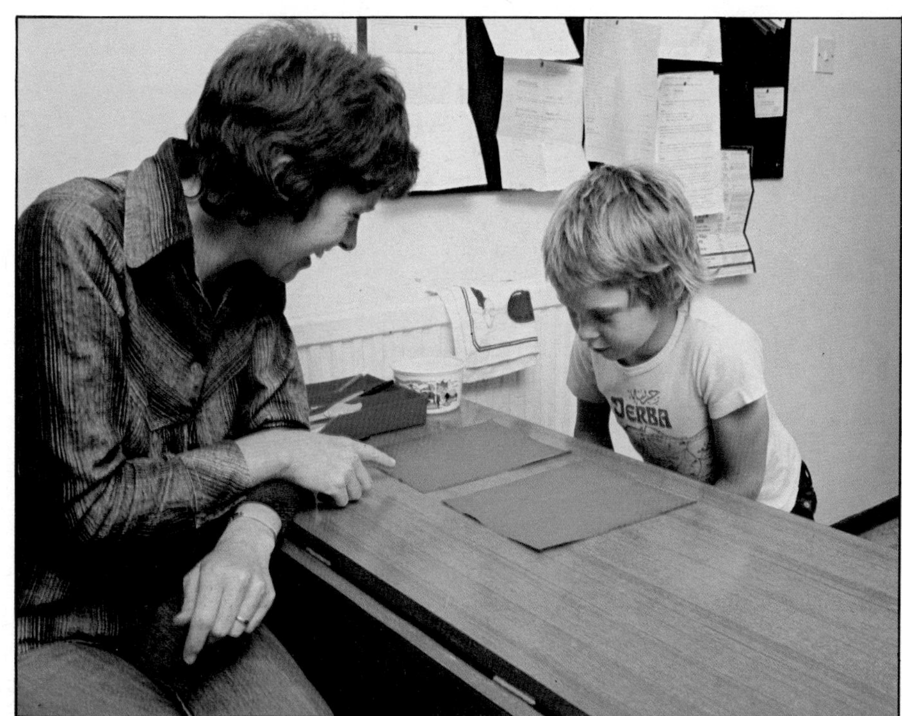

Plasticine balls

What about three-dimensional shapes? Do children go through a stage of thinking that the shape of something affects how much there is of it? Make up two balls of plasticine which your child agrees look the same.

○ Ask him: *'Is there the same amount of plasticine in this ball as in that one?'*

If he agrees, pick one and roll it into a sausage. Do this in his full view. Put the sausage next to the ball.

○ Ask: *'Is there the same amount of plasticine in this ball as in this sausage?'*

Again, the answers fall into three stages. At Stage 1 children will say one shape (usually the sausage) has more plasticine, at Stage 2 they are unsure and at Stage 3 they always say 'the same'. At which stage is your child? □

Generally, it takes children longer to reach Stage 3 in this game than for the straws. They are less sure about plasticine in three-dimensional shapes than single dimension straws. Because the sausage is plainly longer they assume there is more plasticine and ignore the fact that it is thinner.

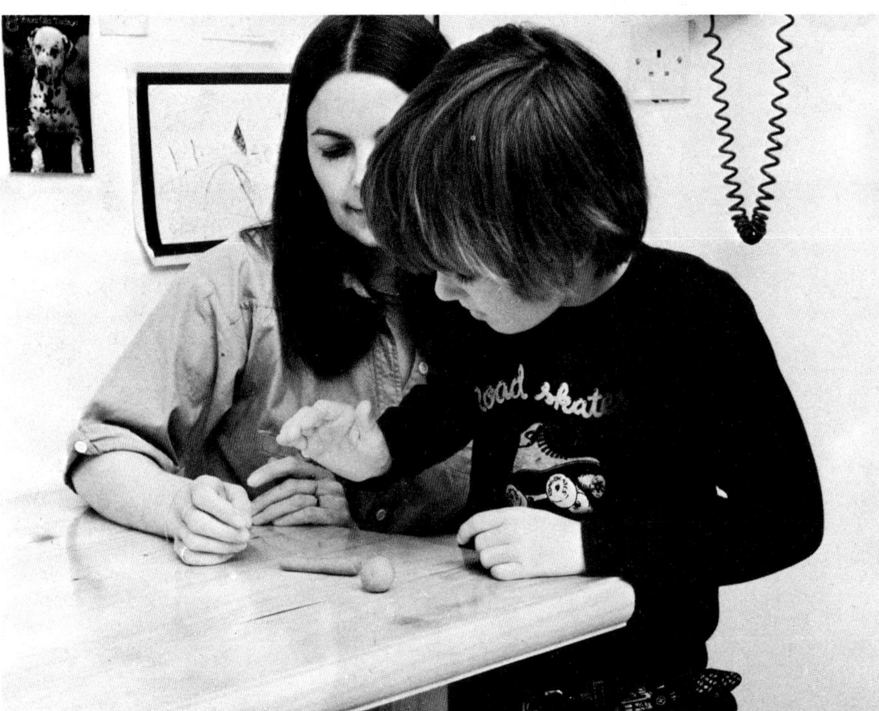

Fair shares

Liquids are more difficult. You can play a similar game with orange juice. You need two identical see-through beakers and one slimmer, taller see-through beaker. (They don't have to have straight sides, but this helps.)

○ Ask your child to fill the two identical beakers so that each person gets the same amount of juice.

○ Check that your child agrees they are the same by asking: *'Is there the same amount of juice in each beaker?'*

Pour the juice from one beaker into the taller beaker.

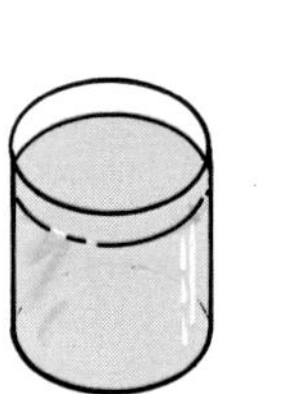

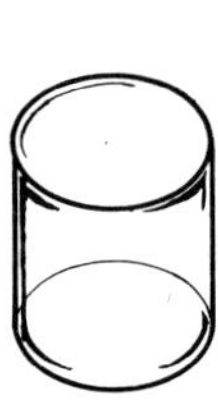

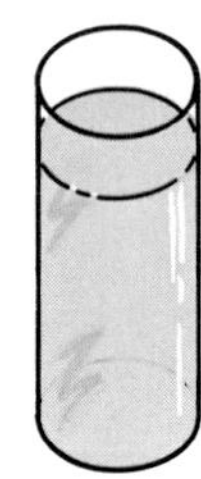

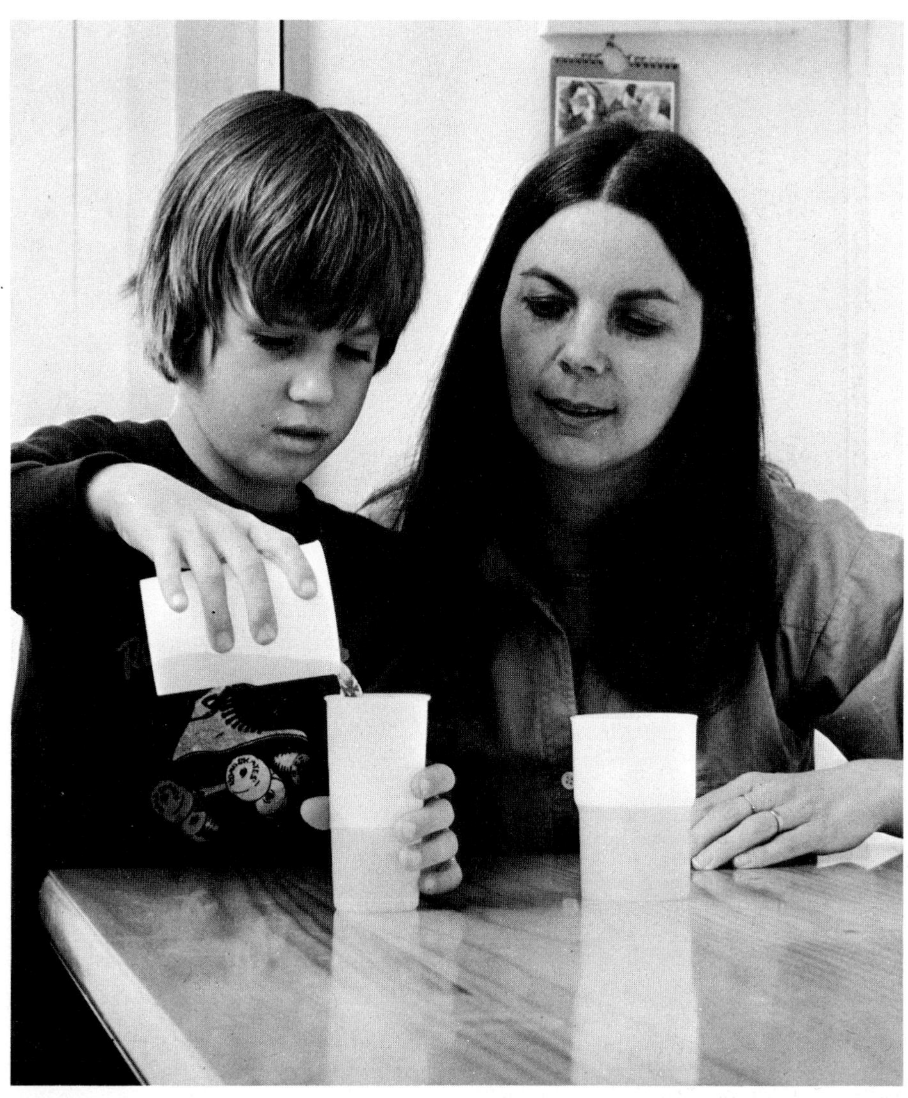

Game	Property that changes	Property that stays the same
Sweets for you and me	Length (of row)	Number of objects
Which straw is longer?	Position	Length
Out to grass	Number (of pieces)	Area
Plasticine balls	Shape	Quantity (weight)
Fair shares	Height and width	Quantity (volume)

○ Ask your child: *'Is there the same amount of juice in these beakers?'* (ie, the remaining beaker and the taller beaker).

At Stage 1, children will say there is more in the taller beaker, at Stage 2 they are unsure and at Stage 3 they know that the amount of liquid does not change and that there is the same in each beaker.

Younger children don't realise that the increase in height is compensated for by the decrease in width.

At what stage is your child in this game? □

What's happening?

What is happening in these games is that some property is being changed and the Stage 1 child assumes that other properties are also being changed. The table on the left shows what is changed in each game and the important property that does not change. The child has to learn that certain properties do not change even if others do.

The child's difficulty becomes clearer to us now. First he must interpret the question in the way we expect him to. Secondly, he must make his decision from what's in front of his eyes and from what he remembers about the set-up before the change.

The child at Stage 3 has solved the problem. He realises that changes in arrangement do not affect number, changes in position do not affect length, changes in the number of pieces do not affect area, and changes in shape do not affect weight or volume. He is sure enough about this to answer correctly every time and can often put into words why he has given his particular answer.

The Stage 1 child reasons from appearance, not from what he knows has happened. When he sees the arrangement of sweets changed, a straw moved or plasticine rolled into a sausage, he does not reason (like the Stage 3 child) that because things were the same before, they must still be the same now. He looks at the objects – they look different, so are different.

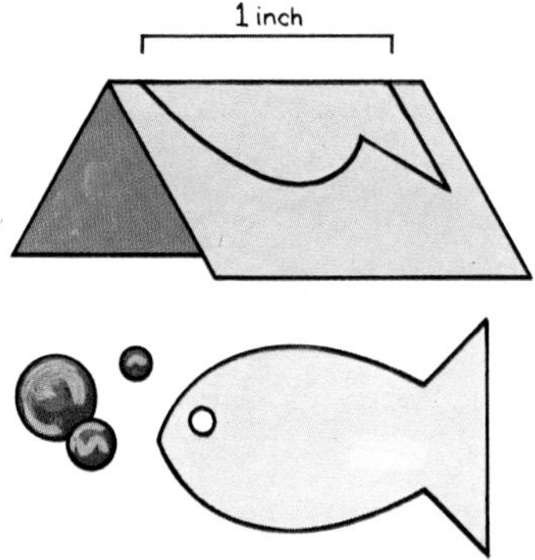

Feeding time

This game involves two sets of objects which vary in length and size. Eight cardboard fish of different lengths must be matched with eight different-sized plasticine 'meatballs'.

You need some plasticine and a sheet of cardboard or paper. Ask your child to help.

○ Fold cardboard/paper in half.

○ Mark out about 1″.

○ Draw fish shape with tail.

○ Cut out fish, open out cardboard/paper.

○ Make the next fish about $\frac{1}{2}$″ longer, and then six other fish, each $\frac{1}{2}$″ bigger than the one before: $1\frac{1}{2}$″, 2″, $2\frac{1}{2}$″, 3″, $3\frac{1}{2}$″, 4″, $4\frac{1}{2}$″.

○ Now separate the plasticine into eight different-sized balls.

○ Spread out the fish and the balls on a flat surface, all jumbled up together (see picture).

Explain to your child that the game is to give each fish the right plasticine meatball. *'Big fish need big meatballs, and smaller fish only like little ones. Each one will only eat its own special dinner.'*

Ask the child to work out which meatball goes with which fish and ask him to put them together.

Watch and encourage him, but don't prompt.

If he doesn't know where to start, point to the biggest fish and say: *'Which do you think this one would like?'*

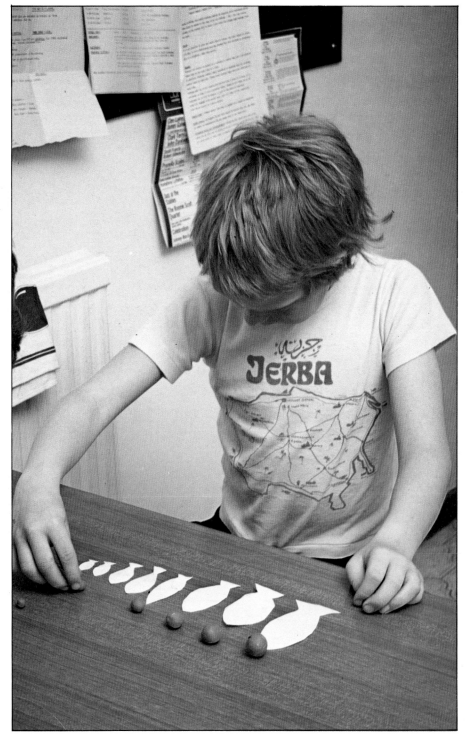

Which of the following stages most nearly describes what your child did?

Stage 1
Tries to match meatballs to fish without trying to arrange the fish in any particular order. May succeed with largest and smallest.

Stage 2
May start as in Stage 1, but may attempt to separate out fish that have been matched with meatballs. Arranges some of the fishes and attempts to match meatballs. By trial and error may get a number of correct matches.

Stage 3
Lines up fish in order of size. Looks for largest (or smallest) meatball and places this by the largest (or smallest) fish, then finds next-sized meatball, and so on until all correctly matched.

What is of interest here is not whether they get it right but how they work it out. What seems obvious to us doesn't seem obvious to them.

Here is what some children did.

Billy charged straight in and started arranging, then rapidly changed his mind. After much trial and error, he got the three largest pairs right, and the smallest, plus two in the middle, making six in all.

Stage? ☐ (write in)

Carolyn thought for a short time, then carefully lined up the fish in order of size. She found the largest meatball, gave it to the biggest fish, and continued correctly down the line.

Stage? ☐ (write in)

Anjali played with the fish and talked to them a lot. She gave the smallest fish the smallest meatball but the largest meatball went to the second largest fish. Most of the other fish got fed in the end, but there was no order in the arrangement at all. Only three fish were paired up with exactly the correct meatball.

Stage? ☐ (write in)

Answers: 2, 3, 1.

Putting things in order
In the feeding time game, the child at Stage 3 realises that each fish is related to another by being bigger or smaller. This means that the fish can be arranged in order. This idea must also be applied to the meatballs, and fish and meatballs matched together. To put the fish in order, the child must be able to realise and manipulate these ideas in his head. He cannot do it unless he understands relationships.

Younger children, however willing, cannot do some things because they can't plan or organise very well. There are many everyday activities that require things to be carried out in sequence (cooking, assembling something). Young children will be unable on their own to do tasks that require them to order and sequence, but that doesn't mean they cannot do it with help. You can help by breaking complicated tasks into manageable parts. As they get older their thinking will develop so that they are able to organise things for themselves.

Asking a child to tidy up his toys or his bedroom is a very good example of adults expecting a young child to perform a complicated task. It may not be that he is particularly difficult or stupid about tidying up. He just doesn't know how to do it. You can help him by breaking it down into smaller tasks. Start perhaps by suggesting he looks for all the jigsaw pieces and puts them in their relevant box. Then pick out another small task, and so on until he has finished tidying up.

Your child's understanding

Your child's results should give you insight into the development of his thinking and if you look again in a few months' time you will probably see changes. To help you do this, place ticks in the summary table to show which stage your child has reached.

Game	1	2	3
Sweets for you and me	☐	☐	☐
Which straw is longer?	☐	☐	☐
Out to grass	☐	☐	☐
Plasticine balls	☐	☐	☐
Fair shares	☐	☐	☐
Feeding time	☐	☐	☐
TOTAL	☐	☐	☐

For each game there is a progression in the child's thinking from Stage 1 through Stage 2 to Stage 3. However, children vary a lot. Some will be at Stage 3 in one game and Stage 1 in another, whereas others will be round the other way. Adding up the ticks in each column will give an indication of the child's overall progress which can be compared with these scores a few months later.

The child at Stage 1 is unable in his head to move from the first arrangement; he simply compares what he sees. When the child reaches Stage 3 this requires him to be able to move from one arrangement to the other and back in his head and realise that this is the most important clue. To be able to hold the thought about an action and to apply and reverse it is a crucial stage in the development of thinking. These thoughts are about concrete actions – the child at Stage 3 is able to manipulate them in his head and to base conclusions on this mental action. Much later the child will learn to manipulate abstract ideas.

It takes children a long time before they acquire this new way of thinking that enables them to see a bit more order in a changing world. It depends what experiences they are exposed to.

So don't worry about trying to speed things up. But make sure your child has opportunities for playing with a variety of objects and materials.

Understanding other points of view

When do children start to see that different people have different views? Our games help you find out.

Children must be able to take account of the views and feelings of others as well as their own. The young child cannot do this. His own views dominate, and these are based on what he alone sees and feels. He does not realise that other people have views different from his own. Only gradually does he learn that he is not the centre of the universe after all.

In this topic there are a number of games you can play with your child. These games enable us to see how much young children understand about other people and how this understanding changes as they grow. We can think of these in three stages.

At Stage 1 the child is unable to take account of the view of others. By Stage 3 he can. Stage 2 is an in-between stage where the child is beginning to realise that others have different views but is unable to work out quite what these are.

These stages do not necessarily match the three stages that mark a child's understanding of the physical world. Children's understanding of the physical world often develops quicker than their understanding of people. The purpose of these games is not to find out whether your child is ahead or behind others. But one of the joys of living with young children is to see their progress and to understand how they are changing. If you play these games again in a few months' time you should notice changes.

Talking about people

A child's understanding of people is based on how he sees them. Does he see them just in terms of their physical appearance and what they do, or does he see that they too have likes and dislikes? If he sees them mainly as objects he is not likely to realise that they have views and feelings different from his own. Usually he'll see more as he gets older.

Here are some real-life examples of children talking about their best friends and worst 'enemies'.

'He's called Jason. He's got a big teddy. He lives next door to me. He's got red hair. His dad shouts.'

'My friend Lynda gives me half her sweets. She's got a new blue coat and a blue hat with a bobble on it. Her big sister brings her to school. We went to the seaside.'

'Henry is seven years and two months old. He has red hair and glasses. His brother is called Tommy and their cat is called Fred. Henry is good fun, we play in the park. He likes watching football and Dr Who. Last week we went to the zoo and Henry got lost. Henry is sometimes a bit naughty at school and makes me laugh.'

'Ahmed is a good friend. He always sticks up for me. He is very good at football and is happy when he gets lots of goals because he wants to play for Manchester United when he grows up. He never boasts about his goals like some boys do. Everyone in the class likes him. Sometimes he is noisy in lessons and is a nuisance.'

'Peter is horrid. His mother shouts at me. He took my ball.'

'Tony is very smelly and nasty and I hate him. He is fat with glasses and ugly and selfish. He doesn't like anything I do and always tries to upset me. His sister is called Margaret and she is very silly too. He is always rude to everyone. Nobody really likes him.'

'Roger is the worst boy in our class. He is always crying and often gets other people into trouble. I think he is mean and miserable and likes to see other people feel miserable too.'

Best friend, worst enemy

Try this game with your child. You should be able to tell the stage he has reached and the stage the children quoted above have reached when you read our explanation of stages in the next column.

○ Ask your child to choose a friend he likes very much.

○ Say, *'What do you think of him? What's he like? I don't mean what he looks like or what he wears, but what he's really like.'*

○ Ask him to write down his answer, or make notes yourself, or use a tape recorder.

○ Don't interrupt him once he starts. You may have to wait a bit while he thinks. You can prompt at the end: *'Is there anything else?'*

○ Then ask him to do the same for a child he doesn't like.

There are three main ways we can describe another person.

By their outer appearance – what they look like, and what they wear.

By what they do and who they know – examples of their behaviour and information about their family and friends.

By making judgements of what they are like, their character, and by giving reasons why they do what they do.

Outer appearance	**Example**	**What your child says**
What they wear	*'he has a red coat'*	
What they look like	*'She has blonde hair and glasses'*	
What they own	*'their cat is called Fred'*	
What they do/know		
Habits	*'she likes drawing'*	
Happenings	*'we went to the zoo'*	
Their family and friends	*'his sister is called Margaret'*	
Judgements		
Character words	*'Peter is horrid'*	
Strings of character words that mean similar things	*'Smelly, nasty, ugly, selfish'*	
Linking character words with behaviour	*'He's happy because he wants ...'*	

Fill in the table above from what your child said. In each case we have given an example.

Stage 1
The youngest children talk mostly about looks and possessions. 'Nice' and 'nasty' are as near as you're likely to get to a character sketch. Usually this is stated as *'She is nasty to me'*.

Stage 2
As they get older they start to use words like 'very'. They give more detail, although this may not always be the kind you would call relevant to a description of someone: *'her dog can play ball'*. People's looks are given as much importance as their behaviour. All behaviour described is still likely to have personal importance for the child giving the description. *'We make cakes.'* Judgements are very definite, black and white. People are awful or wonderful.

Stage 3
The oldest children concentrate a bit more on behaviour and its links with character. They give examples to show you why they like someone, instead of assuming it's obvious. They can give a more impartial description. Life is not so clear cut, people can be sometimes good and sometimes bad, but these contradictions are not usually linked together until the child reaches adolescence.

Which stage has your child reached?
☐

As others see us . . .

How a child describes others gives us some idea how much he can understand about them. The youngest children only report the obvious facts. They know someone's great or nasty and assume you know the same. There's only one possible point of view on the matter: theirs. There's so little detail that it's difficult to tell how much they understand about other people.

Later on people and their family and possessions are seen as closely connected, probably because this is all part of what makes them nice or nasty to be with. Character is still not considered very much. They say of their friend, *'She's got lots of toys and her mum lets us make a mess'* rather than, *'She's kind and thoughtful'*.

Older children know that motives and intentions are important and lie behind our actions. They are not always very good at working these out but then how many of us are! They are starting to look for clues to inner character in their friend's behaviour. They talk less about appearances.

You cannot expect a child to be reasonable all the time about how others treat him, because he does not see them as you do. He cannot understand that people see things differently until he is ready to. You can help by explaining why people do things and that they sometimes do things we like and sometimes things we don't like.

But nobody is all good or all bad. Remind him when he says he hates somebody that only a short while ago he loved them. Say, *'You hate Jimmy now but remember he was very nice to you and helped you tidy your toys.'*

Doll's eye-view

This game involves working out what something looks like from someone else's seat. It may look a bit complicated to set up, but don't be put off!

○ You and your child will each need a set of three toy 'houses'. Each set must be the same. You can use two identical cereal packets, two packets of square biscuits and two of soap powder. Plastic food boxes are quite useful also, as long as they are rectangular. Don't use cylindrical packets like baked bean tins.

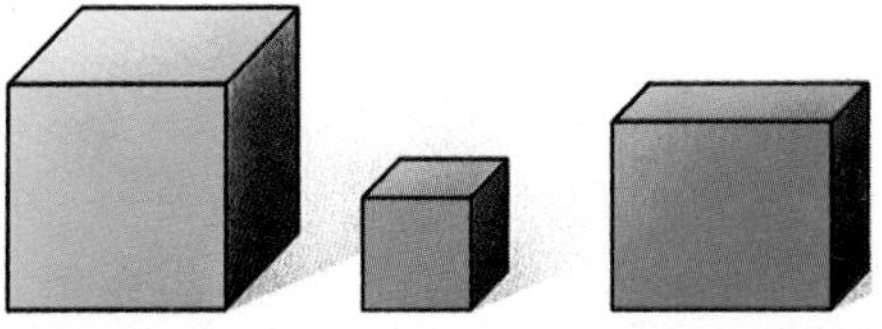

○ You will need a fairly large area of floor space – you can use tables if this is convenient.

○ Find two large sheets of plain paper or newspaper.

○ Select one of your child's favourite toys, such as a doll, a soldier or a teddy.

○ Set out the sheets of paper on the floor (or on tables) as shown.

○ You and your child should sit in the positions shown.

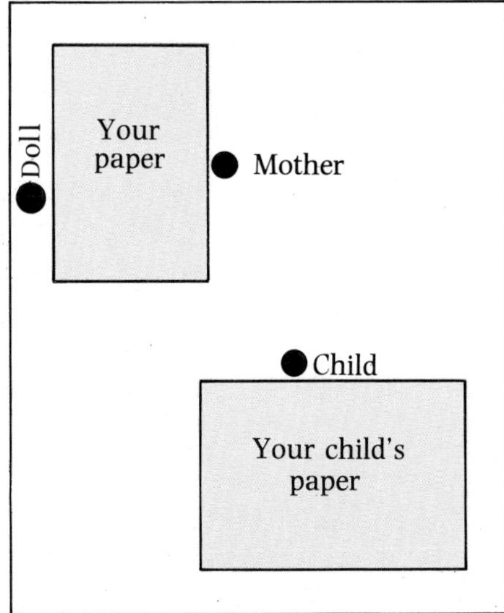

○ Arrange your three 'houses' on your piece of paper as shown.

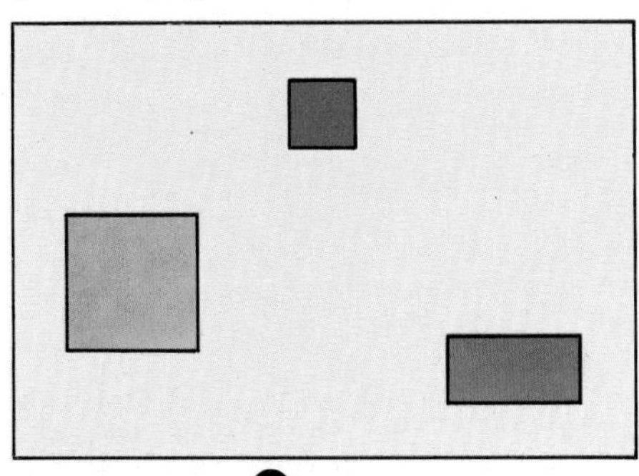

○ Ask your child to walk round your piece of paper and look at the houses from all directions. Then tell him to go back to his place.

○ When he is sitting down in his place, sit your child's doll opposite you, on the opposite side of your paper.

○ Ask your child to arrange his set of houses on his piece of paper so that they look the same as the view the doll can see from where it is sitting. Your instruction should go like this: *'Now can you put your houses out on your piece of paper so they look just like what Dolly can see from over there. Pretend you're Dolly, what would they look like?'*

○ The child is *not* allowed to get up and walk round again and you should not give hints.

○ When he's finally arranged his houses draw round them and compare his arrangement with the original.

This is a difficult task for a child so don't worry if he cannot do it. If he really can't understand what to do let him go and have a look or help him. But probably he's not ready to play, so you could leave it for a few months.

There are clear stages shown in children's answers to this game.

What stage did your child reach? ☐

Stage 1
Your original. A reproduction of your arrangement from your viewpoint. This is not what Dolly would see.

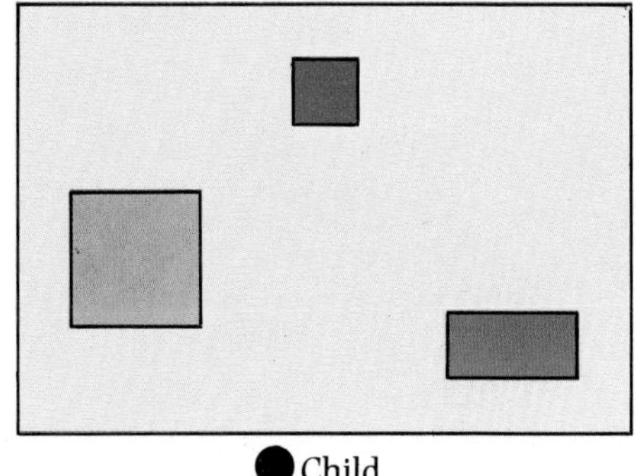

Confusion. The child is aware that Dolly will see something different but cannot work out what this is.

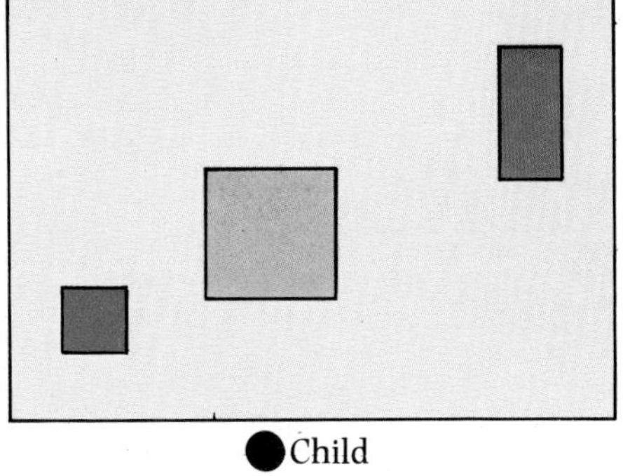

Stage 2
Left-right error. The nearest house is correct. The other two are on the wrong sides and at the wrong distances.

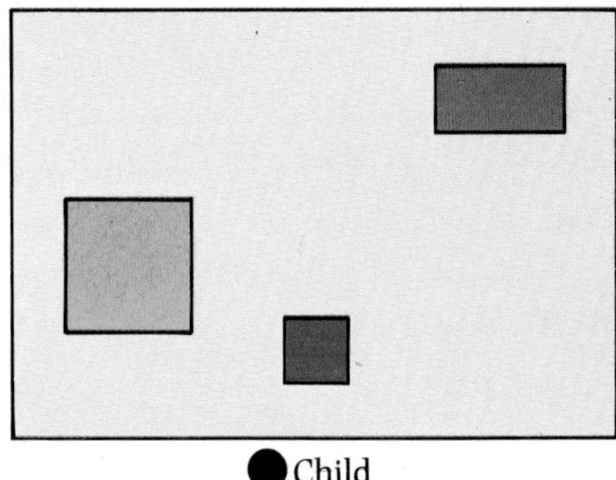

The nearest house is correct and the other two are on the correct sides but at the wrong depth.

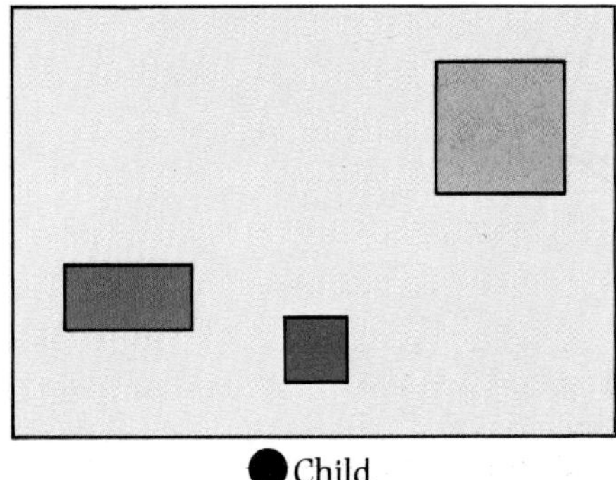

Stage 3
Correct arrangement. The child can move the scene around in his head and come to the correct arrangement.

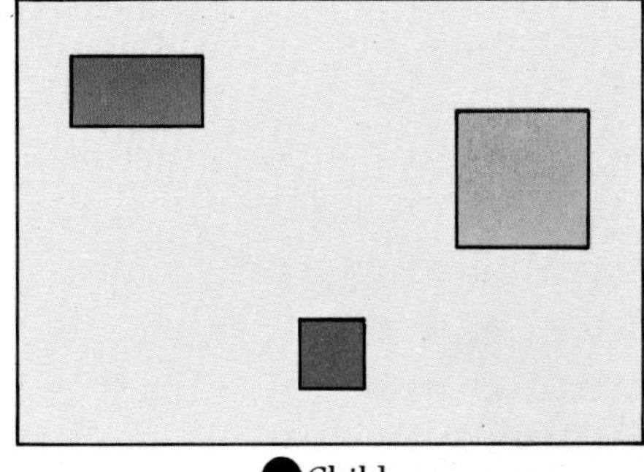

This game requires children to project themselves mentally into the position of the doll. They must be able to represent the scene in their mind and then walk round to the doll's side and look at it in their 'mind's eye'. They can then reconstruct the scene outside. They must not let their own view of your arrangement intrude into this process. The immediate impression created by their view must be kept separate from the doll's view they are trying to reconstruct.

The country walk

Because people have different viewpoints they see events differently. Or they may have less information so they may see only part of what is going on. If a child looks at a series of pictures that tell a story, does he realise that another child who sees only some of them will tell a different story?

○ Ask your child to tell you a story about what is going on in these pictures. Make notes or tape record what he says. Now cover up pictures 2, 3 and 5, so that he can only see pictures 1, 4, 6 and 7.

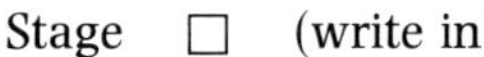

Stage □ (write in)

Example B
'He's going to the park. He's singing. He runs, he sees a tree. He climbs up it. He eats an apple.'

Q. *'Why did he do that?'*
'So the dog don't get him.'

Stage □ (write in)

Example C
'He's walking along and the dog's gonna chase him so he runs. He goes up this tree. The dog walks away and while he was there he's eating the apple.'

○ Choose the name of one of your child's friends. (In the example Peter is used.) Now say, *'Let's pretend it's Peter's turn. If we show him only these pictures, tell me the story he will tell us.'*

○ Make sure he realises that you mean that Peter sees just pictures 1, 4, 6 and 7 and not the complete set. You can ask a few questions if it helps. For example if your child hasn't mentioned the dog at all you could say, *'What would Peter think the dog is doing in this picture?'*

Here are some stories children thought their friends might make up. Identify which stage each story illustrates and check your answers with the chart.

Example A
'A boy goes for a walk so he sees this tree and there's this dog and he climbs up and eats an apple.'

Q. *'Why did he climb up?'*
'Well he . . . he was scared, of a ghost or something.'

Q. *'What will Johnnie think the dog's doing?'*
'He's chasing him.'

Q. *'Does Johnnie know that?'*
'No, but the boy does.'

Stage □ (write in)

Example D
'This boy is just walking along and sees this apple tree. He goes to climb it and eats an apple.'

Q. *'Why?'*
'Just to eat the apple.'

Q. *'What about the dog?'*
'The dog's not doing anything to him. He's just there.'

Stage □ (write in)

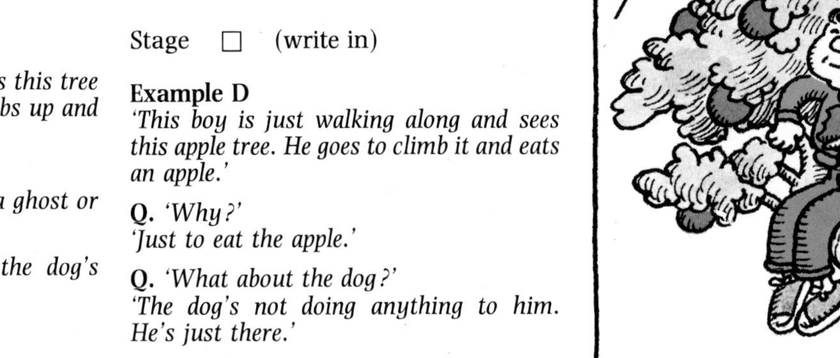

Your child

Stage 1
The younger children find it very hard to see two separate stories in those same pictures. They don't seem to be able to imagine what the friend would see, because their own story keeps getting in the way.
Example B, C

Stage 2
Even when they realise that the friend will tell a different story, they may still have difficulty keeping their own stories out of the way. That's why their versions are often more confused than the less accurate ones in Stage 1. For example, A *knows* the friend can't tell that the dog is fierce, but the idea that fear made the boy climb has stuck in his mind.
Example A

Stage 3
The child has fully understood the task and got it right. He is able to ignore his own version of the story. He understands that a set of pictures can tell lots of different stories.
Example D

Cat up a tree

Understanding other people means more than simply being aware that what they see or know is different from what you are looking at or know about. Feeling and motives are important and a good guide to what people actually do and how you should approach them. How good are children at working out feelings and motives? Read this story with your child.

Polly is an eight-year-old girl who likes to climb trees. She is the best tree-climber in the road. One day while climbing down from a tall tree, she falls off the bottom branch but does not hurt herself. Her father sees her fall. He asks her to promise not to climb trees any more. Polly promises that she won't. Later that day Polly and her friends meet Shaun. Shaun's kitten is caught up in a tree and can't get down. Something has to be done or the kitten may fall. Polly is the only one who climbs trees well enough to reach the kitten and get it down, but she remembers her promise to her father . . .

Ask your child to go on with the the story. You could get him started by asking how Polly feels. How will Polly's father feel if he comes along and sees her climbing the tree? What should Polly do? Here is what some other children said.

Stage 1
'Shaun is sad. Polly will save the kitten. Father will be happy. He likes kittens. I'd save it.'

This little boy said nothing about Polly's feelings – just the immediate action. And he relates the event to himself. He'd save the kitten because he likes them. So he thinks Polly's father will like kittens too and be pleased. When his mother said, 'But her father might punish her,' he said straight away, 'She'll leave it up there.' 'How will she feel about that?' Young children contradict themselves when anyone points out different sides to a story, but they don't seem to be aware they are doing it.

Stage 2
'If her father saw her and didn't know why she was climbing the tree he'd be angry. But if she tells him why he will realise she had good reason.'

A bit more understanding of the story here. Reasons have appeared. This little girl still assumes that father will share the children's idea of a good reason.

'She knows that father will understand. He wouldn't want her to climb. He thinks breaking a promise is worse, but he'd understand that Polly thinks the kitten's life is more important.'

This child realises that Polly knows her father's feelings. He also knows that father could understand *without* agreeing completely. He can see the conflict in the situation.

Stage 3
'Polly will climb the tree. Father will say she was wrong, because she should have called the fire brigade. But he will not punish her because he knows that she thought very hard about what he would say and did what she thought was right. She knows he will care about whether she thought it was right before she did it.'

This child thinks beyond the immediate circumstances for an alternative solution – the fire brigade. She realises that both people know that the other one can also reason about a problem. Also that the other person may not come to the same answer. Both could be a bit right and a bit wrong.

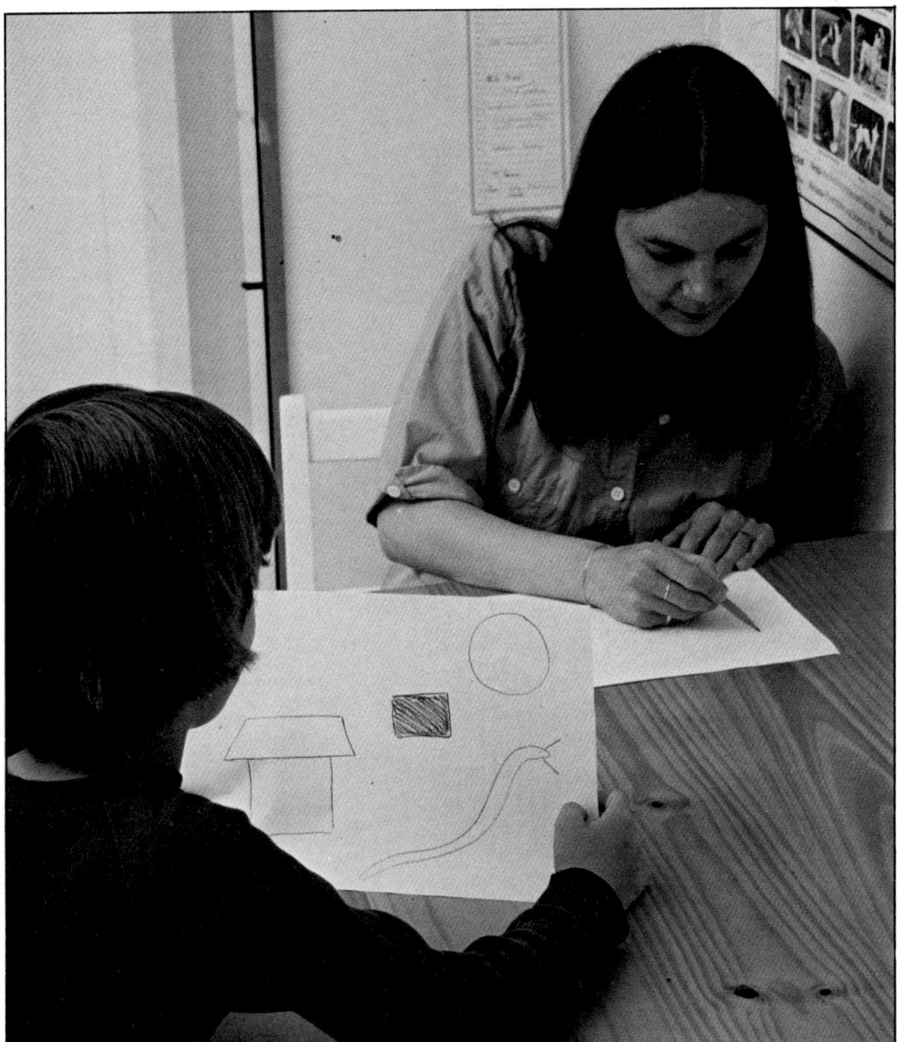

Draw this

This game demonstrates how children use language in a simple game about instructions. Young children find the precise use of language very hard. As they get older, they learn to use words effectively and this requires an understanding of other people. Children learn by experience what effect their words have on other people, and they respond to what other people say to them. They learn to give clear explanations about something that has happened, instead of presuming you know.

Draw a design like this on a piece of paper (or use the one printed here) and give it to your child.

Ask her to give instructions for drawing it to a friend or adult *who cannot see the picture*. The instructions are to be good enough so that the other person can actually draw the same picture, without ever seeing it. Your child should not look at the other person's attempt to see how she's getting on.

Here are the stages that children go through in this game. Firstly they just describe the objects ('a wiggly thing', 'a box'). This is Stage 1. In Stage 2, they see the relationship between one object and another ('next to the house', 'near the bottom'). At Stage 3, they give lots of useful detail, combining position, size and colour of objects ('near the top corner of the black square').

Stage 1 and 2 information wouldn't be enough to draw the picture, because the descriptions of the object are not precise enough, and the objects could be arranged in a number of ways. Stage 3 information would be sufficient.

In general, the older the child, the more useful information she'll give, because she realises that it is needed to reproduce the same picture. The younger ones can't see this yet. They may not really understand that the other child has no idea of what the picture looks like.

You have probably noticed your child saying things like *'What's this?'* when you are in another room and cannot see what he is looking at. Or your child being surprised when you come upstairs and don't know what she wants tying after she has called out *'I can't tie this.'* Later on a child may call from the garden, *'Look! What's this? Mum, come here and I'll show you,'* illustrating that he realises that you cannot see what he is looking at.

Of course, it's quite convenient when a young child is drawing in another room and calls out *'Look Mum'*. You can say, *'Yes, lovely dear,'* and she will be quite happy. But one day she'll realise that you are cheating and she may say, *'No, come and look properly.'*

How can you help?

Any game that uses language, like puppets, charades, etc, helps a child get practice in using words. Guessing games where you need to get the answer in as few questions as possible are good, because the child learns the advantages of organising his thoughts into words. Asking questions that will get you the information you need quickly is very useful in everyday life too.

Let children teach themselves to play box games from the instructions once they are old enough to read them. Then get them to explain the rules to other children or adults who don't know how to play.

Games can be very valuable in teaching children to express themselves clearly so that others can understand. This is important in everyday life too, of course.

The child can understand instructions from others, such as teachers, librarians, lollipop ladies, other children's parents. And the child can tell others what has happened to him. You may be good at guessing this because you know him so well. But this is no help to others, especially if he's in trouble.

But your child will take time to reach this stage of understanding. The table below summarises the skills he will develop between five and ten, and relates them to the games we described earlier. Then it shows how such skills (or lack of them) might be applied in real life.

Your child's understanding

You can summarise the stages your child has reached in these games by placing ticks in the table below.

Game	Stage		
	1	2	3
Talking about people	☐	☐	☐
Doll's eye-view	☐	☐	☐
The country walk	☐	☐	☐
Cat up a tree	☐	☐	☐
Total			

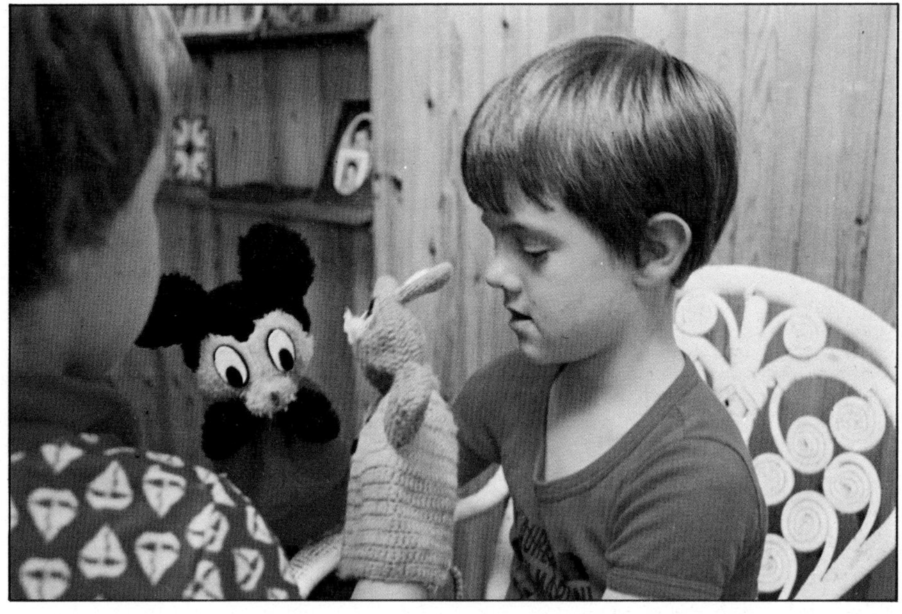

Games	What your child is learning	Example
Talking about people	Ability to identify and describe attributes of people	Mum: 'What's your new teacher like?' Susie: 'Well, she's sort of tall ... and she wears glasses.' (Stage 1)
Doll's eye-view	Ability to leave his skin and project himself mentally into another person's view-point	John is laying the table by stretching across, not by walking round. Although he can put the knives and forks with the handles pointing towards the edge of the table, he gets them on the wrong sides of the placemats (Stage 2)
The country walk	Ability to separate two views of a situation based on different amounts of information	Big boy reading a comic in the playground. Little boy comes along and snatches it. Argument ensues. John sees everything. Mark comes along half way through and thinks the big boy started it, but John knows the little boy did, because he saw it all (Stage 3)
Cat up a tree	Ability to sort out the situation to suit all parties, often by providing the lacking information	Mark is just about to take the side of the little boy when John tells him the whole story. They tell the little boy where lots more comics are and suggest he gets some of them (Stage 3)

Turn back to the summary table at the end of the previous topic, *Understanding the physical world*, and compare your child's results there with his results in this chart.

You may well find your child is at a higher stage on the previous chart. Children usually take longer to develop the skills of understanding people than understanding the physical world.

Learning right from wrong

Children develop their own values from a very early age.

But they may not be the values you expect!

It is always difficult for parents to decide what ideas about right and wrong to pass on to their child. They sometimes seem to forget that children develop their own ideas on this subject between the ages of five and ten. By five, most children are beginning to be aware that justice and injustice exist, but their ideas about it are not always the same as ours. Should we try to influence our children? Or should we let them develop their own ideas?

Chairbusters

Try this cartoon story with your child.

1 Two children, Andrew and Jason, are sitting on two chairs at a table, colouring in books. One says to the other, *'I'm thirsty, let's go and ask for a drink of orange.'* They leave the room.

2 Some bigger children come in and throw chairs about roughly. *'Let's have a chair fight.'*

3 They get bored and put chairs back, *'So no one will know we've been in.'*

4 First two return. Andrew sits down and colours. After a few seconds he leans forward to reach a crayon. The chair breaks. Looks very worried. Jason is still standing up, looking out of window. He says: *'They're silly old chairs anyway.'* He kicks his, which also breaks.

○ Ask your child: *'How naughty was Andrew?' 'How naughty was Jason?'*

If he says either child is naughty, ask how they should be punished. Here is what some other children said.

Dean, age 5 Andrew and Jason were both very naughty. Mother and father would be cross.

Nadia, age 6 Jason was very naughty. Andrew wasn't. Parents would be cross about both chairs but would not punish Andrew, because he was sorry and did not mean to break his.

Fatima, age 8 Andrew wasn't naughty. Jason was very naughty to kick the chair but it might not have broken if the other children hadn't damaged it. The parents would be able to tell what had happened so he wouldn't be punished very much.

Patrick, age 10 Andrew wasn't naughty, Jason wasn't either unless he meant to break the chair. It was important that they were both honest in telling how the two chairs got broken.

Now fill in this table (right) from your child's replies.

At the first stage, the youngest children look most at the results of the actions. This is what matters. They often think quite severe punishments are appropriate, and cannot see any difference between punishments to put people off doing a thing again and punishments aimed at making up for the wrong action. Not being allowed to watch television all the evening when their favourite programmes are on is an example of punishment of the first kind. Saving up pocket money to give towards new chairs or helping father mend them are examples of punishments of the second kind. The youngest children cannot link up actions and intentions. They will learn this gradually.

At the second stage children know that intentions are important, but see them as stronger than they really are. *'He kicked at it – it broke – he meant to break it.'* This later gives way to considering more details and circumstances – it might not have broken, had circumstances been different.

At the third stage, children think it's

	Example	Your child
Stage 1 Judges on *consequences only*	**A** *'Both very naughty'* *'Wrong to break chairs'*	
Stage 2	**B**	
Takes *intentions* into account but authority's view most important. Assumes Jason meant to break chair, can't separate kicking at it from the consequences	*'They'll be cross' 'He was sorry – he didn't mean to'*	
Stage 3	**C**	
Authority will be reasonable and take *intentions* and *consequences* into account	*'Parents will know what happened. Jason was only a bit naughty because it might not have broken'*	
It is important to be *honest* and *truthful* so that authority can consider everyone's intentions	**D** *'Must tell how chairs got broken'*	

important to be honest and truthful. Some general guidelines for living are appearing. You don't 'tell' just because someone will find you out anyway, you tell because it is right to. It matters that other people think you are a good person.

This last is an idea beyond the understanding of a younger child. To him, what's naughty is what you are told off for doing. If you are not told off, it can't be naughty.

Which stage is your child at? □

Being helpful

Here is another story which shows that results and intentions cannot always be considered at the same time.

Pam goes shopping for food with her mother. Her mother has a lot of shopping to do and is getting very tired from walking round the shop. They are almost finished and her mother remembers that she needs a bottle of squash which is right at the back of the store. Mum: *'We've forgotten the squash.'* Pam says *'I'll get it for you.'*

She runs to get the bottle of squash. As she is taking the bottle off the shelf, she drops it. It falls and breaks.

	Whole story	First half (INTENTION)	Second half (CONSEQUENCES)
Was Pam good or bad?			
How good (or bad)?			

○ Show the child the story. Ask if he can retell it, so you can make sure he understood it.

○ Then say, *'Was Pam good or bad? Why?'*

○ If it is not clear why from what the child says, take his verdict and say, *'How good (or bad) was she? A little, medium or a lot?'*

○ Now cover over the second part of the story. Say, *'Tell me the first bit again, this bit here.'* Afterwards try the questions again, as above.

○ Then do this with the second part of the story, covering up the first half.

○ Fill in the results.

Stage 1
Some of the youngest children say that Pam was bad, and some that she was good. They stick to this verdict whichever bit of the story is being discussed.

Stage 2
Some children, when helped by the appropriate bit of the story, can shift their verdict according to whether they are considering the intention or the consequence. 'She was good' in the first half and 'bad' in the second. Their first verdicts are obviously based on whichever they thought more important.

Stage 3
Older children nearly always think intention is the most important, but not if the consequence is very bad; the older ones weigh it up sensibly against the intention.

Which stage is your child at? ☐

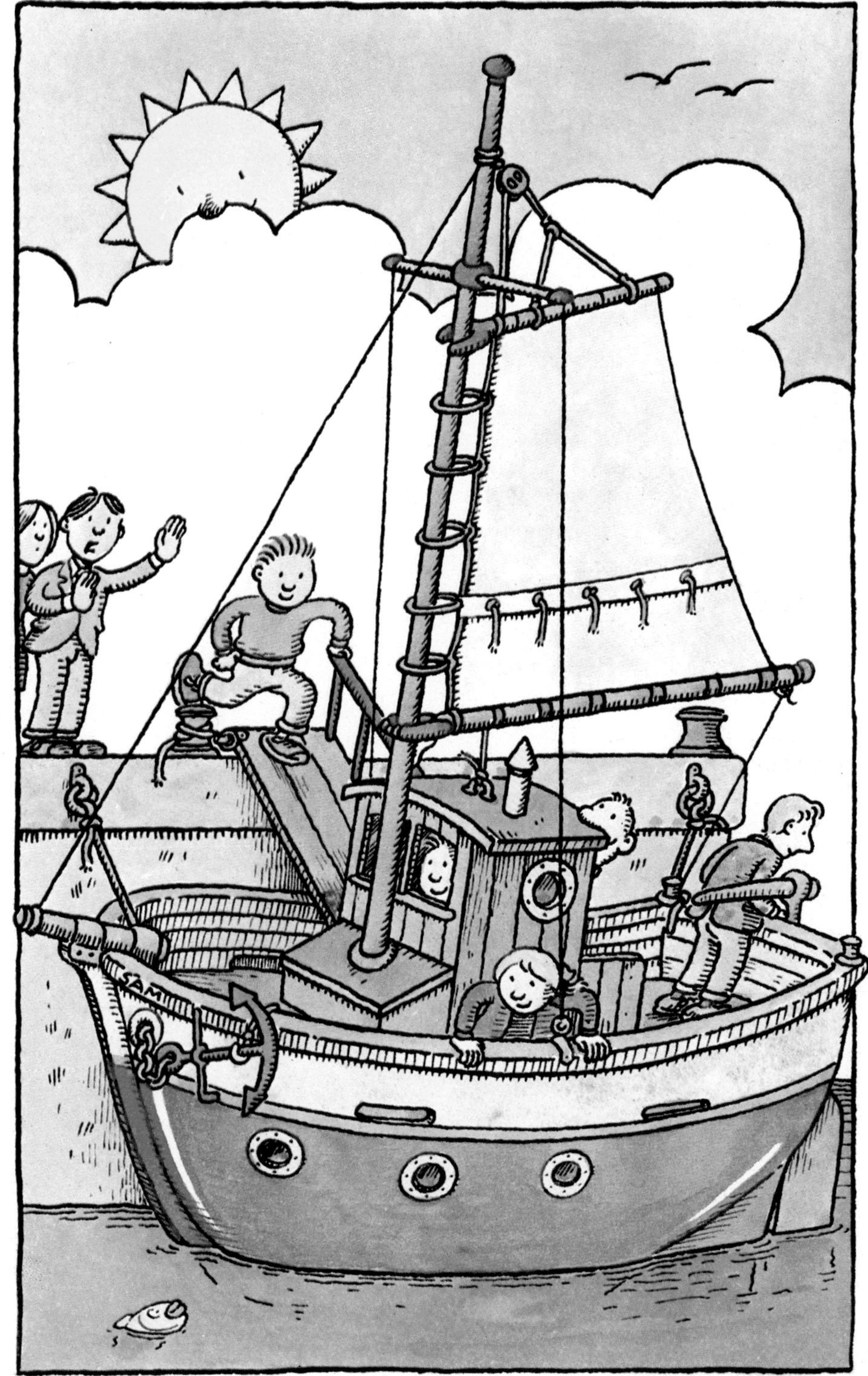

The school boat ride

What's fair to a young child is something that is fair to himself. When older, he can see that fairness must apply to everyone: *'If I am fair at sharing, he will be fair when he shares toys with me.'* Later still, it is realised that being just and honest is worthwhile in itself, as intention, rather than just to get fairness for oneself in exchange.

Here is a story to read and talk about with your child. But if you can do this with several children and let them all have a say, that would be even better. It might be helpful to make notes or tape record the discussion.

A class of children were about to go on a boat ride. They had all been looking forward to it for a long time. The captain of the boat was called away just before they were to start their boat ride. He told the children to stay off the boat, and put Patrick in charge because he was the nearest.

Some of the children were naughty and took no notice of what the captain had said. They climbed on the boat, although Patrick asked them not to. Then the naughty children got off the boat before anyone else saw them.

While Patrick waited for the captain to come back he worried about what he should tell him. Should he tell the captain about the naughty children, or should he not say anything? He didn't know what the captain would say – he might say that the whole class couldn't go on the boat ride. Patrick didn't want that.

○ Ask the children: *'What do you think Patrick should do?'*

○ Encourage them to say why, if they don't give reasons. Don't tell them what you think.

Here is what some children said when talking about the story.

Lucia: *'Patrick must own up.'*

Joey: *'He should keep quiet because telling tales on your friends is rotten.'*

Mary: *'Well, he should keep quiet because no harm was done and what the captain doesn't know won't hurt him.'*

Lloyd: *'The captain might be very cross with Patrick, so he shouldn't tell.'*

Sue: *'Patrick should own up because it wasn't his fault. I think people should be honest and tell, even if it means that the naughty children get told off.'*

Frank: *'Patrick should own up and then the children who went on the boat shouldn't go on the trip.'*

As you can imagine, there are lots of different ideas that can come up. Most of them work on the basis of personal 'hidden rules'. The hidden rules of the children quoted above might run like this.

Lucia's rule: It's wrong to tell lies.

Joey's rule: It's wrong to tell tales.

Mary's rule: If you can get away with something forbidden without hurting anyone, that's OK.

Lloyd's rule: It's better to avoid trouble for oneself.

Sue's rules: It's right to be honest. If you own up when it wasn't your fault, people will understand.

Frank's rules: Owning up is right. Rewarding the obedient and punishing the disobedient is right.

The stages in children's rules go as follows.

Stage 1 In the school boat ride story, smaller children won't get the point. They'll probably agree with everyone else, or say something silly. They don't know what a rule is or what it is for. They can't learn this until they are ready. There won't be any hidden rules in what they say.

Stage 2 The Stage 2 child goes for simple but rather rigid rules. He might think none of the children should go, or, like Mary, that they all should, because no harm was done. He'll probably stick to his view even if others disagree. He's not used to the idea that he can make up his own rule. He often, like Joey, repeats the ones he already knows.

Stage 3 The Stage 3 child is more thoughtful and is more likely to take account of other principles such as honesty and reasonableness. Sue and Frank do this. They know that some rules are more important than others and that rules can be changed.

Which stage is your child at? ☐

Rule chart

Stage 1 child
Not aware of rules as such. But is beginning to notice things that happen regularly. May protest if you try and change these. 'But you always let Teddy have a bath with me.' This is the beginning of an attempt to make a rule.

Stage 2 child
Aware that rules do exist. Has no clear idea of who makes them. May say he doesn't break rules in his games, but he often does. However he doesn't notice this, and is not deliberately lying.

Later: Realises rules are everywhere. Whether it's a game of conkers, how to cross the road safely, what you're allowed to do at school, everything has its rules. They're all very important and must not be broken. Neither can they be changed. Of course, he does break rules sometimes. Thinks it's all right if he gets away with it.

Stage 3 child
Thinks that rules are fascinating for their own sake. Children at this stage invent all sorts of most complicated rules for their own games.

They have realised that game rules are invented by people and for people. So they know some rules can be changed. This can only be done if everyone concerned agrees to it.

They have become aware that some rules are much more important than others. There is a world of difference between making a mistake in a game and stealing the teacher's purse, for example.

They probably still think that school rules and the laws of the country can't be changed, or say that only the head teacher can change school rules and only the queen can change the law.

Making rules

Children's understanding of rules is important because we all need some rules to help us live together without too much squabbling. But until a child can link events together in his head, he won't be much good at rule-keeping. You'll have to tell him again and again, every time the situation is the slightest bit different. For example, you can teach a very young child to say thank you when his granny brings him sweets every week. But he won't think to say thank you when the next-door neighbour gives him a picture book. Until he can group together events that have something in common in his mind, he can't learn rules properly.

At Stage 2, he'll get a bit better at keeping rules, but is likely to confuse what he did with what he thinks he did. The world of his imagination is not yet clearly separate from the real world. He won't be a very reliable rule-keeper.

Later on in Stage 2 the child can learn rules all right, but can't sort out what to do when they conflict with each other. He has no idea about priorities. While he knows what rules are, he doesn't really know what they are for, and does not see them as being useful and helpful. Rules you make need to be definite and easy to keep. There also shouldn't be too many. The rules at school might contradict some of yours and you should make this clear and explain why. One thing that he should not have too much trouble with is knowing that one set of rules operate at home and another at school.

At Stage 3, a child will be interested in your explanations for rules, but he'll probably try arguing with them. But once they're agreed between you, he is likely to try and keep them, even when no one's about to know otherwise. This is because he can see that rules are not made to be a challenge or a nuisance to him, but to help people.

Forming a conscience

That little inner voice that tells a person what's right and what's wrong is conscience. It forms in a child through many complicated processes that are not yet fully understood. We do know that example is very important. 'Do as I say, not as I do' doesn't work. If you often break rules in front of the child, he won't think much of them.

A conscience is somewhat different from the keeping of rules purely because they are there. Conscience means keeping rules because they are right. This doesn't usually happen until a child can see the principles behind rule-making and rule-keeping, at Stage 3. At Stage 2, he obeys mainly to avoid punishment.

Talking about rules and where they might be used as in the school boat ride game is always helpful. It enables children to move from seeing rules as unbreakable towards knowing that they can be useful and that they can be based on everyone's agreement. A conscience based on principles the child understands and ones he can see are followed by the people he admires and loves is a solid guideline for life.

So the biggest danger to guard against is making rules that can't be kept. If a child gets into the habit of breaking many rules before he can really understand what use they are, he might lose any respect for rules. This could lead to him only caring about himself instead of being concerned for the rights of others.

Your child

You can summarise the stages your child has reached in these games and play them again in a few months' time to see how he has changed.

	Stage		
Game	1	2	3
Chairbusters	☐	☐	☐
Being helpful	☐	☐	☐
The school boat ride	☐	☐	☐
Total	☐	☐	☐

A child's world

This chapter is about what it's like to be a child. It asks you to stand back and take a fresh look at the world children inhabit. It's about children's personalities, imagination and play; it's about their friends and their ability to stand on their own two feet. It should help you to get to know your child better.

Knowing your child means a great deal to him and you. It means knowing what he likes, his favourite book or song, what he likes to wear or eat and what he dislikes – thunder or haircutting or Dr Who.

Every parent reponds to these likes and dislikes; it is part of the closeness of the relationship between parent and child. Children feel secure if they know that they are understood by parents. But a child's world is a very different place from the one inhabited by adults.

A child's world between the ages of five and ten is so exciting and varied that it can't easily be summed up in a few sentences.

It's the time when a child has tremendous energy and curiosity about everything around him and an amazing capacity to learn if his interest is captured. But it is also a time when he needs constant reassurance that what he is doing is right.

What others of his own age think begins to matter very much. As well as being part of a family, he's now part of a school class and part of a group of friends. He will work tremendously hard to become good at something and, if he receives approval, he will try even harder. But if he feels he is not coming up to someone else's standards, he may learn a feeling of inferiority.

Since no one can be good at everything, he's going to fail sometimes. So it is important that he realises that *everyone* is good at some things and fails at others. Some are best at sports, some at school work, some at art or crafts and so on.

Every child is potentially talented; every child is an important, unique individual. He needs to feel that you value him as a person, and that this is not dependent on his achievements, even though you will always be proud of these and always give him encouragement.

2

A daily diary

Even when you do the same things, you and your child may have very different memories of your day.

One of the best ways to find out what's important in your child's daily life is to suggest he keeps a diary for a day or two – and you do it too. You'll probably be surprised to find how different your accounts are of his day. Things you forgot about may, however, have made a strong impression on him. Things you thought he would remember he forgets. And, by making it a game, you'll probably find out all sorts of things about times when he was away from you that you wouldn't otherwise have known.

His diary

Ask your child to note down the main things that happen to him for two days. Choose a weekday and a weekend day. If he doesn't want to write things down, perhaps you could use or borrow a tape-recorder and either ask him questions about his day or let him speak into the machine himself.

Your diary

All you need to do is note down the basics about how your child spends his time. Take the same two days as he does. You may find it easiest to keep your diary in the form of a chart, like the one we show opposite, which Mary Durham filled in for her daughter Helen.

The chart has four main sections to fill in.

1 **Time** When he starts and finishes doing things.

2 **Activity** What he does. You might need to limit this to major activities. For instance, simply write down 'play' even if he has played four different games in an hour.

3 **Place** Where he does an activity. First, fill in the particular place, and then make a note whether it's at home, at school or out in the community.

4 **Abilities** We suggest that, for each activity he does, you tick the relevant skills and abilities.

○ Skills (physical, writing, drawing, painting)

○ Understanding the physical world

○ Understanding other points of view

○ Learning right from wrong

So, for each activity tick which particular abilities he is using. For instance, if he goes swimming, that's mainly a skill. If you have a long conversation with him about his friends, he is using his understanding of other people. For some activities he will be using all these abilities and in these cases don't single one out.

Don't worry if you have difficulty in deciding which to tick sometimes. It probably means that you weren't present and don't really know what went on or that several skills were used equally.

You may want to do what Mary did in her chart and write down a few words about an ability that you were particularly struck with, or something in particular which happened. You might find your child doesn't agree with you.

Mary Durham
Weekday chart for Helen (aged 9)

Time	Activity	Place	Skills	Understanding the physical world	Understanding other points of view	Learning right from wrong	Comments
7.45	Gets up	Home					
8.00	Breakfast						
8.45	Sets off for school						Helen looked smart in her new hat
9.00	Class together	School					
9.30	Assembly						
10.00	Writing		✓				
10.30	Playtime				✓		
10.45	Writing, music		✓				
12.00	Lunch and playtime				✓	✓	
1.30	Story		✓				
	Spelling		✓				
	Apparatus		✓	✓			
	Story		✓				
3.30	Reads	Home	✓	✓			She took a long time coming home
	TV			✓			
5.30	Tea						Had fight with Alex over who had more milk. Both had same though
6.00	Brownies	Church hall (community)	✓		✓	✓	Helen lost her Brownie badge again
7.50	Writing		✓				
	TV	Home		✓			
	Music			✓			
9.00	Bed					✓	But she didn't go to sleep for ages

Helen's diary

Here is Helen's weekday diary. It records the same day her mother recorded and contains information about a lot of things that happened at school which her mother didn't know about. Underline any sentences that you think refer to skills and abilities.

7.45 Mum shouts in my ear to get up.

8.05 I get downstairs for breakfast.

8.45 Set off for school with my sister.

8.55 I get to school. Put hat and coat on peg and go into class.

9.00 I get a new pencil and a reading card. I already have a pencil. We did news and decided on names for language. We are going to have birds. We moved places – that was fun. I'm by Hannah.

9.30 Assembly. We talked about Christmas. I didn't say anything. We sang 'If you're happy and you know it'. I don't like that song. We talked about lots of things in class.

10.00 Playtime. I was called names because of my hat. I'm not wearing it tomorrow. They said I looked like Noddy.

10.30 We wrote about the Christmas holiday. I got very fed up. We started some new songs which I like very much especially 'Here comes Grazzo'.

12.00 Second playtime. Someone had taken my sandwiches. I was very hungry. But I didn't like to say in case I got someone into trouble. I played with Tanya.

1.30 The story was the Hobbit. It was good. Then spelling. I am quite a good speller. We *had* to do PE. Tony Green kicked me in the face. Apart from that it was alright. But anyway he said he was sorry. We got on the apparatus. I got on the wooden beam and walked along it really well. I didn't even lose my balance once. Spellings again. We got in trouble for taking too long for putting things away.

3.30 I went home on my own. I threw some rosehips in the canal. My sister told me that water babies live in it and I thought they might get hungry.

3.50 Got home. Read Missy Lea and watched TV. Flash Gordon conquers the Universe. It was good. We had meat pie for tea. I ate two helpings and told my Mum about the sandwiches. She nagged me and said I should have said.

6.00 I lost my badge before Brownies. I had a good time. We played Good Morning Oh King and Ladies. We had a pow-wow about our Christmas Party and were given letters. Tanya fell over and hurt herself. But she was very brave.

8.00 I did some writing. I put Leo Sayer on the record player. I played 'Endless Flight' but Daddy didn't like it. His head aches when he has to listen to pop music.

9.00 I went to bed. I read under the bedcovers. Mum came in and shouted. She said it was 10.30. She switched the light off.

Some points to notice

The things mentioned most by children are often not the same things that concern their parents, and the child knows this. Helen was surprised at her mother wanting to know the names she was called because of her hat.

The parent learns things that might not have come out in general conversation. Helen's mother found out that Helen had been kicked in the face.

Parents tend to write down what happens throughout the day, while the child only comments on highs and lows.

Children in this age group write about facts, things that happened to them. They don't write long paragraphs about how they felt, or what they thought about. They live mostly in the present.

They don't comment much on why other people do things. It's impossible to tell if Tony Green kicked Helen out of malice or not.

Food and TV are both prominent in the child's diary.

There is pride in being good at something. Helen is pleased about walking on the wooden beam and being fairly good at spelling.

Look at the abilities revealed by your child's diary. You're probably finding out that she can do quite a few things you hadn't known about. (Helen's mother didn't know that Helen could walk along a wooden beam.) Does she use particular abilities and skills more in one place than another? Or are all the skills used equally at home, in school and in the community?

Let's take a closer look at the abilities you've noted down and see which ones occur most often in which places.

Skills

School will be the place where your child regularly practises skills she has learnt – in reading, writing, number work, art and craft, music activities, games and PE. Going to clubs and evening activities out in the community would give her a chance to use them there as well. Skills she might use at home are washing up, sewing, cooking, modelling, repairing things and bedmaking.

Understanding the physical world

A good understanding of the physical world and how well a child can find his way round it should be reflected in progress at number work at school. But you could also spot progress at home in the way he tidies his room, the way he sorts his toys and what he does with his

Lego and the kinds of games he plays when he is on his own.

Understanding other people

This is a skill which will be needed everywhere she goes – home, school and community. Most children of this age are not very good at understanding how their teacher or Brown Owl thinks, but they are going to have a pretty good idea why their friends and their brothers and sisters do things.

Some children learn this skill much later than others. By the time your child is ten, though, she should have a pretty good idea about how to get on with other people she meets.

Learning right from wrong

Most children of five and six have an idea about this, even if they choose not to do the 'right' thing. Every time they find themselves in a new situation they are going to have to discover the rules, and what is expected of them. Home, school and the community will provide ample opportunities to learn what's expected.

By the time they get to school they will be familiar with home rules, but will have to learn a whole new set at school, both for teacher (no running in the corridor) and for acceptance amongst children (don't be a sneak). Then, when they go out into the community, there is yet another set to learn (no apple scrumping allowed).

We'll come up against all these skills and abilities again, when we look at other aspects of children's behaviour.

Let's play

When children play, they are testing out the world.

By watching children at play you can see them practising not only their skills but their understanding of their world and people around them. Without realising what they are doing, they continually experiment and try out different kinds of behaviour and expand that understanding.

What is play?

○ It's fun. People enjoy playing.

○ Play is for enjoyment, for play's sake. It's not done specifically to produce anything. Although something *may* be produced, it's an added bonus.

○ Play is spontaneous and it's voluntary. Nobody usually makes you play.

○ Play is active.

○ You can play alone or with other people.

○ There are countless ways to play.

Have you ever considered how your child is involved with the world around him through his play at home, in school and out in the community.

Opportunities

Through their play, children have opportunities to develop their abilities. The following list shows how different play activities exercise each one.

Skills and body co-ordination Skipping, climbing, ball games, riding bikes, playing on swings.

Learning about the physical world Exploring, testing out the shape and size of everyday objects, and pretending they're something else. A stone that is a cake for a tea party can be turned back into a stone again for digging in the garden.

Understanding other points of view Being in teams and secret societies, having to wait for a turn, not always winning or being the best at a game. Children learn that others are quite different from themselves, and that it is difficult, but worthwhile, to share and cooperate and show loyalty. Besides learning about other people, they will also understand more about themselves through pretending to be lots of different people, through making up, or even acting out fantasies about things that bother them or that they are groping to understand.

Learning right from wrong Having to keep to rules in games, seeing that cheating is unfair and meets with the disapproval of other children, making up their own play rules.

Try to watch some children play; watch them at home, and out-of-doors and, if you have a chance, at school. Here are some things you might watch for in particular.

○ Did one child seem to be the leader most of the time?

○ Did the children take it in turns to do things?

○ Did the children play at being other people?

○ Did the children imitate grown-up behaviour?

○ Were there differences in what boys and girls did?

○ Were there any noticeable rules to the game?

○ Was there any punishment or criticism of people who were doing things unfairly?

○ What sort of pretend and fantasy was there?

○ What sorts of physical skills and abilities were involved?

○ What sorts of things were used? Toys? Everyday objects?

Then make a chart like the one we've given here as an example. We have taken games often played by five-year-olds at home, seven-year-olds outdoors and ten-year-olds at school. Each game has been divided according to the abilities it exercises. In your chart, put down the names of the games you saw and divide them up the same way.

Each of these types of play is a very enriching experience for the children and for you.

Not only will you get an insight into the ideas they have about other people and the world around them, you'll also see many aspects of their own developing personalities.

	At home *five-year-olds*	**Community** *seven-year-olds*	**School** *ten-year-olds*
TYPE OF PLAY	Playing at having a tea party	Skipping and chanting	Acting a play about going to a new school
SKILLS CO-ORDINATION	Laying table	Skipping	Making costumes, scenery, posters etc Learning words
UNDERSTANDING THE PHYSICAL WORLD	Using yoghurt pots as pretend tea-cups Pouring real liquids into the 'cups'	Keeping rhythm	Using stage lights and props
UNDERSTANDING OTHER POINTS OF VIEW	Taking turns to take the most popular part in the game Sharing out real food and drink Playing at being different people	Waiting for a turn Seeing that some children are more talented than others Showing off	Seeing the range of abilities of others and that everyone has a talent for something Co-operating to get the work done
LEARNING RIGHT FROM WRONG	Pretending to be naughty or to tell off naughty children	Telling off those who don't take turns fairly	Acting out quite complicated ideas about right and wrong in the various situations of the play

Your child's temperament

What are the qualities that give your child a personality all his own?

By the time your child has reached the age of five, you will have a pretty clear picture of the sort of temperament he has. This temperament will colour his behaviour towards you, his brothers and sisters, his friends and the outside world. But it can be influenced, or even changed, by a number of things:

○ the physical and emotional changes that your child goes through as he gets older.

○ the way he is treated by you, the rest of the family, people at school and everyone else he meets.

○ his experience of life so far.

Temperament has many facets

Because he is still experimenting and testing out different ways of behaving, there are bound to be some inconsistencies from day to day, and changes from year to year. A child may be the soul of generosity one day and a mean old miser the next; a shy, retiring five-year-old may be the noisiest boy down the street by the time he is ten.

However, you know your child better than anyone else, and you will be aware that in general he behaves in a certain way, despite any day-to-day variations.

When you look back and think how he has behaved over the last week or so, you can probably pinpoint things he did that were typical of him – his temperament was showing!

This topic now asks you to look more carefully at several aspects of your child's temperament and personality. If you have more than one child in this age group, include them both when answering the following questions. Distinguish them by using a different coloured pen for each.

You may find interesting differences between your children. They may have seemed similar when they were younger, but will almost certainly have developed in different ways as they got older.

How active?

Andy, nine years old, is one of those children who can't sit still. He's always rushing about. Taking him on a long train journey is guaranteed to try anyone's patience; his parents call him the world's greatest fidget. However, his constant energy is now being used to advantage as he spends every spare moment practising for the junior football team.

Bob, eight years old, was a very good baby, very easy to care for. As he got older his mother found that he remained a quiet child, not as active as most of his age group, but really quite contented. She finds him a restful companion in the house beside his more energetic sisters, but she has one major problem. It has become obvious that he is a real slowcoach. To get him ready in time for anything is a major battle. Now she just sets his clock earlier than everyone else's. He prefers this to constant nagging, which doesn't help because he is doing his best anyway.

Is your child more like Andy? More like Bob? Or is he in-between? Put a tick where you think he falls on the scale.

Andy |__|__|__|__|__|__| **Bob**

How regular?

Betty is a six-year-old child who's never had any problem fitting into a routine. This is useful because her family need to be very organised – both parents work, at different hours, and have a complicated child-caring and car-sharing system. Betty's appetite, the amount of food and sleep she needs, the time she wakes up, and the times she wants to go to the toilet are all rather regular and predictable. So Betty is very convenient and easy to live with. But last year, her parents wanted a holiday with a difference. They borrowed a caravan and set off to explore Ireland, with no fixed plans at all, eating and sleeping as they felt the need. This was greatly disturbing to Betty, who of course felt very hungry, sleepy, etc, at the usual times, and became grumpy and miserable when her needs weren't met.

Caroline, five years old, is a child whose physical needs are very irregular, and always have been. Sometimes she needs very little sleep and will not settle until quite late, only to be up bright and eager and asking to play at some unearthly hour. Other mornings, she's very difficult to wake and stays sleepy all the way to school. Luckily, her parents say they value her strong individuality (except early in the morning!) and accept it, rather than worrying that it is caused by some mistake they've made in her early care. They feel sure that, as she grows older, she will learn to adapt easily to different places and to stand on her own feet without too much stress.

Who is your child more like? Betty? Caroline? Or in-between?

Betty |__|__|__|__|__|__| **Caroline**

How adventurous?

Danny, aged seven and a half, is one of the friendliest children you could meet. He seems to love anything or anybody new and is quite without fear. Because he always looks on the bright side, he copes well when his wants are frustrated. The teacher even noticed him comforting the others when the coach broke down one day and they couldn't go on an outing. There was a danger earlier that he would become an over-bossy leader, but this phase has passed. Now his mother worries a bit that his lack of fear could lead to problems when he starts being allowed out more on his own. But she feels that, on the whole, the common sense he has gained from approaching new experiences boldly will be a great help to him.

Dawn is nine. Her automatic reaction is to withdraw from anything new, whether it's food or an unknown person. Getting used to school was very difficult for her and she still doesn't want to start any new activity, like Brownies or music lessons. Her parents have found, after

many battles, that the best tactics are to persuade her firmly that she must try but that she can give up after five 'goes' if she really doesn't like it. Her father says, 'Well, at least I don't have to worry too much about her going with strangers; and I know that once she's decided she does like something, she'll stick with it, not want to do something else next week as her little brother does. And she doesn't fuss about the latest fashions either!'

Is your child more like Danny? More like Dawn? Or in-between?

Danny |__|__|__|__|__|__| **Dawn**

How emotional?

Emma, five, always over-reacts. When she is excited she laughs and shouts loudly and jumps up and down. If she falls over, she screams the place down, even if she hasn't hurt herself much. Once, her mother, tired after a day of minor disasters, found herself saying, 'Oh shut up and don't be such a baby', before turning to see a really badly gashed knee. You can't easily tell just how good or bad Emma is feeling. But she's so affectionate and cheerful most of the time that her parents find it easy to forgive her tantrums.

Charlene, aged eight, is just the opposite, and it's even more difficult to know how she feels. If another child takes her toys, she just wanders off and plays with something else; if she's hurt, she'll whimper quietly, and if she's happy, there'll be a charming little smile. She's alert and takes in everything that's going on, but you'd need to get to know her to realise this. Her reactions are inside, rather than outside, and she's beginning to write some very clever and observant stories at school.

Does your child show very intense emotional reactions, like Emma. Or is she more like Charlene? Or in-between?

Emma |__|__|__|__|__|__| **Charlene**

How adaptable?

Liam (nine and a half) is a very adaptable child. Whether he takes to something at first or not, he soon settles down with it. He worries a little about his new school class once a year when the forms change, but after the first day he's soon full of the new lessons he has learnt. When his parents moved house it didn't seem to bother him at all.

Johnny, his friend, is about as different as you can get. He takes weeks to settle down every time a change occurs in his life, and his family sometimes wonder if he enjoys holidays at all, although he says he does, because he's so on edge while he's away, and never seems to sleep much in a strange bed. But once Johnny does settle to something, he is seldom bored or restless.

Is your child adaptable like Liam? Or is he more like Johnny? Or in-between?

Liam |__|__|__|__|__|__| **Johnny**

How observant?

Nicky (ten) is a very observant child. He is rather sensitive, startles easily and is very discriminating about food, noticing differences between various brands that his mother could have sworn didn't exist. He also notices every little change in his surroundings. This was often irritating when he was younger, because he tended to make frank comments on people's clothes and houses that they didn't always appreciate, but he has now learned only to do this when his comments are favourable. This has made him very popular, especially with his parents' friends.

Martin (ten) is just the opposite. His mother says: 'He probably wouldn't notice if the house was flooded.' Nothing worries him – he can happily go out with his jumper inside out and he can eat, sleep or do his homework in the midst of absolute chaos. It's useful in a busy family, but sometimes his parents feel that he's so unaware of what's going on around him that he will often have trouble. He did once when he got lost coming home from his friend's new home. 'Oh well, it all looked the same to me.'

Is your child more like Nicky? Or more like Martin? Or in-between?

Nicky |__|__|__|__|__|__| **Martin**

How easily distracted?

Kerry (six and a half) has been described as 'having a mind like a butterfly'. She never stays at one game for long because something else attracts her attention. She is not doing very well at school and her mother worries that she'll never be able to concentrate well. However, she does gain a lot of knowledge about the world from being interested in so many things.

Nina (eight) has always concentrated well. She settles down to battle with her homework whatever else is going on at home. When she was small, her parents were amused and proud at the length of time she'd spend on her building block puzzles. She was determined to learn to read as soon as possible, and used to keep on and on at them to help by hearing her, which was not always convenient as father had a very tiring job and her little brother was teething. When she sets her mind on something she usually gets it because she never gives up.

Kerry and Nina aren't really complete opposites, because distractibility and persistence are not mutually exclusive qualities. You can see this better if you look at Richard, aged eight.

Richard is very easily distracted, like Kerry, but, like Nina, he is also a persistent child. He comes home from school and leaves a trail of untidiness through the house because his mind is on some activity he has started; then he gets bored and becomes distracted by a more attractive activity. But by bedtime, he has usually returned to each neglected pile of belongings and rearranged them. He is the sort of child who has a 'method behind his madness' that you wouldn't expect on first impressions. His mind seems at times to race ahead of his conversations, so that they're rather disjointed.

Who is your child like?

Kerry **Richard** **Nina**

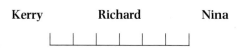

Your child's temperament

As we've tried to show, each style of behaviour can have its advantages and disadvantages. The type of temperament you find most difficult to live with will depend on your own character, and that of the other members of the family. The size of your home may also make a difference.

On the chart (right) you can make up a profile of your child, or children, by copying out the ticks you have put after each example of temperament we gave. Then finish off the sentences at the bottom. This should help to explain the best and worst areas of your relationship. It might be interesting to ask your partner to do this as well, without looking at what you've written.

You might like to keep this chart (right) somewhere and look at it in five or nine months time, or a year. You'll see how some areas of basic temperament can be changed by the child's experiences with his world.

Constantly active	**Andy**		**Bob**	Quiet and slow-moving
Regular rhythms	**Betty**		**Caroline**	Irregular
Boldly approaches new things	**Danny**		**Dawn**	Withdrawn at first
Over-reacts	**Emma**		**Charlene**	Keeps emotions inside
Very adaptable	**Liam**		**Johnny**	Takes ages to settle with new things
Very sensitive to small changes	**Nicky**		**Martin**	Unaware of changes
Easily distracted	**Kerry**	**Richard**	**Nina**	Concentrates very well
		Steady worker if interested		

What I like most about my child is

What annoys me most about my child is

Some children are just difficult to live with, however much you love them. These children usually fall into one of the following groups.

1 'Awkward-minded' children
These children tend to be irregular in their habits (like Caroline), withdraw from new experiences (like Dawn), are slow to adapt to them (like Johnny), show very strong and definite reactions (like Emma). Since these reactions are usually negative, life with such a child is never peaceful.

To succeed with this type of child a parent needs endless patience. He must be consistently firm without exploding or giving up altogether and letting the child always have his own way. It is essential to realise that such behaviour in a young child isn't always the result of your mistakes, or of his determination to annoy you. It may just be the way he is.

2 Children who are slow to warm up
These children, too, withdraw at first from new experiences and take a long time to adapt. Their reactions are mild, though, and they are not particularly active children. This type of child takes a long time to settle into a new school and is often shy and silent while the other children play. Without outside pressure they will join in and adapt in their own time. Parents who value confidence may become impatient, but this only turns reluctance into definite stubbornness.

These children become experts at avoiding what they don't like. If the parents are over-tolerant and indulge these whims, the child will not learn to face the world as it really is.

3 Very distractible children
These children tend to leave everything half-finished, and are very bad at carrying out instructions, although they always mean to do so. But their real problems don't become apparent until they are old enough to be given a bit of responsibility. They are hopeless at tasks like shopping or being left in charge of younger children. Parents who place a specially high value on their children becoming responsible as soon as possible, or completing homework carefully and getting on well at school, will find themselves getting very angry with a highly distractible child. Even when they say quite honestly, 'I'm sorry, I really didn't mean to forget' it becomes very irritating when it happens so often.

Parents who accept that this sort of child is going to take longer than average to become responsible and hardworking are at an advantage here. They can patiently point out that, since he does tend to forget instructions, it's only sensible for them to write them down and give them to him. They can ask, rather than nag, about his unfinished homework.

But as these children grow older, they become interested in particular hobbies or games and their own strong interest helps their concentration.

Remember, they cannot do this until they're old enough to see themselves from other people's points of view, and understand why their behaviour is so irritating.

Not all bad

So some children are more difficult to live with than others, especially if their temperaments are very different from one's own. But every child has his good points as well, and they're all good at something. It's often interesting to hear an outsider's view. Many a 'little terror' is a 'little angel' at school, and some are the other way around. They're trying out different ways of behaving. And in the process, each is showing you that he is a unique and complicated individual, and needs to be treated as such.

This trying out of different roles is a vital and necessary part of growing up.

Boys and girls

Born to be different – or just taught to think they should be?

Being a boy or a girl is a major influence on what happens in a child's world. From birth, boys and girls are treated differently. Both society in general and families in particular have definite expectations of the sort of behaviour they should get from boys and the sort they should get from girls. By the time they reach school age children are pretty clear what is expected of them and they do indeed behave differently in some respects. But are boys and girls *really* different or are they just doing what is expected of them? Have they simply learned to be different?

Differences in behaviour?

Here is a list of differences in behaviour between boys and girls. Some are true, some are false. Tick which ones you think are true and which you think are false.

		True	False
1	Girls are more social than boys; they spend more time with other children	☐	☐
2	Boys are usually more aggressive	☐	☐
3	Girls don't try and achieve as much as boys	☐	☐
4	Boys are less easily persuaded to do things	☐	☐
5	As they grow older boys show greater mathematical abilities	☐	☐
6	Girls are better at rote learning and simple repetitive tasks	☐	☐
7	Boys are less likely to be timid and self-conscious about their appearance and abilities	☐	☐
8	Girls are more dependent on those who look after them	☐	☐
9	Girls have greater verbal ability than boys; their conversation is more fluent; they can explain themselves better	☐	☐

Of course, regardless of whether they are true or false, a great many people believe each of these statements. And once people believe a statement, they behave accordingly. However, research has shown that statements 2, 5 and 9 are generally true, and that statements 1, 3, 4, 6, 7 and 8 are generally false.

Some real differences

Many researchers have studied large numbers of boys and girls and have suggested ways in which they do seem to differ. We give some of them (right). But always remember that these are averages. The average man is taller than the average woman, but very many women are taller than very many men.

The tests that yielded these findings were conducted with a great many children, so they only provide averages. Individual children vary. So it's not likely that all of these things will apply to your child.

Not so different

A recent survey found there were few differences between girls and boys when it came to:

- ○ whether the child had a best friend or not.
- ○ preferring to play alone or together.
- ○ making friends easily.
- ○ being able to stand up for themselves.

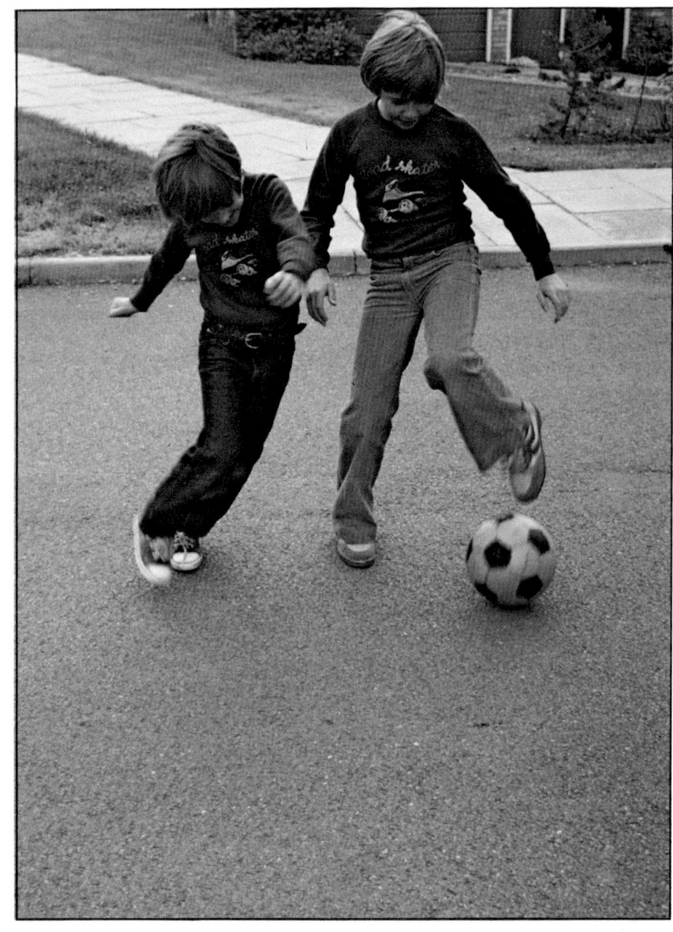

○ quarrelling with friends.

○ fighting with brothers and sisters.

But
○ Boys were more likely to come to physical blows with their friends.

○ Parents of boys were more likely to discourage a friendship their sons had made.

Branching out

Your child does not have to follow the general trend and do what's expected of that sex. Many children, when offered the opportunity to develop skills suited to their abilities rather than to the traditional view of what is suitable for their sex, seize it with both hands. It is far better to encourage them in doing what they enjoy and are interested in than to force them into traditional roles which may not be so 'natural' after all.

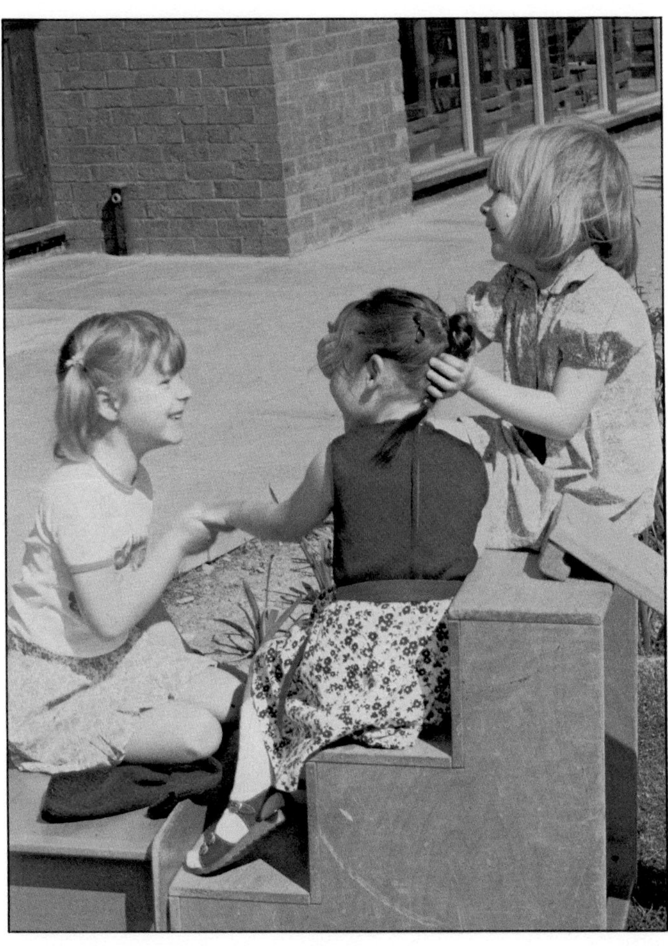

Girls		Boys
say their first words sooner use longer sentences, are more fluent	TALKING	
learn to read sooner	READING	more boys than girls need remedial reading (4 boys to every one girl)
spell better	SPELLING	are not so good
learn to count at an earlier age	COUNTING	learn to count later than girls
	ARITHMETIC	do better with arithmetic tables
are not so good at fitting things together and judging how large things are	SPACE AND AREA	are better at tasks involving fitting objects together, and accurate judgement of space and area
grow slightly faster reach puberty younger	GROWTH	are slightly slower and more uneven in their growth reach puberty at a later age
will sometimes play with boys tend to be more organised and co-ordinated	PLAY	will rarely play with girls (more noticeable as they get nearer ten) tend towards more rough and tumble
tend to perform as well as they can at all subjects tend to evaluate own abilities and performance less realistically tend to show more interest in sewing, cooking, art	SCHOOL	tend to do better in subjects that they have an interest in tend to evaluate own abilities and performances more realistically tend to show more interest in sports, mechanics, science
are more conventional; try harder to fit in	SOCIALISING	are not so worried about conforming

Friends

The making of friendships early in childhood is crucial to loving relationships later in life.

The older a child gets, the more important friends become. Once at school your child may spend more time in the company of other children and adults than with his family. He gets a lot of happiness from doing things with friends of his own age, especially if he is an only child. And he is also learning to 'get on' with people outside his family – something he will need to do all his adult life. So it's important to start early.

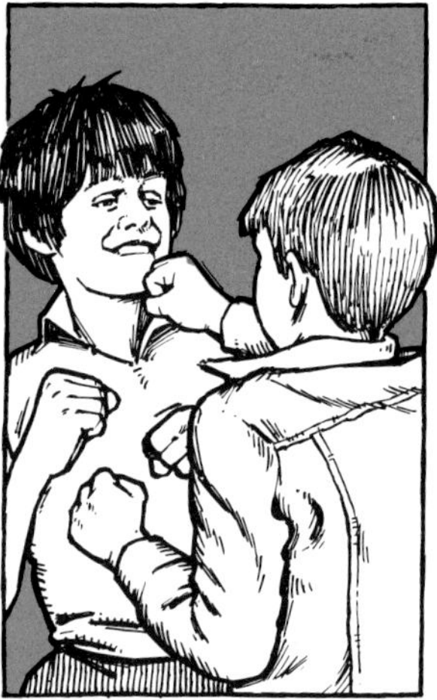

Child of four	Child of seven	Child of ten
He sees himself as the centre of the universe, he's the most important person in his social world	He can see himself as a member of someone else's social circle; aware of choosing friends and being chosen	By now, he will probably have one or two best friends; may also be a member of a clique or gang
Few children to choose friends from; under adult eye most of the time	Wider circle to choose friends from; less adult supervision of play	A lot of activities take place out of adult's view; identifies with older children a lot of the time; greater independence
Gets involved in scrapping rather than fighting – hair-pulling, pushing	Fights – and more serious ones – break out more often	Individual fighting may be less frequent; but groups may 'gang up' on one another
Talk about friends is rare; mostly self-centred	Learns new language from friends – nicknames, jargon of games, abuse for enemies	Language is adopted from older age groups

Patterns of friendship

Making friends seems to be the easiest thing in the world for some children. For others it is hard, or they take a little longer. Some children may have a wide group of friends, others spend most of their time with one best friend. Some children actually prefer to play on their own a lot of the time, or only with their brothers or sisters.

On the right are some of the differences in friendships formed between the ages of four, seven and ten.

Follow the leader?

Is your child usually a leader or a follower? Or is she both – at different times? Watch your child playing with a group of her friends and answer the questions below by ticking the appropriate boxes.

Does she take the lead in most games?

Yes, often	*Sometimes*	*Rarely or never*

Does she try to take the lead in most games, but not succeed?

Yes, often	*Sometimes*	*Rarely or never*

Is she ever the leader?

Yes, often	*Sometimes*	*Rarely or never*

Is she happy to be a follower?

Yes, often	*Sometimes*	*Rarely or never*

In a survey of seven-year-olds in Nottingham, parents were asked similar questions. The answers these parents gave are shown in percentages in the diagram on the opposite page.

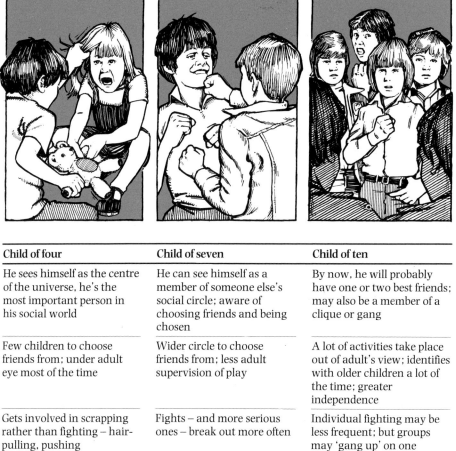

Perhaps you can see these various types of children among your children's friends?

Almost half the parents felt that their children fell into the category of 'givers and takers'. Let's hope they weren't giving too rosy a picture! We'd all like our children to fit in well with others, but this can be a difficult skill to learn. Not only that, but you'd have to be a saint to get on with *everyone* you meet *all* the time. Because each child is an individual, developing in different areas at different rates, and having a distinct personality, there are likely to be some problems somewhere along the way. That's normal, and only to be expected. Don't forget – it takes all sorts.

Us versus them

While your child is making new friendships he sometimes does things that go against the grain with his family. You might get the feeling that by joining up with friends he is ganging up against you. 'Being friends' can show itself in ways that upset parents. On our chart overleaf

29%	8%	46%	17%
The boss	**The failed leader**	**Giver and taker**	**The follower**
Succeeds in leading others His ideas are followed Generally has things his own way	Can't express his wishes in a way that gains the acceptance of others May choose to play with younger children that he can lead	Happy for leadership to change hands Takes different roles from day to day	Doesn't want to take decisions Prefers being led and is happy with this May play with older children so that he can take this role

is a list of things that some parents said about their own childrens' friendships. Tick the boxes for any that you recognise as being like things you've said.

Then look at the other columns and think about the behaviour from the child's point of view. What is he doing that helps him fit into his group of friends? Tick again what sort of behaviour you think it is. Do you still think that what he did was entirely wrong?

It takes all sorts

You may think your child is too bossy, but his friends seem to enjoy his good ideas and leadership. If they found it a problem, they'd stop playing with him!

You may worry that your child is too easily led. But if he seems happy, why try and change things?

If your child doesn't seem concerned, ask yourself what you're worrying about. If he *does* seem unhappy, in what ways can you help?

Nobody likes me!

Children who have some difficulty making friends seem to fall into three groups.

Those with communication problems These children haven't yet learnt the right way to act when they're with their friends. They might be too loud and boisterous, or never listen to what the others have to say. They might over-react to things the others say and do, and frighten them off.

Those suffering from shyness Children who are shy may have one or two good friends but are not outgoing. They immediately retire into a shell if confronted by a crowd of children they don't know very well.

Those who are too bossy Bossy children are usually good at getting other children's attention at first but are then too tactless to become popular.

Learning the right way to make friends and keep them is hard work and some children seem to take a long time to find suitable tactics. It helps if you are able to

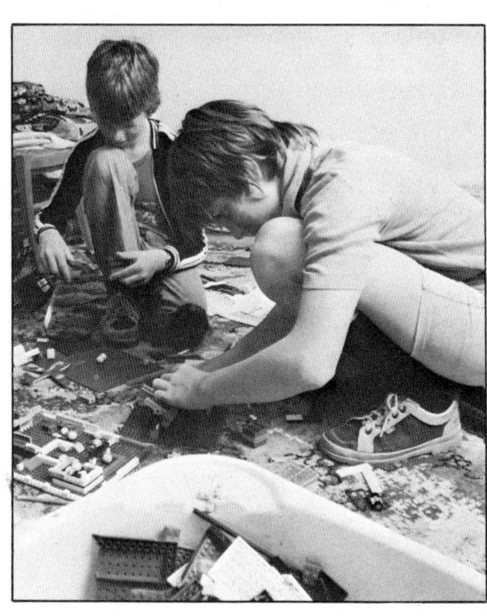

I don't like the fact that:	My child was: enjoying companionship	doing things the others do	obeying rules	becoming more independent	being loyal	learning to give and take
○ as soon as she gets with her friends she's different, she'll be louder, bossier, sillier. Whatever the others do she's got to do it too. It's as though she didn't have a mind of her own ☐						
○ he just won't tell on his friends. A window was broken the other day. I knew he hadn't done it, but even after a shouting match he wouldn't tell on the little so and so who had ☐						
○ he'll be cheeky and disobedient if his friends are there and I tell him to do something. He'd never dare to speak to me like that when we're on our own ☐						
○ the others seem to be making her grow up too fast. She's pop mad. She moons around her bedroom looking at some pin-up. 'Everybody thinks Donny's fabulous' ☐						
○ he never wants to come out with us. He just wants to be with his friends all the time. We can never go out unless we take at least three of them with us ☐						
○ he gave away two action men yesterday. The gang thought there ought to be fair shares a bit more ☐						

point out what's going wrong though you'll need to be very tactful.

A shy child may need to be encouraged to talk about what frightens him when he meets people he doesn't know; but it may be that he is never going to have more than one or two friends, if that is how he is most comfortable.

A bossy child may need to be shown that other people need to lead sometimes too.

The importance of friendship groups

There are things a child learns from being with his friends that he can never learn from his family.

○ He learns about the companionship and intensity of friendships.

○ He learns the ideas and behaviour typical of his age group. If there's a marbles craze, he will soon know all the rules and may be playing like an expert. If he didn't learn things that are important to the group he wouldn't be counted as a member.

○ He learns a set of rules which he must keep if he's to be a member of a group. If the rules are broken quite severe punishments may be meted out by the others.

○ He learns to be more independent. His family is not the only influence on him, now that he has his friends. And this can make life both easier and more difficult for parents.

○ He learns about loyalty and not letting people down.

○ He has to give and take. He doesn't do this because an adult tells him, but because he realises that he *has* to consider the others, if he wants to be counted as a friend. He cannot always put himself first.

○ Friends don't have to tolerate behaviour that parents would, so he has to learn to earn their affection and to keep it.

The earlier he learns to get on with others the better he'll fit in when he grows up.

In a world of their own

There are lots of real-life benefits that come from playing at make-believe.

Watch a young child at play, on his own, completely absorbed and seemingly miles away. He's in a world of his own, we say.

That's what imagination is all about: getting into a world of your own inside your head, where you can try out different ideas and think yourself into different situations. Children are busy making up different worlds all the time. Make-believe play is one of the ways they explore and try to explain the grown-up world to themselves. Young children play like this on their own; as they get older they involve their friends, or their brothers and sisters.

Language becomes the tool for their imagination. They use words to turn the table into a mountain and the space behind the door into a monster's cave. As they play, they talk a lot, using language to help them act out the way they feel.

Because a lot of the action takes place inside their own heads, it may be hard to find out exactly what is going on. You could listen in or, if you've got the sort of child who doesn't mind talking about her fantasies, you could ask.

What do you think?

Parents vary in the amount of make-believe play they consider right for their children to indulge in. Where are you on this scale?

- I allow unlimited make-believe play
- I allow quite a lot of make-believe play
- I allow some make-believe play
- I don't allow much make-believe play
- I don't allow any make-believe play

How much do you actively encourage make-believe play? You can do this by providing varied and unusual toys, reading stories and providing books which stimulate such play, and talking to your child about it. Where are you on this scale?

- I encourage make-believe play a lot
- I encourage make-believe play a bit
- I don't actively encourage or discourage it
- I'm not very keen on make-believe play
- I actively discourage it

If you are near the bottom of each scale, you might care to consider some of the ways in which make-believe games are said to help children to develop creativity, intellectual growth and social skills.

Make-believe games lead to:

- heightened concentration.
- improved self-awareness and self-control.
- better appreciation of how others feel and why they do things.
- development of co-operative skills, since make-believe play in groups needs give and take.
- better use of the child's environment for play.
- greater capacity for abstract thought and for generalisation.
- release of tension by working out problems, defeats and frustrations in make-believe play.

Stories set the imagination free

Children and adults need to make things up. When we read stories in books or watch plays on television or talk to our next-door neighbour about the exotic holiday we would like to have, we are thinking about experiences we may never know in our own lives. We all need to daydream and have our private fantasies about the different things in life that we might have done. Thinking about things as we would like them to be helps us to cope with things as they really are.

Daydreams are stories about ourselves

When Peter was seven and a half he wrote in his school story book, *'When I grow up my profession would be a footballer or something sportish like that. I want to get in the school football team because I'd really love to do that.'* But Peter is a pretty realistic child. Two years later he wrote, *'Last year I was very slow and the PE team I was in usually lost and I think I'm getting too fat.'* He knows his limitations. Now he writes football stories instead, like the one below.

'Cheers of delight came from the Santown team as they mobbed Kevin. It was now 8 o'clock and Kevin went over with the rest of the team to their manager Bert Shawdon. Well done lads, he said, especially you Kevin, even Gordon Banks would be astonished at that save. It was now getting near half past eight so Kevin got on to his secondhand Halfords racer and went home …'

Do you think that Peter would like to be Kevin in this story? Writing stories like this helps Peter to live with the fact that he is never going to be a great footballer or even be in the school team. This sort of story writing is important because it helps the child to sort out what kind of person he or she really is. At the same time, it's a way of trying out what it would feel like to be a different kind of person.

Playing is about life

When we do stand back and let children get on with it, we get a very special glimpse of what it is like to be in their world. Their early games are to do with exploring the safe world of home and family. As they are given more freedom, so their games move into the outside world and further away from you. The games become much more complicated and may need much more careful preparation and equipment.

The list on the next page will give you some idea of the different kinds of games that children may be playing at different

stages. It covers only a few of the possibilities. You will find that you can add to it and alter it. But remember, no two children play the same way.

Homes and gardens

'Mummies and Daddies' is a favourite, particularly when only two children play together. This game is usually very comfortable and involves all the everyday routines of getting up, eating, dressing, shopping, visiting and chatting. As you listen to children playing these games you will be interested, or horrified, to hear them talk like you. You may not like the way you seem to be treating a harmless teddy bear but for the child it is a way of trying out how you feel and what makes you tick.

These games are untidy and can involve emptying the tool shed or hanging blankets over the dining room table. A small tent for the garden or a Wendy house are often a good base for games of this kind, and it's best to put away things you don't want to find made into something they are never intended to be!

Batman and all that

Television makes an enormous contribution to children's imaginative play, both in the playground and at home. Don't be surprised if you get a spate of Batman. You will just have to live with it and resign yourself to the fact that it will be Tarzan next week and that's even noisier. Space Sentinels, Dr Who, Wonder Woman, Scooby Doo, the Pink Panther will all be part of their play. In these TV series the goodies grapple with the baddies and, led by a super-hero, always win; the kids find them rivetingly exciting. Don't underestimate the contribution which they will make to your child's imaginative life.

You may sometimes wonder whether these violent and noisy models for your children's play are a good thing. Should you turn the TV off? It's difficult to tell which programmes are likely to be disturbing for a particular child and which are not. You know your own child and it's best to ask him when you feel it's getting a bit much. And they need to be able to turn to you for reassurance. *'Is that man really dead or just acting?' 'That's really just a man dressed in a plastic mask, isn't it?'* If you are around you can explain anything that seems just a little too strange or alarming.

When they are playing, children use and adapt ideas from television programmes.

Don't worry that they may go too far, imitating the special powers of Wonder Woman or Tarzan.

If you are there to talk about these programmes they will ask you questions and you can explain why normal people in the real world can't fly or dive headfirst through closed doors. Children can accept straightforward answers.

'Let's play schools'

As school is part of their life, it is also a very important part of children's play. With their friends and their toys, they play at being different kinds of children and different kinds of teachers. It doesn't matter how pleasant school is, nor how kind and gentle their teacher, you are sure to hear them playing at being teachers who speak strictly and threaten punishment.

No matter how well behaved your children are, you will hear them playing at being cheeky and disobedient. These fantasies about school probably come from real feelings of uncertainty about school. Playing at being naughty helps them to decide what they think naughti-

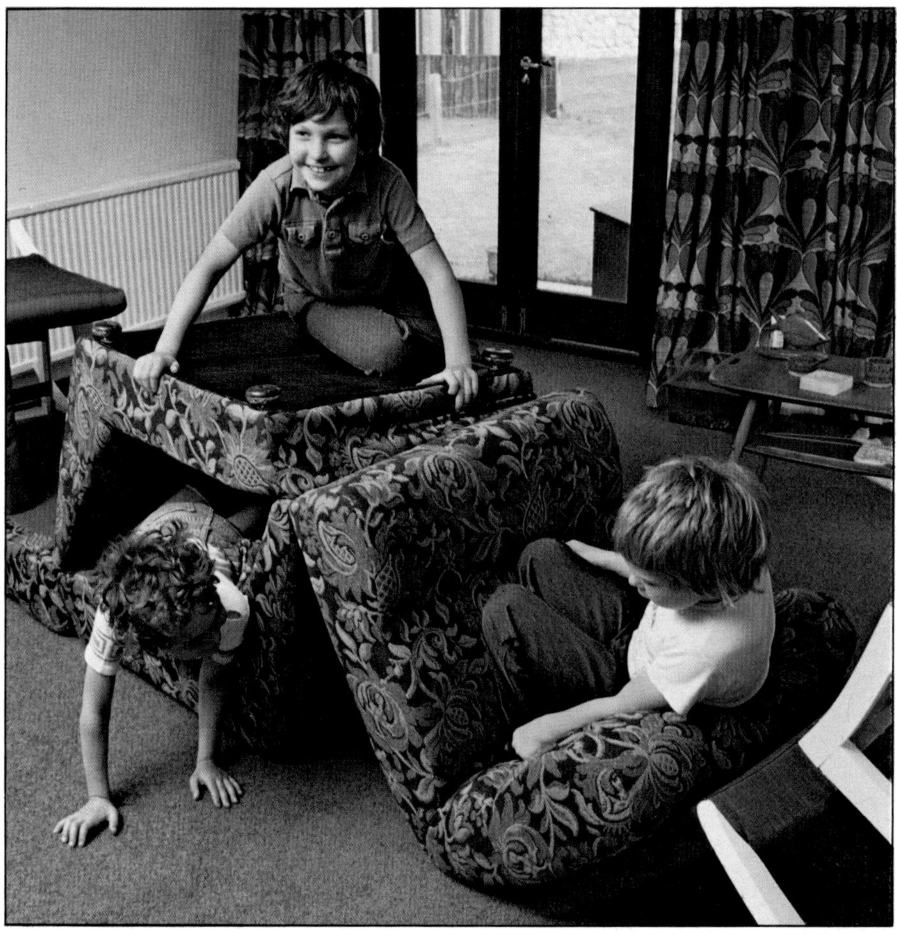

ness is and playing at being a strict teacher helps them to cope with ideas of authority.

Witches and ghosts

When children don't understand or are frightened by something they often turn to spooks or magic.

A ghost in the bedroom cupboard can be useful. When you say *'Pop upstairs and get your shoes'*, your child replies *'No, I can't, I'm frightened, there's a ghost in the toy box/a wolf under the bed/a giant behind the door/a witch on top of the wardrobe.'*

There are times when children's real fears about witches and ghosts get out of hand and they need reassuring and comforting. Don't get annoyed at unreasonable fears as this will not help. Be sympathetic and talk through the fear, and show that, really, there is no ghost or witch in the cupboard at all.

Gangs and secret societies

From about seven onwards you may find notices like 'PRIVATE' or 'KEEP OUT' or 'Nowun under 8 allowed in here'. Small camps, tree houses, dens and hidey holes appear, which are often the HQ of some secret society, places for adventures. Here is an account by an eight-year-old of how he organised a gang.

'On Thursday afternoon I went down to Glenn's house to play and when I went home I asked Andrew if I could borrow his book. I wanted to borrow it because it had something about secret agents and detectives. In the afternoon on Friday I tried to get a detective club up but everyone was playing with Glenn so I didn't bother . . . but on Saturday morning I went shopping and I bought a note book and a torch. I'm the secret agent Andrew's the spy Rodney's the detective and Glenn the assistant. Andrew is going to make up some real radios.'

This game took three days to set up and each member of the group has his own special role.

Such games often involve sending messages in code or inventing secret writing; they can also involve collecting all kinds of equipment and may last for several weeks. Whatever happens, playing relies heavily on the group's ability to talk and listen to each other and to use ideas from stories, TV and comics.

Keep out! Do not disturb!

Despite the warning notices, you *are* needed; as a listening post, consultant and provider of goodies. Cowboys, soldiers and explorers need gun belts, helmets and packs, filled with things like pencils and notebooks, string, a compass, maps and all sorts of personal bits and pieces. They may help themselves if you don't. And if you don't want blankets and pillows taken off beds then it is better to find something else. Getting them ready to go out to play may seem tiresome but it can be the most important part of the game, when they plan and look forward to it.

Come to the show

Play becomes much more private from seven to ten. You may be allowed to pack up the picnic or hear stories about what went on in the 'secret' garden, after the event. But eight, nine and ten-year-olds often want you as an audience as well.

Most shows are not very elaborate and some happen on the spur of the moment. For others you will have to buy a ticket and sit on uncomfortable chairs in the dark. The end product may not be spectacular but the effort put into achieving it is worthwhile.

Toys

Anything can be a toy – as long as it's fun.

Different people have different ideas about the meaning of the word 'toy'. Some people think of big equipment from shops. Others think only of wood toys. Others think of dolls and jigsaws. And a few think of junk. Toys are all these things and more. A toy designer once said, 'Anything is a toy if I choose to call what I'm doing with it play.' Left to their own devices, children would agree: they'll enjoy a wide variety of toys.

Toys help children explore, test, invent, role-play. Toys help them be flexible, adventurous, aware. Toys don't always have 'rules', though when children play board games, or games like marbles, they have to observe rules.

Let's look at some different kinds of toys and the different opportunities they offer.

'Getting around' toys

It's not just learning *how* to climb ropes or ride a bike that's fun. It's the pride and sense of achievement that a child gets from being able to do it that's important. 'Getting around' toys give a child a sense of control. Some common 'getting around' toys are bikes, go-karts, skateboards, swings, climbing frames with slides, climbing poles.

Pretend play

Children enjoy trying on the adult world for size. What is it really like to be a spaceman, a mum, a bossy teacher? Acting it out helps them to find out. Pretend play also helps them to come to terms with their own fears and uncertainties. Big dogs may seem less frightening if a child has a tame pretend one of her own. Hospitals are less threatening if she is the doctor in charge. Pretend games may need pretend equipment (a cardboard box cooker), 'real' equipment (medical kit, shopping trolley, dustpan and brush), dolls that can be different people, or tools, like screwdrivers and spanners.

A small world

A child may pretend he is someone else, or lives somewhere else. He might construct a house for himself and his friends or his brothers and sisters, too small for adults to get in to. Or he may be the dictator of a world made up of model houses, schools, farms and model people. The models he uses might be little dolls, meccano or lego, wooden bricks, plastic animals etc.

Learning skills

Children are keen on learning grown-up skills, like knitting and making models. Being able to make things like Mummy and Daddy do is good fun – especially if you can make something really useful at the end. Popular craft kits are model-making, french knitting, macrame, patchwork and engraving.

This and that ...

There are all sorts of other odd toys around, each with it's own special function, like kaleidoscopes. And there are things children like to collect, saved more for the pleasure of getting the whole set, rather than the value of each individual item – things like dolls' clothes, toy vintage cars and matchboxes.

Think of all the toys your child likes to play with. Which of our categories do they fall into? Note them down on the chart on the right and also say how your child uses them.

Here are some other ideas you might also like to think about.

○ Why do you buy toys? To help play – or as a reward, or pay-off? To get the children out from under your feet?

○ Can you give a child too many toys? Would you prefer your child to have more friends or more toys?

Kind of toy	What your child uses	What does he/she do?
'Getting around' toys		
Pretend play		
A small world		
Learning skills		
This and that		

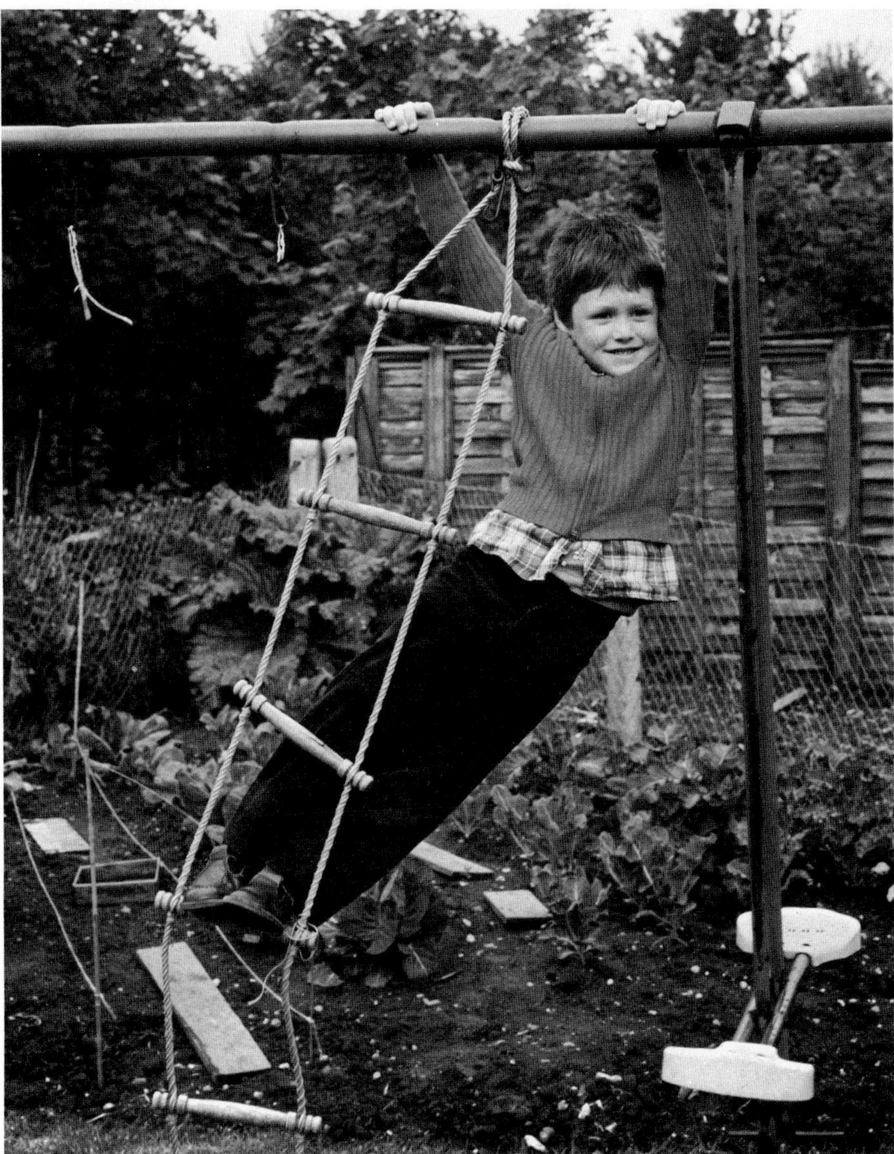

○ Who should choose toys? Care for them? What about sharing them?

Things to avoid

○ Getting in a rut – always buying the same kind of thing – 'he likes cars . . .'
○ Buying your child what *you* wanted but never got when young (unless you are sure he wants it too).
○ Buying what was popular when you were young, or what you miss most from your childhood – times change.
○ Buying the latest toy as advertised on TV.

Counting the cost

When a toy costs a lot, you are probably most concerned that it should be cared for – and used a lot. Otherwise it is a waste of your money. But five to tens are less concerned than you about appearances, less able to foresee that something will rust from being left out in the rain, and less aware of how much £10 to £20 means in the family budget. And it certainly doesn't follow that the most expensive toys will be the most loved, or the most usable. Here are some ideas for controlling costs.

A swap-shop for books, jigsaws and board games which never appealed, have lost their appeal or have been outgrown.

Making wooden toys, dolls clothes – when there's time but not much money to spare.

Buying for all the family toys which will appeal to most members of the family for a number of years. For example: bricks have different uses from twelve months through to twelve years.

Buying toys with lots of uses for example, building systems, or 'building shells' rather than toys that you can only do one thing with.

Making the most of junk old clothes for dressing up, wood for building, card-board boxes and computer paper for construction and drawing.

Doing-it-together bulk-buying for supplies, especially in the pre-school years, but why not after too?

Children's folklore

A trip back into the rhyming world of children.

You hear people say of teenagers, 'They've got a whole separate world of their own.' They seem to have words, styles of dressing, entertainments and interests that no other group of people share. But what about five to ten-year-olds? Are they really any different?

In their world, too, there are special things that give them pleasure and excitement; things that younger brothers and sisters, teenagers and adults, even parents cannot share or appreciate.

If you could disguise yourself as a child and walk into a crowded playground, you wouldn't know the games and rhymes and the actions that go with them. Can you skateboard, or even understand the words for the tricks that can be done with one? Have you got a collection for 'swaps'? Do you know all the characters on their favourite TV programmes?

You'd be a stranger in their world, and they must sometimes feel like one in ours.

Here is a selection of children's folklore. Some you may remember, some may be new to you. Ask your child to tell you some of the rhymes he knows. They will give you an insight into the world he lives in.

Rhymes

For ball bouncing	'Shirley Temple is a S–T–A–R' 'Playsies, clapsies. Round the world and backsies. Touch your heel touch your toe and under we go.'
For skipping	'Vote, vote, vote for Margaret Thatcher...' 'All in together girls, never mind the weather girls, please jump in your birthday, January, February, March, etc'
Tale without end	'There was an old man called Michael Finnigan, he grew whiskers on his chinigan' 'The bear went over the mountain...'
Just for fun	'Oh my finger, oh my thumb, oh my belly, oh my bum'
Ghoulish	'It's not the cough that carries you off, it's the coffin they carry you off in' 'The worms crawled in and the worms crawled out, oo-oo-ah-ah. In at the mouth and out at the snout, oo-oo-ah-ah'

Smut

When Suzie was a baby, a baby Suzie was:
She went ga. ga. ga. ga. ga. ga. ga. ga. ga.

When Suzie was a toddler, a toddler Suzie was:
She went tod, tod, etc.

When Suzie was a schoolgirl, a schoolgirl Suzie was:
She went 'Miss, Miss! I wanna go piss,
I don't know where the toilet is!'

When Suzie was a teenager, a teenager Suzie was:
She went 'Ooh, ahh, I lost my bra,
I left my knickers in my boyfriend's car'

Law

Calling a truce	pax / kings / screase / crosses / fainites
Keeping a secret	'Cut my throat and wipe it dry, if I tell I'll surely die'
Possession	'Findings keepings, taking backs stealings'
Swapping	'Touch teeth, touch leather, can't have back for ever and ever'
Bargains	'It's a deal, double quits, easie-peasie...'
Truth	'Cross my heart and hope to die, drop down dead if I tell a lie'

Half-beliefs about luck

Avoid stepping on the cracks in the pavement

'Find a feather, pick it up,
All day long you'll have good luck'

'Step on a beetle, it will rain;
Pick it up and bury it, the sun will shine again'

'Touch your head, touch your toes,
Hope I never go in one of those.'
(hearse or ambulance)

'Every time you see an ambulance hold your collar until you see a four-legged animal'

Riddles

What gets wet when wiping?	A towel
What turns without moving?	Milk
What's the difference between a warder and a jeweller?	One watches cells and the other sells watches
Why did the cowslip?	Because it saw the bullrush
Why does Prince Philip wear braces?	To keep his trousers up
What did the big tap say to the little tap?	You little squirt
What's black and white and red all over?	A newspaper

Pranks

'Knocking down Ginger/'Ring-bell-scott/Rat-a-tat-tat'

'There's a knock on the first door. When it opens the string knocks the second door... and so on. This is how you cause a row between two neighbours.' (Child's description)

You will probably enjoy recalling some of the rhymes, but we're not suggesting that you need to become an expert on your child's world. Just remember that it's there and it's all part of being a child. No adult teaches these games to children, they are passed down from one child to another, changing slightly all the time, so children in one area sing one version of a song while those in a neighbouring area sing a different one.

Fashions and fads

A fad may be a passing fancy but it is also more significant than you think.

Fashions and fads are an important part of the child's world, even if parents don't always think so. By the age of five, children have usually worked out that parents are likely to let them have something if *everyone* considers it vital. So they will often work out very elaborate and – they hope – persuasive reasons as to why they should be given what they want.

Here are two examples of children who want to keep up with the latest fashion. If you were James' or Michelle's parent, what would *you* do?

James wants a stunt kite

James hasn't got a stunt kite, so he thinks he can't join in with his friends, who've all got them. He implies that you alone are the cause of his being an outcast. You feel guilty. Your partner says that anyone who opens James' toy cupboard is in danger of being crushed to death. Your mother says you spoil the child. On a TV programme someone states that stunt kites are good for children, they learn things from them and get out in the fresh air. You go into the park and nearly get your eye poked out by one. They cost several pounds. Of course you want your child to have fun but is a stunt kite the answer to everything, when six months ago a skateboard was? That skateboard hasn't been out of the cupboard under the stairs for three months.

Would you:

a take James down to the toy shop and get him the latest model?

b tell James that he can save his pocket money for the next month, and if he still wants the stunt kite you will buy it together then?

c point out that he has got an ordinary kite and he could make do with that – look what happened to the skateboard craze?

d say no – and that you are sick and tired of buying him the latest gear just to see it thrown away the next week?

Michelle wants high heels

When it comes to summer sandals time, Michelle says that *all* the other nine-year-olds in her class have got sandals with high wedge heels rather than the sensible, flat crepe-soled sandals you were proposing to buy. Michelle has always been rather an odd one out, and she now seems desperately keen on trying to be like the others. Although the sandals she wants seem strong enough, and are made by a reputable manufacturer, you dislike the style, especially as you hate to see children wearing copies of adult styles. You start to wonder whether it is really you who is making Michelle different from the rest of her class – or would she be, whichever sandals she wore?

Would you:

a go and buy the sandals she wants without any further discussion of your own views?

b try to find a compromise style which looks modern but is still basically the type of sandal you prefer?

c point out that Michelle could twist her ankle and would be uncomfortable in high-heeled sandals?

d say no, I decide what sort of sandals are suitable for little girls?

'a' answers
If you have ticked these for James' and Michelle's requests you are accepting the important part fashions and crazes play in your child's life and letting them have what they want without question. You gave in rather easily, though, considering your reservations.

'b' answers
These answers are compromise solutions which let the child know that you are considering their point of view, but haven't lost sight of your own.

'c' answers
You're turning down his/her request, but for what seem to you to be good reasons; with luck, your child will see your point of view.

'd' answers
These may be the first ones that occur to you, but are going to seem unreasonable to the child, since, indirectly, you are criticising him as a person, and his friends as well.

Copycat, copycat

Why *do* children get so carried away by the latest fashion? It feels good for your child to be like the people he likes. Then he is liked by them!

Being like friends means wearing the same sort of clothes, enjoying the same games and interests, having the same sorts of ideas. It means collecting the same sorts of picture cards, having the same hair cut, being able to climb as high as everyone else.

But being different is painful – it's having to go in at 5.00pm when everyone else goes in at 6.00pm. It's not having a bike or a t-shirt with a picture of The Who on it when everyone else has.

Your child will want to conform because he enjoys it. He doesn't see himself as a sheep! At this age having an identity doesn't mean being different from others or having a mind of one's own; identity comes from being part of a group. So it is worth weighing your child's need to fit in with his friends against your own views on common-sense buying. A little bit of give and take on either side is no bad thing.

Collections and crazes

Between five and ten, children often develop a single-minded interest in collecting things. Sometimes lots of children are collecting the same sort of things at the same time and they get a lot of fun from comparing notes and swapping.

But collecting can be a solitary business too, where a child is revelling in an activity that is all his very own.

Collecting is fun and useful for several reasons. When a child collects things he begins to learn how to tell that things are different. You may only notice the difference between a long shell and a round shell. Your child sees their different colours, shapes and textures and he knows their names, too.

Collecting helps a child to develop certain skills, such as sorting things into different groups because some match and some don't.

The child has control over what he collects and he is the one who does the organising. It is all his own responsibility. He also begins to see that there are special words for things he collects and whole sets of words that refer to particular aspects of them.

Gradually he becomes an expert. Being an expert is great. People ask you about things and you can tell them all they want to know, and more too! Your child will gain in confidence once he understands that everyone can be an expert in something.

Any old rubbish

Most young children are hoarders. Yours probably wants to keep as many objects as possible and often it's quantity that counts rather than quality. The idea is to have the biggest collection. You might notice this after a day out, when you suggest he leaves 'those dirty old stones' behind. 'No, please, I *must* have them, they're mine.' It doesn't matter how useless or ugly the objects seem to you, they're his very own, found by him, and this makes them special. Who knows what memories they may hold for him?

Soon his room starts to overflow with pebbles, feathers, twigs, old boxes or whatever catches his eye. 'It's like living with a human magpie', complains an older sister.

Somehow the collection takes more shape, and eventually you realise he has started to specialise. Many children have several different collections at once, all very important to them, and you're expected to understand this.

These are popular items for collection: stamps, dolls, football cards, flowers, leaves, popstars' pictures, matchboxes, china ornaments, little boxes, car and train numbers, stones, glass and plastic animals, soft toys.

There's no accounting for tastes. And you can't force children to start collecting 'sensible' things. You may get cross when your child has been given a stamp album for Christmas but shows no interest in stamps whereas he has hours to spare for collecting worms. Don't worry too much about what the collection is: spotting, sorting out, and putting into groups are all useful things to learn, whatever the item they are learning from.

Three collectors

Alison is a five-year-old. She has a little corner by her bed where she puts objects she calls her treasures. There are things like a silver painted fircone from Christmas, some bird feathers, pictures, shells and a Spanish fan. She gets so upset if they are moved for dusting that her mother found an old tray for them to stand in.

Simon is a seven-year-old. Like many other boys in his school class, he collects football cards, toy soldiers, train numbers, petrol stickers and badges.

Sandra is a ten-year-old. She belongs to a fanclub for her favourite pop star, and has lots of pictures, posters and badges with his name on. But her special collection is of tiny little dolls in national costume from all over the world. She makes most of their clothes herself, copying style from pictures in books and magazines. This hobby began when relatives who travel abroad a lot gave her a few dolls as a present. Her parents' friends are often surprised at how much she knows about foreign countries.

How to help

You may find that your child has a number of things that are teetering on the brink of becoming a collection. Perhaps by finding him two more little bottles or another few matchboxes you can start him off in earnest.

Help him find a special place for his collection – a display on a wall, boxes to put different items in. This will make his room easier to clean as well.

When the collection is building up, ask him about it. So much the better if you don't know anything about it – he's the expert. Try to ask questions that get him to describe how he groups things, how he spots differences, why certain things are special.

If you reach the stage of asking questions that he can't answer, or if he wants more information, go one stage further.

○ Encourage him to go to the library.

○ Suggest he asks his teacher.

○ Find out if there's a local society interested in what he's collecting.

○ Check on services in newspapers and specialist magazines where people write to have queries answered.

Standing on their own two feet

A child's life is not all play. She has responsibilities to learn too.

Parents have different ideas about how soon their children should take on responsibilities. And some children are much more ready than others of the same age. No one knows your child better than you do. If you watch carefully as she gets older, you'll be able to tell when she's ready to try new activities. Here are some 'responsibilities' to think about.

	Your child can now	I would expect a ten-year-old to
Set an alarm clock, wake up and get up on time		
Choose suitable, clean clothes and put them on. Keep dirty clothes separately		
Choose a meal for the family and maybe help to cook it		
Do homework without prompting, and collect special things needed for school on certain days, e.g. games kit		
Make own bed		
Run the bath, have a bath, put self to bed and turn off light after reading in bed		

Taking care of herself

Learning to take care of yourself is part of growing up. There are many little things you can do to help your child to be more independent in her everyday life. It means letting her make some decisions. Your aim is to help her to be competent, rather than to cossett or criticise.

By the time your child is ten she should be pretty good at looking after herself. How many of the things in our chart can she manage now? How many would you expect her to do when she is ten?

Remember, no one's perfect, and even if she does all this, she probably won't keep it up every day. She still needs you to praise her when she does.

To help her work towards these ten-year-old achievements, try to get her to take some control over the following things.

Waking up Let her wake herself up. An alarm clock is more controllable and less hostile than an 'alarm mother'.

Dressing Choose clothes which she can manage by herself – front openers, pull-on shoes and tops. Expect children to get dirty – choose easy-wash clothes, rather than have rows about dirt on clothes which need a lot of looking after.

Breakfast You're not running a hotel. But you can give the choice between a whole or half slice of bread, toasted or not, eggs scrambled or boiled. You set the limits, she makes the choice.

Rush hour Tell a child to hurry, and she's sure to go slow. Say: 'You have ten minutes before the bus' or 'It's half past eight now' and she may see you think she can be ready, rather than doubting her. If you think she is going to forget something, try reminder notes or a timetable on the wall.

Play time Care of toys is her job – they belong to her. If she leaves them around, agree a 'dump' for them – don't do her putting away for her. Set clear times for when she must be in from play and how much TV she can watch. Help her choose her programmes – and some play projects.

Homework/practice Some children need help with this when they first start, as it's hard to fit school things in at home. But once your child has got used to the idea, help her get on with it by fixing a time and place, and leave her in peace. Don't check up on her or police her. If she doesn't do it, it's up to her to explain to her teacher.

Ready for bed Getting clean should feel good; being clean should be a pleasure too. She'll find this out if you can bear to let her decide when she needs a change of clothes or a bath. Some children in this age group will never worry about little details like clean shoes, though, so if it worries you, you will have to clean them.

Bedtime She lies in her bed, so let her make it. She will, if it's uncomfortable. Duvets are much easier for children to handle than traditional bedcovers. Give warning before lights need to go out, followed by a kiss or a chat. At the end of the day, she's not all that grown up.

Who chooses?

Learning to choose is a skill. Here are some suggestions to help you involve your child in choosing something to buy. When you've read them, look at the chart overleaf.

Pick your time Do the choosing together when you've got time and patience, not every day, or for everything, but sometimes.

Say what you can afford Your child won't know otherwise. Then you can say 'no', or rule out costly choices without feeling unreasonable. And it is good for a child to learn about the value of money.

Give your child a voice Let your child have a say in what's needed, and let her say what it should be like. Talk about the limitations – why white jeans aren't practical, for example, and question them.

If she wants a blue dress and you prefer the red, why do you prefer the red? Does colour matter more to you than letting your child have a say in the choice of her clothes?

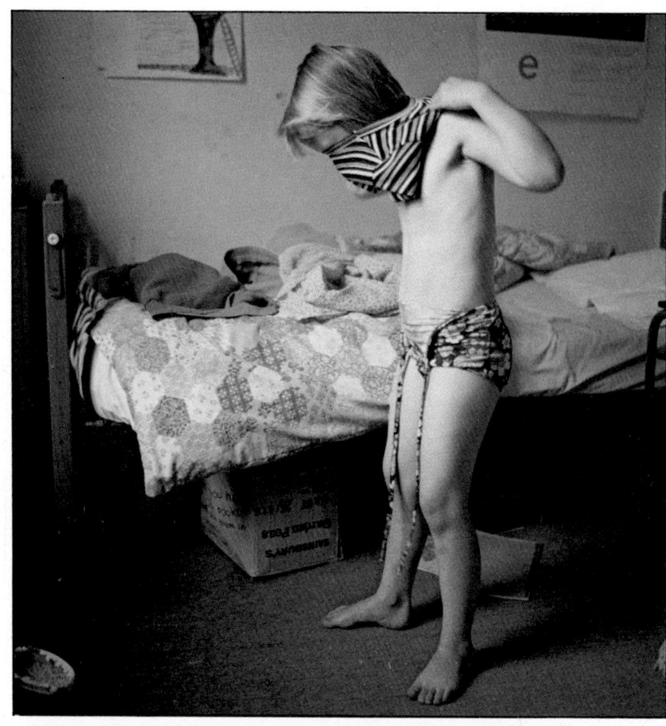
e

Who decides what's needed?	Could your child help you make a list?	Could you ask your child about fashion?	Could you let your child have a say about the decoration of his room?	Could he sometimes choose his own presents – like a bike?
Could you discuss main requirements?	○ different brands ○ value for money ○ tastes ○ packet sizes	○ colour ○ style ○ fabric ○ size	○ pattern of paper ○ washability ○ how it'll be hung ○ quantity	○ size of bike ○ how long it's got to last ○ general style ○ roadworthiness
Could you talk about money?	Tell your child about your housekeeping money	Discuss what's most important if there's not the cash for everything	Explain why you only let him look at pattern books within your budget	Discuss why, if a toy is expensive, you expect him to look after it and maybe contribute some of the cost
Could you let your child have the final choice? For example, choosing...	○ flavours ○ brands ○ sizes ○ what to eat for tea tomorrow	○ colour ○ style ○ trousers or skirt	○ pattern ○ colour	○ type of bike ○ one from a particular range

Who can do what?

Any five to ten-year-old should be able to do something from each box in our chart. So why not let her use her brain next time you shop? It saves using yours, even if it's a slower business and you need lots of patience.

Helping with shopping

These questions help you to tot up how much practical help your child gives you now, or could give you if you let her.

Before going shopping could your child help you:
remember what's needed?
write a list?
estimate the cost?

At the supermarket could she:
find where things are?
read the labels?
ask for what you can't see?
put the goods in the trolley or basket?

At the checkout could she:
unpack?
pack up sensibly . . . so the eggs don't break?
sort out the right money to pay the bill?
check the change?

Back at home
unpack the bags?
remember where things go?
decide what to have for tea?

Running errands

This quiz helps you assess the amount of support you need to give to your child when you let her do things on her own. Choose one answer for each question. Ring the appropriate letter and think why you chose as you did.

If your child goes to the shops round the corner you'd want to:
a go with her all the way?
b see her past any dangers and wait?
c let her go on her own?

You need to get a message to a friend two doors up. Would you:
a go there with your child tagging on?
b send a note with your child?
c tell her what to say, trusting her to remember?

You need some biscuits for tea and your child knows the shop. Would you:
a give your child a note and the right money?
b tell her what you want, and give her the right money?
c tell her generally what you want – but let her choose the brand and flavour and trust her with the money?

The ice-cream van comes. Would you:
a go out with your child to be sure to get what's wanted?
b send her with firm instructions?
c let her choose for the whole family?

All 'a' answers? She's not getting much of a chance. Is it too dangerous? Is she too young to cope? Or are you worrying too much?

All 'b' answers? These answers are bridges between not letting her do anything, and letting her do it all. They are ways you've thought of to help your child take responsibility gradually.

All 'c' answers? You've got a confident child with a lot of skills. But remember – she'll still like to know you appreciate her efforts. Don't take her for granted if you want her to go on helping.

Your answers were probably a mixture. We suggest:

○ Where you put 'a' try 'b' as soon as you can.

○ Where you put 'b' try 'c' as soon as you can.

○ For other jobs around the house, think of b-bridges you could build in to help your child to do more herself. Of course, a ten-year-old can do much more than a five-year-old. Don't expect too much of the little ones, but do help their skills to grow.

Taking responsibility for a pet

Children – and adults – get a lot of real pleasure from having a pet of some sort. Taking care of a pet is good for a child who hasn't been used to responsibility. But there are certain questions you should consider very carefully before you rush off to the pet shop.

How do you feel about it?

If it escapes, is sick on the best carpet, or suddenly becomes ill when your child is at school or in bed, are you prepared to cope?

What about the rest of the family? Is anyone allergic? Is it safe with babies and toddlers, or any other pets?

Do you know about the animal?

How long does it usually live? For example, caged animals like rabbits often only live a year and then the child has to get over its death. On the other hand, a cat or dog may live fifteen years, and remain with you when its owner has left home.

What does it eat? Can you buy its food easily? Does it need bedding? Where do you buy this? How much time is needed to look after it properly?

How much room does it *really* need? (Pet shops usually keep pets in very cramped conditions.)

Get a leaflet from the RSPCA or a book from the library and find out. Better still, let your child find out for you. That is the way she'll learn.

Can you afford its upkeep?

Remember, there's no National Health Service for pets. The Blue Cross and Peoples' Dispensary for Sick Animals do admirable veterinary work for small donations but they are very busy, and don't stay open 24 hours a day. Find out how much its food, and such possible extras as cage, bedding, collar, licence cost. Is it going to need inoculations? If it is wise to have it neutered, how much does it cost and when should it be done?

What about holidays? It is an offence to leave most animals alone whilst you go away for the weekend or over Christmas. Can you get reliable friends or neighbours to look after it or will you need to pay for it to be boarded out? This needs to be booked in advance and can be expensive. A vet or the RSPCA will recommend suitable places.

What else should you do?

Make sure that your child really wants a pet, that it isn't just a passing fad. Try to 'borrow' a similar pet to look after for a few days. Schools sometimes let children take animals away for the school holidays; neighbours may let your child help look after their pets.

Family patterns

In the next two chapters you'll be looking at your family and where your child fits into it. He's no longer a baby lying in a carry cot but a full member of your family with his own rights and responsibilities. Exactly what those rights and responsibilities are will depend on the people in your family, their hopes and expectations, how they see themselves and the way they have lived their family life up till now.

We'll ask you to look back over family events and patterns, and try to work out how your family has grown to be the way it is today.

Family life has its practical aspect too. There are plenty of jobs about the house children can carry out – how many of them do *your* children do? And is pocket money a reward for work done or for good behaviour? Are there too many rules and regulations in your house, or not enough?

We will also look at the important subject of mothers who go out to work (there are more and more every year) and suggest some ways of eliminating all but the most essential work that has to be done at home, after hours.

3

Family life

It isn't only children who grow and change.

Parents grow and change too.

Today thinking is far less rigid about what it means to grow up and become adult. Emotional growth, unlike physical growth, doesn't stop at 21. This means that parents as well as children are continually changing and developing as they grow older.

Once we realise this, we can look at families in a different light. Instead of seeing parents as adults fixed in their development and just helping their own children to grow up, we can look at the family as a group of individuals all facing new challenges as they grow older. This means that the family, as a group, has to change as all the individuals change within it.

The life cycle

This chart shows the kinds of concerns which bother people at different stages in their lives. Can you think of any others?

	Infancy	Pre-school	Schoolchild	Adolescent
Concerns	Can I trust them?	Will they let me?	Can I do it?	Who am I?

Some couples get married young, others may wait till their mid-thirties. So children between five and ten can have parents in the 28–40 age group. The age of the parents will affect the family and the way they relate to each other and the children.

Parents and children closer in age may do more 'growing up' and fun things together while parents of an older generation may be less adventurous but offer instead much more security and certainty.

Of course not all young children have two parents. Many will be in single parent families or be part of step-families. Some will have older brothers and sisters already in their teens, others will have to share their parents with very young children, who are more demanding on their time.

Family organisation

Families have to organise themselves to try to meet the needs of each family member.

But that can be hard as, often, different individuals want different things from the same family. Consider this, for example.

- Father has problems at work, so he wants peace, quiet and support at home.
- Working mother wants her family to be able to cope for themselves.
- Children aged five to ten want lots of activities with parents' support and participation.
- Very small child wants routine and supervision.
- Teenager wants more freedom to do as she wants.

You probably know from your own and others' experience the sorts of difficulties that arise if all these people are in the same family! Father comes in harrassed wanting a nice supper and a relaxed evening. Mother comes in expecting supper to be started and the washing to be already in the machine. The children want to be taken to the swimming baths, the teenager doesn't want to tell anyone where she is going and it is the baby's bedtime.

An exaggerated picture, but it makes the point that families have to try to adjust to what individuals want and need.

If no adjustments are made at all, family life feels uncomfortable. People become unhappy or the children play up. Father may start to take his time about coming home from work, stopping off for longer and longer drinks at the pub and not getting back till late.

Expectations have to be adjusted too. Often parents can be one step behind their fast-growing children. The five-year-old who enjoyed family games is suddenly seven and wants to play with his own friends. It can be hard to accept that children grow up. It is a process of letting go. The skill of parenting is in realising and accepting when that time has come and then knowing how much to let go.

Teenager	Young adult	Adulthood	Middle-age	Old-age	Death	
Can I get away?	Can I commit myself?	Am I doing what I'm supposed to?	Is there enough time?	Have I done the right thing?	It's up to them now	Concerns

Date	Jim 28	Sheila 26	Janet	Simon	Comments
1970	*Marriage*				
	Moved into new home				
		Changes job			
1971	Promotion at work	Changes job Pregnant			
1972	*Have first child*				
	Pressure at work	Depressed	Normal birth		I didn't realise the strain we were under *(Jim)*
1973	Changes job	Joins mother/baby club			
1974	*Move to bigger house*				A lot happening, I think Janet's tantrums were really a reaction to birth of Simon *(Sheila)*
	More time at home	Pregnant	Temper tantrums		
	Have second child			Calm baby	
1975	Away a lot on business	Mother stays, causes tension	Doesn't like going to playgroup		
1976	Promotion				
1977	Working long hours		Starts school		
	First family holiday				
1978	Father dies and mother stays for two months	Feels tense and depressed	Confused, slight difficulty about settling in at school	Starts nursery school	Having someone else in the house all the time is difficult *(Sheila)*
1979	Promotion	Takes very part-time job	Learns to read and makes friends locally		
1980		Takes on more work	Changes school	Starts infant school	
1981	Takes up sailing	Health poor, lots of headaches	Always out with friends. Joins Brownies	Unsettled	Simon needs more of Jim's time *(Sheila)*

The family event chart

Here is a chart which one family has filled in. The columns across the top represent each member of the family. Down the side are the years the family have been together. This family is a fairly traditional one. The parents have remained married and have had two children. They have not had any big problems or disasters.

By looking at each column you can see how each family member is coping.

Jim is establishing himself in his career and providing for his family. He has to face a conflict between the demands of home and work. His own father dies when he is 36 and for a time he feels responsible for his widowed mother. Work appears to dominate Jim's life but at 39 he takes up sailing and appears to be even less involved in the family than he was before.

Sheila soon loses interest in work after marriage and embarks on motherhood. Caring for the baby leaves her tired and quite lonely. A second baby follows shortly after moving house. But extra help and a holiday relieve the situation. Mother's presence causes tension. Once the younger child reaches school age, Sheila can consider her own needs again.

Janet arrives at a convenient moment when parents have begun to establish themselves. At three she suddenly has a difficult phase of tantrums. She takes her time settling into playgroup but at five has no real difficulty with school. Her progress is smooth and uninterrupted apart from the death of grandpa which causes some distress.

Simon's arrival is well timed. The family have a larger home. He is happy enough until he hits an unsettled period at six, and his dad is not often at home.

Now make your own chart

Draw up your chart by putting the names of everyone in your family across the top. Down the side put the date of your marriage. (If you have had more than one marriage start with the first and include both.) In the space for each family member trace major events up to the present. Ask other members of your family to help. Make sure you haven't left out important details by checking through the list of life events below. (But there are bound to be some events in your family's life that are not in the list.)

Life-events checklist

Marriage
Pregnancy
Birth
Moving house
Changing job/promotion
Changing school
Serious accident/illness
Depression/breakdown
Redundancy/unemployment
Death of close relative
Death of family pet
Long separation
Divorce or reconciliation
Debt/money problems
Serious rows
Marriage problems
Child leaves home
Wife beginning/ending work
New member of family
Trouble with law
Windfall/win on the pools
Becoming famous

When you have completed the chart look through it with the rest of the family. Look for connections across the columns. When one person is having problems or doing new things differently, how are the others reacting?

Family patterns

If you look across the lines of each year you may be able to see links between events. On our chart, the arrival of Janet in 1972 required an adjustment for Jim and Sheila. Later, in 1974, Janet's temper tantrums coincided with a move to a new house and Sheila's second pregnancy. All these factors may be linked. Tantrums are common at three but the move unsettled Janet, and Sheila, being pregnant, felt less able to cope. Janet's reaction to Simon's birth was to be unsettled at playgroup.

The family had to adjust to a new member when Sheila's mother came to stay. 1979 was a good year for everyone. 1980 was full of changes and by 1981 things were not going so well, at least for the parents. Janet's interests were now outside the family but Sheila might have been missing her. Jim was less often at home and Simon may have been missing him.

All families pass through phases like these and difficulties do seem to coincide. A child's problems in school may be linked with its parents' marital problems or illness in the family. Family relationships have to change in an attempt to keep pace with individual changes.

Looking ahead

What are the next steps for each person in your family? Let's go back to the family who filled in the chart.

Jim will need to decide how he can spend more time with the family. How can he balance what he wants with what his family wants?

Sheila, at 37, has to adjust to the fact that her children are taking less of her time. She may wonder what has happened to her relationship with Jim.

Janet is moving towards adolescence and will begin to assert her independence.

Simon is moving towards junior school. His energy is directed towards mastering new skills.

What are the next steps for each member of *your* family? Write them down on a separate piece of paper.

Now look at what you have written and consider what effect these events will have on each of the other members of the family. Let's look at Jim and Sheila's family again.

At the time that Janet is asserting her independence Sheila may be feeling she is now middle-aged and useless. Her tension may express itself through rows with Jim and this could make Jim feel he is better off sailing than being at home. Simon could feel even more left out.

Events that occur to individuals affect the whole family. It is like a chain reaction. Everyone is dependent on each other. That is why it is so worthwhile looking at your family as a whole.

Families are . . .

Families come in all shapes and sizes.
How does that affect family life?

Mr and Mrs Average have two blond children, a semi-detached house, a dog, a garden, and a fairly new car. They eat hot soup on cold days. They don't argue and fight. They seem to like getting up in the morning because of the sunshine that breakfast brings into their lives. Grime comes easily off their floors and germs never pollute their sinks. They eat chocolate and it doesn't rot their teeth or stain their clothes. And when they go to bed their bedtime drink assures a peaceful sleep before another perfect day.

Or that's what the adverts would have us believe!

Most of us know that life for us isn't much like the life that is shown in advertisements. But perhaps, in the back of our minds, we *do* think that other people lead perfect lives. Maybe it's only we who bicker and row and get on each others' nerves. So how do we build up our picture of what a family should be?

We have our own family. We see the families of neighbours and friends. And we see the types of families that TV, newspapers and magazines show us.

A typical family?

Take a look at the list (left). Which one do you think is the 'typical' family? Mark it with a cross. Which is the family closest to your own? Mark it with a tick.

Different families

1	Single parent + 1 child	☐
2	2 parents + 1 child + grandma	☐
3	Parents + 2 children	☐
4	Step family	☐
5	Family with handicapped child	☐
6	Mixed marriage, half-caste child	☐
7	Older family + 1 small child	☐
8	4 children in care (no parents)	☐

Take a separate sheet of paper and for each family think of a couple of things that might have a good or bad effect on five to ten-year-olds in each family. For example, if the children live with their mother only, they may have no-one to play football with them. Then look at these ideas.

1 **Single parent families** Did you know that one in eight families in Britain are headed by single parents? It can mean less time for the children because there is only one parent to provide it. There may also be less money coming in. But maybe there are fewer rows and less unhappiness. If a boy lives only with his mother he needs a male figure to identify with. But it's not the end of the world if father is not around. Children are resourceful and may model themselves on an uncle or grandfather or teacher. (The reverse will be true for single fathers of girls.)

2 **Grandparents in the family** Many families have one or more grandparents living with them. For children it can feel like having three parents or they may develop with a grandparent a special relationship that is very precious and different from that which they have with their parents.

3 **Two parents, two children** This is the 'average' family. But one in two marriages end in divorce, so it may not be 'average' for long. For children it means having the attentions of both parents but it doesn't mean there are no problems.

4 **Step-families** As there are many re-marriages involving children there are many new step-families each year. For children it means getting used to a new parent, or having two parents every day and a third parent outside the family.

5 **Handicap in the family** Families with a handicapped child can be under much strain. Of course handicaps vary from mild to very severe. Inevitably much of the parents' time is taken up with the handicapped child and that leaves less time for the others. But it also means that the other children have a chance to learn more about tolerance and patience.

6 **Mixed marriages** These can be either of a racial mix or a religious mix. For a child in a racially mixed family the most marked effect may be his colour – which parent does he look like? Whom does he take after? It can be hard on a child who is neither black nor white.

7 **Late arrivals** The 'afterthought' has a very special place in a family of parents and young adults. He may be spoilt and made a fuss of but it can also be a lonely place in the family. There is no one close of his own age.

8 **Children in care** Some children are only in care for a few weeks (perhaps if a parent is ill). For others it can be permanent. Brothers and sisters in care still identify as a family. The issue for them is where is home and who can they depend on?

Now look at your own family. Describe your family on the lines below.

What are your five to ten-year-olds losing out on?

What are they gaining?

If the losses are heavier than the gains, can you do anything to change that?

Who fits where?

Younger children are very interested in how all the people in a family fit together. Alex Walsh wrote this about her family.

○ I am my sister Laura's sister.
○ Grandma Wilson is my Mum's mum.
○ Grandma Walsh is my Dad's mum.
○ Uncle Julian is my Mum's brother.

Older children may be more interested in where people in the family live. This is

Grandma lives in Worthing, and is very nice, and her house is lovely and big
She cooks lovely ham and has a big garden
She has a box with a black wooden cat in it and old coins and things
Tante Kate and Onkel Hans, live in Germany, and I like going to see them
They have a wishing well in the garden, and there is a nice budgie called Heini
Grandma and Grandad. They live in Cleveleys. We see them most of all our relations
Grandma takes us to feed the ducks and swans
Grandad does bowling, he's won a lot of cups
Once when we were at Cleveleys we met Uncle Raymond and Uncle Ronnie, they are twins
Uncle Julian and Aunty Vieda. They live next to Watership Down, and have 4 children – Anna 22, Camilla 20, Juliet 19 and Oliver 16
They have a red setter called Jonah
Mummy's relations
Daddy's relations
Sometimes when we go to Grandma's we see Aunty Gladis. She lives in Ingleway
She has got a lovely fishpond
Aunty Dorothy lives in Scotland
Aunty Doris, she lives in Reigate, she's coming to see us soon
She makes us lovely nighties
Sometimes I get her mixed up with Aunty Dorothy
Uncle Peter and Aunt Rohanna. They have children and live in Manchester
The children's names are Hanafiah 9, Djurahiah 11, Andy 7 and Irmani 2
We have never seen them
When we go to Grandmas we always go to see Great Grandma. She lives in Blackpool
She has lovely ornaments in her house

the map that Kay Walsh drew, with her Mum's help, to show her family and how far away they all lived. When they'd drawn the map, Kay put down how often they contacted people in the family and anything she especially liked about them.

Mapping out the family

Help your child to draw a map of the family.

○ You will need a large sheet of paper, scissors, felt tip pens, glue.

○ Start by cutting up small pieces of paper and writing a name on each one. Get your child to try to think of the names.

○ Then show the child how to make a family map. Start by sticking down the names of the immediate family and then move outwards.

○ Try using different colours for each side of the family.

○ Put in the relationships between family members and anything your child remembers.

○ You can do your own map, too, and compare the differences.

How much are the two maps you have drawn alike? Look at the two maps together. Are there people that you know but whom your child has only heard of? You will see that your map may be different from your child's. There may be people whom you've fallen out of touch with, whom your child would not even think of as family.

Some families have strong ties, others don't. Many people keep in touch with friends far more than family.

Family portraits

Try drawing a picture of your family. See if you can get other people in the family to draw pictures too. Write a few words about your picture. And try and get your child to describe his or her picture.

On the right are the pictures drawn by seven-year-olds of their families in Liverpool.

What do you notice about them?

They are not accurate well drawn pictures but they give an impression.

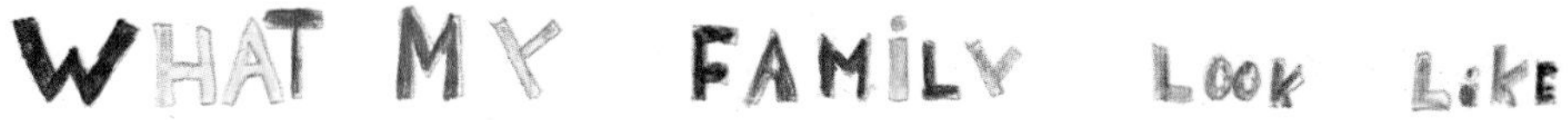

○ Notice the size of the different figures. The biggest is usually most important (at least to the child).

○ Notice the colour – brightest colours are happy, dark may be sad.

○ Where are the spaces?

Family scrapbook

Look at all the changes your family has gone through by glancing at family snapshots. They will give a strong impression of the experience of childhood for different generations.

Family roles

Children learn about families from being in them. They form their ideas from what they see.

What are your children learning in your family? Stand back and look at your family to try and see what they see.

Families have changed since today's parents were children. Many more mothers go out to work, especially when children start school. The advantages of washing machines and convenience foods mean there is less to do but if you are a working mother there is even less time to do it in. Fathers nowadays tend to be more involved in the day-to-day care of children and this helps build closer relationships. So today's five to ten-year-olds have a different experience of what parents do and the way families are run. They may have, therefore, a completely different idea of parental roles. What is the experience of your own children?

Fill in the chart shown on the right. There are no right or wrong answers. But different patterns of ticks mean different family lifestyles. Below we describe what these different patterns mean.

Sharing tasks
Everybody in the family gets an equal share of ticks and most people have a go at most of the jobs in the list.

This is a fairly typical pattern for families nowadays. Both parents contribute to family life in an equal way and there is no clear division about who does what.

Equal but different
Here the ticks are under father or mother, but not both. Many parents share what has to be done but take responsibility for different things. For example, father organises the garden and home repairs. Mother always does the cooking and shopping. But they both share the care of the children.

The division of work in this family may seem fairly traditional. It is attitude that is not. 'Male' work is not given any more importance than 'female' work by the parents.

While accepting that men are better at certain things than women, and vice versa, in this type of family the male is not considered in any way superior.

How is your family organised?

Answer the following questions by putting a tick in the appropriate squares.

	Father	Mother	Children	Other
Who earns in the family?	☐	☐	☐	☐
Who makes big decisions?	☐	☐	☐	☐
Who organises what happens at home?	☐	☐	☐	☐
Who does the chores?	☐	☐	☐	☐
Who is responsible for the shopping?	☐	☐	☐	☐
Who does the cooking?	☐	☐	☐	☐
Who looks after the children?				
(a) weekdays?	☐	☐	☐	☐
(b) weekends?	☐	☐	☐	☐
(c) when they are ill?	☐	☐	☐	☐
Who comforts and cuddles the children?	☐	☐	☐	☐
Who disciplines them?	☐	☐	☐	☐
Who looks after the car?	☐	☐	☐	☐
Who does the garden?	☐	☐	☐	☐
Who does the repairs around the house?	☐	☐	☐	☐
Who sews on buttons?	☐	☐	☐	☐
Who pays the bills?	☐	☐	☐	☐
Who plans family holidays?	☐	☐	☐	☐
Who organises the children's clubs?	☐	☐	☐	☐
Who writes out the Christmas cards and sends presents?	☐	☐	☐	☐
Who goes to see the teacher on parents' days?	☐	☐	☐	☐

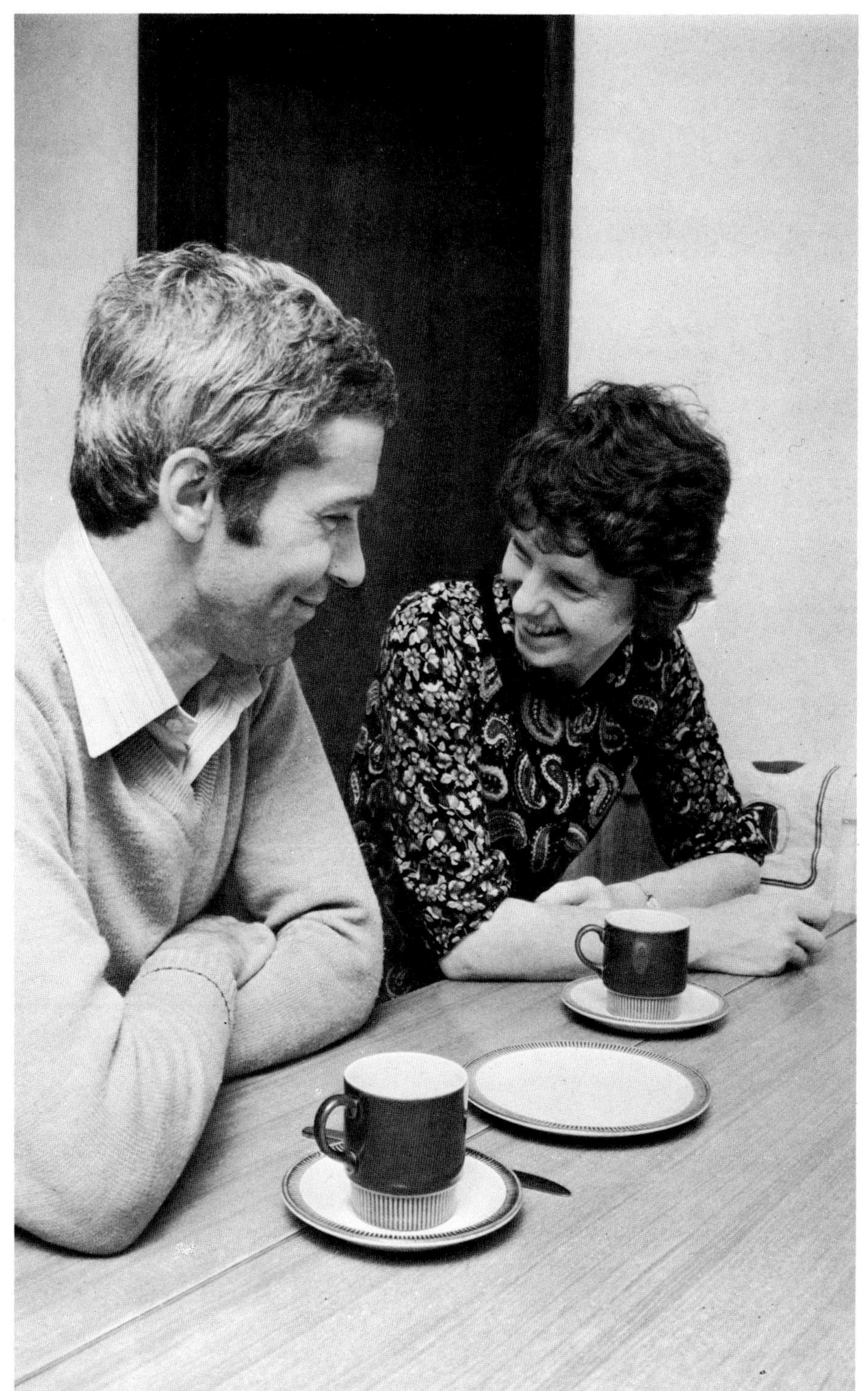

Traditional pattern
Father's ticks are against earning, big decisions, paying the bills and looking after house repairs, the garden and the car. Mother's ticks are under all the other tasks, from organising the home down to sewing on the buttons.

Here roles are very clearly divided into male and female. Father works and takes authority and major decisions and the wife has control of the home and children – a pattern which is disappearing.

Single parents
Here there will be a long unbroken column of ticks under father or mother, with some help from the children. No choice here about how things work out unless they bring in help from outside.

Three generation families
This is where you may find several ticks in the 'other' column, as well as under mother and father.

If your grandparents are living with you, then arrangements are bound to be complex. There has to be a lot more negotiation and at times there is likely to be conflict over who decides what.

Problems can arise if members of the family have not sorted out who does what and why. One person may feel over-burdened, another that they are not important or listened to. It's worth thinking about for, if you feel unhappy the chances are your partner does too. It can also feel very unbalanced if one parent hands out discipline and punishment, while the other offers all the support and caring.

In most families, someone is:

○ the organiser
○ the decision maker
○ the care giver
○ the one who smoothes it over
○ the blamer
○ the scapegoat
○ the rescuer
○ the clown
○ the sick one
○ the useless one

Can you add any more?

Sex roles

From an early age, children make sense of their world in terms of what is expected of them as girls or boys. That is something they learn, not something they're born with. If you are not sure how much you influence your child's ideas about what boys and girls are like, try the following quiz.

Sugar and spice

Look at this list of words and divide it up into those that you think apply to boys and those that apply to girls. Don't spend a long time over it, just mark it according to your first thoughts. Put a tick under the boy or girl column.

		Boys	Girls
1	soft	☐	☐
2	tender	☐	☐
3	impulsive	☐	☐
4	handy	☐	☐
5	dependent	☐	☐
6	passive	☐	☐
7	anxious	☐	☐
8	aggressive	☐	☐
9	gentle	☐	☐
10	brave	☐	☐
11	bold	☐	☐
12	quiet	☐	☐
13	naughty	☐	☐
14	peaceful	☐	☐
15	timid	☐	☐
16	clean	☐	☐
17	untidy	☐	☐
18	dirty	☐	☐
19	noisy	☐	☐
20	stubborn	☐	☐
21	rough	☐	☐
22	shy	☐	☐

You have probably divided the list up without much difficulty and may have something like this:

Boys: 3, 4, 8, 10, 11, 13, 17, 18, 19, 20, 21

Girls: 2, 5, 6, 7, 9, 12, 14, 15, 16, 22

Now go back over the list and look through it picking out the words that apply to one particular boy and girl you know. You may not get results that match your first set.

Of course, it's not an insult to use any of these words for either sex – everyone knows quiet men and dominant women. But each sex in general seems to have a set of particular descriptions associated with it. These are often called stereotypes and some people encourage their children to fit these stereotypes.

Boys' ways, girls' ways?

Here are a collection of things children do. Mark with ticks any you would be concerned to find a son doing. Put ticks by any you would be concerned to find a daughter doing.

	Boys	Girls
Playing with dolls	☐	☐
Accepting a dare	☐	☐
Picking a fight	☐	☐
Taking an interest in clothes	☐	☐
Dressing up in lipstick and high heels	☐	☐
Wanting to be kissed and cuddled	☐	☐
Not wanting to leave mum	☐	☐
Coming in from play very dirty	☐	☐
Pushing and shoving	☐	☐
Playing doctors and nurses	☐	☐
Playing with guns	☐	☐
Saying dirty words	☐	☐
Telling tales	☐	☐
Being cheeky	☐	☐

Look back at the list. Do your marks reflect the traditional view that it's OK for boys to be rough, get dirty and be naughty, as long as they are 'manly' and strong, and that it's only OK for girls to be gentle, clinging and feminine? Or do you have a more easy-going attitude?

Basically, what does seem to worry many parents is that their child is going to become a deviant of some sort – or that they'll suffer later on, if they don't 'conform' to their sex role.

'Sex' objects

Here are a number of objects. Ask your children whom they would go to – mummy or daddy – if they wanted to ask a question about any of these things.

Vacuum cleaner	Tea bags
Power drill	Clean clothes
Television	Tin opener
Sewing machine	Scouring powder
Garden spade	Tea towels
Lawn mower	Paint brush

By the age of five, every child has a fixed idea of what boys and girls are (often more conservative than their parents' view because they still see things in black and white terms). Children of this age sex-type each other and themselves.

Try asking your children about the future, about what they think they will all be doing. Probably they will tell you boys will be lorry drivers, explorers, doctors and girls will be mothers, nurses, secretaries. Already they have a view of sex roles which they may carry with them through life. These are reinforced by what they see around them.

Outside the family

Other people besides parents provide children with strong messages about how men and women should behave. Children often find this fits in with their own views.

Children's books usually uphold traditional views about sex roles. Women are not often the leading characters. They are usually background figures whose activities are limited to watching, loving and helping. Boys solve problems, have adventures; girls just have mishaps. Boys have fathers who are engineers or carpenters or professors; girls just have mothers of whom perhaps a few are secretaries or teachers.

Even in animal stories, the stereotypes are kept up – male animals are lions and tigers. Female animals are soft and fluffy cats or a silly goose, or a big fat hippo with long eyelashes.

What children learn in school or see on television reinforces these ideas. Change is slow despite the efforts of the women's movement. Do you think there should be change at all? Do you think that perhaps sex roles are too restricting for both girls *and* boys?

Family work

Family work usually means housework and most of it is done by mother.

How many hours a week are spent on work on the home and by whom? Fill in the table to show the work done each week and the amount of time each member of the family spends on it.

Time spent

It is very difficult to estimate the time spent each week on housework. What may be work to some may be 'fun' for others, for instance, gardening, decorating or repairing the car. Understandably, when there are younger children at home there is more time spent on housework. Also there are big differences between working and non-working wives. Working wives have to stick to essentials; they do less cooking and cleaning and may actually have paid help. Working mothers may or may not get help from their husbands and children.

A newly married couple is likely to have a smaller home, fewer possessions and share most of the household chores. Yet even when men are used to looking after themselves, women often take on the traditional role of housework when they marry. Husbands 'help' wives and wives 'thank' them, as if they should really be doing all chores even if they both work full-time.

As soon as the first child arrives then the wife tends to take on even more of the traditional tasks and these increase as her family grows. Whether she works or not all the household chores are seen primarily as her responsibility.

Yet housework is part of family life and an opportunity for children to join in and learn to take responsibility. It's not all fun and games but children can learn a lot by taking their part. Are you ready to let them?

Job	Hours spent per week			
	Mother	Father	Children	Other
Shopping				
Organising household				
Record keeping – bills etc				
Food preparation/cooking				
Washing-up				
Cleaning house				
Looking after car				
Repairs to house				
Gardening				
Washing/ironing/ mending				
Physical care of family members – baths, hair etc				
Other tasks (fill in)				
TOTAL				

Attitudes to family work

How is family work divided up in the home? Look at these three ways (opposite) of dealing with household jobs.

How do people develop their attitudes? Partly from what they learned as children.

When you were a child . . .

Think back to when you were aged between five and ten and tick on the chart on the right who did these jobs in your household. Add any other jobs that you remember always being done by one person.

Look at the jobs *you* did. Did you feel happy about doing them or resentful? Which ones did you try to get out of? Do you remember having to do different jobs as you grew older? Did you resent a brother or sister's set of jobs?

What happens if children don't ever join in household jobs? Perhaps:

○ they think that children don't have any responsibilities.

○ they fail to see how much time and effort it takes to keep a household going from day to day.

○ they don't find out how much effort it takes other people to look after them.

○ they miss out on that feeling of accomplishment of a job well done.

You may not have strong views about housework and children's role in it. Or you may have made some very conscious decision. 'I always had to do jobs when I was little and it never did me any harm. So it won't do Peter any harm either.' Or 'I had a hard life when I was small and I'm determined that Peter's not going to suffer too. Let him have it easy while he can.'

Some enjoy acting the martyr, and others are quite happy to watch them suffer. Jean doesn't really expect her family to do anything. She gets her satisfaction from feeling put upon.

Some people don't like handing work over to others. They think they can do it better and more quickly. Mary doesn't expect her family to do anything but feels very satisfied at doing it all herself.

Some people think it's quite natural that other people should be involved in housework as well. Linda feels that her family have a part to play because they are the ones who get the benefit of a clean house and cooked meals.

	Mother	Father	Children
Mending clothes			
Washing-up			
Drying-up			
Washing			
Ironing			
Cleaning			
Painting and house repairs			
Window cleaning			
Cooking			
Looking after small children			
Gardening			
Putting things away			
Bed-making			
Cleaning the car			
Mending electrical gadgets			
Other tasks (fill in)			

One thing is certain, your own ideas have a major effect on your child's developing attitudes.

Jobs for small hands

Here is a list of jobs that most people do once a week, or more. Because they get done again and again, these sorts of jobs are ideal for children to help with. If they aren't too good to begin with, you only have to live with the results for a few days!

Polishing	Hanging out washing
Dusting	Ironing
Washing-up	Laying the table
Hoovering	Washing the car
Washing clothes	Making beds
Sweeping	Putting away shopping

Most children start out wanting to copy what mum or dad does. So if yours *don't* want to help, think what you might be doing to put them off. If you always say, 'No you can't', or criticise and nag, you should not really be surprised if they don't want to know. Here are some ways to help them help you.

Explain why Children need to see why jobs are worth doing – because it feels good, looks good or whatever. So talk about that. They'll probably think cleanliness is less important than you do, though.

Recognise feelings If you see your child struggling, tell him so. 'That looks as if you're finding it tough …', 'You've had enough of that …' An idea for doing it differently will then go down a lot better.

Give praise 'That's a smashing job you've done!' General criticism, such as 'you can do better than that', puts backs up. Praise first if you have to criticise. 'The socks are lovely and clean, but your T-shirt needs a harder rub.'

Share the work Work alongside your child, so he gets the chance to talk, to see what you do – and to comment.

Lower your standards In the end you have to decide which is more important: the people you live with, or the place you live in. Does it really matter if things aren't perfect once in a while?

Do-it-together

The less often you do a job, the more important it is that it's done well. So children helping with DIY can be a problem. They aren't as handy, or quick, or fussy as you are. But they need to learn – and can do so if you help them. Look at the different aspects of do-it-yourself jobs.

Design If it's something for the children, consult them. For example, the height of shelves, or the site of the swing.

Preparation Rubbing down, washing, digging are all mucky activities where a lot of energy is needed. Can be enjoyed by older children.

Helping There are always small parts of the job that need doing. 'Find me the …', 'Hold the …', 'Turn the …' etc. It may seem boring to you but to your child it is fun.

Doing-it-himself Sometimes there's only one right way to do things, like wiring a plug. And sometimes only you can do it. In which case, say so. But sometimes you can teach your son or daughter to do-it-themselves. Like sewing and sanding wood, using a plane, pricking out seedlings, smoothing concrete. *You don't know what your children can do till they've tried.*

You can help your child learn by showing him or telling him. You can guide with your hands or in words. Either way, he's learning your skills – and that you like him to help. If he wants to stop helping, he'll be happier than if you never let him in on the activity to begin with.

If the worst comes to the worst

Just think about this for a moment.

If you were ill, what would need doing in the house? And who would do it? Would five to ten-year-olds be able to help? What sort of supervision would they need to be able to do important jobs? The answer to these questions will give you two guidelines:

○ the minimum that needs to be done to keep the household going.

○ the ability (or lack of it) of your family to fend for themselves.

If you *always* have to have a grandparent, aunt or neighbour in when there's an emergency, perhaps it's time your family had a chance to step in.

Cooking for boys and girls

Why shouldn't all children learn to cook? Later in life they may choose not to. But that's different from growing up not being able to do it at all – or boys expecting girls to do it for them. Many junior and middle schools now teach both boys and girls to do woodwork, sewing, pottery and cookery.

There are some simple recipe books written especially for children. But there are lots of things you could teach that you know already.

Things that don't need cooking Like salads, sandwiches, cold drinks.

Simple cooked dishes Like beans on toast, boiled eggs, hot dogs, party buns. You can easily cover all the basic ways of cooking – boiling, grilling, frying, roasting, baking.

Getting it all ready This is quite a skill and it's educational too. You can compare the length of time that different things take. Laying the table is all about the numbers of things needed and where you place them. If your child likes writing, suggest he makes a menu card.

How to help them learn

Do suggest things that are likely to be a success – don't let your child get over-ambitious.

Do break the job down into little steps, explaining as you go. That way it's more likely to work. For example: (a) find the ingredients (b) weigh them all out (c) chop or mix (d) turn on stove (e) clear away any mess.

Do help him when needed, by saying what's to be done, or showing him – don't hover over him worrying.

Do praise his efforts, but don't go overboard in ecstacy if the sandwich is falling apart and he forgot the butter.

Do let your child get tea ready for the family when you've got the time to help and not fuss. Don't expect him to do it every day. Even though he's got the skill, he won't want all the responsibility. It's *worksharing* remember.

Time and place

Sometimes you may not want to give jobs to other people, because it's quicker to do it yourself or other people make a mess of

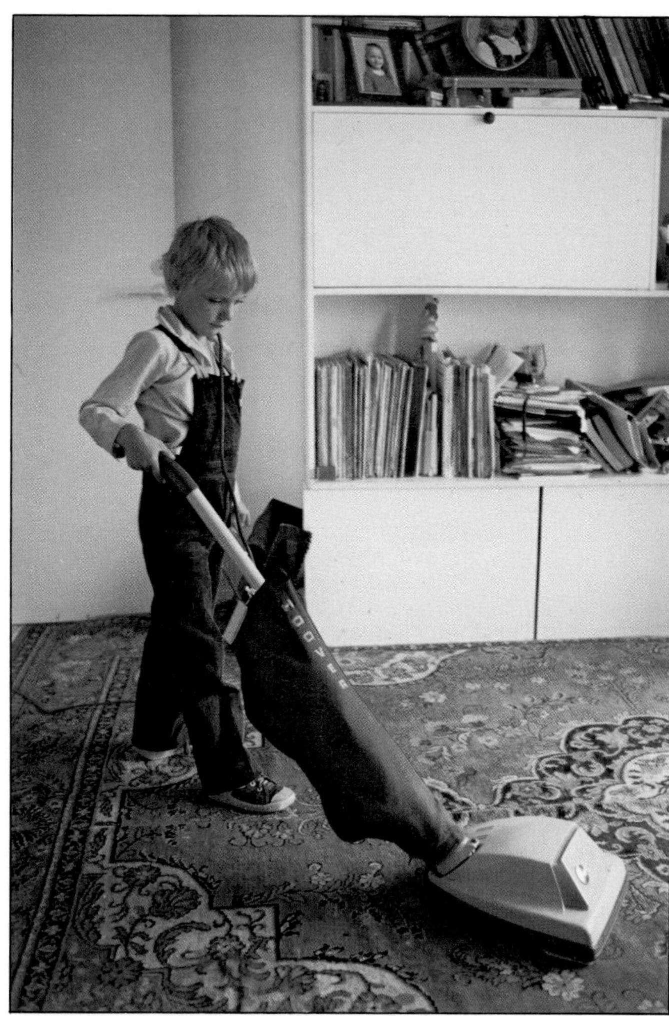

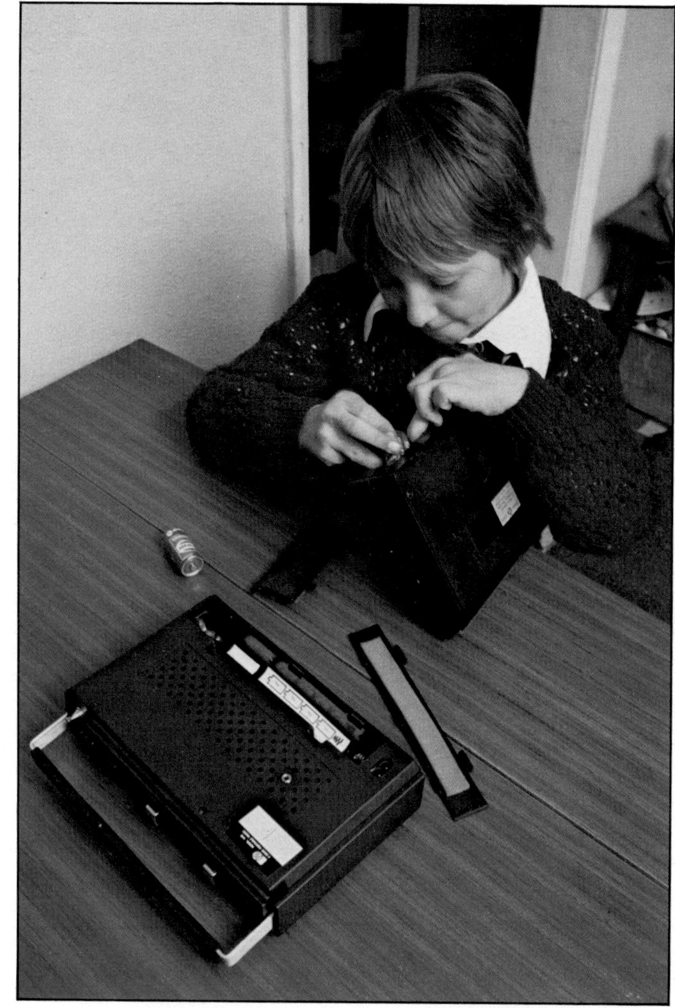

things. But the more you do jobs for yourself the more people let you. However, sometimes your own convenience is bound to win the day. When you're rushed off your feet, the baby's got flu, your partner's going out, then you can't stop to pick the garden flowers with your seven-year-old.

Think of a couple of jobs that you might like your children to do when things aren't so hectic – and then answer the questions in our chart as though you were going to hand out the jobs you have chosen today.

We have filled in what Mary Jones wrote and left two columns for you to fill in.

You will see that some jobs can be given to your child now. For others, you may need to make a few adjustments to your own schedule.

For instance, if Mary has no time to supervise her son mowing the lawn today, why not leave it till tomorrow, when she can, instead of getting her husband to do it that night, when he is tired from work anyway.

	Our example				*Your example*			
Do you want your child to...?	**defrost the fridge**		**mow the lawn**					
	YES	NO	YES	NO	YES	NO	YES	NO
Have you got the time to let your child do the job?	☑	☐	☑	☐	☐	☐	☐	☐
If the job needs supervising have you got time to do that?	☑	☐	☐	☒	☐	☐	☐	☐
Can your child do the job at his own pace?	☑	☐	☑	☐	☐	☐	☐	☐
Is your child willing to do the job?	☑	☐	☑	☐	☐	☐	☐	☐
Is the job simple enough for your child to do it all (if supervised)?	☑	☐	☐	☒	☐	☐	☐	☐
Is your child likely to think the job is fun?	☐	☒	☑	☐	☐	☐	☐	☐
Is there a reward for the job?	☑	☐	☐	☒	☐	☐	☐	☐
Are you prepared to put up with mistakes?	☑	☐	☐	☒	☐	☐	☐	☐

Working mothers

For many mothers there is still a conflict between the need for identity outside the home and the need to be a homemaker.

Should mothers go out to work? Society gives conflicting answers. On the one hand there is belief in the traditional role of housewives and mothers as home-makers. On the other hand there is the view that you are only someone if you have a paid-full-time job.

Over the last 30 years more and more married women have gone out to work, and there is no sign that this upward trend is levelling off or declining.

During the 1970s the proportion of women with dependent children who worked part time rose from less than thirty per cent to nearly forty per cent, and seems to be still rising.

Following the Equal Pay Act of 1970 women's average earnings rose relatively faster than those of men so financial incentives have improved.

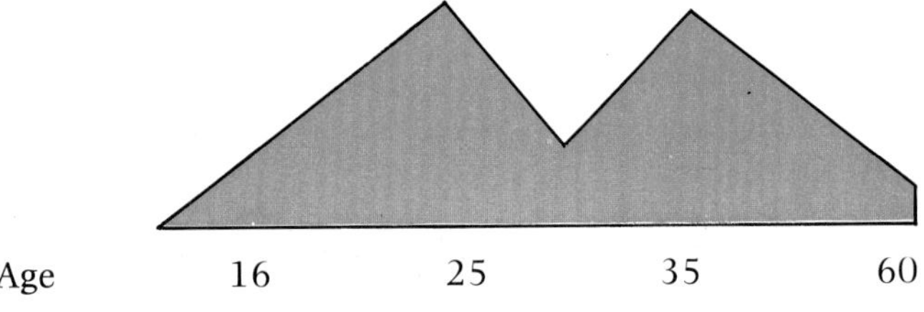

The overall trend is for the number of working women to fall off between the ages of 26 to 35 – the age when many women have children and stay at home to look after them. But during the 1970s fewer women left work after their first child was born and those that did returned to work quite quickly.

Why do mothers work?

Most mothers of five- to ten-year-olds have jobs or would like to work. Many need the money. Others say they'd go on working even if they didn't need the money. Simply, they enjoy it. We all need time off and a change of pace – so mothers need a break from mothering. Having a paid job can reduce housewife depression.

Some people say that children's needs should come first. But the number of hours spent with a child is no measure of the benefit the child receives. It is quality, not quantity, that counts. A happy working mum and a good minder probably benefit a child more than a miserable home-bound mum.

Some mothers want to work but their husbands won't let them. Some feel they ought, but don't want to. How do *you* feel? This quiz will help you sort out what you feel about working. Answer each question honestly. Put a tick if your answer is Yes, a cross if No. If you're not sure or if the answer is sometimes Yes and sometimes No put a question mark. Then look at our comments overleaf.

Your job	Yes	No
1 You enjoy what you do		
2 You enjoy the cash it brings		
3 The family's OK with you at work		
4 You feel better for being at work		
5 If the pools came up, you'd still go on with it		

The daily round	Yes	No
6 Getting everyone out in the morning is a big problem		
7 There's too much to do when you get home from work		
8 You feel rushed and jumpy by the children's bedtime		
9 You are desperately tired at bedtime		
10 The family expects too much of you		

Which of the following has happened to you in the last month?	Yes	No
11 You decide the house is too untidy to live in		
12 There are no clean undies		
13 You run out of five or six staple foods		
14 'Overnight' your child grows out of everything		
15 You realise no-one has had a haircut for three months		
16 You say no to an invitation because you're tired		
17 You fall asleep watching TV		
18 You miss a school parents meeting because you're at work		
19 You get upset because you forget to wash some clothes that were needed		
20 Your child says, five minutes before school, she needs eggs, milk and apples for cookery or Miss Smith will kill her		

Do you worry about ...?	Yes	No
21 Half-listening to your child because you're busy		
22 Not doing anything special with your child in the holidays		
23 Telling your child to put herself to bed		
24 Doing housework at the weekend, late at night or early in the morning		
25 What your child's up to when with the baby sitter		
26 Feeling too tired to let his/her friends come round to play		

Do you worry about ...?	Yes	No
27 Sending your child to school when he just might be sickening, because it's hard to get time off work		
28 Having to get the supper started before you've had time to take your coat off		
29 Spending work time worrying about the work to be done at home		
30 Putting off going to the dentists/doctors/shoe shop because there's never enough time		

Contentment
Questions 1–10 are about how content you are. For questions 1–5, score: 2 for each ✓, 1 for each ?. 0 for each ✗. For questions 6–10 score the opposite: 0 for each ✓, 1 for each ?, 2 for each ✗. Enter your total here: ________.

The more points you have, the better, If you score low, think again: what *does* your job bring you? Is it worth the cost of your not feeling content?

Organisation
On questions 11–20 score one point for each question you *didn't* tick. No score for ? or ✓. Enter your total here: ________.

The more points, the better organised you are. (But can you add in other panics of your own?) If you score low, look overleaf at 'What's to be done'.

Concern
On questions 21–30 score one point for each question you *didn't* tick. No score for ? or ✓. Enter your total here: ________.

The more points, the better – it means you worry less, though we're sure you can add worries of your own. Some points listed are just to do with children and the household, some to do with you or your partner.

It's less important whether you *do* these things than whether you *worry* about them. Worry makes you feel bad. And the rest of the family can catch your anxiety. Some people are worriers by nature. If they stopped work, they'd worry about that too.

Do the children of working mothers suffer?

Probably not, especially if the mother is happy about working and can find suitable care for the children. That's the evidence so far. But there have been few long-term or large-scale studies. Of course, you and your child are individuals. Only you know if everything is all right. But in general terms recent studies do stress the following:

The importance of mother's attitude
Content and satisfied mothers, whether working or not, tend to have 'well-adjusted' children.

The importance of alternative care
Children do need a reliable and secure form of alternative care outside school hours and during holidays.

All mothers work

Remember, all mothers work at running a home and family. All mothers need to organise themselves and their families, and to be free of them at least sometimes.

A paid job is one sort of 'extra' thing to be done. Studying or doing volunteer work are others. All mothers who take on extra loads, for whatever reason, share worries about time and finding care for the children.

Helping children understand your work

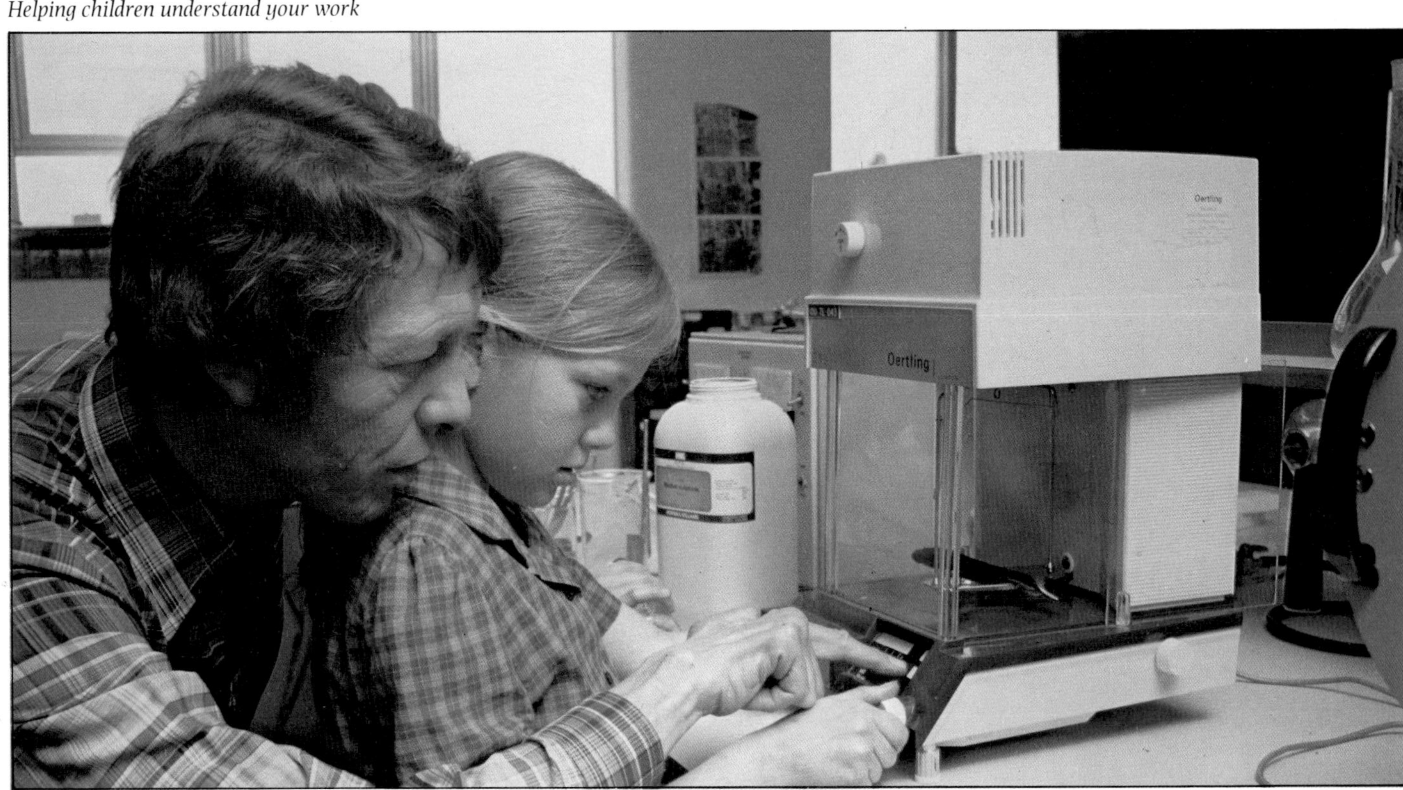

What does dad do?

A recent survey showed that whether or not their wives worked:

○ 1 in 3 dads never read to their children at all.

○ 1 in 4 dads never put their children to bed.

○ 1 in 6 dads have never looked after their child on their own, even for part of a day.

And even when their wives work full time, three out of four dads don't take time off if their child is ill, and don't fetch the kids from school. They don't see this as their job.

Younger wives tend to get more help. But most of today's fathers grew up with the idea that 'success' means ability to support a family. A working wife is a threat and helping with housework a blow to his pride.

He may well not be willing to admit it though.

What's to be done?

Here is a list (right) of things you could do to make your job easier. Tick each according to how important you think it is. For items 1–8 write in the 'help' column who you get help from now. Then tick if you'd like help, or more help, with such tasks.

Items 1–4 are essential to keep a household running The family should be able to help, if you want them to. Don't use any time saved for more chores.

Items 5–8 are important once in a while But you can live without them. On the other hand they may be one of your pleasures – especially if not done too often.

Items 9 and 10 are essential to keep family life happy Take another look, if needed, at your priorities. How do you divide your time between yourself, the family and the chores?

Items 11–12 are signs of how your working is affecting you If you ticked both as essential, you need to look again at the way you organise your life, and at how you feel. You can't feel tired and guilty forever.

At least one of items 13–16 (or a similar personal interest) is essential to keep you going Putting TV before the polishing isn't lazy (even if your mother might think so). It's good for you. And it's good for the family to see you have your own needs to think about, quite apart from meeting theirs.

		Essential	Important	Not important	Help from	Would like help
1	Basic cooking for family					
2	Day-to-day washing of clothes					
3	Housework – barest essentials, eg washing-up, hoovering					
4	Shopping – basic needs					
5	Special cooking involving more time					
6	Washing blankets, curtains					
7	Housework – polishing, dusting etc					
8	Shopping – clothes, special purchases					
9	Time to relax with children					
10	Time alone with partner (if applies)					
11	Frequent, lavish treats for partner or children					
12	Regularly going to bed early because you're tired					
13	Seeing friends					
14	Going out to pub/films/sports					
15	Watching television, reading					
16	Home hobby – sewing, knitting, etc					

Helping children understand work

If you are asking for help to make life around the house easier you can offer things in return. Showing your children your workplace is one. Your five-year-old can have a realistic picture of where you are when you are not at home and what you are doing. Your seven-year-old can see the office or machinery – how it works, what it can do. Your ten-year-old may like to see whom you work with and find out more about what exactly you do.

We are not suggesting employers should welcome your children often! But the occasional visit helps your children build up a picture of you as someone who has a responsible job and who is not just a parent to them.

House rules

Do you have rules for the children at home?

For whose benefit are they?

As your family alters, the way your home is used will alter as well. The rules you have when your children are babies are different from those you insist on when they can walk and talk and interfere. You don't often have to tell your seven-year-old not to throw food about. You don't have to keep all your valuables and breakables hidden away on a high shelf.

But your home may still be a battlefield. It is just that the troops' tactics are changing!

Young children want more space. They don't always want to be where you are. Family members want to do different things and that may mean sharing the same area or going somewhere else to do things.

How are you using the available space in your home?

A tour of your house

Draw a rough plan of your home. Where do people go in it? What worries you as a result? Go through a day or weekend and try to remember what you said to various people in terms of dos and don'ts in various parts of your home.

Here is Mary Jenning's map to give you an idea.

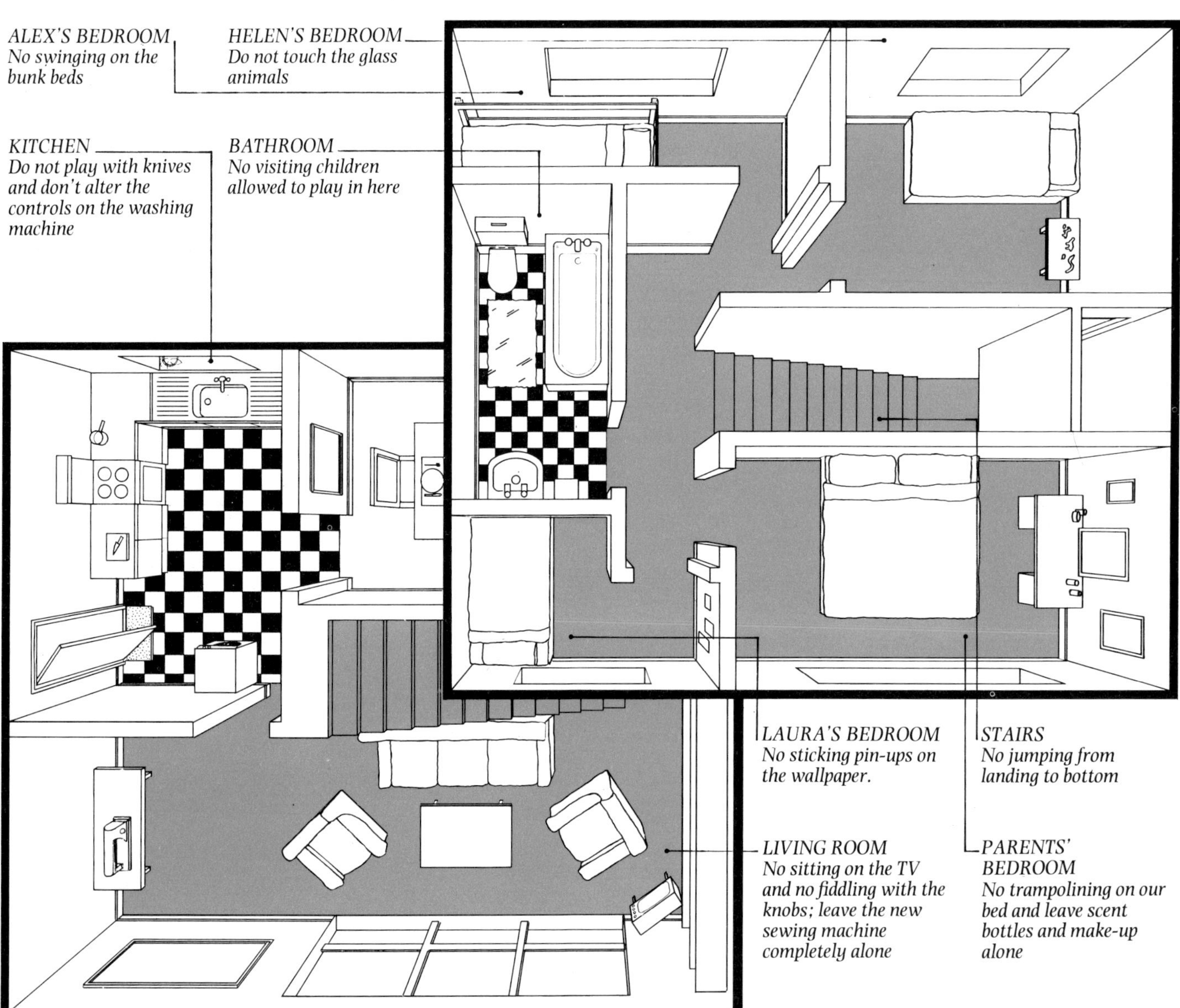
ALEX'S BEDROOM
No swinging on the bunk beds
HELEN'S BEDROOM
Do not touch the glass animals
KITCHEN
Do not play with knives and don't alter the controls on the washing machine
BATHROOM
No visiting children allowed to play in here
LAURA'S BEDROOM
No sticking pin-ups on the wallpaper.
STAIRS
No jumping from landing to bottom
LIVING ROOM
No sitting on the TV and no fiddling with the knobs; leave the new sewing machine completely alone
PARENTS' BEDROOM
No trampolining on our bed and leave scent bottles and make-up alone

Personal nightmares

What does worry you?

1
You only feel happy when they are in your sight.

2
But when they are out of your sight you worry that they'll make a mess and break things.

If you look at your map you'll probably see that it boils down to a set of rules for children to keep. If so, you could ask yourself for whose benefit the rules have been made. Some rules are crystal clear. Not letting children play on the balcony of a high rise flat is for their safety. But not all your worries and rules will be about basic safety issues. You may find your children obeying rules which are mostly for the benefit of other people.

What effect do rules have?

Below is how one family's rules affect the people in it. Look at them and then in the space on the chart write down how two of the rules in your family affect people.

Clearly the younger child is the one who gets the raw deal in our example.

Father	**Mother**	**1st child**	**2nd child**
Rule: Children keep out of living room when dad comes home from work until after tea			
I need a bit of peace and quiet for half an hour and this is the only way I can get it	My husband remains happy for the rest of the evening which is great	It's good in the summer 'cos I don't get called in between the end of school and tea. But the winter's not too good because I can only go to my bedroom	I go to bed early so that I never really get to see my dad when he comes home from work
Rule: Eight-year-old is allowed to watch 'Incredible Hulk' and 'Startrek' every week			
Doesn't worry me. I just drop off to sleep	I get to finish the washing-up in peace	It's the two programmes I'm sure to get to see. I have to ask to see everything else	I have to go to bed before. And it isn't fair 'cos the things I want to watch are while dad's asleep in the living room
Your rules:			
Your rules:			

In your own case you may find the rules don't satisfy everybody.

Look at your own rules and see what you could do to make things more comfortable for everyone. Here are some suggestions.

○ **Time** Can you change the timetable in your home – change meal times, have special times to do things?

○ **Place** Can you alter the rooms at all – put more things out of the way, make them safer?

○ **Rules** Can you change the rules from negative ones, stopping people doing things, to positive ones? For instance, instead of saying 'You can't play ball in the kitchen', you could say, 'The kitchen is for sitting-down games like drawing and painting'.

The family in the example could perhaps:

○ have a special time for the children to do quiet things in the living room while dad's there.

○ allow the younger child to watch television while dad drops off.

○ make sure tea-time is a special occasion where the kids get to talk to their dad.

Rules of the House

You've probably seen one of those joke posters, 'Rules of the house'. They usually tell people not to spit on the sawdust and to keep their fleas to themselves! Make up a list of your own – but not a jokey one.

To fill it in:

○ go over the rules which annoy people in your home. Look back over what you have done so far, see what can be changed.

○ discuss them so everyone is fairly happy. This might involve offering to ease up on one rule so as to get people to obey another one.

Compromise is always worth considering if it helps you to get your way over something that is more important.

Broken rules

Why are rules broken? Most people disobey rules for two reasons.

1 They do it as a way of saying something to the people who made the rules.

2 They do it because rules get in the way of what they want to do.

Children between five and ten will break rules for both these reasons. They are testing you out. What will you do if they break a rule? They are also testing the world out to see how it works. Sometimes rules get in the way of that.

Here are some broken rules. Why do you think they were broken? Read them and then look at the table below.

1 June told her son, Sean 9, that he had to be quiet in the living room when other people were watching TV. He carried on playing his recorder.

2 Mary told daughter, Jane, only to take one paper hankie at a time. Jane told her later that there were more than ten hankies in the box. All the paper hankies are now on the floor.

3 Philip told his son, John 10, to clean up his room before tea. But John was making a model aircraft and didn't bother to do it.

4 Think of a rule that your own child has recently broken.

There are four questions in the table below. Put YES/NO in the space provided.

Now let us take a look at what these children were really doing when they broke the rules of the house.

Sean was testing out his parents The more people to annoy the better. If he really wanted just to play the recorder he could have gone to his bedroom.

Jane was testing things out How many paper hankies are there in a box? Take them out and see.

John was absorbed in what he was doing and the rule got in the way. He was saying model aircrafts are more important than a clean room right now.

What was your child doing?

Your child's friends

Between the ages of five and ten children are learning most about the outside world. Friends are very important to them and they will want to bring them into the home.

Are you clear what your rules are? Do the children have to be invited by you? If they come to play do their parents know where they are? Who stays to tea? Perhaps most important, are your children clear about what your rules are?

Everyone has a different style when it comes to how their home is used. Some enjoy an informal 'open-door' approach. Others prefer privacy and invitations. Either style is fine provided the children know what is expected.

	Sean	Jane	John	Your child
Was the child testing out his parents?				
Did the rule get in the way of something he wanted to do?				
Whose convenience had the rule been made for?				
Was breaking it actually putting anyone out?				

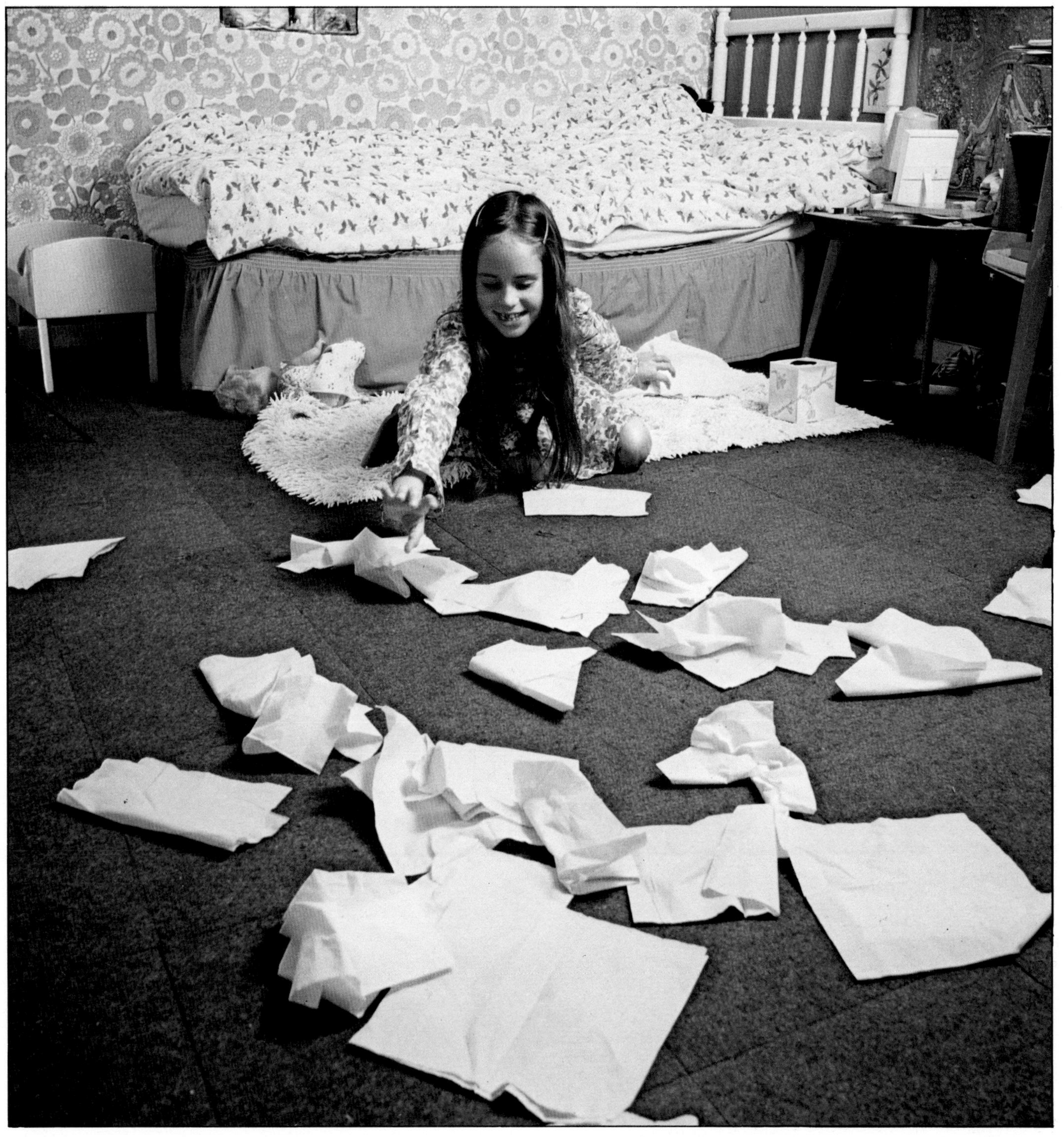

Pocket money

Is pocket money a right or a privilege?

Money is part of family life whether we like it or not and pocket money can be a real issue for children.

Attitudes to money vary from family to family. How do you handle money? Does everyone get an allowance – by right or as payment for chores? Your answers matter because your attitude to money will directly affect your children's views on money.

Money can be used in many ways. It can be exchanged for goods and services. It can be freely given and withdrawn as a punishment. It can be a weapon used by parents, some with more success than others. Start this topic by thinking about your views on money.

What are your values?

In this quiz, tick in column 1 the things you have and do. In column 2 tick the things you believe in for children aged five to ten.

	You	Children should
1 I have a regular income, from wages or entitlements		
2 I save regularly because it's a good thing to do		
3 I save up when I want a special thing		
4 I budget by the week, month or year		
5 I buy, sell or swap second-hand goods		
6 I have a small gamble now and then – raffle, lottery, bet		
7 I have a good idea what most things I need will cost		
8 I borrow money – buy now and pay later		
9 I have a special extravagance I insist on indulging		
10 I have even once used money to bribe or threaten		

Q1 covers all the knotty questions about pocket money. It's quite basic whether you think children should have some money as of right or whether – like adults – they must 'qualify' for it in some way.

Q2, 3, 4 concern long-term attitudes towards money. (And the will-power to keep to what you decide.) Children are more likely to see the point of saving if you *do* it, rather than just talk about it. It makes most sense when they can see a good short-term pay-off. They'll save to buy a special toy in three weeks' time more willingly than they'll save for nothing special – or save to pay for the broken window.

Q5, 6 If you save or make money these ways, it can be doubly hard for a child to see why he shouldn't. Why not sell his bike or play shove-ha'penny? It could be more help to talk with him about how to bargain and what's legal: to supervise rather than suppress these activities, especially if you do something similar yourself.

Q7, 8 Children need practical experiences to learn about money. An empty purse is much easier to understand than debts.

Q9, 10 Money *is* an emotional issue. We don't always spend sensibly. And money is part and parcel of our relationships with other people. Can you still remember a row with your parents over pocket money? Many can – showing how deep the feelings can run.

The pocket money pay code

Pocket money gives children freedom to spend. Or does it? Most pocket money systems involve pay policies worthy of a government think-tank.

Our chart on the right lists some of the questions parents must decide. Tick the points you agree with. Then look at the quiz and circle the letters of statements you agree with.

The answers you give to the quiz questions indicate your kind of control. If you circled mostly **'a'** your attitudes are strict, punishing and restricting. Your child feels anger and frustration at you instead of learning anything about money.

If you ticked mostly **'b'** you give little control; money is free and easy. What happens when it runs out?

Ticks for **'c'** mean you give a child most help to decide for himself. You advise without taking over. And between five and ten, children need your help over money matters.

Cash claims

Try filling in this chart on the far right with your child. Just writing things down can help you both see and talk about danger-spots. Cross out sections which you agree don't apply. If you find it helps, use it once or twice a year to review pay claims.

Issue	Examples	Quiz
1 A right or a privilege?		
It's a right if there are no strings attached	**Jimmy** gets 10p per week	**Your child breaks a toy**
… and it's regular and consistent	**Kerry,** his sister, gets 20p as she's older – not, as his parents need to make clear, because she's better, or more loved	Would you: **a** stop his money to pay for the toy? **b** replace it yourself? **c** suggest he buys a gift to say 'sorry'?
… and/or is given as a reward or withdrawn as a punishment	**Peter** gets his money stopped for being 'naughty'. He learns to be good just long enough to get paid	
2 Linked to duties?		
Pocket money has to be earned	**Sam** is supposed to clear away after tea. He usually does	**Your child cleans your car badly**
Extra money for extra chores gives a child choice to earn more. Clear contracts avoid blackmail …	**John** cleans his shoes and makes his bed. Some weeks he helps clean up to get more	Do you say: **a** he'll get on with cleaning it, or no money? **b** you'll pay him this once? **c** it's time for a review of money and jobs?
… as can happen with money for favours and nothing expected for love	**Lindy** is so used to odd pennies for fetching dad's slippers, and so on, that she bargains over every request for help	
3 What should it cover?		
As they get older, children can cope with larger sums	**Jo** (aged 5) gets pennies for sweets and papers only	**Your child wants more money**
You can help a child choose what it covers	**Lyn** (aged 8) gets money to cover fares – but can choose to walk and save that money	How do you reply? **a** You get quite enough for your age **b** OK, what's the going rate?
When a child has some idea of saving and budgeting he can be more responsible for himself if you wish	**Mark** (aged 10) gets money to cover all small toys and some of his special clothes	**c** Tell me what the others have to pay for with their money
4 What can it be spent on?		
Strict rules don't give a child the chance to learn to decide for herself	**Pam** wants to buy what her mother calls rubbish. It's now so attractive partly because it's forbidden	**Your child wants rubbishy toy** Would you: **a** say no? **b** let her have it even though you know it'll only last a day?
But no control can also be harmful	**Nicky's** teeth suffer from the amount of sweets he buys	**c** point out something else to buy instead?
5 Are extra earnings allowed?		
Legally your children can't work. But they can make themselves useful at home and outside	**Colin** runs errands for a neighbour, who sometimes gives him a tip	**Your child gets paid for a job for a neighbour**
Do you keep an eye on standards?	**Darrell's** customers find he can't reach to wash the top of the car – trade's falling off	Would you: **a** tell him off for taking money? **b** say 'fine'? **c** keep an eye open to make sure he did the job well?
Do you rule out sharp practice?	**Paul** rules the game by insisting (his) conkers are sold	

££ OUR PAY DEAL ££

1 Rights

I/We will give ______________________ (child's name)

The sum of ______________________ pocket money

On ______________________

This money will not be paid if you:

1 ______________________

2 ______________________

2 Duties

In return for this money I/we expect you to:

1 ______________________

2 ______________________

3 Coverage

This money will cover:

1 ____________ 3 ____________

2 ____________ 4 ____________

4 Spending

You may not buy:

1 ____________ 3 ____________

2 ____________ 4 ____________

5 Extra earnings

You can earn extra money by:

1 ____________ 3 ____________

2 ____________ 4 ____________

Family feelings

When there are five to ten-year-olds in the family, days are so busy with doing things that it is easy to overlook the emotional side of family life. This chapter gives us a chance to look at family feelings. These may not be very comfortable at times and certainly it is not always easy to face up to difficulties. But by looking carefully at what goes on under the surface in your family, you may uncover strengths you were not aware of and find new ways of coping with the difficulties that come your way.

Family lifestyles vary enormously and so we begin by describing different ways families have of organising day-to-day life. You can compare your own with those described and it will give you an opportunity to think about the choices you perhaps unconsciously make in family living.

In the five to ten age group, children are very conscious of family relationships and emotional ties. They question it all as they try to make sense of complex relationships and no longer take it all for granted.

Questioning and finding out are major tasks for this age group. This includes finding out how far they can go, how far they can push you. It is important for you to know where you stand on discipline and limits. Parents need to have clear ideas and get them across to their children. Of course standards of discipline are largely a personal matter. Problems can arise when the standards you apply with your child conflict with those your neighbour sets for her child, if the two children often play together. There are no easy answers but a few possible approaches are suggested, in the topic called *Strictly for the family?*

Very often conflict is not outside but inside the family; brothers and sisters row. No one who has grown up in a family escapes family jealousy and it can feel very painful. Recognising and accepting jealousy as part of family life is an essential task for parents. The ways we talk to our children are important for making it easier to live with and understand. The topic called *Words matter* covers this important area.

All families face crises from time to time and the last part of this chapter looks at some of the difficulties. Identifying what is a crisis and understanding the kinds of stress you are under are explored. Family break-up is also a fact of life for a number of five to ten-year-olds. This chapter cannot attempt to cover all aspects of divorce and re-marriage but the thorny problem of what to tell the children is touched upon.

Having read through this chapter you may want to make some changes in your own family. *Family change* is about one family's attempt to alter parts of their lifestyle. You may pick up some ideas. The rest is up to you.

4

Inside the family

Families should be warm and giving, understanding and sharing ... or is that just too much to expect?

In this chapter the emphasis is on the family as an emotional unit and the way members of the family, especially the children, have their emotional needs met.

There is a common belief that families should be warm and giving, that everyone within them shares thoughts and feelings. But is this expecting too much from families?

Do we expect too much?

Work down the following checklist on the right filling in either the 'father' or 'mother' columns. Put ticks for items you agree with and items you think your partner agrees with. Add any important items which you think have been left out. Then cover up your answers and hand it to your partner to fill in. When you have both finished look at your answers together.

You and your partner may not agree on all points. Discussion may clear up some misunderstandings, but differences are likely to remain. You can agree to disagree and still have a meaningful relationship.

You may find you disagree because one of you has the idea that a 'good' family has intimate, sharing, caring relationships. But many people haven't been brought up to share feelings and therefore don't find it easy.

Sharing isn't an automatic virtue. Some things may be best kept hidden if making them explicit will do more harm than good. Telling a child you feel uncertain in a crisis may simply cause alarm and always telling your partner exactly what you think of him is rarely helpful. Sharing feelings can mean expressing hatred and disappointment as well as love and trust and not everyone copes equally well with these feelings. Finally, not all families have lots in common, in which case enforced sharing would do more damage than good.

Expecting all our satisfactions to come from the family is unrealistic and unwise. Many needs can best be met by important outsiders.

Mother		Families should:	Father	
I think	He thinks		I think	She thinks
☐	☐	be put above all else	☐	☐
☐	☐	agree about most things	☐	☐
☐	☐	should share most things	☐	☐
☐	☐	do most things together	☐	☐
☐	☐	be the people you can really talk to	☐	☐
☐	☐	have a few secrets	☐	☐
☐	☐	include grandparents	☐	☐
☐	☐	give you time on your own	☐	☐
☐	☐	have lots of interests in common	☐	☐
☐	☐	talk about feelings	☐	☐
☐	☐	be clear about who's in charge	☐	☐
☐	☐	aim for material comforts above all else	☐	☐

Conflict in the family

Every family has its share of conflict. How could it be otherwise when several people are trying to live together, often wanting different things at the same time? Conflict is a natural part of life, so it is natural in families too. Don't think that, at all costs, it must be avoided.

Many people are brought up to think conflict is bad, that conflict means trouble and should not occur in a happy or 'good' family.

In fact conflict is just a signal of some form of disagreement, and can be a very positive thing.

It gives families the chance to face up to difficulties that may not have been recognised before. Dealing with conflict can help a family to adapt to new situations, to grow.

Conflict is only bad when families are continually fighting and not sorting things out. A husband, for instance, may spend more time in the pub with his mates than with his wife. He does it because his own father did. But his wife thinks it means he doesn't love her. If she tells him how she feels, they might be able to sort out the problem – and the misunderstanding – and be better able to meet each other's needs. But if they don't discuss it, the underlying resentment will make matters worse. Eventually it may grow so large that it bursts out in the most unholy row – and everyone ends up miserable.

Family style

Take a look at the following three families. Do you recognise yourselves in any of them?

Family A

Nine-year-old Terry is watching out of the window. 'Mum's here,' he says. He, his sister Anne, aged seven, and their

A – The closed family

father all go down to the kitchen where mother is starting to unpack the shopping. 'Help your mother,' says father. Soon everything is put away. Terry notices some chocolate and reaches towards it. 'Not now,' says his mother, 'After lunch.' Everyone helps to get the lunch ready. Then father breaks up portions of chocolate according to age and mother hands them round.

Family B
'What shall we have to eat this weekend?' asks Mrs B, getting ready to go to the supermarket. 'Anyone any suggestions? Those who want to come shopping – I'm going in ten minutes or so.' Mr B calls out that the children's room needs to be cleared up otherwise someone will fall over the mess. 'I'm going shopping,' says Peter, aged ten. 'So am I,' says Jo, aged six. 'Now wait a minute,' says mother 'What about the mess upstairs?' 'I'll do it later,' says Peter. 'If you and Jo can manage to do it in ten minutes I'll hang on,' says mother. The children agree and Mr and Mrs B decide how much food they will need and guess how many extra people will stay for meals over the weekend.

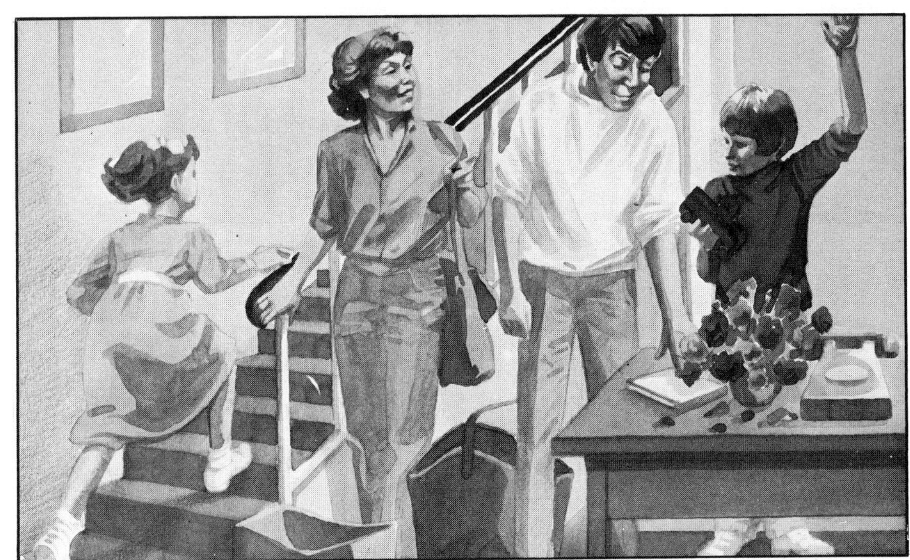
B – The open family

Family C
'The tap is leaking again,' shouts Mrs C. I'll mend it,' says John, aged nine. 'Don't worry, son, I'll be there in a minute,' says father. (That's what you said last week, thinks mother). John is actually better at fixing things than his father. Julie, aged seven, is practising gymnastics in the sitting room while father tries to change the light bulb. There is a smell of burning from the kitchen. Mrs C hardly notices. She is busy getting things ready for her trip to the bring-and-buy sale. 'Get what you want to eat,' she calls, 'Sorry the pie is burnt.' John annoys Julie and a squabble breaks out. Mrs C quietly makes her exit. Mr C decides to take the car to pieces. 'When's Mum coming back?' asks Julie but no one knows. They are not even sure where she has gone. 'Let's give her a surprise, let's cook a cake,' says John. Father agrees it is a good idea. They decide to watch TV at the same time . . . but there isn't enough space.

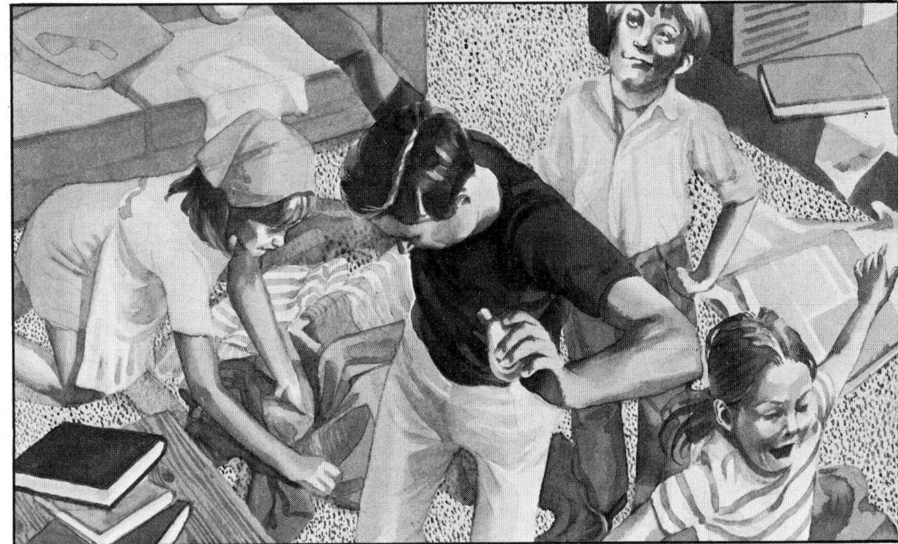
C – The random family

Organisation is the key in Family A. Everything has its own place. There is plenty of encouragement for doing well and both Anne and Terry do well at school. Family interests always come first and there is order and method in everything they do. Discipline is firm and the children know what is expected of them. This is a 'closed' family.

Routines are flexible in Family B. Patterns exist but people and their interests come first. Tidiness is not a first consideration and sometimes things get out of hand. No pressure is put on the children to achieve but they are given plenty of encouragement. Discipline is not strict but the children are expected to behave. This is an 'open' family.

Family C does not worry about organisation or routine; in fact, they have none. Tidiness is irrelevant to them. Everybody is more concerned with themselves than with anyone else. The children are expected to amuse themselves and they have a lot of freedom and encouragement. Knowing what is expected of them can be difficult because they do not often find time to talk together and even when they do they don't get clear instructions. The atmosphere is **unpredictable** and therefore they are a 'random' family.

What kind of family style do you have? Tick the statements that apply to you.

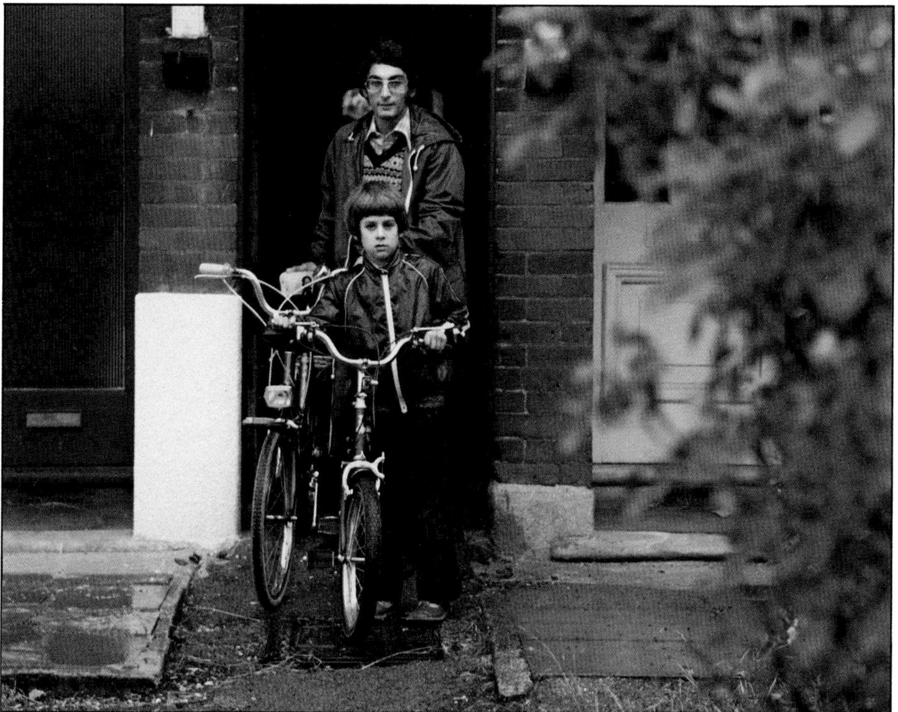

The closed family

- Parents are always in charge ☐
- We always arrange family outings ☐
- There is a lock on the bathroom door ☐
- Bedroom doors are shut ☐
- Privacy is important ☐
- We know exactly who comes in and out of the house ☐
- We monitor all the TV the children watch ☐
- Childrens' friends don't come in uninvited ☐
- Mealtimes are fixed ☐

Children know their bedtimes ☐
We hate waste and irresponsibility ☐

The open family

We keep an open house ☐
We try to decide things together ☐
We are involved in the community ☐
We punish only as a last resort ☐
Experimenting is important ☐
We encourage personal responsibility ☐
Mealtimes vary and we try to fit in with everyone ☐
Children usually go to bed at about the same time ☐
We don't believe in unlimited freedom ☐
Children are encouraged to think of others ☐
Children's behaviour isn't all we could wish ☐

Random family

Everyone does as they want ☐
We are always fighting ☐
We don't manage to sort things out ☐
We believe in individuality ☐
We don't believe in timetables ☐
We eat when we are hungry ☐
Children go to bed when they are tired ☐
Punishment is hardly ever used ☐
It is important to find out for yourself what you like doing ☐
Crises are almost routine with us ☐

Did you find that most of your ticks fall within one group? If so that is likely to be the style that your family uses most. No one style is right, all have advantages and disadvantages.

Sub-group	When and where?	What happens?	What they learn
Father and son	Sunday morning	Swimming	Son has dad to himself, sees dad on his own as well as learning swimming. Learns about how men behave on their own. Sees dad less as an authoritative figure, more as a chum
Father and mother	Evening/bedtime	Relaxing without children	Opportunity to have time together without the children around
Brother and sister	After school and weekends	Play and quarrels	Sharing and competing. Learn about being children in the family on their own without adults

Family identity

Families have an identity as a whole. But individuals have their own identities within them.

Jimmy Jones is always going to be a Jones: the son of Mary and Brian. This is an important part of his identity. Being the father of Jimmy and the husband of Mary is important to Brian's identity. Everyone's identity is influenced by belonging to a particular family and by their particular place within it.

The sense of being a separate person from the rest of the family is slower to develop. As child and family grow, the child gains a feeling of being independent and separate in so far as the family allow him to do things for himself. In every family there is a 'space' for each child. Being Jimmy is different from being a Jones.

Sub groups

Not only does each child have his own identity and his own place in the family group but he has a place in several sub-groups within his family. Every family carries out part of its function in smaller groups. Individual pairs like husband-wife, mother-child, brother-sister are all subdivisions of the family group. These sub-groups can be formed by generation, by sex, by interest or function. Each may meet at a different time and sometimes a different place; patterns of activities are different and the members learn different things from being in each sub-group.

List the sub-groups in your family. When and where do they take place? What are the children learning? There are some examples in the chart shown above.

Each sub-group is maintained by rules governing who joins the sub-group and how, where and when it meets and what it does. To be successful, each sub-group is dependent upon those *outside* it respecting its existence and not interfering. They can do this if they know they have a place within their own particular sub-groups and a place within the family as a whole.

Strictly for the family?

When it comes to discipline, you set the limits.

But do you know where you stand?

Whatever your views on children's behaviour, there are very many occasions when you need to make it clear that you're in charge. Individual children react differently to discipline and limits – some accept it with the minimum of fuss, others fight it all the way. If you want to succeed you need to be clear where you stand.

A	B	C
Children must learn good manners ☐	Children have to learn to behave themselves ☐	Children will be children, you can't expect perfect behaviour ☐
Children must show respect to elders ☐	Children must learn to be polite to their elders ☐	Adults should learn to approach children in the right way ☐
Rules have to be firm ☐	Children need guidelines for behaviour ☐	Children should be brought up with the minimum of rules ☐

What are your views on discipline?

On the right are a number of statements. Tick those that are closest to your views. Just a glance will show you where you stand on the discipline scale. A expresses a traditional view, B shows more flexibility while C reflects a much more permissive attitude. All three have pros and cons.

○ If you have ticks all in one column, you are consistent and your children know what to expect.

○ If you have a tick in more than one column, you like to show some flexibility.

○ A tick in each column suggests you really haven't made up your mind about where you stand. Is your uncertainty getting through to your child? Children sensing parents' weakness and uncertainty can exploit it without mercy.

Interest or indulgence?

To be child-centred seems to be a present-day virtue but it can very quickly lead to over-indulgence and that's not a virtue at all. Everyone indulges their children – but do you want it to be an everyday occurrence? Spoilt children are not popular with anyone inside or outside the family. There's a big difference between being easy-going and being indulgent.

Being an easy-going parent means allowing children to shout and make a noise when it won't disturb anyone else; letting them have a pillow fight but not jump on the bedsprings; allowing them to sleep in the tent in the garden on a fine summer night but sticking to their usual bedtimes.

Being an indulgent parent means never saying no to a request for sweets; allowing a child to stay up as long as he wants; watching him scribble in all his books without saying anything.

Children benefit from an easy-going attitude that enhances their confidence and feeling of being accepted for what they are. Children who are overindulged may end up feeling extremely anxious that no one can control them, and that includes themselves. They fear that their own imagined power may cause real damage.

OK, not OK

Traffic lights are a useful way of explaining to a child what is allowed and what is not.

RED means no, never, forbidden.

YELLOW means it may be tolerated for specific reasons.

GREEN means it is quite all right to do this.

Here are six activities children may wish to indulge in. We have put R, Y and G at the top of the chart (right) to indicate red, yellow and green. Tick which you think applies.

	R	Y	G
Scribbling in reading book	☐	☐	☐
Playing with garden hose	☐	☐	☐
Breaking a plate	☐	☐	☐
Picking flowers in garden	☐	☐	☐
Playing vets with a knife and the cat	☐	☐	☐
Using telephone without permission	☐	☐	☐

'Green' and 'red' are easy for children to understand. They are simple yes and no. Yellow is not so easy, because here it isn't the activity itself that's important but the circumstances. A broken plate may be tolerated if the child is trying to help with drying up; throwing a plate in anger is taboo. Total bans are certainly easier to operate.

Try this game with your child. Make a list like ours, with traffic lights at the top. Think up different situations for yourself and then get your child to put a tick for each under one of the lights. Compare your views. It's a good way of checking what your child understands.

Getting it right

If you are going to set limits, make sure your child knows what they are.

Be explicit 'Not too much mess' isn't good enough. Children and parents can vary in their views on 'too much'. Make clear, authoritative statements such as, 'painting is only allowed on the kitchen table', 'You must wear your overall'.

Don't bother with all the past history 'Remember last time, all that water, that's why I don't want you in the dining room' – is fussy and confusing. The child wants to know about today, not what happened last week. He can't go back and put that right but he can get it right next time – with your help.

Don't try and solve everything in one go 'Most other children manage to paint without making a mess. You have to muck up everything, even your clothes. As for your bedroom – it's a disaster, you are going to have to learn to be a lot cleaner and tidier.' When a child hears that, what can he do but feel a failure? As a request, it is confusing and overwhelming. All he can do is ignore it. So break down requests into small steps he can manage. If it is messy painting that bothers you, stick to that. Leave the bedroom mess until another day.

Enforcing discipline

When instructions are quite clear and said in a simple non-threatening way, most children conform. But some don't. In that case, parents need to be firm, not to give way and certainly not to lose their tempers.

○ Don't get drawn into long arguments. No one ever wins.

○ Don't debate the fairness of the rule. If you make it, stick to it.

○ Don't go in for long explanations. The chances are your child will find a loophole to exploit. It's unnecessary to explain why windows must not be broken or the dog not kicked.

○ Avoid a battle of wills. Don't get into a yes/no battle. But acknowledge the child's feelings and the conflict he is experiencing. 'I know it's very hard to go to bed when you were having such fun downstairs.'

When children disobey, their anxiety mounts even if they don't show it. A child needs a strong adult to take charge. Too much talk conveys weakness. Threats only make things worse and then both parent and child get anxious.

Spare the rod and spoil the child?

Children don't usually hit their parents but what about parents hitting children?

Fifty years ago it was believed that corporal punishment was good for a child but times change and today's parents are not so sure. Tick the statements you agree with in the quiz below.

In a survey of the parents of seven-year-olds, nearly half thought smacking was good for children and less than a quarter thought it was just routine. The rest considered it 'unfortunate but necessary as a last resort'.

Smacking carries a message of 'I know better than you' or perhaps just 'I'm bigger than you'. It's the message the smack carries that is important and not merely how hard you smack.

Smacking is far less common between five and ten than it is with under-fives. It's not surprising really. It does get easier to reason with children as their understanding improves. Less than a tenth of seven-year-olds in the survey mentioned were smacked every day. A quarter were smacked about once a week and a third about once a month. Rudeness and bad language were the most common reasons for smacking.

It is interesting that nearly three quarters of the parents interviewed said they felt guilty and upset when they smacked their children. Hardly anyone felt relieved. It seems most parents want to be thought easy-going and do not like to be strict. But what emerged clearly was that their strictness and their smacking depended more on their own mood rather than the child's behaviour.

All parents want well-behaved children and those who believe in smacking say it helps produce well-behaved children. Other parents get by just using disapproval or battles of words. Still others withdraw privileges. The least effective method is to make threats which are never carried out. Children quickly see through that one.

Those parents who smack and those who don't all have the long-term interests of the child at heart. The issue of smacking has to be decided by what feels right to you and what works.

There is no clear evidence that smacking does great harm or has any benefit. It is the overall relationship between parent and child that counts.

What do you think about smacking?

- ☐ It's good for children
- ☐ Just routine
- ☐ Unfortunate but necessary as a last resort
- ☐ Never should be done

How does it make you feel?

- ☐ Relieved
- ☐ Nothing in particular
- ☐ Guilty and upset

How often do you smack on average?

- ☐ Daily
- ☐ Weekly
- ☐ Monthly
- ☐ Less than monthly
- ☐ Never

What do you smack for?

- ☐ Disobedience
- ☐ Rudeness
- ☐ Bad language
- ☐ Other

Children's fights

When children squabble they are learning the art of bargaining and negotiation.

Children growing up in the same family fight, squabble and generally jockey for position. Why should we expect anything else? They often spend long hours together without any choice in the matter and they often have to compete for the time and attention of parents. It seems children of the opposite sex and those with a bigger age difference fight less. But if your children are squabbling from the moment they wake up till the moment they go to bed, take heart, they are not unusual.

How children get their own way

Most children are skilful manipulators and they practise their skills on their nearest and dearest, the unsuspecting younger members of their family.

Threats can be used by older and stronger children. They are often unspecific about what they are threatening – they hope their bluff won't be called. Young children can also threaten, but will usually cry and bring in the grown-ups.

Telling tales has a double standard: it's a jolly useful ploy when you're in a corner but it is sneered at by all other children.

Beating-up/brute force is not a last resort, more a second line attack. Said to be more commonly used by boys, but girls may just be more skilled at being discreet about it.

Bargains and promises tend to be a last resort – they are not always held to. Children recognise that they are temporary bait. They can then use a broken promise as a bargaining tactic in the next round.

Tears and anger are not easily controlled by children and there are usually two results. Either the other child retreats from the battleground and a truce called, or an adult is brought in to sort things out.

Is there any value in fighting?

Children should be able to 'let their hair down' especially with each other. Conflicts are bound to occur and children do have to learn to sort things out for themselves. But if one child consistently comes off worse, you may wish to teach him or her new tactics. It is important that parents keep a sense of fair play, which is not the same as treating all children equally. Children are not equal in age and position and differences should be maintained and respected by parents.

However much brothers and sisters may fight, squabble or ignore each other at home, don't despair of their ever having the sort of relationship you would wish. For, outside the family, in other groups of children, you will find brothers and sisters side by side sticking up for one another.

But parents must not allow children to bully each other. Attacks can cause physical harm to the victim and the attacker. Children need to be stopped and told firmly that you, the parent, will not allow them to harm each other. This is reassuring to the children – to know that someone is in charge and they will be stopped if things get out of control. Their own sense of control can feel very shaky at times.

A fighting hour?

Should you ever try and stop children fighting? Well, if you do, it's for your benefit – not theirs. You may need some peace and quiet. So what about a fighting hour, at a time to suit you, when all the quarrels of the day are sorted out, perhaps in the garden if you have one. The condition is no fighting the rest of the day! All squabbles have to be saved for the special hour and absolutely no exceptions.

This quite often has the desired effect – children soon forget a grievance and find it hard to fight to order; the bonus is peace for the rest of the day for all the others in the family.

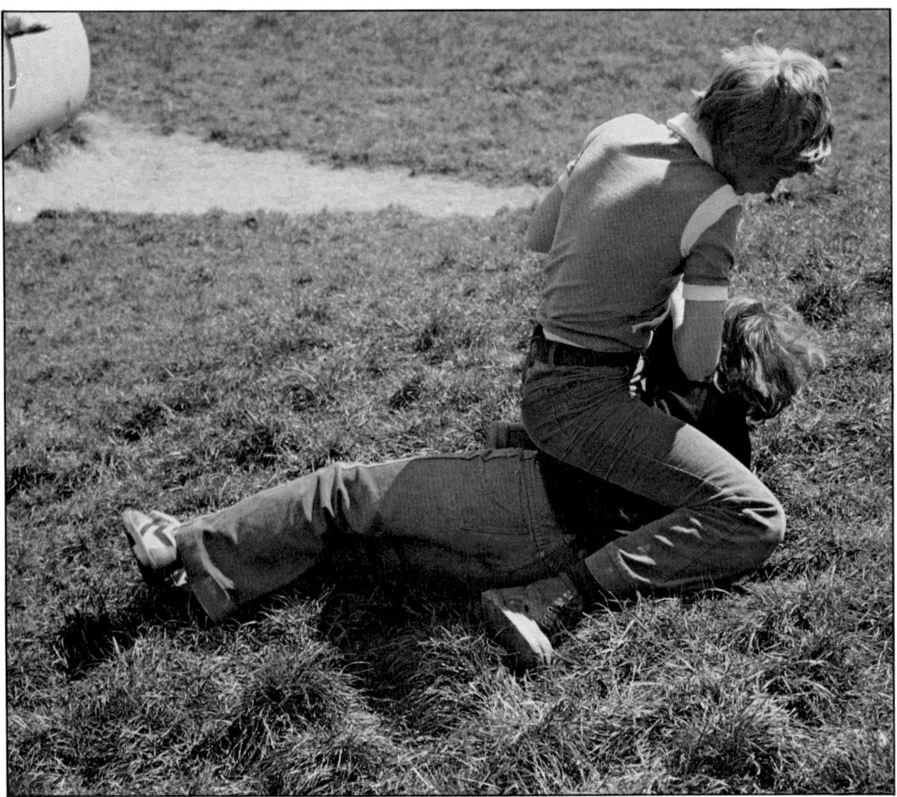

Fights and quarrels outside the family

Knowing *when* to help is as important as knowing *how* to help. Unfortunately there are no simple rules.

Physical hurts
If your child tells you that he has been hurt by another child, you probably check out the story before you rush in. Your child may have started it. If he comes home with stories of being 'set upon', you probably don't take it all at face value. It may be the sort of teasing everyone is subjected to. And he may be describing his fears about what *might* have happened rather than what did happen.

Emotional hurts
Hearing or seeing that your child is being left out, is shy, or seems to have difficulty making and keeping friends can be very distressing because you are emotionally involved.

But, you wonder, is your child exaggerating? He might be left out of one game and included in many others. Or you may think he has got the problem out of proportion. You know your child may not be the life and soul of the party, but he has got one or two good friends. Some children go through a solitary phase and only if it persists and distresses him should you seek professional help.

Children sometimes take a long time to learn how to get on with other people.

Parent problems
You may be caught in a real dilemma if you don't like your child mixing with a neighbour's 'little menace', although in the end, you probably put your child's interests first and take the risk of offending the other parent.

It is even more upsetting to find out that other parents don't 'like' or 'approve' of your child. Parents differ in the way they think children should be brought up. So there are bound to be disagreements between parents that occasionally come to the surface when children play together.

Helping or interfering?

How can you distinguish between helping and interfering? You can't always. Sometimes the line between the two is so fine that it's impossible to know what to do for the best. And what is 'helping out' to one set of parents may be 'interfering' to another.

Circumstances change fast. Children can be best of friends one minute and hate each other the next. Later the same day they'll have made it up. It's their parents who worry and are left feeling confused!

Think before you rush in to act. Try to take stock of things from a distance.

○ There are other ways of intervening apart from going in in person.

○ Talk to the children about what worries *you* in a quiet moment.

○ Talk to other parents if the problem persists; or your child's teacher if he/she is sympathetic. They may have some ideas. It always helps to share worries.

○ Your child is always going to meet people in life he doesn't like. Toleration is learnt very slowly.

You can set guidelines for your child on how to behave towards other children. You can teach him the rules. But you can't play the game for him.

Parents frequently have different ideas on what to do about quarrels among children. Six typical approaches are given on the right together with their popularity among parents who had used them, and the parents' comments. Before you read them, try to recall the last two squabbles you got involved in and fill in the chart. If you think about what you do when your child fights with other children, you may find that you use one of these methods more than the others.

Putting the pieces back together

When you next decide to intervene in a quarrel involving your child, try out our technique shown in the cartoon sequence. It is an argument among a group of four children where the parent of one intervenes as a 'peace-maker'.

What children did	What you did/said	Comments
1		
2		

Now compare your approach with those used by these parents.

Method	Score (% of parents using)	Advantages	Disadvantages
INTERFERE IN PERSON 'If they start fighting, I bring them all in here and I give them a good talking to'	25%	Gives you a chance to arbitrate, see things are done fairly. Prevents smallest and weakest always losing out	Child may come to rely on you for defence
URGE RETALIATION 'If they've kicked him and he comes in crying, I say – well, go and hit them back then – the same as they've done to you'	25%	Self-defence is an art that should be learned	Tit for tat rarely solves anything. Someone may get hurt
REFUSE TO GET INVOLVED 'I say that's up to her. If she causes arguments, she can patch them up again'	23%	Throws child on to own resources	Child may not always be able to sort things out alone
TRY REASONING 'I say, now look here, you can't expect the boys to play with you if you will insist on having your own way'	10%	Helps child develop ideas of right and wrong	May be difficult for child to accept. You and he may have different ideas about what's 'fair' and what's not
URGE WITHDRAWAL 'I tell her to be kind, and if they aren't kind to her, to leave them, just not bother to play with them'	8%	Physically safest. Avoids confrontation	May not always be possible. And child may not learn to solve disputes if always opting out
URGE DIPLOMACY 'I always say to him if he knows he's in the wrong, then he should admit it and say that he's sorry and then everything's OK again'	6%	Practical way of recovering the status quo	Difficult for a child to do. And he may become over-obliging, especially if he is the only one doing this
Other strategies	3%		

Stage 1: *Sorting it all out*

This is where you start to act as the diplomat. Go over the problem carefully and they will have time to think it over. Tempers will have a chance to cool. Show that you are concerned to get the problem sorted out rather than 'pass judgement'. A situation is rarely black and white anyway.

Stage 2: *Mediation*

By saying something neutral or sympathetic about both sides ('Kevin's unhappy', 'Paul was kind') this will get them thinking more positively, rather than merely shouting further accusations at each other. They both need an 'escape route', a way that's fair and that doesn't involve a loss of face for either of them. By now they should have 'unwound' sufficiently to allow 'peace talks' to begin.

It may take a while for children to learn to make positive suggestions, as in the cartoons. You can suggest things yourself, but don't push if they reject them. They may make some totally impractical suggestions which you'd have to point out would not work. But you may be surprised at the inventiveness of children once they do set their minds to the problem and look for solutions.

Of course, fresh quarrels may break out ten minutes later, but then that's life. Try the same method again if necessary.

There is no one method of preventing children arguing or fighting. But there are certain advantages to this approach.

○ You can get away from the idea that someone always wins, and someone else has to lose. It is usually possible to work out a compromise that is acceptable to everyone.

○ The emphasis is not on punishment, but on everyone 'giving' a little to everyone else.

○ The children who are arguing are responsible for sorting out their own problems. They can't depend on adults to find all the answers for them.

○ Once they get used to it, children may begin to think along these lines themselves even when an adult is not around to act as a go-between.

○ For the adult who intervenes, it's a positive approach. Because you don't go in as judge and jury, it's easier to keep your temper. And you don't feel so irritated by yet more fighting between the children.

You can try this method not only with a group of children who are quarrelling, but even in an argument between yourself and your child. It's surprising that even in situations which seem to be terrifying battles of wills, sometimes there *are* alternatives apart from the obvious ones of you imposing your will on your child or him imposing his on you.

Stage 3: *Reconciliation*

Notice that the children themselves are involved in working out their own solutions to their problems. Because they are not having these solutions imposed on them by adults outside their group, they may be more committed to making them work. In recognising each other's needs, however grudgingly, they are taking the first steps on the road to a peaceful compromise. You, as the grown up, have to direct them away from 'getting revenge'.

Facing ups and downs

You can't protect children from crises.
But there are ways in which to cushion the blow...

Parents of five to ten-year-olds have already coped with huge changes in their family as they moved through early married life, had their first baby and lived through the pre-school years. Many parents would like to go on protecting their children from life's ups and downs as they did in the pre-school years. But life itself is full of changes – and the simple fact that everybody is getting older ensures that nothing stays the same for very long. Children are aware of ups and downs in family life. Crises can occur *inside the family*, when relationship problems occur or they can be generated by *outside events*, such as moving house or unemployment. Children cannot always be sheltered from crises.

Planned or unplanned

Some events bringing changes are planned; the move to a new house or starting school. Others arise quite unexpectedly, a handicapped baby, a serious accident, father made redundant.

Some crises can be predicted even if the timing is uncertain. All parents know that children will be sick sometimes, play up occasionally and that there will be minor problems with the car. But no one can foresee serious illness or accident or indeed the house burning down. And there are some events that creep up so slowly that we fail to see them until they are really serious: marriage problems for example.

Sympathy or criticism

Some events such as serious illness or losing your job bring sympathy and understanding from people outside the family. Other events such as divorce or truancy are still a crisis for the family but may bring criticism on them. The way people outside the family respond will make a difference to the way the family is able to cope.

Keep these elements in mind when you think of stresses in the family.

○ Inside/outside family.

○ Planned/unplanned.

○ Sympathy/criticism.

	(1) Inside family	(2) Outside family	(3) Planned	(4) Unplanned	(5) Sympathy	(6) Criticism
Arrival of new member	☐	☐	☐	☐	☐	☐
Break up of marriage	☐	☐	☐	☐	☐	☐
Serious illness of parent	☐	☐	☐	☐	☐	☐
Death of member of family	☐	☐	☐	☐	☐	☐
Quarrels with someone	☐	☐	☐	☐	☐	☐
Father's redundancy	☐	☐	☐	☐	☐	☐
Car accident	☐	☐	☐	☐	☐	☐
Fire/flood in house	☐	☐	☐	☐	☐	☐
Starting/changing school	☐	☐	☐	☐	☐	☐
Moving house	☐	☐	☐	☐	☐	☐
Promotion	☐	☐	☐	☐	☐	☐
Winning the pools	☐	☐	☐	☐	☐	☐

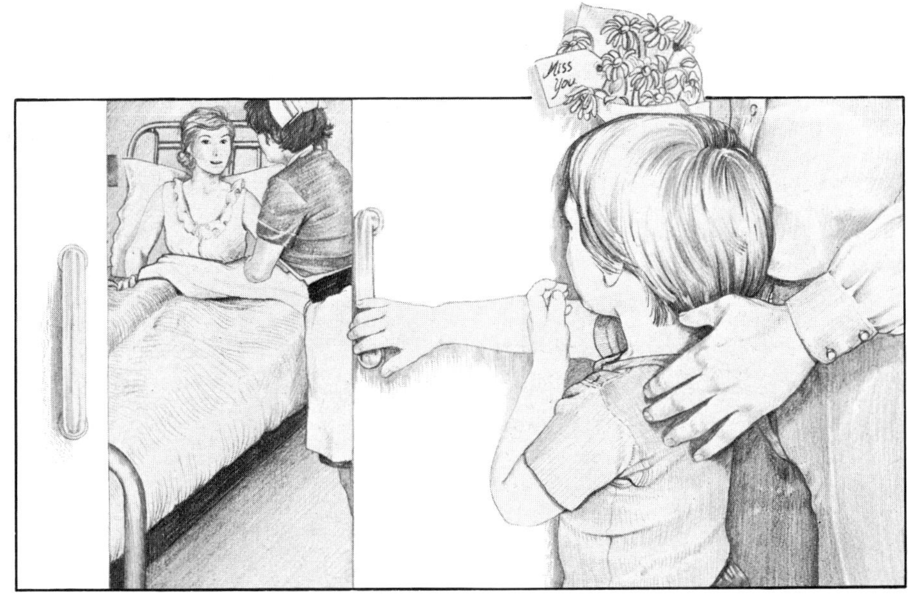

Stress events

Look through the list on the left. Tick the appropriate columns for the events that apply to your family. We show you below the events Sheila picked out from her life.

Sheila's events

Jim's father's death
This was the biggest shock we had to deal with *(outside family)*. It really jolted us. We had no idea it was coming *(unplanned)*. He wasn't old – we didn't really know what to do or say. Everyone in the street rallied round to help *(sympathy)*. Janet understood a bit. She was upset because we were. Simon was just puzzled. Jim kept most of it to himself. It is not something you get used to.

Simon going to nursery
This affected my day *(inside family)*. I looked forward to getting them both off my hands for a few hours *(planned)*. I knew it would happen and had it all planned what I'd do. Yet I felt quite upset and our family changed a lot. It took a lot of adjusting to. I like the work I do. It gives me an interest outside the home.

Moving house
We chose the house *(planned)*, as we needed the space. The family were pleased and we had four months to get used to the idea. Yet we all felt unsettled and took ages to settle down. We love this house now – Janet and Simon hardly know anywhere else as home. Funny to look back on the problems it caused at the time.

How do children cope?

We have looked at crises for families but what about the reactions of individual children?

Jonathan and Diana are two eight-year-olds. Here are some details about them and their families. When you have read them, fill in the tables (right).

Jonathan, aged eight, an only child, lives with his mother in a small flat in a London suburb. They moved there about a year ago from a house with a garden because they could no longer afford to keep it. Jonathan had to change his school. His parents have been divorced three years and his mother now works full time. Jonathan goes to a childminder after school and during the holidays. He likes going to his grandparents quite often and he sees his father for part of most weekends. Jonathan reads a lot and has joined the cubs. He is a typical eight-year-old and has made a lot of friends. He enjoys school and is doing well. In many ways he is independent, able to go to the local shop on his own and help around the flat. He and his mother enjoy doing things together when they can. Mother is very pleased with Jonathan's progress.

Diana, aged eight, lives with both parents and a brother aged five. They have always lived in the same comfortable house in a country town. Father is a professional man working locally and mother devotes herself to looking after the home and the children. There are no money or health problems. But Diana is a great worry. At eight she still wets the bed and cries very easily if she doesn't get her own way; she has tantrums more like a three-year-old. Diana is also a worry at school as she has not begun to read yet. She doesn't make friends easily and is very jealous of her younger brother.

Her mother doesn't know what to do with her. They do not get on. Diana will not listen and that makes mother shout all the more. She feels guilty about the way she shouts but she feels she cannot trust Diana to do anything herself. Father disagrees with his wife and says she is 'too soft' with Diana. But he is not often there. Both parents want Diana to do well as they know she is bright. They try to get her to read each day and tell her what a disappointment she is. Both parents argue and quarrel a lot of the time. This family do not enjoy week-ends at all.

Securities and stresses

These are two very different situations yet Jonathan copes and Diana doesn't. Why has this happened?

Take a look at the family patterns and events these children have faced and put a tick under the name of the child who has had to cope with them.

	Jonathan	Diana
Single parent		
Going to childminder		
Divorced parents		
Changing school		
Moving house		

No doubt you have put a column of ticks under Jonathan's name. So much seems to be loaded against him while Diana has not had to cope with any of these changes. Why is she suffering?

Look again at these children, this time at their relationship with their families and put a tick under the name of the child who faces these stresses.

	Jonathan	Diana
Unhappy relationship		
Difficulties at school		
Unable to make friends		
Jealous of brother		
Pressure to do well		
Quarrelling parents		

This time a different picture emerges. Diana is the child with very unhappy relationships despite a seemingly secure background. Her behaviour and bed-wetting are signals that this family is in distress and needs some help.

Jonathan's relationships are what helped him cope with all the changes he faced. He still sees both his parents although they live apart. He also has a close relationship with his grandparents. He gets on well with his mother even though she is not there all the time and he behaves appropriately for an eight-year-old.

These examples show that stress and change need not be disastrous provided the child feels secure in the relationships within the family. But, as in Diana's case, a child can be under stress in the most stable family if the relationships are poor.

Finding the balance

Security can balance distress. Does this apply for your child? Tick the relevant statements below and add any others you think of at the end of each list.

Stress	Security
Moving house ☐	Good friends ☐
Changing schools ☐	Happy at school ☐
Pressure to do well ☐	Good relationships with parent(s) ☐
Unhappy at school ☐	Good relationship with wider family ☐
No friends ☐	Stable home ☐
Divorce or separation ☐	Happy parents ☐
Unhappy relationships with parents ☐	Knows parents are pleased with him ☐
Quarrelling parents ☐	No abrupt changes at home ☐

No parent can protect a child from every kind of stress. But it is worth looking at the chart to see if your child needs extra help in terms of your time or energy in order to cope. Every child is different, even in the same family. Personality as well as life experience count.

How do you cope?

Individuals and families deal with events in different ways. Perhaps most of us respond to crisis by trying to put the clock back, by attempting to get back to the way things were. Others actively look for change to bring variety constantly into their lives.

We all know the sort of person who looks for a new house the minute he has sorted out his present home.

How closely events follow one another also affects our coping. If crisis follows crisis the cumulative effect will be greater than if there is time to deal with each separately.

The resources we have affect how we deal with change – not only financial resources but practical and emotional ones too. Some problems are helped by money, others require skills of patience and living with uncertainty.

Which of the following patterns is most like you?

You fail to notice anything different

Do you overlook all the warning signals? This kind of approach is bound to fail. Events will just overtake you. If John is not learning to read at eight, he may still be unable to read at ten and 'suddenly' it will be a problem. Granny spoils Mandy and she demands she has her own way. Her parents say that 'Granny and Mandy have such fun.'

You notice something different but choose to ignore it

Sometimes it goes away but more often things get worse. So it doesn't help to notice John isn't reading but say it will come in his own time. Or see granny is in difficulty with Mandy but presume 'she knows what she is doing'.

You notice something has happend and just live with it

Mother and father 'help' John by reading to him and not expecting him to try. And perhaps all grannies behave like Mandy's and spoil children.

You opt out

Father stops going to see John's teacher. Parents leave granny and Mandy to sort it out.

You get rid of the offenders

John with reading problem is sent to boarding school. Granny is not invited to stay.

You attempt to deal with it yourself

Mother buys all the books she can find on reading problems. Mother makes attempts to control Mandy.

You use family resources to find a solution

Family discuss John's problem all together and resolve to give John as much time and help as he needs. Parents involve granny in talking about how to deal with Mandy.

You get outside help

Family decide to get a remedial teacher for John. The doctor is asked about Mandy's behaviour problems.

You try to draw attention away from the real problem

John's mother begins to complain about the size of classes at school. Mandy's parents worry about their youngest child, Philip, not getting any attention.

Finding help

Families and friends are the first source of help when it comes to a crisis. But many people feel ashamed to ask for help. Having a problem is bad enough, but not being able to cope by yourself is a real personal failure. Or is it?

Where do you turn?

○ Involve your family – can grandparents or aunts or uncles help?
○ Talking to friends can help too.
○ Family doctors may be sympathetic.
○ Teachers are concerned.
○ Child guidance clinics specialise in family problems.
○ Social services help families.
○ Marriage Guidance help with marriage problems.
○ Health visitors are interested in all children's well-being.
○ In emergencies there are the Samaritans.

27

Words matter

What you say and forget today a child may carry inside for the rest of his life.

Words play an incredibly important part in your dealings with five to ten-year-olds. They are getting more skilled in listening to and taking notice of words. At the same time, they are often unsure of themselves and what they can do. So words harshly used can easily undermine them.

For both these reasons, words matter. You need to choose them carefully, so that you encourage when you talk, especially about feelings. 'Sticks and stones may break my bones but names will never hurt me' goes the old saying. Sad to say, it's just not true. We all have experiences of being hurt by a chance remark or verbal attack.

Helpful talking requires two things: respect and skill. Respect means accepting children have all sorts of feelings. You may not agree with them, but you can acknowledge them. The skill lies in listening, and in being clear and direct when you speak. Words and feelings need not be a tangle if you take time and trouble in learning the skills and passing them on.

How wires get crossed

No parent wakes up in the morning planning to make his child's life a misery. No parents swears 'Today I'll shout and nag and muddle my child'. Yet, in spite of good intentions, it can happen.

Below are some of the ways parents cross wires in talking with their children. Which, if any, do you use? What happens when you do? Are there any you wouldn't use on your own or other children? Why?

Threats and bamboozling – 'If you do that again…'
Threats are an invitation to misbehave. Only the meek child knuckles under. Most take a threat as a challenge. 'Bamboozling' is a bluffing sort of threat, like 'I'll get the police / leave home / send you away'. A young child may take bluff seriously. They may start to mistrust parents who use it. They soon see through your threats.

Bribes – 'If you do this, then you'll get such-and-such'
'If … then' suggests doubt about the child's ability to do better of his own accord. Short-term it may work. Long-term it can lead to a spiral of blackmail and bargaining, to being 'good' just long enough to get his pocket money. The child never learns there are satisfactions in pleasing others, without material reward.

Promises – 'Promise me you'll…'
If parent and child trust each other, do they need to add promises? 'Unpromised' words should be trustworthy as well. Sometimes things turn out unexpectedly, and you cannot do what you said. Children need a basic trust in parents to do their best without having the back-up of a promise.

Sarcasm and abuse – 'Are you deaf? You clumsy idiot'
Sarcasm and abuse are attacks on the child's personality and his personal worth. They invite counter-attack ('you should know, you're my mother'). It is not a response you want your children to copy. It can undermine a child's confidence in his new found confidence and skills.

Detecting – 'Where's your new doll then?'
If parents know it's broken or swapped, they shouldn't play detective by asking misleading questions. It could push children into dishonesty. If parents know the answer, they don't need to ask the question or at least the question should be different. 'Does your doll need mending?' 'Did you really want to swap it?'

Rudeness – 'What do you say when you get a present, then?'
Parents want their children to be polite. But it's easy for parents to be less than polite when trying to teach manners. Children watch adults to see how they behave and follow them. Common courtesy towards children helps them to learn good manners.

Most parents use some of these ways of talking at some time. No one behaves in a way they would like all the time. Short-term they can backfire on you: 'but you promised!' It is an awkward situation but no long-term harm is done. Used regularly, they pass on to your children unhelpful, sometimes hurtful, ways of talking. It's not easy to be an accurate judge of what you're doing. *Would you dare tape record yourself for a day?*

Listening to feelings

John goes home from school cross because football was cancelled.

Mother: *'You look disappointed?'*

John: *'Yes.'*

Mother: *'You really wanted to play, didn't you?'*

John: *'Yes.'*

Mother: *'And it had to go and rain.'*

John : *'Oh well, maybe we'll play tomorrow.'*

John goes out happily.

Stephen's mother says: *'No football? Well you hadn't cleaned your boots had you?'*

Stephen: (Sulks)

Mother: *'No use whining at me.'*

Stephen: (Sulks)

Mother: *'Sulking will get you nowhere.'*

Stephen stomps out of the kitchen.

John cheers up, Stephen is crosser than before. Why? Stephen's mother ignores his feelings and nags. But that doesn't make Stephen's feelings vanish, it just makes them worse. John's mother listens and accepts his feelings. Often that's enough to make a child happy again. Other times, it's the first step to take, before going on to discuss or suggest things. Below are suggestions for listening to feelings.

When a child tells you he is upset it often helps to talk about his feelings. You can try to sort out what they are by careful attention
Mary comes home in tears: the teacher has told her off. *'It looks as though you had a rough day'*, or *'Did you feel cross inside?'* will comfort her with understanding. Then you can begin to discuss why she was told off.

It soothes a child to hear his feelings reflected in your words. If you can accept his feelings, he'll then more readily accept your questions, judgements, sympathy or suggestions
Tom sulks when he turns on the television and sees the film has been changed. Instead of getting irritated his mother tries: *'You must feel cross!'* Tom flings his arms around her and says: *'What can I do instead?'*

Children don't always know what their feelings are. You can help by giving feelings their names. Then they're less frightening. They can be shared and discussed and got through together
Anna wants to go on to the school camp, but she's worried about it too. *'Make up your mind'* is just what she can't do. *'You want to go and you want to stay'* airs her mixed feelings so they can be discussed.

When a child tells you about something that has happened it's often because the people involved are important. So talk about the relationship, and the feelings, rather than about the event
Kerry says she's had fewer new clothes lately than her older sister. Is she worried by clothes or her sister? Mother tries a big hug, saying: *'But I love you just as much as Tina'*. It may be enough to send Kerry off happy again.

When a child says something about himself, it often helps to add details that show you understand. Make more of what he says about himself, rather than judging or just agreeing
Mark says he's no good at sums. Even if true, agreeing won't help. *'They're not easy. Do you worry about the tests, or what teacher says?'* is a start. It splits the problem into smaller parts that can be dealt with.

Helpful ways of putting your view

All families show their feelings differently. A small smile in one family may mean the same as a big hug in another. What's important is that all the family know and respect each other's feelings. As a parent, you'll have your own ways of telling your children what you think and feel. Simply ask yourself: could I be any more helpful in getting the message across? Here are some ideas.

Praise: when it's due
Helpful praise is realistic praise about what a child has done. He can think over what you say and draw his own conclusions about himself. When he's done a good job, or really helped you, say so. Most people's heads don't grow bigger when they are given praise and thanks that are due.

If instead you praise him for what he does by saying 'you're good' or 'I love you', it can be less helpful. A child often has doubts about himself or his family. If he feels he's really bad, he won't be able to accept your praise. or he may worry that your love depends on what he does, not who he is.

Criticism: deal with what's been done
When you criticise, deal simply with the event that has sparked it: the spilt drink, the poor work, the open gate. If you are rude about the child ('you naughty, stupid brat') you may find he is rude back. Or he may think he is always bad. Be specific. 'You must shut the gate to keep the dog in' or 'if you sit down to drink you don't spill' is more help than 'you know better than to do that'.

Responsibility: help your child take it
Your child wants to do something and you're happy to let him. Rather than say 'yes' yourself, use a 'freedom phrase' that lets your child decide. For example: 'If that's what you'd like/you decide/it's up to you/whatever you choose is fine by me.' Being trusted by you to decide makes a child feel good inside. He needs to feel that way if he is going to take responsibility – for a pet, or homework, or tidying his room. Nagging doesn't work.

Your own anger: watch it
Sometimes anger is the only way to show you care. But anger frightens some children. And it does no good to be lashed with harsh words. So watch out when you are angry. Don't attack your child's personality, or make him feel at fault for things that have nothing to do with him. Do try to show your child exactly what you are angry about.

Give warning: *'I feel annoyed.'*

Repeat if needed: *'... really annoyed ...'*

Add reason why: *'When you lot push off and leave me with the dishes all the time, I feel really cross...'*

Family tension

Everything may seem fine on the surface.
But what's going on underneath?

Growing up in families involves everyone in tension. Sometimes just one person is affected but more often it can dominate the whole family. People living together are bound to have conflicts because they want different things from each other. Tensions arise if they don't face them.

What are the signs of tension?

Body posture and behaviour Anxious tense positions, fidgeting, nail-biting, finger-drumming, teeth-clenching.

Physical symptoms Frequent unexplained mild headaches, stomach pain and sickness, some skin problems and all kinds of minor ailments.

Troubled moods Anxiety, depression, agitation, muddled thinking and lack of concentration.

Note down on a chart like ours the tension signs familiar to you and your family.

Under 'comments' put down what you thought the behaviour meant before you realised its real cause. An example is given to help you see the kind of reaction we mean.

Family member	Tension sign	Situation	Your comments
Husband	Irritation	He yelled at children in the evenings for making too much noise	I thought he was being unreasonable until I realised he was under stress at work

Everyone feels under stress at times. It is a normal reaction to the pressure of everyday life. It can get out of hand if no one recognises it and if it continues day after day with no let-up. Learning stress signs in those close to you alerts you to the fact they may need extra attention and support.

Reaction under stress

Sometimes tension is too uncomfortable to face and so people may use these tactics to try and avoid it.

Withdrawing either by going elsewhere or being silent.

Preoccupation with other things. You may be there in person but unavailable to take part in what's going on.

Aggressive behaviour towards other people can be an outlet for unresolved tension. But it doesn't help solve the real problem underneath.

Illness can be an escape from tension. One family member may be unable to take any more and the rest of the family may be all too ready to blame their problems on that person's illness.

Relationships under stress

Understanding each other is not always easy at the best of times. In a tense situation misunderstandings are frequent.

Everyone wants to hold on to the fairy tale notion, 'they got married and lived happily ever after'. Regrets that real life, and marriage in particular, can never be like that can only add to the disappointment and guilt when things don't work out.

People get married for a variety of reasons besides love – to leave home, to feel wanted, to escape from loneliness, or because they are pregnant. Some marriages get off to a good beginning, others start from less than ideal circumstances. Whatever the beginnings, difficulties will occur.

Sadly, marriage stress is not always kept between husband and wife. When the relationship between them is unstable a child is often brought in to balance the relationship. This allows them to forget their own quarrel and concentrate their attention on the child. It's only fleetingly they notice they no longer talk together as husband and wife, only about the children.

The difficult child

Children can recognise that parents have difficulties being together and may divert attention away from those problems and on to themselves by being difficult, refusing to do what they are told, having tantrums or insisting on sleeping in their parents' bed. Parents then find it easier just to stick to the parental role. They join together to do something about their 'problem child'.

But they may disagree even here about what they should do. Tension mounts and the child plays up even more to try and hide from himself the differences between his parents. For some families these cycles go on indefinitely.

Joy was a six-year-old who refused to do anything she was told. *'Please sit down,'* her mother would say but Joy refused to hear. *'Joy, don't be naughty,'* she would carry on. *'Don't nag the child,'* said father. *'You get her to sit down,'* says her mother. *'What for?'* father would say. Joy by this time would be chasing round and round the room in a frenzy. *'I wish you'd do something about that child. I can't hear myself speak,'* – father. At that point both parents would get together and yell at the child to calm down. Joy calmed down once her parents were in agreement about what they wanted her to do. But Joy was always ready to use awful behaviour to provoke parental conflict.

Smothering closeness

Another model is the one where mother and child are locked in a close relationship where no one else can intrude. The intensity means that all responses are exaggerated. Mother responds to the child with a mixture of devotion and exasperation. The child responds with difficult behaviour and mother cannot control him.

Father is called in to help deal with the child. Father succeeds in giving clear instructions and getting what he wants from the child. Mother then criticises father for not doing it the way she wanted. She may even threaten to walk out and leave him to it. Father responds to mother by giving up. He cannot succeed in coming between mother and child.

Mother and child are again locked in a mixture of devotion and exasperation and this continues until they reach loggerheads once more. Father again comes in and the sequence begins all over.

The child can become the means of communication for the marriage and all issues may be dealt with in this way, as a means of avoiding the threat of real issues.

Effects of stress

Sometimes a wife under stess goes to one of her children for comfort and support against the father. This traps the child into the uncomfortable position of being mother's ally against father.

Whole families can be changed by one member's stress. If the husband is under stress as a result of losing his job, then the family organisation may alter completely to ensure the family survives. Father may stay at home and take over some of the housework and looking after the children while mother goes out to work to support the family. This is a sudden reversal of roles and may require a change in the authority structure. Another family might bring in granny to look after the children whilst both parents go out to work. Problems arise if the family adopts a rigid pattern and refuses to give her authority she needs to do the job properly.

The single parent and grandparent

This is a three generational problem involving grandparent, mother and child. It may well occur when a single parent returns to her old home following divorce. The sequence is as follows.

○ Grandmother looks after the grandchild all the time protesting that mother can't do the job properly. Indirectly grandmother is siding with the child against mother.

○ Mother moves further away from child, letting grandmother take over.

○ Child responds to mother's withdrawal by misbehaving or being sullen.

○ Grandmother protests that she shouldn't have to look after a young child. She has already brought up her own family and the mother should do the job.

○ Mother starts to take more care of child. Grandma criticises her for not doing it properly and says she is irresponsible. She takes over again 'for the sake of the child'.

○ Mother moves away again because it is simpler to let grandmother take over. Child reacts by misbehaving.

This too is a cycle that can go on for ever unless deliberately interrupted.

Letting go

A child growing up finds he also has a place in a world outside the family. He has to be recognised as more independent and his parents have to learn to relate to him in a different way. He may no longer wish to be included with a younger brother or sister.

If a parent refuses to recognise this change, the child may react strongly in an attempt to safeguard his freedom. Parent/child conflict could divide the marriage and cause an uncomfortable situation where one parent sides with the child against the other parent.

The introduction of someone new into the family requires an adjustment from all existing members. The new person could be a baby, a foster-child, step-parent or grandparent. To stay the same is to keep that person right outside. The family has to readjust to give them a place whilst at the same time keeping continuity with the way that they all were before.

Family jealousy

Children know all about jealousy. It is a very important feeling that crops up time and again in legends and family stories. The theme is usually the same; a parent shows favouritism to one child and the others plot revenge, forcing the favoured child to flee or be killed. As adults, jealousy conjures up all sorts of unpleasant associations and feelings which lead us to avoid acknowledging it unless it is forced upon us.

Maybe we hope that it does not exist in our own families because we love all our children. Children themselves don't see it that way. Inside every child is a wish to be the only one – the favoured child. It is not just small children who feel jealous. Most parents have thought about preparing children for the arrival of a baby and expect a certain amount of jealousy for a while.

But all children go on feeling jealous. Rivalry and envy between brothers and sisters is certainly part of the lives of five to tens. These feelings can stay with us for life.

How can you recognise jealousy?

Children can feel ashamed of their jealousy or fear that it won't be understood. If they then try to hide it, it can come out in different ways.

Jason couldn't put his jealousy into words and it came out in nightmares. He was jealous of his brother Paul – he too wanted to be the little one and have all the attention.

For other children the jealousy might be even more disguised – wetting the bed, getting tummy aches or biting their nails.

Being destructive is not uncommon – some children break up their own toys, or other children's, some even attempt to break up the home. Destructive behaviour, like throwing toys or pulling books to pieces, might represent what they would like to do to the brother or sister but they know it is forbidden. If they could only say in words how they are feeling, these children would be helped a lot.

Feelings into words
Parents can encourage children to talk about how angry or lonely they feel. Knowing how their child feels helps them to do something about it. The child that feels lonely and unloved needs extra time and attention. The angry child can be encouraged to work off his anger kicking a football rather than his sister.

Don't undermine
Children feel very strongly towards each other. These ferocious feelings need to be accepted, not denied or encouraged. It is not helpful to blame or criticise. Accusing a child of shameful or cruel behaviour can do no good. It can only undermine the child's confidence and further convince him that he is unlovable.

The following sentences may give you ideas on how to tackle your child's strong feelings.

'Everyone likes to feel they are the only one. I bet you wish it was just the two of us. But I don't love you any the less, you know. Just tell me when you feel very angry/lonely/sad and I will make more time for you. Then you'll feel better inside.'

Don't pretend jealousy doesn't exist That can only make a suffering child feel even more miserable. It helps a child to know his feelings are understood even if little is done about them.

Don't give special preference to the eldest or youngest Of course being older brings advantages, just as being the youngest has privileges, but don't ever emphasise one at the expense of the other. For many families there will be one in the middle who also needs to feel special sometimes.

Don't overvalue a special ability or talent Particularly in front of brothers or sisters. It can be recognised but treated as normal, otherwise it will be seen as favouritism and arouse a great deal of envy in the other children. And they may well take their feelings out on the child.

Don't try to treat all your children the same It is not what they want. They are all different and have different positions in the family. Older children get more pocket money and stay up later. These are things to look forward to as you grow up. Inequality is a natural part of the family's life which children have to cope with.

Don't ask children to give up things for the other children At least not too often. Sacrifice does not endear one child to another and many would rather watch the other one suffer. Saying, *'Timmy is not a baby any more and he needs your bed, you'll have to sleep in the other room now'* can leave a child feeling furious and rejected. Turn it around. *'Now that you are getting bigger you need a room for yourself and a new bed'* has a very different ring to it.

What is likely to upset everyone?
Equal measures of fairness. If parents always have to do and say exactly the same to each child then something is missing. You should be able to give one child the last spoonful without uproar because everyone knows their turn will come.

Children don't want to be equal; they all want to be someone special and like no one else. No parent loves his children in exactly the same way. Loving them in different ways gives a child a feeling of being unique – of being the centre of attention if only for a short time.

As long as everyone in the family is favoured sometimes then the balance is about right. At least that way no one is left out.

shreddies

Family break-up

How do you tell your child?

Ending a marriage is painful and sad. There is no such thing as a painless divorce. Hopes of what the marriage might have been are dashed to the ground. In the place of those hopes come a sense of failure, accusations directed towards the other partner and bitter recriminations.

The marriage seems to have been a waste of time, useless, no good. But the children are a direct result of the marriage, reminding you of the investment you made in the relationship. The problem for divorcing parents is how to manage the continuing relationship as parents. Parenting does not necessarily end with the marriage though sometimes to attempt to share parenting may result in the fight going on and, unhappily, children become part of that fight. It is a way of prolonging the relationship however unhappy.

Family break-up causes distress all round and deciding what to tell the children can be a real additional problem. Is there a right way to do it? Below are a list of common fears many parents have and, unfortunately, these fears stop them telling the children about the separation in an appropriate way. Think about what fears you would have. Put a tick by the ones that bother you and then add a couple of your own.

- ☐ He will be so upset
- ☐ He will blame me
- ☐ He might want to live with his dad/mum
- ☐ He will play me up
- ☐ He won't understand
- ☐ He will think we don't love him
- ☐ He will worry about what is going to happen to him
- ☐ ____________________
- ☐ ____________________
- ☐ ____________________

Fear	Why are you worried?	What reaction would you anticipate?
He'll be so upset	Ben worries too much already	Tearful clinging behaviour
He'll blame me	He already thinks I'm a bad-tempered old witch	He won't do what he is told
He might want to go and live with his dad	He worships his dad	He will be lost without him
He'll play up	Already difficult to handle	He'll expect his own way all the time
He won't understand	He won't listen to what I tell him	He'll behave as if nothing has happened
He'll think we don't love him	All our quarrels have made him rather insecure	He'll think he has caused the break-up
He'll worry about what is going to happen to him	He won't know what to do because he knows he's important to both of us	He'll keep asking why can't we all stay together

Kate made a list (above). Her son Ben is nine and she and her husband are about to separate.

Kate's list is full of very common worries that affect all parents who are about to split up. She is trying to protect Ben from as much of the pain as she can even though she is going through a lot of stress herself.

Are her fears realistic? What does family break-up mean to children?

He'll be upset
Undoubtedly Ben will be upset at the break-up. But he has probably been worrying for a very long time if the family has been going through a lot of ups and downs. For some children an actual separation can bring relief from family tension. They can begin to adjust to a new situation without fearing calamity is just around the corner. The tearful clinging behaviour may become less after the event.

He'll blame me
Children can be very accusing of parents. 'How could you do this to me?' But often underlying the protestation is a real fear that they have caused the break-up and are responsible for the unhappiness. Children in this state of mind need reassurance and concern from parents, not defensive reasoning.

He might want to go to his dad
This is a fear about whom does he really prefer. Everyone makes the comparison occasionally but it is important not to let it get out of hand. It's all too easy to put children in the impossible position of having to choose between parents. This they cannot do because they want their parents together, not split up.

He'll play up
A realistic fear. Children under pressure do play up – it is a signal that they feel confused and unhappy. Always making allowances is not going to help. That can lead to Ben playing Kate off against her husband. It is worth alerting the school to difficult family situations. School work can deteriorate under stress. Teachers can make allowances if they know what is going on.

He won't understand
That is quite true, he won't understand why his parents can't live together. It may be hard for him to understand all the adult emotions – but that should not be an excuse for not saying anything. Ben

COPY of an
e Marriage
cts,

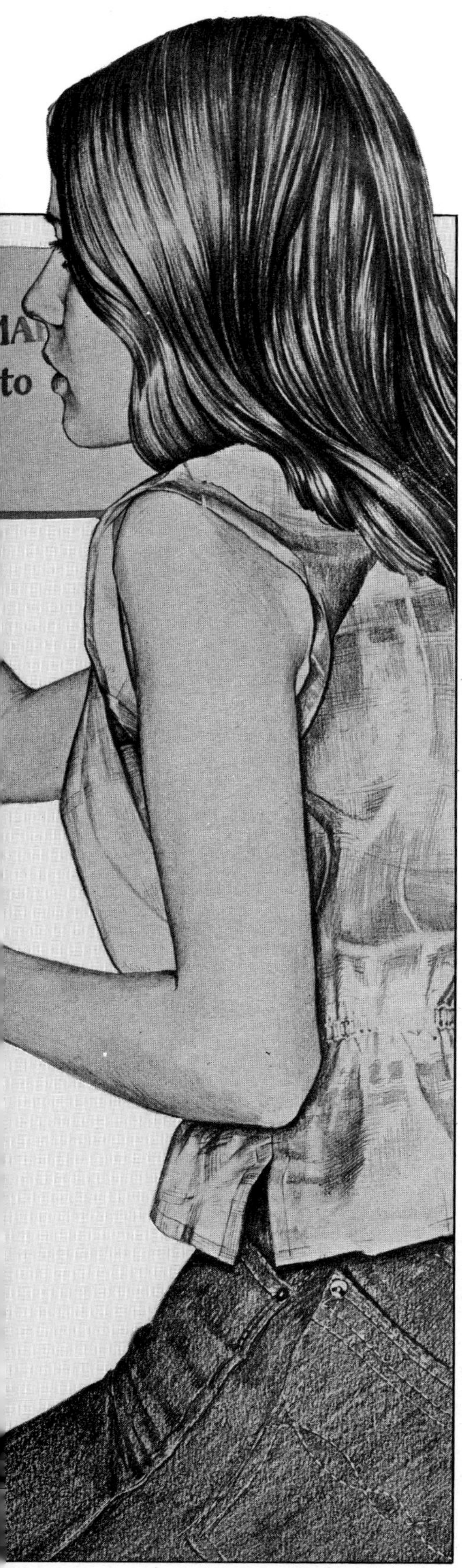

probably knows far more than Kate thinks. He needs simple explanations of what is happening, without being over-burdened by Kate's fears and worries.

He will think we don't love him
Children's logic is such that they often think they have a lot of power and may have caused the family break-up themselves. They may not say this outright but fear it. It is as well to keep reassuring children that they are still loved and wanted even if the marriage is coming to an end.

He'll worry about what is going to happen to him
Ben may know where his home is but he will need to be told over and over again. He will see his father and go and stay but his home is with Kate. Some children are not as lucky as Ben and parents bring them into their own battles and fight over them. It can only do harm. Children need love and cooperation from their parents and these need not disappear because the marriage is ending.

What does breaking up mean?

Breaking up means a whole new way of life. Being a single parent, in charge of a family, is a huge area far beyond the scope of this chapter. Practicalities are enormously important and there are groups and organisations with a lot of expertise in this area. But until the feelings that lead to break-up are acknowledged it can be difficult to make headway with the practicalities.

When and how do you tell the children?

Kate listed her fears but she still had the problem of talking to Ben. Should she involve his father? Should she do it alone? Should it be a special announcement or just dropped casually? There seemed to be pros and cons whichever way she looked. But she decided to talk to Ben first, so when they were making the bed one day she said that his father and she had decided that they could not live together any more because they made each other unhappy but they both still loved him.

He was hurt and unhappy and said no more about it. Kate thought she had made a great mistake. But later on he asked his father about where he was going to live and what he would do. That gave him a chance to hear that his father still loved him. Most parents find a joint telling just too painful and artificial. If they are still fighting then it just turns into another battle. If they are hardly speaking then it can be impossible.

Occasionally one hears of parents who manage to hide their disagreements and then suddenly tell their family they are splitting up without any warning. For children that can be as traumatic in its unexpectedness as it is always to be in the centre of family rows.

What reaction can you expect?
Grief and sadness as well as behaviour problems and fall-off in school work are normal reactions to stress. They do pass as things calm down and parents should not take all the blame and feel guilty. The appropriate action is to inform school and other important people in your child's life so they can understand what is happening.

Playing parents off one against the other should not be tolerated in the same way. Children are quick to see where they can gain and may play on parental weakness. Whatever you think of your partner, give them the benefit of the doubt before siding with your child.

Behaviour can seem puzzling. A child may refuse to visit the parent who has moved away. The refusal may not be a rejection of that parent but a kind of loyalty to the parent he thinks is vulnerable and needs him most. He may be willing to cut himself off from one parent in an effort to protect and please the other one.

Divorce and separation can seem like a minefield – and you probably can't avoid a few explosions. The best protection for the children is to keep them out of the fights, whenever possible. We can't give personal help in this course but professionals like the Marriage Guidance Council are available.

Family change

You don't have to stay stuck in a rut.

Learn how to plan for changes.

In taking this course Vicky got really excited about all she read about family life. She recognised a lot of familiar situations, she learnt about some new ones. She had a lot of high expectations about what a difference it would make to her family.

But reading all about the family was one thing. It changed her ideas but made little or no difference to the family's daily life. Vicky could have given up at that stage. But she wasn't put off. She soon realised global changes do not come about overnight, and certainly not without planning. She made a decision to plan for the changes she wanted.

You too can follow the process Vicky used – if you plan to make some changes in your family.

Tomorrow it will all be different!

It is easy to be over ambitious and imagine you can achieve all you want in one easy step. Vicky had rather grand ideas about how her family was going to change. She had a picture of her family suddenly calm, herself never losing her temper again, all the family getting excited by the chores and turning them into exciting projects.

Trying to get help with the washing-up proved to be rather different. She came up against resistance. No one wanted to know about her new ideas. Vicky realised very quickly that changing anything needs a lot of thought and careful planning.

What did she do?

Vicky decided to begin in an orderly way by listing all the topics in chapters three and four and noting the changes she wanted to make in those areas. Notice Vicky only says 'I'. She knows that attempting to change other people never works. You must start with yourself and what you want to do. And then other people may start to respond.

Vicky's plan for change

Chapter 3	
Family life	I want to be more sensitive
Families are...	I want to meet more of the family
Family roles	I want to be more open-minded
Family work	I want the children and me to learn new skills
Working mothers	I want more time for myself
House rules	I want to be flexible
Pocket money	I want a clear contract on pocket money

Chapter 4	
Inside the family	I want to improve communication
Strictly for the family?	I want support for clear rules
Children's fights	I want to understand why
Facing ups and downs	I want to know what to do in a crisis
Words matter	I want to calm down
Family tension	I want to leave them alone
Family break-up	This doesn't apply
Family change	I want to change some small things

Vicky realised that her goals, although laudable, were too vague and ill-defined, so she decided it was all too much at once. So she sorted her big list into three smaller, more manageable lists, and set realistic time-scales for her goals.

Short term	Medium term	Long term
Give children a chance to learn new skills	I want to meet more of the family	I want to be more sensitive
I want a clear contract on pocket money	I want more support for clear rules	I want time for myself
	I want to know what to do in a crisis	I want to be more flexible I want to improve communication I want to calm down

Vicky now decided that her long term goals depended on her having achieved the short term goals. She wanted to start by making practical changes, which would also give the children a chance to learn new skills. She decided her first step would be to set a clear contract about pocket money.

Vicky decided to take a risk and make an open suggestion about setting rules for pocket money. She knew why the children always wanted more – she had not set clear limits.

So she had to start talking about her ideas with the family. Sharing and getting their cooperation was vital. She could not do it all on her own. She needed support. She decided to put across her ideas to the rest of the family by emphasising how they would benefit. Vicky also knew that if she changed the way *she* did things, the family could not help but change in response.

Starting off

First she spoke to her husband about pocket money rules, pointed out the advantages and eventually got his backing. It

was not as easy as she thought. Finding time to talk at all was a problem. Vicky wanted a time when the children were not around which was a limitation. Her husband did not get the point straight away. She said he wasn't concentrating. *'I always listen to you,'* he said in a rather hurt tone and immediately went back to what he was doing.

But Vicky persevered and said she wanted them both to make a decision about the children's pocket money. *'You decide, you are so good at that sort of thing and I will support you,'* said her husband. Vicky felt frustration building up and she knew that she was going to have to find another way. Later on she tried again and met with the same response.

She felt angry. Why was it always left up to her? So this time instead of bottling up her angry feelings she told her husband she felt angry and unsupported when he said *'you decide'*, and that she wanted him to help. She did manage not to blame him too much.

Vicky's outburst gave him quite a jolt and he looked rather confused. Then he said he had no idea she felt like that but *'wasn't she making a fuss over nothing? It was only pocket money after all.'* Vicky stuck to her point, she wanted his help and support over pocket money. He agreed and they had a useful discussion.

○ They decided the amount of pocket money they thought was reasonable.

○ The children were consulted about the amount and what was expected of them, if they were to receive it.

○ To Vicky's surprise the children were full of ideas, not all of them realistic, and they accepted her limits and suggestions. They were delighted to have both parents so concerned.

Results

Vicky now felt less pressurised. The pocket money issue had been settled and agreed by them all, so she could stick firmly to the rules. Vicky was surprised at the improvements she noticed. There were fewer arguments, fewer groans, fewer occasions when she and her husband felt manipulated by the children's demands.

For many families what is important is how they get on with each other. If they feel things are better, then they probably are. No hard and fast rules exist to measure levels of satisfaction. A lessening of tension and anxiety means that people feel better. For Vicky, other signs of improvement she noticed were her own enjoyment of the children and also the children's willingness to co-operate with her. Even her sceptical husband had to admit he was impressed.

Maintaining success

When making any kind of changes, it is important to keep up momentum. The problem is that at the first setback many plans are abandoned. Vicky knew that her children would challenge her pocket money rules before long. Despite their protests she stuck out for the agreement they had made. She tried to curb her temper and instead listened to the children's complaints, trying to understand what they felt. Then she explained her own views. At first they did not listen and Vicky had to persevere in getting them to listen. The children got cross and the atmosphere at home was tense.

Vicky felt under pressure to abandon the plan but she kept telling herself to ignore the failure and carry on. It was very hard but she reminded herself that, if she gave in now, the going would get harder. The children forgot the scene sooner than Vicky and she felt very pleased to hear the children telling their friends quite proudly their rules for pocket money.

Vicky thought a great deal about what had happened. Pocket money was just one of several issues affecting her and the family. Behind even this simple issue lay a whole process of family communication. Vicky went back to her original list. She saw that each other medium and long term goal depended upon a scheme of getting across to the whole family what she wanted and beginning a process of negotiation. She knew what her next goal would be. Better communication, which she had seen as a long term goal, was really vital for even short-term aims.

Better communication

Listening is taken for granted by most people. But really listening requires a great concentration and is a real skill. Family and friends tend to make assumptions about what each other are saying based on what they expect to hear, from past experience. Vicky decided she wanted to change her way of listening. Instead of giving half an ear, while washing up, she would really try and hear what was being said and find out the feelings behind the words. So when the children talked to her, she asked them how they were feeling and made sure that she had understood what had been meant, not what she thought it meant.

The children took it all in their stride and made their own attempts to say clearly what they wanted, instead of assuming grown-ups could read their minds.

Adults find it harder to change patterns of a life-time and Vicky's husband was suspicious. He thought it was a bit of a game. Vicky worked very hard to share her feelings with him but he took a long time even to begin to talk about his own feelings with her. Vicky suspected he was a bit frightened by all the talk of feelings and did not attempt to force him to share more than he wanted to. Even so, she made sure they had a few minutes each day away from the rest of the family just to talk to each other.

Vicky took responsibility for:

○ letting the rest of the family know how she felt.

○ telling them when they had particularly pleased her and why.

○ telling them when anything displeased her and why.

○ telling them when she was confused.

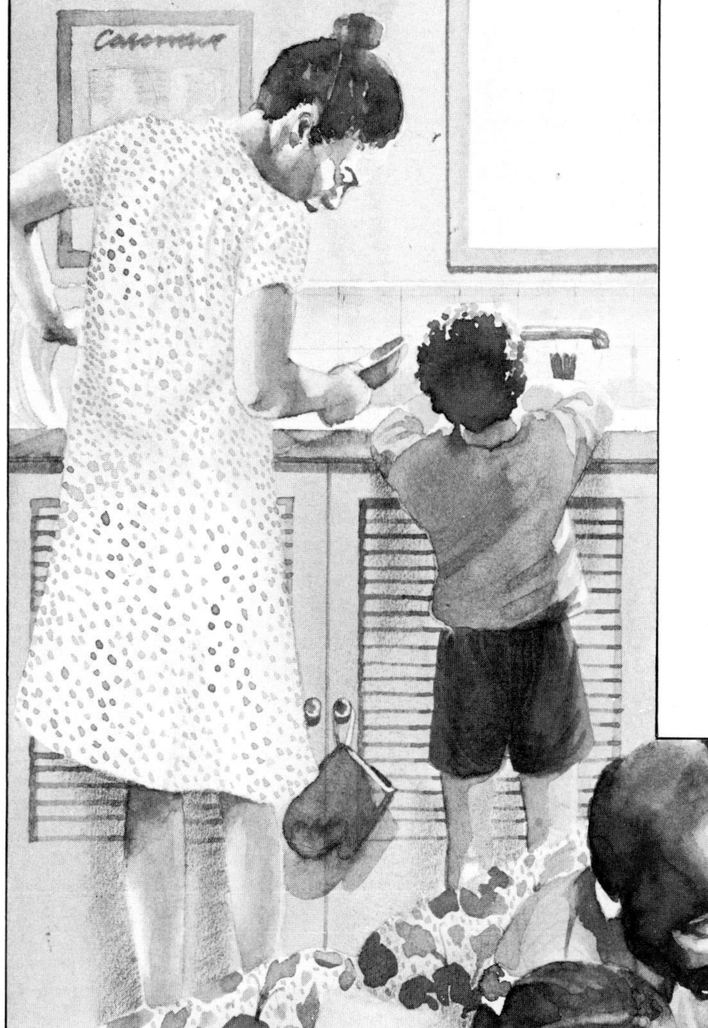

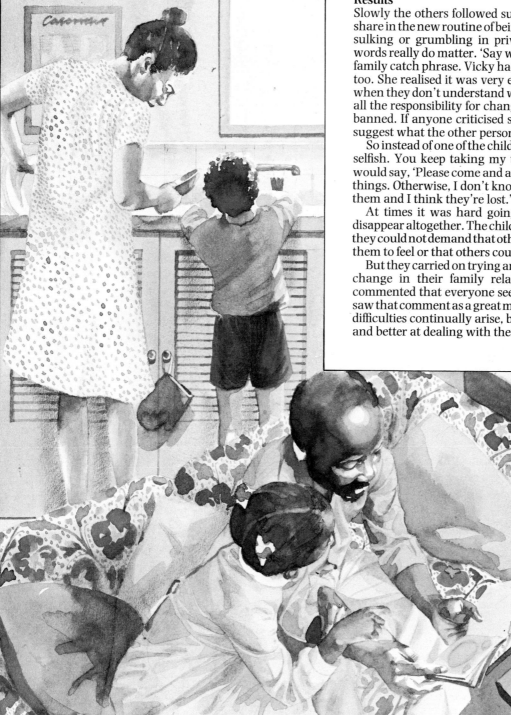

Results

Slowly the others followed suit. Even her husband began to share in the new routine of being open about things, instead of sulking or grumbling in private. Vicky had evidence that words really do matter. 'Say what you really mean' became a family catch phrase. Vicky had to make some rules for all this too. She realised it was very easy to slip into blaming people when they don't understand why they're wrong and pushing all the responsibility for change on to them. So blaming was banned. If anyone criticised someone else, then they had to suggest what the other person should do instead.

So instead of one of the children saying to the other, 'You're selfish. You keep taking my things when I want them,' he would say, 'Please come and ask me if you want to borrow my things. Otherwise, I don't know where they are when I want them and I think they're lost.'

At times it was hard going and family tensions did not disappear altogether. The children found it hard to accept that they could not demand that other people felt what they wanted them to feel or that others could not always read their minds.

But they carried on trying and Vicky is now delighted by the change in their family relationships. Even her husband commented that everyone seemed to be talking more. Vicky saw that comment as a great measure of success. Tensions and difficulties continually arise, but the family are getting better and better at dealing with them.

Learning the basics

'I think school is very good because you go to the baths and you do PE and the teacher learns you things. They learn you sums and english. I can nearly swim and you do take-aways and adds. For english we do diarys.'

'I like school because we go on trips and we do PE in the hall and I like doing Maths and I like doing english and I like playing rounders in the yard, some times the girls win and some times the boys win, and we watch the television at school. I think school is very good we play out in the playground and I like the teachers because the teachers learn us and we have a party every year.'

Swimming, English, the teachers, maths, rounders, trips, TV and other children; all of them are equally important parts of school life to children. Children don't usually think about the full range of things going on at school, but concentrate on what they think is important. So you may not hear much about lessons when you ask your child about school!

In this chapter that's what we're dealing with – what happens in the classroom. As each school subject is considered we shall also be looking at how you can support and supplement your child's school work at home. How can you give your child practice in the reading skills he has learnt at school? What practical experience of mathematics can your child get from everyday activities like shopping, cooking and gardening?

Since there have been a lot of changes in recent years in the way maths is taught, making it hard for parents to find out just what their children are doing in maths lessons, we take a look at some of the new methods to see how they differ from old ways of doing sums.

5

How schools are organised

Because no school, teacher or classroom is the same there are very big differences in what is taught and how.

The only way to find out fully what happens on a day-to-day basis at school is to go on a visit, talk to the teacher, and talk to your child about what she does in school. You may well find things work very differently from the way you remember school. Here are some of the modern methods you can expect to find.

Open-plan classrooms

The first and most obvious difference between classrooms of twenty years ago and the modern primary classroom is in appearance. Our photographs show a classroom in the 1950's and one in the 1980's. It is not just recently built schools that use the latter type of classroom. Many of the older schools have been redesigned inside to provide a spacious, interesting and varied working environment. An open-plan classroom will usually include:

○ a reading corner filled with books that children can select for themselves.

○ a writing table covered with felt-tip pens, paper, word and alphabet cards, and sometimes a typewriter.

○ a science area usually containing live animals like gerbils or hamsters, as well as plants, rocks, thermometers and magnets.

○ a maths corner with work surfaces holding weights, counters, measuring cups and scales, and sometimes an oven for use under adult supervision.

○ an art corner where the children can model clay, work with water colours and collage material and cut out pictures from old magazines and newspapers. Simple musical instruments like recorders and drums might be found here.

The integrated day

This is the term used to describe the method of teaching where the children are allowed to choose, from a range of activities, what they will do and how long they will spend on it. When using an open-plan classroom with sufficient equipment, activities like creative work, reading, writing and mathematics can take place at the same time throughout the day. Children are free to move about among these activities according to their individual abilities, interests and concentration spans.

For the teacher this system involves careful preparation

work, organisation, and record-keeping for each individual child. In the classroom she will move between individuals and small groups giving information and encouragement and drawing out learning experiences from the various activities.

Very few schools allow children this amount of freedom all day. Most classes will spend some time as a group to learn the basic skills of reading, writing and maths; and they get together for PE, story-telling or a class discussion. How your own child's teacher divides her time will depend on the teaching methods she prefers and on the facilities available in the school.

Breaking the day up between individual activities, small group activities and activities involving the whole class provides children with a variety of work experience, all of which can be equally useful and enjoyable. But whether your child's class teacher prefers using an integrated day, or teaching the whole class together, or a combination of these, what really matters is not the method used but how successfully the teacher makes it work.

Team teaching

In some primary schools the whole school has been turned into one big open-plan classroom in which all the children can move freely between areas designed for particular purposes – reading, writing, and arithmetic, craft activities, music and games. Each teacher will have responsibility for a set group of children, but for most of the day they will move about the school helping any number of different children individually or in small groups as the need arises.

Working as a team allows teachers to develop their own areas of interest and specialisation. One teacher may be particularly good at teaching remedial reading to children who are in danger of falling behind the rest of the class. Another may specialise in handicraft, another in music, and so on. When it is working well, this system allows the children to benefit from each teacher's best abilities.

Family grouping

Family grouping, or vertical grouping, as it is sometimes called, is a modern method of organising children, based on a traditional idea: in old village schools children of different ages were in the same class. So family grouping means that a child starting school will join a group or class with children whose ages range between five and seven, (or, in small schools, from five to ten). Sometimes brothers and sisters will be placed in the same group.

Older children can then help younger ones settle into school life and find out what to do without having always to ask the teacher.

This system means that a child may have the same teacher right through infant school. Because of the age differences within a family group, a school operating this system will generally use the 'integrated day' method of teaching.

Streaming

'Streaming' or 'setting' means putting children in one class because they are all roughly of the same ability. Very few primary schools still use any form of ability streaming, except in areas where the 11-plus exam still exists.

Teachers have come to recognise that separating young children by ability rarely helps them to learn and frequently prevents them learning as quickly as they would if they were allowed to develop at their own speed. Classes which do not stream children by ability are normally described as 'mixed ability classes'. A variation on streaming, usually called 'setting', is sometimes used for particular subjects. The class may divide into reading groups or language groups for part of the day. These groups may include a number of children working on the same material, or they may be decided on the basis of reading or writing tests, to group children of the same ability.

Some schools, particularly in inner city areas, have 'nurture groups' or 'sanctuaries' where children can withdraw from the busy active classroom to a quieter area and be given more individual attention.

Following progress

'Well, I don't think they learn them very much. That new scheme they've got up there – where they play and learn to do it with play, you know – the teacher thinks he'll benefit from it, but I don't think that they get anywhere. I mean I did know my ABC when I was seven, but he can't get his ABC at all; and it makes me wonder sometimes if it is a good scheme, and I think I'm a bit disgusted to think that he can't say his ABC like that, you know.'

This mother in Nottingham is voicing a common concern of parents who see their children given the freedom of an open-plan classroom: if they have the freedom and opportunity to learn everything, don't they also have the freedom to learn nothing?

What it comes down to is that any teaching method is only as good as the teacher who uses it. Some open plan classrooms look chaotic and *are* chaotic. But often what looks to the visitor like chaos is in fact a varied and carefully supervised learning experience for a whole classful of children.

One way of telling the difference is to look at the sorts of checks the school is keeping of the progress of individual children. A good teacher using an 'integrated day' will have to keep accurate records of each child's progress. She knows that it is much more difficult to follow the progress of each individual child when they are all involved in different activities and at different stages of development.

Detailed records, including folders of the child's work and progress checks on the basic skills of reading, writing and mathematics, ensure that steady progress is being made in all these areas. Check that your child's school uses these, if this is of concern to you.

Learning at school

There's an awful lot to learn from having fun!

Let's take a look at what children learn, and how they learn it. Look at these pictures of children in first and middle schools.

Here are some lists of the skills children need to learn and to practise between the ages of five and ten. Tick off the ones you can identify as being taught or practised in the school pictures on the left.

1 Talking and listening skills: picture 1

- Talking about how they feel ☐
- Talking about what they would like to do ☐
- Talking about what they're thinking ☐
- Telling a story to a friend ☐
- Talking about a group project/using discussion – both talking and listening – to complete a group project ☐
- Asking the teacher questions ☐
- Listening to the answers ☐

2 Reading skills: picture 2

- Working on graded reading cards or graded reading books ☐
- Using reading skills to interpret instructions ☐
- Using reading skills to read a story book ☐
- Using reading skills to find things out ☐

3 Writing skills: picture 4

- Practising letter writing by copying ☐
- Developing skill with fingers and hands by playing with clay and play-doh ☐
- Playing with pencils, crayons, felt tips and paint ☐
- Using writing skills to record information. Writing notes and letters to friends or to the teacher ☐

4 Number skills: pictures 5 and 6

- Learning counting skills by matching numbers to objects like beads or bricks, shells and buttons ☐
- Learning the basic skills of adding, subtracting, multiplying and dividing ☐
- Discovering and practising number skills by solving practical problems ☐
- Practising number skills by recording experimental results ☐

5 Experimenting skills: pictures 1, 3, 5 and 6

- Comparing and grouping objects and materials by size and shape, length, volume, weight and proportion ☐
- Carrying out small experiments ☐
- Observing and recording what they have seen by talking, writing and drawing ☐

6 Social and creative skills: pictures 1, 4 and 6

- Drawing and modelling using materials like:
  - chalk ☐
  - wax crayons ☐
  - fabric ☐
  - wood ☐
  - clay ☐
- Learning to work and play with others, to contribute towards a group effort ☐
- Learning to control their own feelings ☐
- Sharing new experiences and information with others through conversation ☐

What did you see?

Besides the skills shown in these pictures, children doing these activities will be learning other things too.

Picture 1 Language skills are essential if children are to be able to communicate with each other and with adults. This means developing reading and writing skills but it also means learning how to talk and listen. The children in the first picture are practising using words as they talk together about the objects they are playing with on the table.

Picture 2 Learning to read is not something that comes as naturally as talking and listening. Children need lots of encouragement and guidance but, most important, they need to have a real interest in finding out what letters mean on the page.

A teacher uses a variety of techniques to help a child with his reading. Talking to children, telling them stories and reading to them all help to maintain their interest and develop a familiarity with words. If books and reading cards *look* interesting children are more likely to want to know what's in them.

The children in the picture are using cards from a graded reading programme. Having read what's on the card they then answer a few simple questions about it. If they get the questions right they can move on to a slightly more difficult card.

Picture 3 Young children need the opportunity to explore what's around them. They need to use their natural curiosity to investigate all sorts of objects, smells, sounds, plants and animals. The child in the picture is watering a plant and noting down how much it has grown over the past week. Next he will write down in an exercise book the amount of water he has given it.

This sort of activity develops a variety of skills – the mathematic skill of measurement, writing skill in recording the results, and it introduces the scientific methods of observation and analysis.

Picture 4 The child in this picture is modelling with clay – finding out about shapes and textures as well as developing the control of his fingers and hands which will later help him hold a pencil to write with. Materials like clay impose a natural discipline on children since the nature of the material places limitations on what can be done with it.

Picture 5 Children need to be able to think and communicate in numbers as well as in words. They need to learn to apply these skills in practical situations. The children in this picture are playing with coloured cubes to discover how addition, subtraction, multiplication and division work.

Picture 6 In this picture, the children are working on a model of their school. This involves a whole range of learning experiences; measuring, designing and drawing skills, as well as imagination and the ability to work co-operatively with a group of other children. Projects like this are useful for teaching because children understand better when they explore every aspect of a subject, instead of trying to learn the facts in isolation. They are also learning about social relationships, widening their experience of other people by making friends, talking, working and playing in a group.

Talking

Talk is important for all sorts of learning.

But don't leave it all to the teacher.

Five year olds arrive at school already equipped with a range of language skills. Most can make themselves understood, and understand what is said to them. Here is a list of things they may be able to do.

Describe *'I'm making a big castle.'*

Find out *'How did you make the cake pink?'*

Plan *'I'm going to put the blue ones up there.'*

Imagine *'Pretend I'm Mummy.'*

Give reasons *'I put it there so pussy can't get it.'*

Make guesses *'That will be too big.'*

Compare *'Her lolly's bigger than mine.'*

Speculate *'If he climbs up there, he might fall off.'*

It is an impressive list of skills, and plenty for the teacher to start work on. Children need to use words to find things out; and their desire to know also helps them learn to use words.

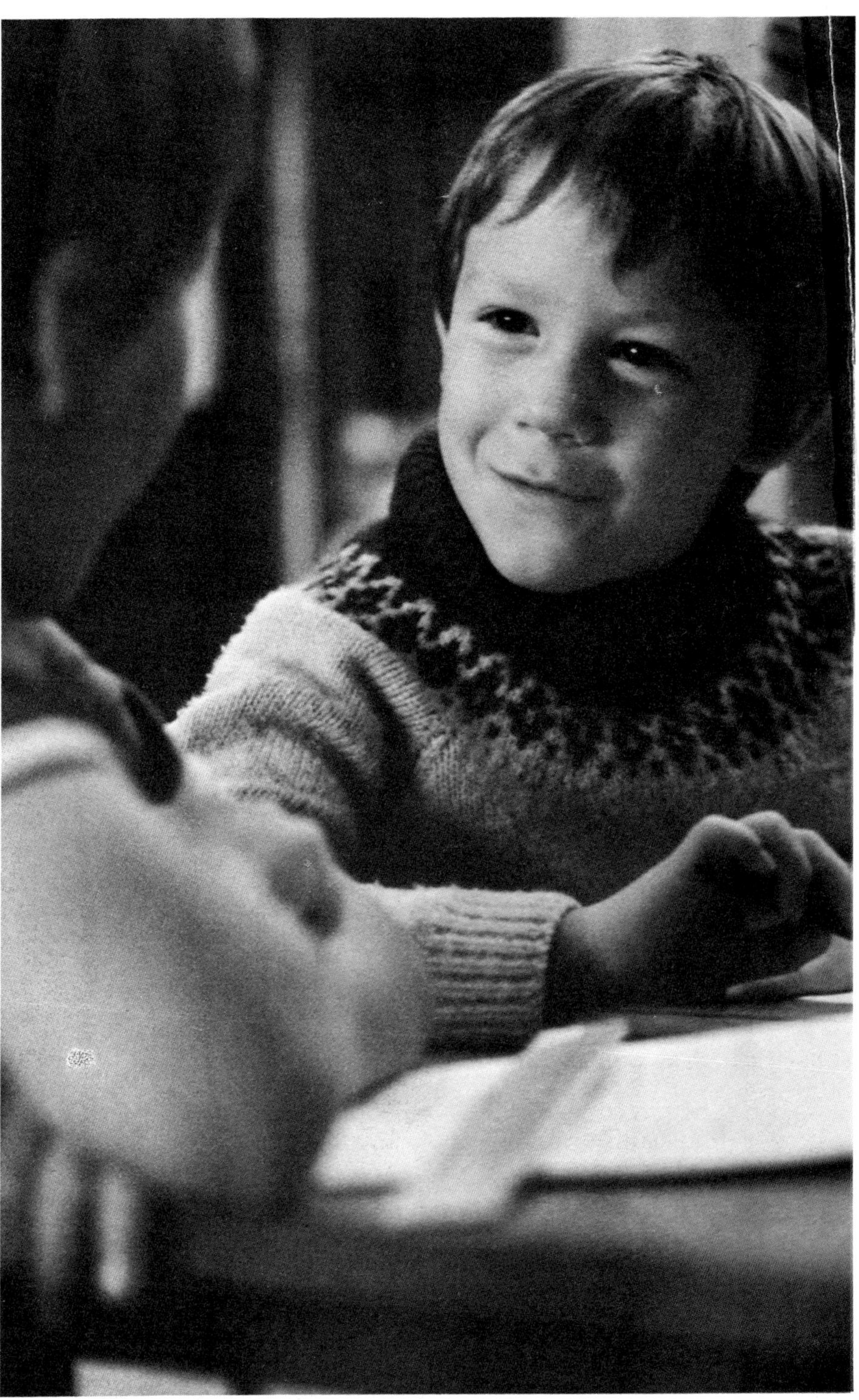

Talking in class

Children often sit in small groups round tables. Teachers want them to be able to work together, as well as on their own. By sitting like this they can talk to each other and exchange ideas.

Teachers want children to find out as much as they can for themselves. By making guesses, asking questions and trying to find their own answers, children discover that there isn't always one right answer but a lot of different ones. When they begin science they look at things closely and talk about what they can see.

In the following passage, Abdul (seven), Emma (eight) and Sally (nine) are looking at two snails and discussing what they are like. Notice the careful way the children search for words. They are talking very slowly, and painstakingly, trying out different ways of saying what they can see.

Look for the words and phrases which show that the children are exploring and wondering as they try to describe what the snails look like.

Emma: *That one's ... like silk ... go on snail.*

Sally: *Looks ... funny underneath.*

Jason: *Looks like it's plasticine.*

Sally: *No it doesn't, it looks like a sludge of something.*

Emma: *Dark green, a bit of a pond, dark... when ... you ... look ... at ... it ... when ... it's ... very ... still.*

Sally: *Put it down ... like that!*

Emma: *Ooh ... the bottom on this one is a yellow green.*

Sally: *Yes, look at this one, it's come ever so far. This one's stopped for a little rest.*

Jason: *It's going again!*

Sally: *Mmm ... good!*

Emma: *This one's ... moving ... slowly.*

Jason: *Look, they've bumped into each other.* (laughter)

Emma: *It's sort of like got four antlers.*

These are some of the expressions you may have noticed:

like silk	*a bit of a pond*
funny underneath	*a yellow green*
looks like it's plasticine	*it's sort of like got four antlers*
like a sludge of something	*dark green*

The children are using previous experience to help them to describe what they see: plasticine, ponds, antlers. All of them use language inventively, but the words are familiar ones they have probably heard at home. As they talk they are helping each other to notice and explain things.

Try eavesdropping on your own children to discover more about how they use language.

Does your child talk in class?

When you visit the school, look out for signs that the kind of 'talk-with-a-purpose' illustrated by the discussion about snails, is encouraged in the classroom.

○ Do the children work in small groups?

○ Is there work on display which suggests that talk-with-a-purpose is going on? For instance, a model made by two or three children together?

○ Is there a table with things to talk about: pebbles, feathers, fossils and things the children have brought in?

Some children are naturally more talkative than others but it is not always the noisy children that develop language skills quickest. A shy quiet child within a group is still learning the use of language even if he has difficulty in getting a word in edgeways.

Accent and dialect

The government's 'Bullock Report' on the teaching of language and reading has this to say on accent and dialect:

'The aim (of education) is not to alienate the child from a form of language with which he has grown up and which serves him efficiently in the speech community of his neighbourhood...'

Many teachers are now using children's local dialect to enrich their language work in school, rather than dismissing it as 'incorrect English'. Of course it is important for children to be able to write standard English, but in some of their school activities, for example drama, talking about different variations of English and when they are used can help children understand the richness of the English language.

Talking at home

Children learn to speak and listen at home, before they start school. By talking to your child, reading to him, and listening to what he says, you have already done a lot to help him when he starts to read and write.

Some research has shown that once children begin school some parents do not keep up this good work. You should not feel you've handed over all the

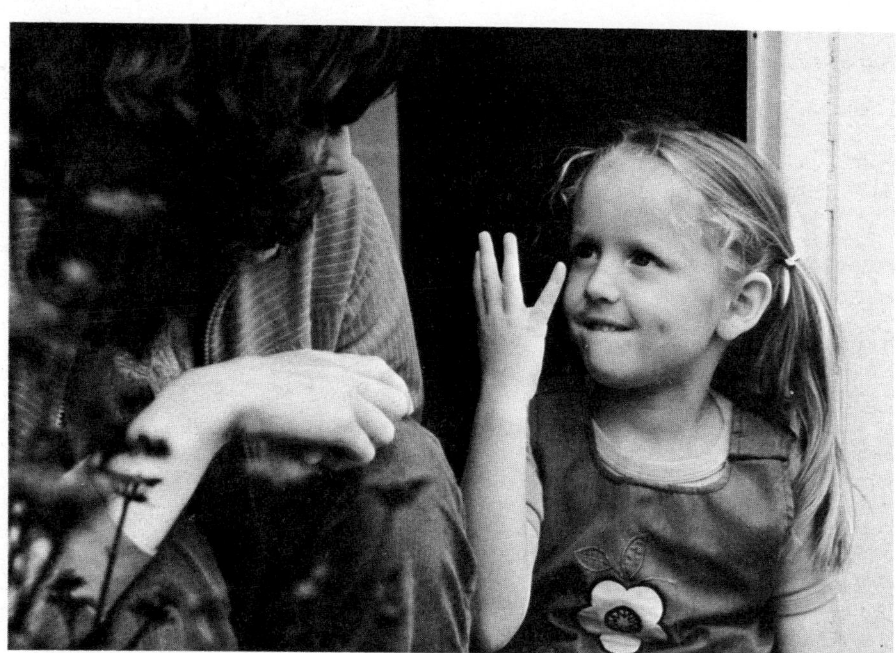

business of communication to your child's teacher. The more you talk with your child about the things that interest her, the more this will help her language and learning in school.

This is what a first school head felt about parents talking to their children.

'I think the most important thing is for parents to just enjoy sharing their children's experiences and achievements. And they can do this by listening and talking to them. Children desperately try to communicate, and I know it can be hard work listening to a child as he gropes from one idea to another, but this is the best way to learn about how the child is thinking, what he feels. So many people just talk at children, and the child answers 'yes' or 'no', and gets no chance to have a real conversation.'

Often, communicating with children requires the skill of seeing beyond the words to understand the emotions the children are trying to convey. The same teacher said:

'Children find it difficult to talk about what they are feeling. They know they are unhappy but they cannot say why. They will say, 'I don't like school', but what they may mean is they don't like lunch times because they are not with their own teacher but with someone else.'

So you have to probe further to find out what your child means and not just take words at face value. Here are two examples of children talking with their mothers. Think about the differences between the two conversations, and the reasons for them.

John is not yet five. He and his mother are in a train going over a bridge.

John: *We're going fast now. Look, there's a river now – and some boats.*

Mother: *It's the canal, I think.*

John: *Isn't it a river? It looks like one.*

Mother: *Well, the river would be at the bottom of the hill, wouldn't it? Can you see the canal is on the side of the hill?*

John: *Why is it there?*

Mother: *Well – because someone decided it would be a good thing to have it there, so that the boats could go through the town.*

John: *Do the boats go through the town?*

Mother: *Some do, I think, but they used to bring all the coal from the mines in big boats.*

John: *Coal – for the fires?*

Mother: *Yes – like we burn on the fire.*

John: *Where do they get coal?*

Mother: *Don't you remember? You saw men in the mine on the telly?*

John: *And they had lamps on their heads so they could see.*

Mother: *Yes, that's right.*

Karen is six. She is talking to her mother at home.

Karen: *Oh dear what a mess.*

Mother: *What's that?*

Karen: *Help mummy!*

Mother: *What's the matter?*

Karen: *All my paper's got stuck round my stick of rock.*

Mother: *That's nice.*

Karen: *Look at it.*

Mother: *Yes.*

Karen: *When I got it, it was about that long.*

Mother: *Oh, yes.*

Karen: *And I got it after dinner.*

Mother: *Well.*

Do you notice how, in the first conversation, the mother listens carefully to John and builds on what he has said in her replies? John is developing all sorts of language skills, while all the second child may be learning is that what she has to say is of no interest or importance.

There are times for all of us when we are busy and respond like the second mother, but it shouldn't happen all the time. Recent research has found that the quality of children's conversation with their parents has a most important influence on their progress in school.

Your conversations

Jot down a list of the conversations you have had with your children today. Do they fit into the descriptions listed below?

Organising daily activities 'Get up', 'Get dressed', 'When do you need your football shirt?'

Controlling 'Don't do that', 'What do you think you're doing?', 'If you don't stop that...'

Consulting 'What do you think about this for an idea?' 'Which lamp do you think will be best?' 'Can you think of a better way of doing this?'

Discussing Talking about things your child is interested in.

One-sided conversation One person contributes little more than 'mm', 'yes', 'that's right', and so on (like the conversation between Karen and her mother).

Opportunities for talking arise all the time, on buses, in shops, at the launderette, whilst watching TV, on the way to school, at meal times and bedtime. Look again at your list of conversations. How well do you feel you use the opportunities for talk with your child?

Learning to read

Even before the time your child starts school he will be learning to read in all sorts of different ways.

Reading is a hard won skill. A child has to be able to work out what is on the page – and realise that writing represents spoken sounds.

Handling books and getting familiar with the language used to describe books and their contents is important.

Without this experience children can be forgiven for not understanding what we mean by page, letter and words. After all, a letter is something which the postman brings.

Can you remember what it was like when you first started learning to read? This exercise may give you some idea of what it feels like for a child coming to grips with this new language of written words:

As carefully as possible, copy the following examples of coded symbols in the boxes provided.

Which symbols caused you the most confusion?

The signs in 1 and 2 differ only in detail – like 1 and t. The signs in 3 and 4 are similar, but different ways around, like b and d, or n and u.

Not all children are ready to start learning reading at the same time. Don't worry. It's a big jump from talking to reading and it can be very slow.

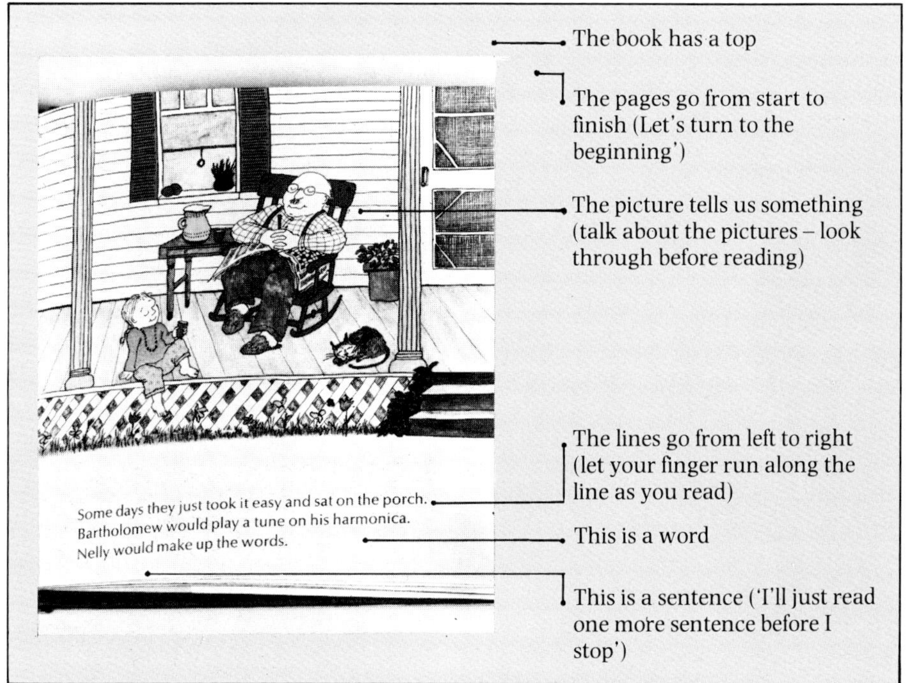
The book has a top
The pages go from start to finish (Let's turn to the beginning')
The picture tells us something (talk about the pictures – look through before reading)
The lines go from left to right (let your finger run along the line as you read)
This is a word
This is a sentence ('I'll just read one more sentence before I stop')
Some days they just took it easy and sat on the porch.
Bartholomew would play a tune on his harmonica.
Nelly would make up the words.

How it's done

Try to find out how they teach reading at your child's school. There are lots of different methods, so ask your class teacher to explain which she uses. Ask to look at the books and equipment they use.

Remember, it's not so much the scheme as the teacher who matters and teachers are more successful using the methods they feel most confident about. The list below will give you an idea of the most popular schemes. You will probably find your child's school uses several of these. Talk to your child's teacher about this.

Look and say
In the early stages of reading, teachers often use word cards to help children recognise words or even sentences and their shape. These are called 'flash' cards because it is believed that when they are held up before children for only a few seconds, the child forms a mental picture of the word or sentence. You may be surprised that your child can recognise the word 'aeroplane' but stumbles over 'pony', which he hasn't yet been introduced to. When children have learnt a group of words in this way they are introduced to their first reading book which contains the same set of words and has many pictures which help children to make informed guesses at words they are uncertain about.

Most children are successful at their first attempts at reading by this method. This gives confidence which helps them through the next stage. From the beginning, children can read the meaning of the story with understanding.

Phonics
Some teachers combine this approach with activities to help children to recognise the sounds of letters as they meet them in words. Children become familiar not only with the sounds with which we commonly link letters, eg, *c* as in *cat*, *castle* and *canary*, but also *c* as in *celery* and *c* combined with *l* as in *clock*, *clown* and *clothes*.

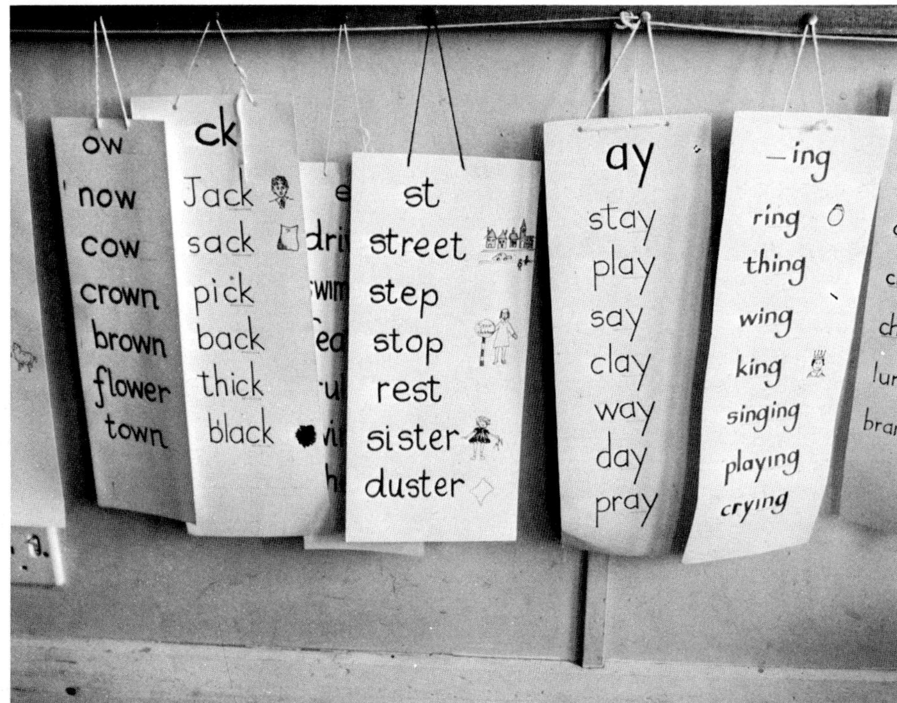

Phonics ▲

By combining this and the previous method, teachers are able to overcome the disadvantages of using either of the methods alone. This means that children gain confidence early on by using the whole word method. Meanwhile they are gradually learning about the sounds of individual letters and groups of letters, such as br, tr, th, ch, ing, end, etc. This knowledge helps them to sound out new words which they may not have met on flash cards.

Building up words by 'sounding' letters is not easy. There are 26 letters in the alphabet but 44 different sounds. Try breaking down the word *breaking* into its letter sounds and see what you get! Rules help children to deal with letters like br/ea/ing. You'll see lists hanging on classroom walls to help them.

Initial teaching alphabet (i.t.a.)

This is another attempt to deal with the problem of the 2000 different ways of writing 44 sounds. It looks pretty peculiar but is easier for children to read. The alphabet is based on the sounds used in spoken language. Children can become fluent readers of i.t.a. quickly, giving them a confidence and enthusiasm for reading. This system is no longer very common in infant schools, mainly because of the problems that sometimes arise when a child moves from a school which uses i.t.a. to one that doesn't, or from a school that doesn't use i.t.a. to one that does.

If your child uses this method you should talk to the teacher about how it works and where you can buy story books in i.t.a. Sometimes your local library will stock them and it's worth asking them to, if they don't.

wun dæ chicken-licken

went tω the wωds for fωd.

whiel shee wos thær an æcorn

fell on her pωr littl hed.

▼ *A sentence maker*

Breakthrough to literacy

This system does not start with printed books but uses the child's own spoken and written language.

Children begin by working with the teacher on a large, plastic folder called a sentence maker. Two pages of the folder have spaces for 130 commonly used words, though they may not be given all these words at once. The third is a store for their own words, written on card by the teacher.

To make sentences they choose words from the folder and slot them into a plastic stand in the right order. They read them to the teacher, to make sure they are right, and then copy them into their books. This way, they write their own reading books, drawing on their own language and experience.

Reading to learn

Once your child is ten years old he should have worked his way through most of these forms of reading.

Most teachers use a *reading scheme* to help them structure their teaching of reading. Books in reading schemes are organised so the child moves on in easy stages, each a bit more difficult than the last. A teacher tries to listen to children reading from the scheme as often as possible, using this as an opportunity to talk to them about the book and find out if they have any particular problems.

Many schools have *reading labs*. These use workcards through which children can work at their own pace, progressing in easy stages.

Topic and *project work* also call on a whole range of reading skills from knowing how to use the library to being able to find the right chapter and page. Research has shown that children can use books far above their reading level when they are really keen to get particular information.

Here is a ten-year-old's chart for finding the right book – notice all the skills it involves!

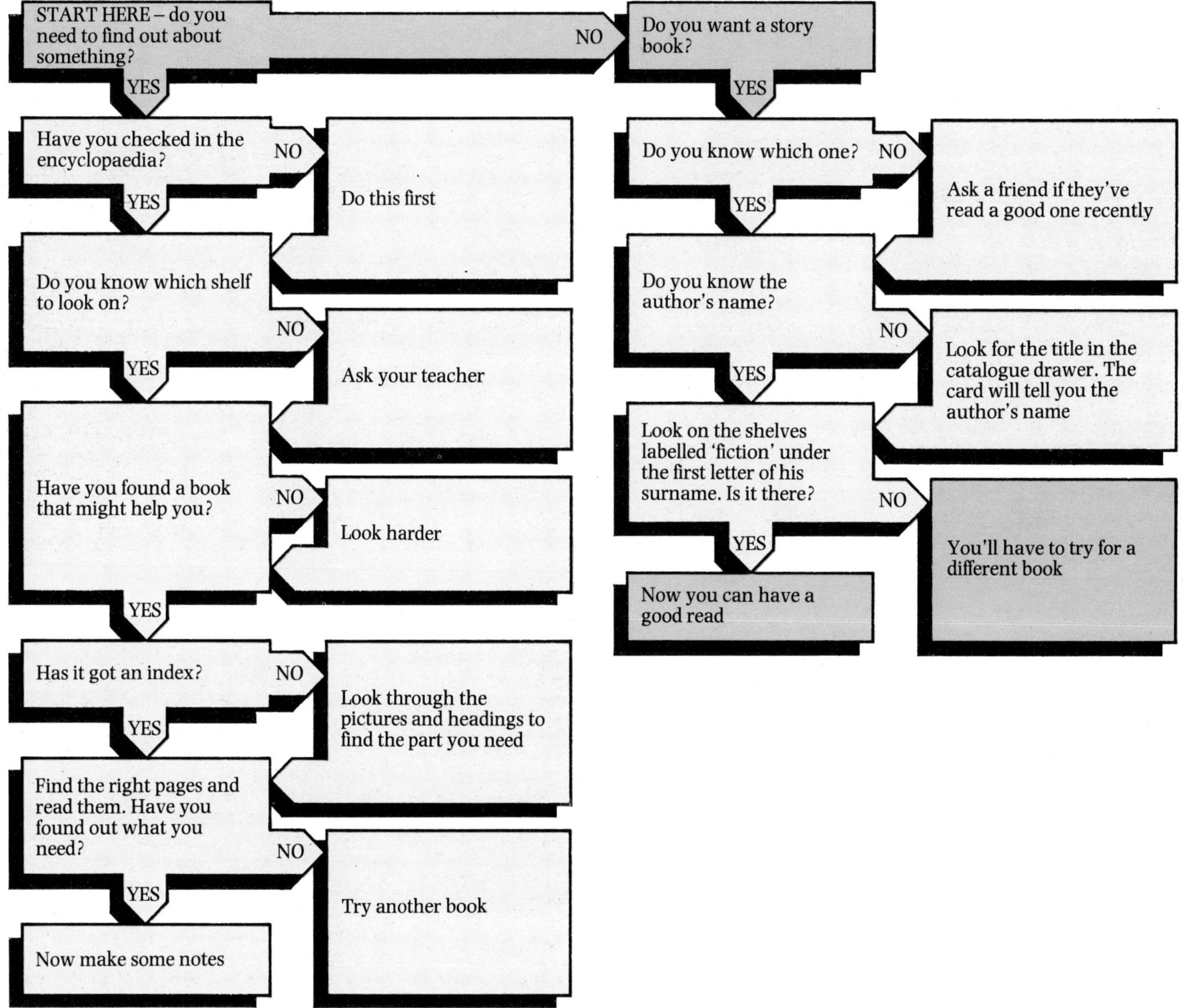
START HERE – do you need to find out about something?
NO
Do you want a story book?
YES
YES
Have you checked in the encyclopaedia?
NO
Do this first
YES
Do you know which shelf to look on?
NO
Ask your teacher
YES
Have you found a book that might help you?
NO
Look harder
YES
Has it got an index?
NO
Look through the pictures and headings to find the part you need
YES
Find the right pages and read them. Have you found out what you need?
NO
Try another book
YES
Now make some notes
Do you know which one?
NO
Ask a friend if they've read a good one recently
YES
Do you know the author's name?
NO
Look for the title in the catalogue drawer. The card will tell you the author's name
YES
Look on the shelves labelled 'fiction' under the first letter of his surname. Is it there?
NO
You'll have to try for a different book
YES
Now you can have a good read

A child may also have to be able to read *instructions*, like these.

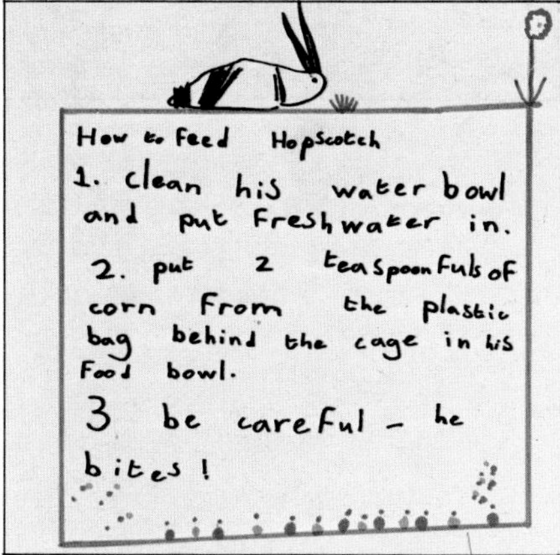

How to Feed Hopscotch
1. clean his water bowl and put Freshwater in.
2. put 2 teaspoonFuls of corn From the plastic bag behind the cage in his Food bowl.
3 be careFul – he bites!

Your child may be given *workcards* to help him practise particular reading skills – to find a piece of information from within a passage, or to show he has understood the idea behind what he's reading. See if you can do this exercise yourself.

It is designed to help children to extract information for a particular purpose – in this case, map making.

Pirate gold by Barbara Chamberlaine

The pirates anchored their ship in a small bay. Captain Jake and ten of the crew rowed ashore and landed on a sandy beach in the north of the island. They walked south until they came to three trees. There they turned west and walked on until they came to a large black stone sticking up out of the sand. From there they travelled south again, crossing a stream, until they came to a small stone hut. They went north east until they came to a deep ravine. They crossed it and turned north. They went through a small wood and came to a hill. On the top of the hill they planted the pirate flag. Then they went straight back to their ship. *'At last we have hidden the treasure safely,'* said Black Jake, *'And we will be able to find it easily when we want to.'*

When Black Jake got back to the ship, he made a map so he would remember exactly where the treasure was.

Try to draw the map – remember to show which direction north is, and make a key if you are using symbols.

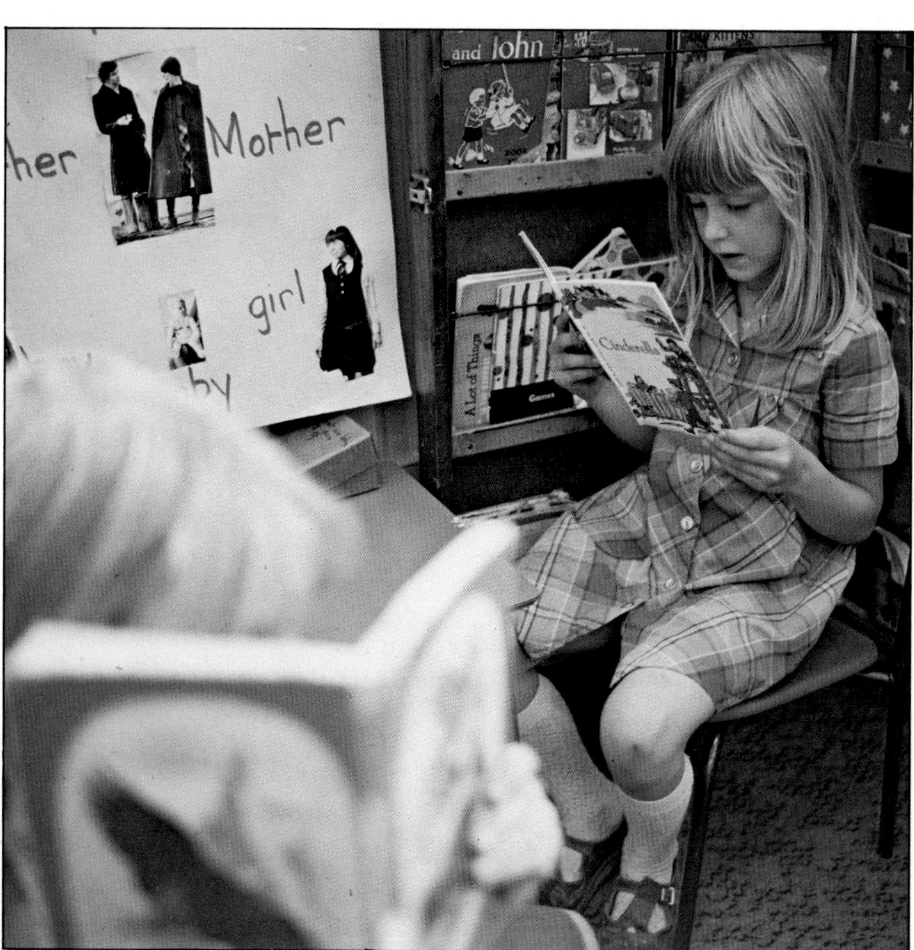

Is your child reading in class?

When you visit the school, take this list of things to ask about and look out for.

○ What reading scheme does your child's school use, and do you understand how it works?

○ What level has your child reached and what reading books might be useful to have at home?

○ Is there a well stocked class library?

○ Are the books in good condition?

○ Is it comfortable to sit and read them?

○ Does your school have a club with regular book sales?

TV and radio programmes for schools

Since more than half first and middle schools show lessons from TV and radio to their pupils, your child will probably be watching or listening to at least one series. Maths, music, reading, movement, even foreign languages can be taught in this way.

Try to watch two or three programmes from a series which interests you. You will see they are not just entertainment and the child is not supposed to lean back and goggle. He should be actively involved, either giving answers when cued to do so, joining in songs or preparing work based on what he has seen or heard.

Reading at home

How can you help, without getting your child confused?

A recent survey among parents of young children showed that four out of five wanted to help with their children's reading. But they were not sure what to do, and they didn't want to interfere with school work. This topic looks at some ways all parents can safely help their children to read.

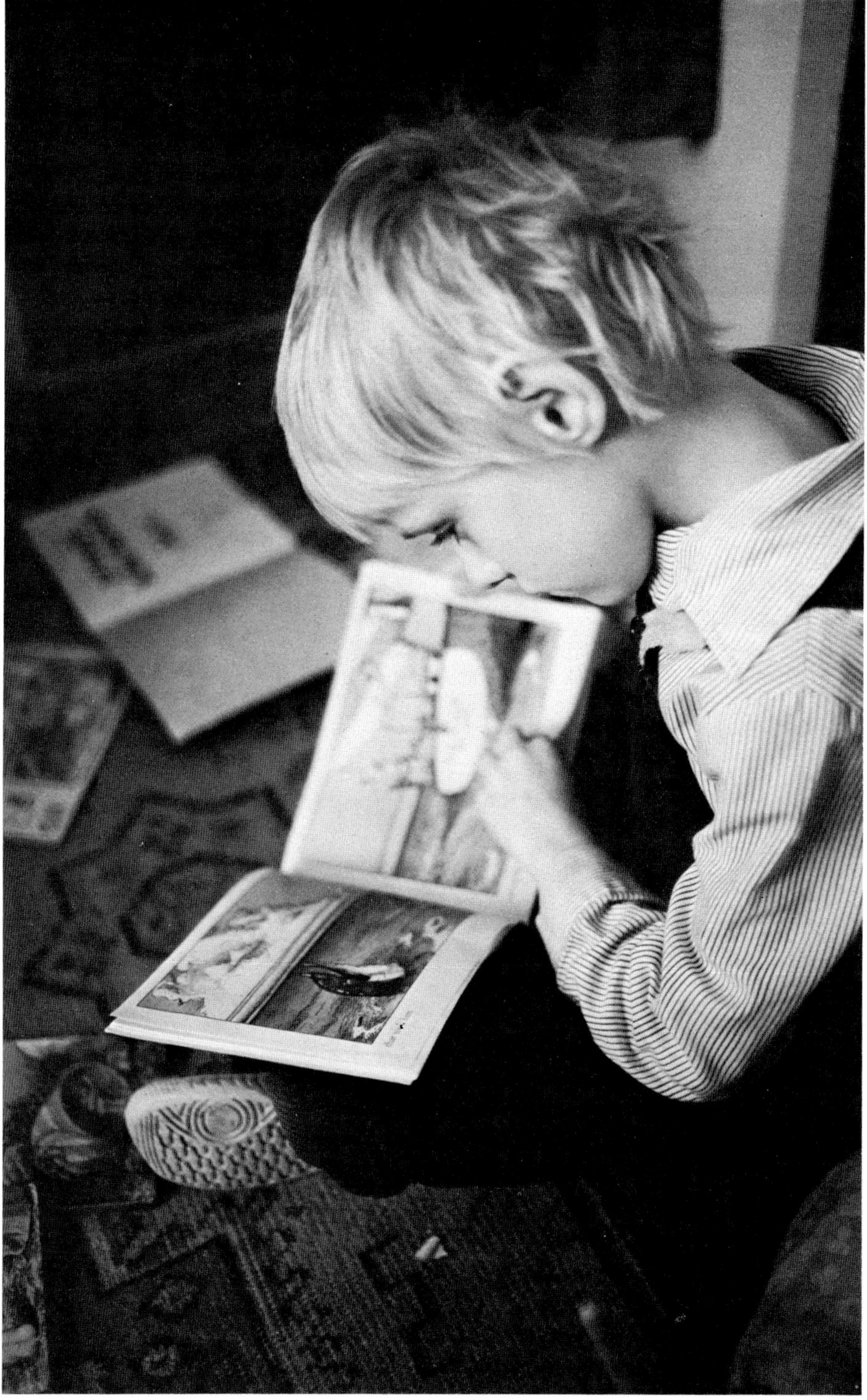

What is reading?

Studies show that five-year-olds have some pretty vague ideas about what reading is, and what it's for. They don't understand the terms adults take for granted, like sound, word, sentence. See this for yourself by asking four, five or six-year-olds the following questions.

Question	Studies of five-year-olds show:
1 Can you read?	Some aren't sure; others say 'no, only a bit'
2 What is in books?	Few say writing, words, or stories; some say pictures, some aren't sure
3 Can parents read?	Again, few are sure
4 What do they do when they read?	Fives are practical – 'sit down', 'say go away'. Few say they look at the words and pictures
5 How does the postman know which house letters are for?	Again, vague: some will point out number, only a few name or address
6 How do we know which bus to catch?	Some mention number, few name destination or direction
7 Which of these is a word? (top, p.139)	Children tend to have no clue at all; or think all bar

(a) brrr	(a) are words; or
(b) O	all bar (a) and (b)
(c) milk	are words
(d) fish and chips	
(e) dad is in the garden	

With questions 4 and 6, children's answers change if they're shown a book or model bus. Then they're more likely to point to words or the name-boards.

Reasons for reading

Children need to see there is a reason for reading. Show your child that being able to read is the key to finding things out by gently drawing her attention to what you're doing. For example:

○ explain why you're reading something: 'I'll just read the timetable so I can find out when the bus is due.'

○ make it clear that reading can answer a question for you: 'I wonder what's on TV? Let's have a look at the paper.'

○ if your child has begun reading, ask her to help you – it may take a little longer, but she will be able to see how useful reading skills are. Ask her to look:

In the newspaper 'Can you find the advert for special offers at the supermarket for me?'

In a recipe book 'What does it say I have to add to the pudding mix now?'

In the TV guide 'Is there anything you want to watch on the television?'

For younger children

Learning to read is quite a task. The rules of reading a page from top to bottom and from left to right, and the skills of recognising and interpreting the shapes of letters are much easier for a child to grasp if she has had some practice with similar exercises.

These games won't 'teach reading', but they will help the eye and brain to look for shapes that are the same or different.

○ Jigsaws.

○ Matching games, like snap or picture dominoes.

○ Sorting games – grouping look-alikes together (use toy cars, or buttons, or cans in the larder).

○ Puzzle books for games like find-the-hidden-picture or spot-the-odd-man-out.

○ Copying or tracing shapes.

Sounds

Some letters of the alphabet make more than one sound (c as in cat or in icing). And some sounds need more than one letter (ch, th, sh). You probably learned ABC at school. That comes in useful for looking things up in dictionaries and libraries, but is not a very good guide to how to sound out written words. It's more help to your child to focus on the sounds in words he already knows. Try these activities.

○ Playing 'I spy sounds'. Eg, *'I spy ... something beginning with the sound sh.'* Possible answers: *sh*oulder, *s*ugar, *sh*ip. *'I spy ... something ending with the sound k.'* Possible answers: sin*k*, ti*ck*, boo*k*.

○ Making up rhymes.

At home, and when you're out and about, you can look together for objects that are familiar words.

For example, you could play 'I spy' with posters. You say *'I spy ... Cornflakes'* and your child spots where they are.

In shops you can say, *'Can you see the baked beans?'*

On the way home ask, *'Which is our bus?' 'What does the street sign say?'*

Talking about words and sounds

The most important thing you can do to help your child with her reading is to talk to her about it. Try talking about words and sounds. For example:

○ discuss the different sounds of letters: 't' uses your tongue, 'sh' pushes your lips.

○ find interesting words – ones that sound funny, or are extra long, or sound like something ('purr' for cats).

○ answer your child's questions – 'What does coincidence mean?'

There are often opportunities for discussing the origin of words, eg, sub/marine – 'sub' means under and marine means sea, so a submarine is a kind of ship that can go under the sea.

Gradually help children to see other links, for instance, mariner means sailor – a man who goes to sea.

Beginning reading

If you have a child who is just starting to recognise words, try playing this guessing game when you next sit down to read a book with her. Stop at the last word in a sentence, and just pronounce the first sound: 'Jack climbed up till he reached the top of the tr...' Point to the word so the child will probably guess the word from the meaning of the rest of the sentence, or from a picture in the book. How would you respond if your child guessed that the word 'tree' in the example above was 'tram'? How would you respond if she guessed 'try'?

The first answer is a really sensible guess within the meaning of that sentence; it's the right sort of word to go in that gap. In the second answer, the child is concentrating on the sound of the word without thinking about the meaning – when you read the sentence again, putting in 'try', she will hear immediately it doesn't sound right. In any case, don't put any pressure on the child: praise her if she's right; give a clue or just read the word if she hesitates.

No nonsense

Children of this age love puns and nonsense rhymes – try reading them together, like this modern version of the Hare and the Tortoise:

A rabbit raced a turtle,
You know the turtle won;
And Mister Bunny came in late,
A little hot cross bun!

Young children love hearing about characters with ridiculous nonsense names, and your older children will already have their own favourite puns and riddles – all this play with words greatly encourages reading and writing.

Listening to reading

Your child may bring his school reading books home to read to you. Reading requires:

○ a happy reader – don't do it if it's a struggle.

○ a sympathetic listener, who is interested and helps but doesn't criticise.

○ helping out when your child gets stuck on a word – tell him what the word is before the flow of his reading is interrupted and the meaning of the sentence is lost.

○ checking he understands – by talking about the story afterwards, or asking questions: *'Was the little girl sad?' 'What will happen next?'*

Don't interrupt the flow. Expect to hear toneless reading for a while. It's hard enough reading each word at a time. Putting together the words in a smooth flowing sentence comes from an understanding of the sense of the story, and will come with time and practice.

Reading scheme books often have rather dull stories, because they are only using a limited number of words. This makes it all the more important for you to go on reading stories and nursery rhymes to your children long after they've started reading themselves, as well as encouraging them to look at other books themselves. But do be careful not to force your child to try and read a book that's too difficult or it may put her off reading completely.

Keep reading

You don't need to be a wizard at reading or funny voices. Being read to by *you* is far more special than being read a story on the TV or radio because:

○ you're a special person.

○ you can be interrupted with questions.

○ you're a familiar voice – and lap or arm.

It's tempting to stop as soon as your child can read for herself. But for years you'll be able to read her things that she'll enjoy but couldn't manage herself. So keep on reading, even when she's past ten.

A word of warning
There are lots of practical ways you can help your child with reading. But one thing that doesn't help is to show you're worried about her reading. If she knows you're anxious she may feel it's better not to try in case she fails.

Remember that the best way of helping your child to read is to show her that every day presents all sorts of useful and enjoyable opportunities for reading: like learning to read a colourful seed catalogue so that she can help you choose what flowers to grow.

Choosing books

Make a point of visiting the library with your child and talking about what sorts of books she likes. Children often select a book because of its cover. You could read extracts, especially to the youngest ones, to give them an idea of content.

Five-to-tens are interested in a wide range of things:

○ **non-fiction** information books about things, the world, people.

○ **fiction** story books about familiar things, amazing things, even frightening things.

Books in libraries are usually divided up like this. The five-to-tens need both – one to increase their direct understanding of the world, the other to increase their understanding through imagination and fantasy.

Books for information

Look for books which help children to find out rather than just fill them with facts. They need ideas as well as answers. Make sure that the information is concise and simple to follow and that there are colourful illustrations. And think – what is the book wanted for?

○ Projects at school or home?

○ To satisfy their curiosity about a topic?

○ To get ideas about things to do and make?

Investing in an encyclopaedia?
Don't imagine you'll get the whole of human knowledge if you pay a lot. Do you really need one? Encyclopaedias can be expensive and a volume suitable for an eight-year-old will be useless when she is ten.

Look for cheaper single volumes, like the Octopus General Knowledge Encyclopaedia or Pears Encyclopaedia and use reference books for more detail. Remember, the younger the child, the more important the pictures.

Make and do
Books for colouring, cutting out, and constructing can be very attractive and challenging. Older children enjoy books, like the *Practical Puffins*, *Strange Things to Do and Make*, or the *Armada Lions' Magic Tricks*. Football and ballet annuals, *The Guinness Book of Records*, *Young Naturalists' Handbook*, *The Blue Peter Book* are all part of a balanced reading diet.

Choosing stories

Beginning to read alone is a big step. This can be the moment when some children stop reading fiction altogether. Try the Ladybird series of *Easy to Read* stories, and the *'I can Read'* series published by World Books. There are titles suitable for five to eight-year-olds, many in paperback. Here are some more ideas to help you to help them.

Good for a laugh
Look out for funny books. Children like stories that take the mickey out of real life.

Comic books
Comics are cheap and fun to read. They can be swapped about among friends and they often deal with up-to-date people and events – such as television and football personalities. Some of the titles will probably be familiar from your own childhood, like *'Dandy'* and *'Beano'*, and some will be new, like *'Shoot'* (for football fans) or *'Fun to do'*, which is full of games and activities.

Shivers down your spine
Ghosts and things that go bump in the night are popular. Look out for books like *Ghosts and Bogles* by Dinah Starkey (published by Good Reading), and the Armada series of ghost books.

Wizards, witches and wolves
Younger children like witches who are funny, like Meg, in the books by Helen Nicoll and Jan Pienkowski (Penguin), whose spells go wrong and Catherine Storr's Stupid Wolf, who is tricked by Clever Polly (also in Penguin). Older children can face tougher stuff.

Myths, legends and folk tales
These are good for reading aloud. You can move on from their pre-school favourites to well-illustrated versions of Grimm, Hans Anderson and Andrew Lang's fairy tales.

Adventure stories
Help them choose by reading the summary of the story inside the cover. Younger readers still need pictures and not too many words.

Happy endings
This age group enjoys heroes and heroines with ponies and bikes, boats and caves and an unrealistic plot with a bit of magic or crime. Try introducing them at eight or nine to series like *The Children of Green Knowe* by Lucy M. Boston, and *The Little House in the Big Woods* by Laura Ingalls Wilder (both published in Penguin). Girls often aren't interested in stories about boys, but there are plenty of books available now with girls as the heroines, such as *'Pippi Longstocking'* by Astrid Lindgren (Penguin).

Science fiction
We've got space-age kids. They're Dr Who, Star Wars and Superman fans. Of course, they'll look for stories like these – and probably find them in comics as well as the book-of-the-TV-programme.

TV and books
TV serials are a good guide. Sometimes a book like Worzel Gummidge or the stories by E. Nesbit are serialised; at other times the serial is turned into a book, like Grange Hill Stories (the story of a comprehensive school) by Phil Redmond. A reluctant reader may be drawn to the book, having seen the story on TV.

Book clubs

Book club catalogues are a good guide to what is available in children's books even if you don't buy through the club. Their catalogues are usually divided up under age groups. Most adult book clubs sell children's books, and there are now clubs selling only children's books. These often advertise in newspapers and magazines.

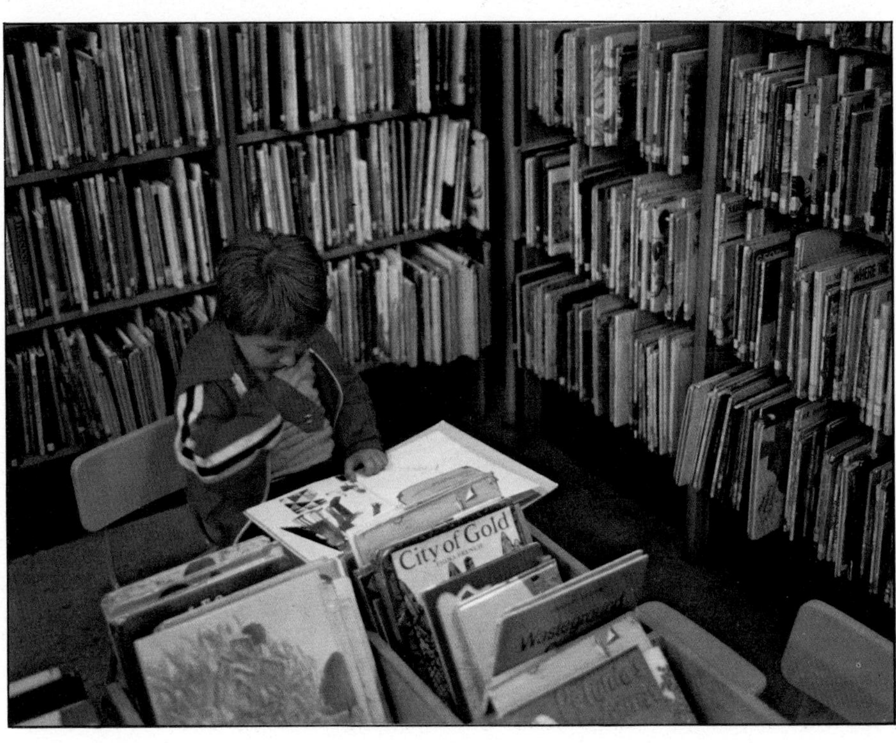

Writing and spelling

Writing is a form of self-expression.
It doesn't just have to be neat!

Learning to speak is seldom a struggle. Learning to write is much more difficult. What a child can *say* is five years of mental development ahead of what he can *write* when he starts. Watch a five or six-year-old trying to write. What she wants to say takes second place to the struggle to control the paper and pencil.

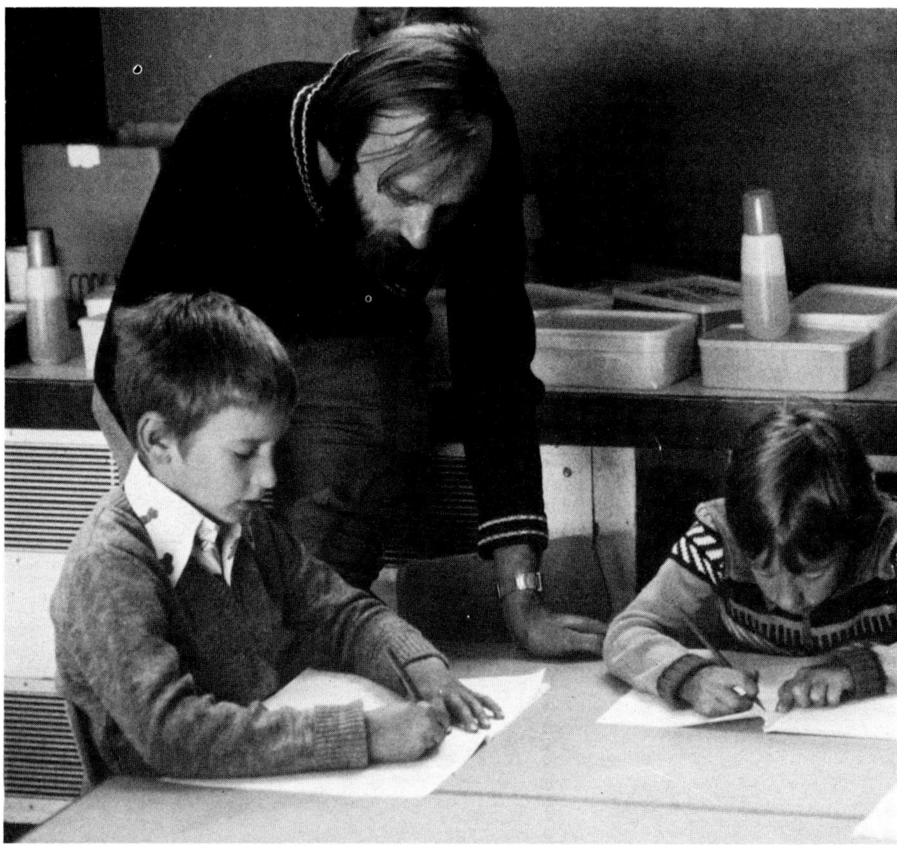

First steps

To begin with writing is very slow. Children are busy copying words they have had to ask for or find for themselves. Then one day, when their reading is getting confident, they get impatient and start writing on their own. It is an adventurous step and needs a really good audience. What do you think this sentence says? *A urpan is fling in the sci.* (An aeroplane is flying in the sky.)

Once the first step in writing on their own has been taken, talking, reading and writing become inseparable. The better they are at reading, the more confident they are about writing; and the more talking they do, the more ideas they have!

What do they need to write for?

Writing makes something you want to say permanent. In school it is one of the means by which children put on record what they have learned. Like talking, writing has many different uses in school. Children need to write:

- to record information.
- to tell others about their experiences and describe real events.
- to make up stories and describe imaginary events.
- to explore the way they feel, in poems and plays.
- to give instructions.
- to solve problems.

Find out what different bits of writing your child has done in school in the last few days. Ask her what it was about and who was meant to read it. (Look at the chart on the right.)

Writing	It was about	It was read by
My magazine questionnaire	What you like in magazines (We're going to make one)	Tracy and Jason. They answered the questions
Instructions	How to work a cassette recorder	People who haven't used it before
My ghost play	A haunted house	Darren and John and Helen acted it with me
Invitation to a party	Robert and Andrew and I are giving a party	Mrs Johnson
My project	What to feed your dog on	Me and my teacher
Measuring	How to measure our notice board	Me and my teacher

Monday	Tuesday	Wednesday	Thursday
bet	**torn**	**ago**	**with**
enter	**look**	**win**	**hide**
bleed	**lump**	**chain**	**rush**
best	**make**	**slap**	**clay**
begin	**bake**	**skid**	**upset**

Write the sentences beneath the pictures.
Choose words from the lists to fill the spaces.

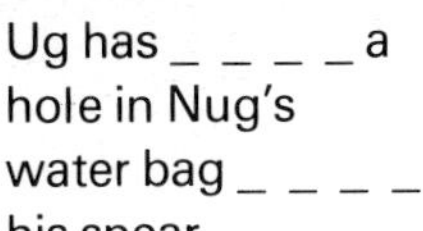

Ug has _ _ _ _ a hole in Nug's water bag _ _ _ _ his spear.

Nug hits him over the head with a _ _ _ _ of _ _ _ _

Ug is _ _ _ _ _ _, but Nug says, '_ _ _ _ at this hole in the clay!'

Nug puts it to _ _ _ _ in the fire to _ _ _ _ a clay water jug.

Spelling at school

On the left is part of a page of a work book a little boy called Mark has been using to learn from. As you can see there are activities designed to help children to understand and learn selected words. If you try to work through this page you will get some idea of the experience that a child has in learning spellings in this way.

Other ways to learn

Using exercises like these is one method of teaching spelling which is fairly common. Some teachers prefer to select for each child a few words which he has misspelt in his recent writing. This is a more individual approach. The words may be written on card and kept in a box or folder which becomes the child's personal word store.

Sometimes children record words they are learning to spell in notebooks, arranging them in alphabetical order. This is similar to a dictionary and practice in finding the correct page to write a word on should help with future use of alphabetical lists such as dictionaries and telephone directories.

How to remember

Teachers use several techniques to help children to memorise spellings. These may include:

- saying the letters aloud.
- writing the word several times.
- 'drawing' the word in the air or on a surface with their finger.
- tracing or crayoning over the word in different colours several times.

In the classroom there will also be simple dictionaries, both published and school-made, word lists and charts to which the children can refer.

What matters?

Spelling is not usually a problem for younger children since the teacher writes down words for them to copy. This is done to provide the children with a model and to help them with the difficult task of letter formation. Most five-year-olds lack the muscular control and co-ordination of older children and controlling a pencil and forming letters is enough for them without having to worry too much about spelling.

Spelling becomes more important as children start to write stories on their own. Even at this stage, emphasis on correct spelling is less important than encouraging the flow of self-expression through writing. The message, a story or facts which the child is trying to convey, is most important and most teachers are careful not to inhibit children by demanding an unrealistic standard of spelling. If children have to check every word they write they soon learn to play safe, resulting in repetitive stilted work.

Teachers value children's writing primarily for what it conveys, though they will, of course, encourage and help children to overcome spelling difficulties. This is why you may sometimes see work with spelling errors in it displayed in schools.

Writing and spelling at home

The best help you can give your child at home is to show him you find writing is useful and fun and that you're pleased if he does too. Neatness and good spelling can come later.

Try making a list of all the writing that you do during an ordinary day. It may look something like this:

- ○ notes for the milkman.
- ○ shopping lists.
- ○ paying bills by cheque.
- ○ ordering goods.
- ○ letters to family.

Are there any things on your list that your children could contribute to? Does the Gas Board really mind if the address on the envelope is written by an adult or a child, as long as it is legible and they get paid?

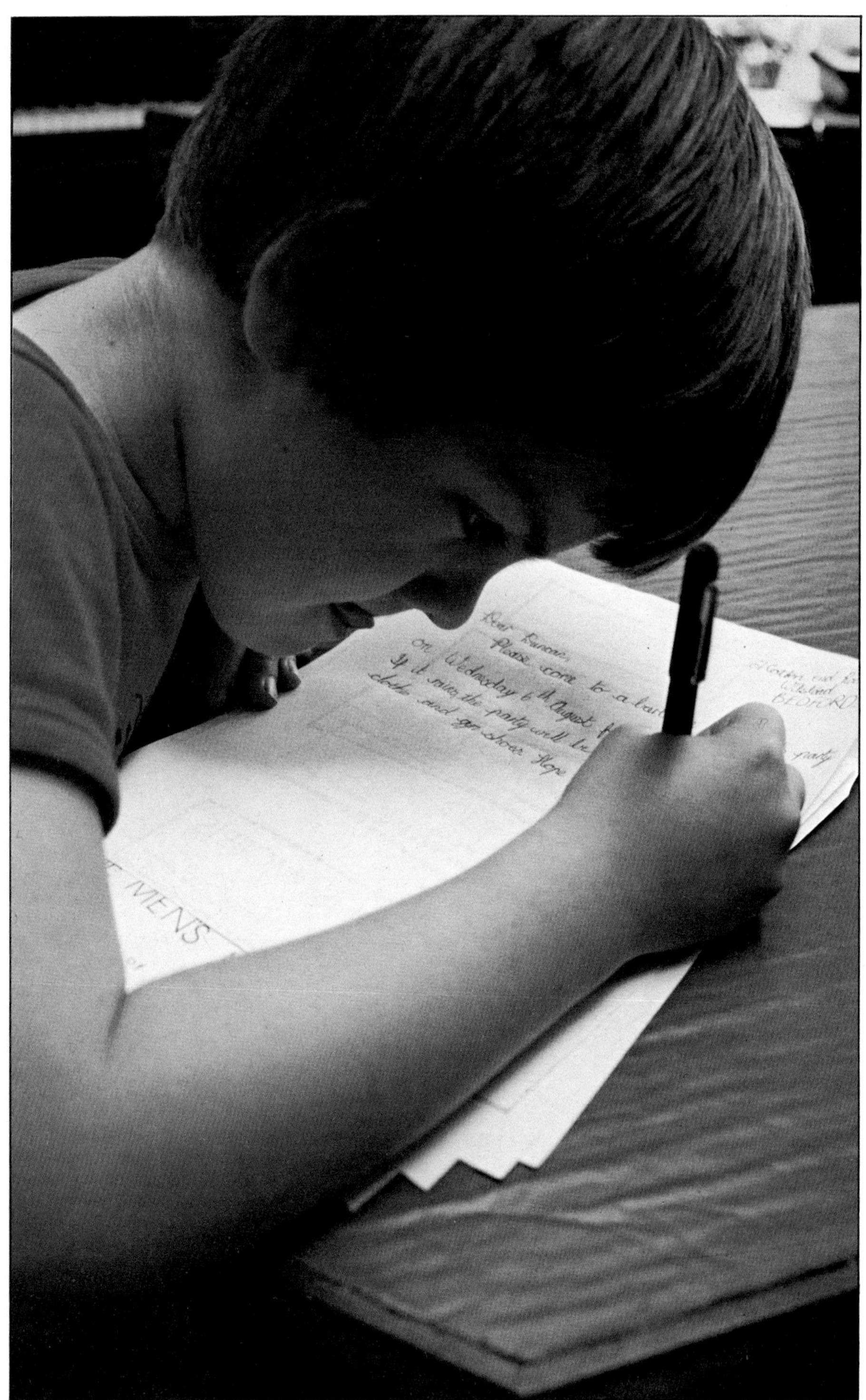

Sometimes you have to leave a written message for your child – like this note on the door:

'Gone to telephone – back soon, Mum.' Are there times when they could leave a message for you?

Practical problems

Parents sometimes worry about the development of their children's writing. Most problems resolve themselves with time. If you are worried, see your child's teacher rather than worry your child. Some common worries are these.

Mirror writing

In writing about the camera she's made out of a soap box, Sonya, aged six, has used some capital letters, and reversed some other letters. The letter 'e' in 'pretty' is even written upside down. There is no need to be too concerned about reversal – young children know a cup is still a cup whichever side the handle is on, so it takes a while to get used to the fact that 'd' and 'b', for instance, are very different. Some children continue to reverse the odd letter up till age ten or longer.

Left-handers

Don't have to be a problem. Two or three children in a class will be left-handed – and no one should force them to change. It makes little difference, and teachers will help left-handers to write clearly.

Sudden untidiness

May appear if a child is unwell or under stress. Or he may just want to write down his ideas so quickly he hasn't time to be tidy. Gradually he'll be able to cope with ideas *and* be neat.

A lack of style

Most schools don't worry too much about style, particularly in the early stages. They are most concerned that children should be able to get their ideas down quickly, easily and clearly. Your child's writing style will change as he experiments with his new found skill.

Writing letters

Letters are based on patterns, like these. Draw them for your child to copy – going from left to right. This will help your child to control his pencil.

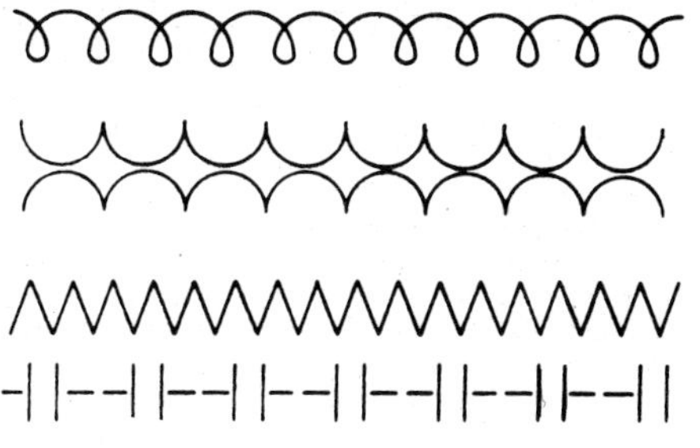

Infants learn to print first, using small letters. Capitals come later. Practise yourself: all letters are made up in one movement unless more than one arrow is numbered. Remember: write for your child to copy – it's always easier than spelling it out for them. There is no need to write extra large for children.

It helps to point out the similarities between some letters; for instance a, c, g, q, and d all have common characteristics. Fun can be had by making patterns with letters or even decorating them.

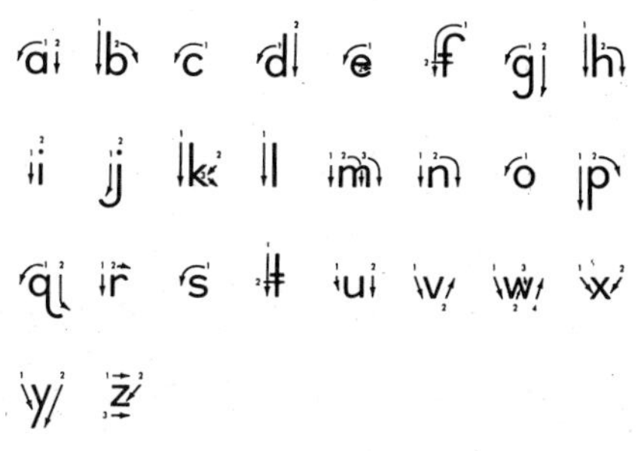

Writing materials

There are lots of different ways to help your child learn how to control a pencil.

Fingers

need exercise to develop the control needed to draw and write with. Plasticine and play-doh, sand and hammering are fun – and they help the fingers too. So does seeing how many funny shapes you can wriggle your hand into. Writing isn't just about pencil and paper. Try chalk, finger paints, sand – lots of variety to get fingers itching to try it.

Tools for writing

depend on the child's skills. Start with chubby soft pencils, wax crayons, or felt tips. Thin pencils, biros and ink pens should wait till a child is about eight. Help him hold a pencil between thumb and forefinger, resting on the third finger. A child's first letters are wobbly and large; they get smaller as he gets more skilled. So start with large sheets of unlined paper. Kitchen paper and lining paper are useful at this stage. Lines help at junior stage when writing is more controlled.

Hands and eyes

need to practise working together. Tracing or copying what you have written on the paper is easier than looking up at a board. Neatness comes from hand and eye working together.

A proper place

for writing helps. This can be any flat, steady surface that a child can sit up to. However, children often press hard, so put a magazine underneath if you want to protect the furniture.

Things to write about

1 Tell me about your picture
You print what your child tells you. (Don't correct him.) He can trace over your letters, or copy them below. Later he'll be able to write it all himself

2 Saying hello
Your child can draw his own greeting cards, or glue-and-stick pictures on. Help him write a very short message. 'To ... Love from...' is the limit for many young ones. The thrill of getting a reply will encourage him to do another one

3 Cartoon comic
Help your older child make a comic strip. It's a familiar style for children. And it shows how thoughts use words too

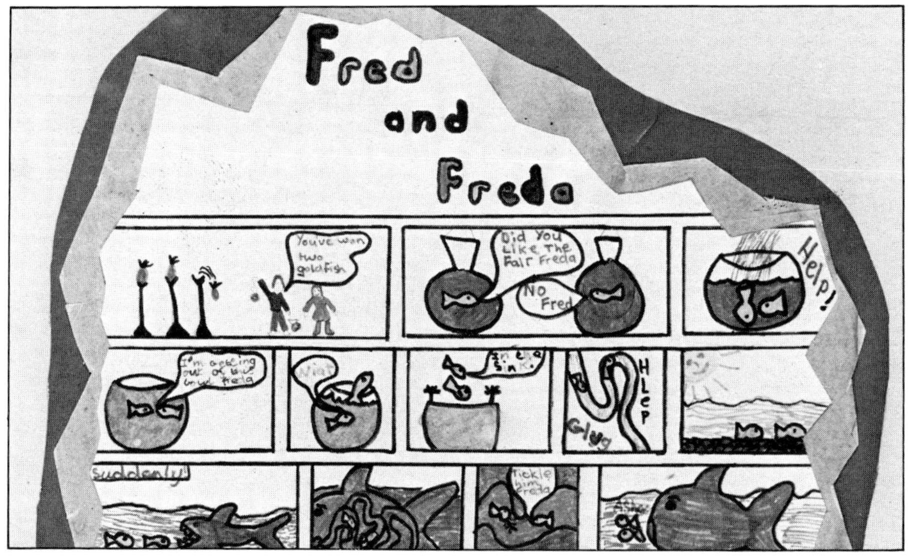

4 Shopping lists
Most children will enjoy helping with the shopping list if they want to add lemonade or ice-cream to it. At first this may just be a drawing with the name of the item copied from a label on a container

5 Coupons
Let your child fill in his name and address on a special offer coupon – it could be something for the family, or for himself. It is always exciting getting something in the post

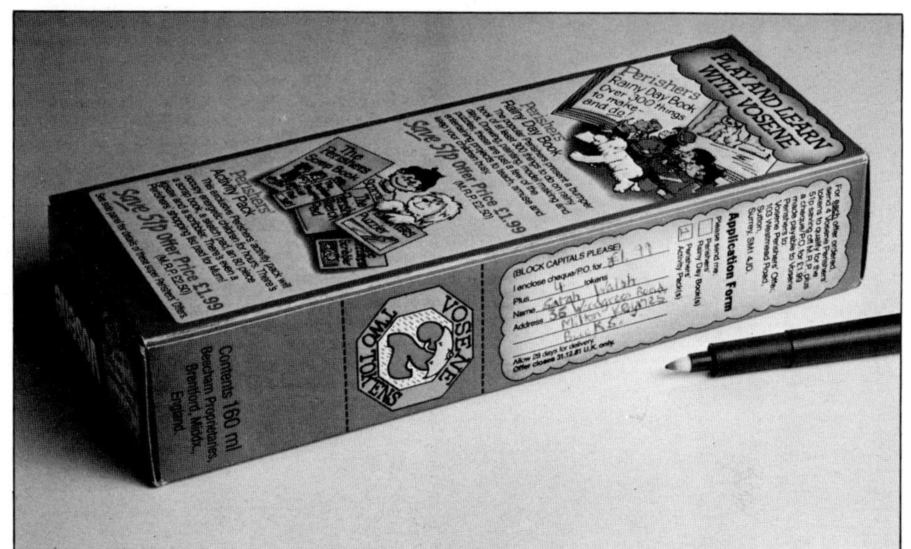

6 Story books
The best known characters for a child are himself and his family. But he may also like stories about pets, princes, Mr Men – or his own made up people. Let him choose how much to write and what about. Children don't usually start on short stories before they are seven or eight

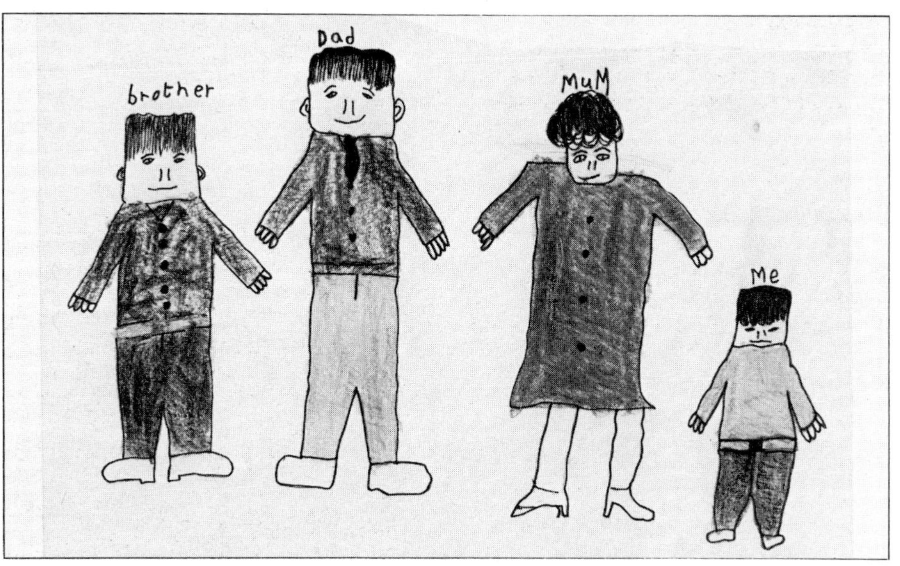

These are all ideas you might like to try out with your child. Remember that the best way to encourage children to write is to make it enjoyable – so don't push too hard. Writing is an effort. It is often slow and frustrating, so don't expect too much too soon. Choose things that your child will be able to cope with and always show that you appreciate the efforts he makes. And don't push him – or he may start to lose interest in learning to write and spell.

Maths at school

New methods of learning maths don't have to be a mystery for parents.

David and Marjorie England are visiting their son Michael's school for a Parent's Day. They have already looked through Michael's project book on pond life, read his poem called 'Snow' pinned on the classroom wall, and are now chatting with his teacher about how well Michael is fitting in with the rest of the class. Suddenly Mr England says: *'There is one thing that bothers me, Miss James, Michael is ten now, nearly eleven, but he doesn't even know his tables. In my job I often have to work things out in my head but if I ask Michael to do a sum he's lost.'*

Maybe you've had the same doubts as David England that the basic skills aren't being taught to your children. You wouldn't be on your own. Of the three Rs (reading, writing and arithmetic) it is the teaching of arithmetic, or mathematics, that is cause for most alarm. Often that is because parents don't understand the point of the methods used – and no one has bothered to explain to them.

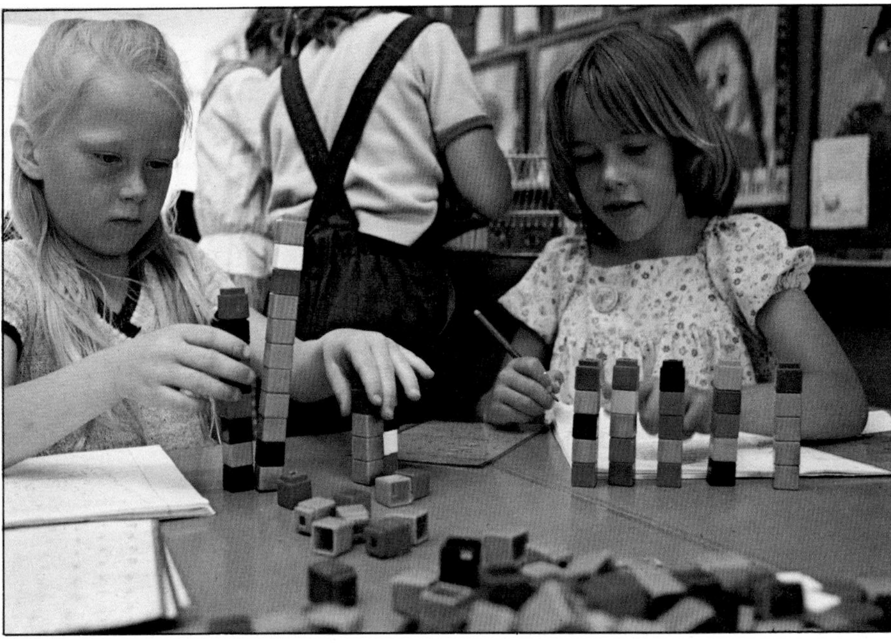

What are you worried about?

Listed on the right are some of the typical concerns about maths expressed by parents. Read through the list and decide whether or not you share these concerns. For each of the statements in the left hand column put a tick underneath the reaction that most suits your own feelings.

	Agree strongly	Agree	Disagree strongly	Disagree
Basic skills are neglected	☐	☐	☐	☐
Too much time is spent on games as a way of learning maths	☐	☐	☐	☐
Too much practical work rather than pencil and paper work	☐	☐	☐	☐
Too much individual work causes children to progress slowly	☐	☐	☐	☐

Now compare what you put with what most of the parents of children in a Buckinghamshire first school said. They agreed that basic skills were neglected; strongly disagreed that too much time was spent on games and on practical work; and agreed strongly that individual work caused children to progress too slowly.

Other worries were: *'too much variation in the work too soon'* ... *'not enough mental work'* and a rather heartfelt *'I just don't understand the work my daughter is doing.'*

It does help to say what worries you. Once you have a clear idea of what your worries are it's much easier to look closely at them and decide what to do. As you work through this section you may feel happier and more confident about the maths teaching methods used in schools, or you may feel it's time to talk to the teacher and find out some more.

Maths at school

The teaching of maths in primary schools has changed since the 60s. Most likely when you went to school it was all about 'adding up', 'taking away', 'dividing', and 'multiplying'. These processes simply had to be memorised. Remember the rule for doing this sum: $\frac{3}{4} \div \frac{1}{2}$? Probably it was something like this: 'turn it upside down and multiply', so $\frac{3}{4} \div \frac{1}{2}$ became $\frac{3}{4} \times \frac{2}{1}$ which is $\frac{6}{4}$ or $1\frac{1}{2}$.

Maybe you still use this rule, but do you understand it? Does it help you when you try to work out day-to-day problems like 'how many rolls of wall-paper do I need?' or 'how much do I owe the newsagent?' In the primary classroom maths is presented as a method of solving everyday problems rather than as a set of rules that have to be learned by heart. Children must still use the basic skills of arithmetic to solve them but, more important, they are learning to understand what they are doing.

On the right is part of Mark's workcard 'Words and Numbers'. The problems which he has to do are shown in pictures and words, to help him to see that they are about real things. In the past, when children always saw problems presented in an abstract manner ($3+4=\quad$, $4+5=\quad$) they had difficulty in seeing that what they were learning applied to real life too.

This is what Mark produced in response to the first two problems.

Work through one or two of the problems on the workcard yourself.

Mark has also done some work on multiplication tables. Many parents are anxious because their children don't learn tables in the conventional way, that is, by reciting them. The old system of teaching tables by rote learning has been criticised because of the way it relies on memorising lists without a real understanding of numbers. This formed a shaky foundation for later learning. The low interest in maths at higher levels, as shown by the number of pupils who dropped maths as soon as they were able to, does indicate that that method of teaching did not work well.

Any work which involves children in analysing numbers is contributing to their knowledge and understanding of the content of 'tables'. For example, a young child might be set the following task.

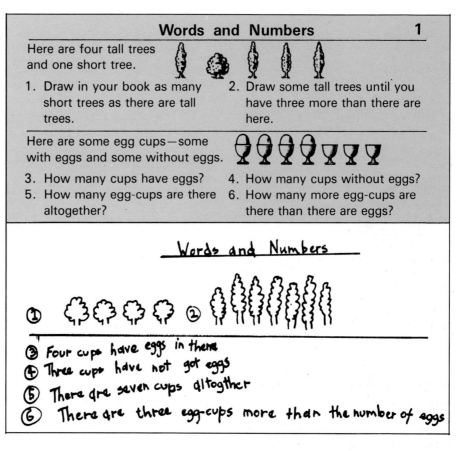

Words and Numbers 1

Here are four tall trees and one short tree.

1. Draw in your book as many short trees as there are tall trees.
2. Draw some tall trees until you have three more than there are here.

Here are some egg cups—some with eggs and some without eggs.

3. How many cups have eggs?
4. How many cups without eggs?
5. How many egg-cups are there altogether?
6. How many more egg-cups are there than there are eggs?

Words and Numbers

③ Four cups have eggs in them
④ Three cups have not got eggs
⑤ There are seven cups altogther
⑥ There are three egg-cups more than the number of eggs

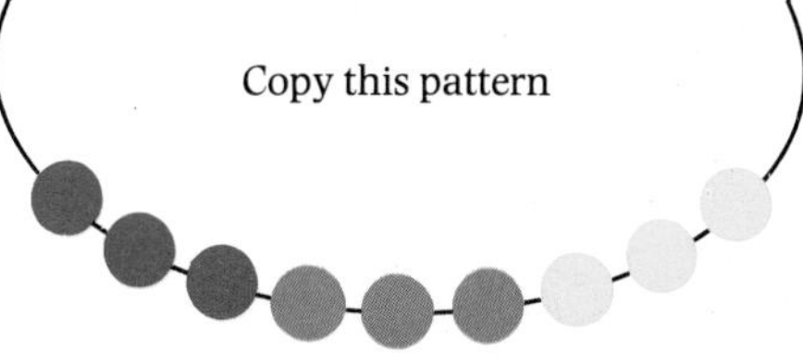

There are nine beads

By doing this he is gaining experience of reading and colour matching as well as learning that $3+3+3=9$ and $3 \times 3 = 9$. He will also have understood these combinations of numbers without writing them all out:

$$1+1+1+1+1+1+1+1+1=9$$

$3+6=9$	$9-6=3$
$6+3=9$	$9-9=0$
$9-3=6$	$9 \div 3=3$

New words for old ideas

The methods used to teach children maths today are often very different from those most parents were taught. These new methods involve new terms and ideas which are unfamiliar to many of us. This makes them seem complicated, and so parents feel that they are unable to help their children with their maths. However, when you look a little closer at the new methods, they are quite easy to understand.

Take, for example, the idea of 'base work'. At first sight this looks like a complicated new area of maths, but it is only a new way of looking at the familiar old maths. We are all used to writing numbers in 'hundreds' 'tens' and 'units'. The number 26 actually represents 2 tens and 6 units.

When we add two numbers, we first

add the 'units' and as soon as we reach '10' units we transfer this to the 'tens' side. This transfer from one side to the other when you reach 10 means we are working to 'base 10'.

Here is an example of addition in base 10

26 +
37
—
63
—

It is the same as the addition that we understand. (We first add 6 and 7 giving 13 or one '10' and one '3'. We transfer the one '10' across, leaving 3 in the units column. We then add the tens, 2 + 3 + 1 giving 6.)

But not all things in real life are expressed in base 10. So in base work, the base is flexible. For hours and minutes the base is 60, for instance. By using the new methods and thinking in terms of 'bases' we will find that these numbers can be added and subtracted in just the same way.

There are 60 minutes in one hour, so if we are adding hours and minutes we will be working in base 60, as follows: add 1 hour 43 minutes to 6 hours 28 minutes.

1 . 43 +
6 . 28
—
8 . 11
—

43 plus 28 is 71 or one '60' and 11 'units'. Transfer the 60 to the other column and add 6 + 1 + 1 = 8. The answer is eight hours and eleven minutes.

Below is a problem which has been used in a test for a ten-year-old.

Rather than using familiar terms like hours and minutes, the problem uses 'tocs' and 'zigs'. However, the methods that you need to use are just the same. See if you can answer it.

This addition sum is correct:

tocs	zigs
1	1 +
1	3
3	0

So how many zigs make a toc? Answer: 4.

Which of the following came closest to your own reaction in attempting this sum?

'Easy' You understood the principle involved in the first sum, and were able to transfer this to the second calculation. Just as 12 inches make 1 foot, so 4 zigs must make 1 toc if the sum is to work out.

'A pointless exercise' In fact this example illustrates the principle behind using different sizes of units: 100 centimetres = 1 metre, 7 days = 1 week, 4 zigs = 1 toc, etc.

'I realised that zigs were a smaller unit of tocs and experimented until I worked out that 4 of them added up to a toc' This kind of thinking involves exploring numerical values. Teaching approaches like this which encourage children to think and explore for themselves are often used in schools. Much learning takes place through activities which appear to be play. Although there is an element of play and pleasure in what the children are doing, playing with coloured bricks is not always what it seems.

'I found it easier to talk it through with someone else' Talking over a problem is a good way to get your own ideas straight, and it also brings in other people's ideas on what the answer might be. Group discussions of all sorts of problems involving basic maths are a common sight in the primary classroom.

Work involving different base values gives children a great deal of flexibility in handling numbers, familiarising themselves with multiples of 2, 3, 4, 5, etc, and seeing relationships between numbers. Achieving this by working it out via a thinking process has obvious advantages over the rote learning of tables. Children discover and learn in very similar ways to adults; they look, ask and discuss. The primary classroom is designed to help them to do these things as much as possible in their maths lessons.

Maths out of maths lessons

Maths teaching is not confined to maths lessons or even to school hours. As part of a project on the human body, Mark had practical experience of measuring his classmates' feet, heads, height, weight and area. This led him not only to measure but to make comparisons and find different ways of recording and presenting the information. Many of the skills acquired in this way will be useful to him in adult life.

In his report, Mark used a lot of mathematical words: heaviest, lightest, tallest, smallest, longest and shortest. Experience of 'mathematical language' is important to the development of mathematical concepts and can be encouraged at home.

Group projects can also provide opportunities to reinforce maths learnt in the classroom, as well as being useful in themselves. This extract (right) from a local paper describes a project tackled by nine to ten-year-olds. Using what you know from reading this far, go through the article and underline the exercises where some form of mathematical thinking would be needed.

It is clear from the articles that the children were involved in *measurement* of *length*, and *time*. They *collected* and *analysed data*, so they will have needed to *count* and *add*. They needed to *calculate* such things as *speed* of cars, *prices* of cakes and the *total amount* needed to purchase the armbands – so both *division* and *multiplication* would have been used.

It is not just project work that provides the opportunity for children to use mathematics. The lively active primary classroom provides a rich context for making use of mathematics. Such things as cooking, or weighing out food for the class pet also provide mathematical experience in the pleasantest possible way.

Your own child's class

Your child's teacher would probably welcome a parent showing interest in what he or she is doing. So try to arrange a visit to the school during lesson time and then have a chat to the teacher. While you're there these are some of the things you might look out for in your child and ask the teacher about.

○ When is formal work started?

○ Is he able to use materials and start from practical activities?

○ Does he usually find the work relevant and get involved?

○ Does he learn reasons and an understanding of processes rather than mechanical rules?

○ Is he encouraged to discuss mathematical experiences with other children and the teacher?

○ Does he have the opportunity to practise and apply ideas that he understands?

Always *ask* about what you don't understand. As a parent you are the most important influence on the progress of your child. The teacher knows this and is anxious to involve you in the learning environment of the child.

SCHOOLCHILDREN WITH ROAD SAFETY IN MIND

IN THESE GRIM early days of 1981 we can all learn a lesson from the children of Cherry Hill Middle School. Unperturbed by the apparent failure of their campaign to convince the authorities of the danger of children crossing the road at the busy London Road roundabout, they decided to do something practical about it themselves.

On Tuesday afternoon they held a mini-fete in the school hall to raise the £25 or so needed to give all the pupils who have to cross the busy London Road a pair of luminous armbands to make the crossing of that road a little less dangerous.

Ten-year-old Roy Davis was one of the children who had worked hardest in the campaign and he told the Advertiser about its chequered history.

"It all started in the classroom early last term when Mrs. Jones, our teacher, told us that last year her class had done a traffic census down on that road and we all thought that we should do another one," he said.

"As we went down there time after time, we all began to realise just how dangerous it was for children to cross the road there.

"So we set about gathering information to send to the County Council and other authorities. We measured the width of the road and the amount of time it took for a car to stop travelling at average speed on that road.

"We also measured the visibility for a driver coming from Birmingham, because there is a slight hill just before you come to the roundabout and this would stop the driver from seeing far enough ahead.

"We put all the information together and found it was completely unsafe for children to cross the road there," said Roy.

Mrs. Jones took up the story. "We sent a letter to all the parents on the estate and when we had a parents' meeting it emerged that in several cases Mum has to come with her child and cross the road with him. Some of the younger Mums have babies to look after as well, so you can see how difficult it is for them."

Continued Mrs. Jones: "The trouble is that there is no speed restriction at all there, no sign warning drivers that school children cross the road at the point. Ideally we would like to have a lollipop person there in the morning and in the afternoon, but apparently the school itself would have to pay his wages. We simply can't afford to do this. Also it seems there aren't enough children to have a pelican crossing."

The children set about making a collection in the school for all the old toys and books that someone else might want. For a penny a go you could play a table version of skittles and they had made cakes and tea for all the Mums who turned up for the afternoon.

As Roy Davis said: "All we got were just promises on paper. We felt we had to do something now, ourselves, and then just hope that something will be done to solve the problem properly."

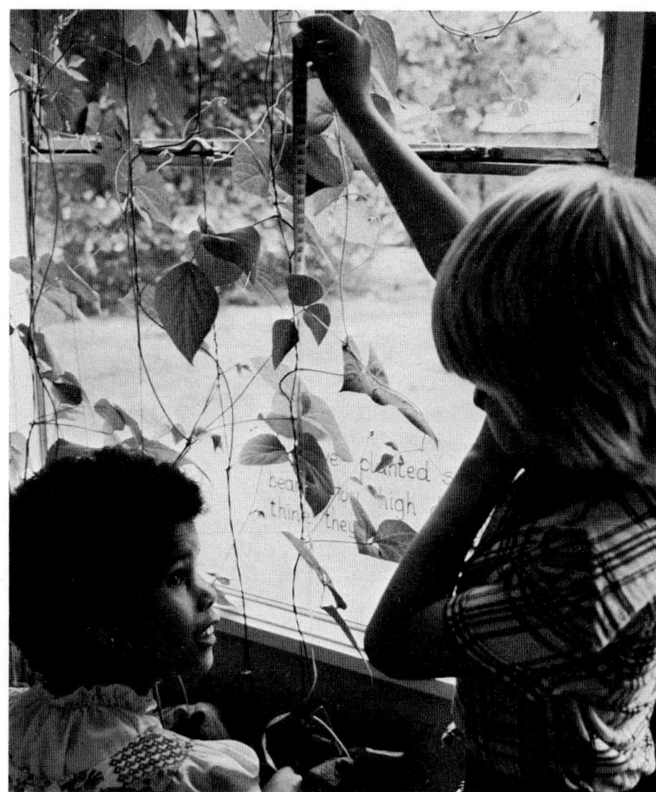

Maths at home

Many of your daily tasks involve you in maths – though you may not realise it.

The important thing to remember when helping children with maths at home is to build mathematical learning into everyday activities.

Think about the last time you had to do a mathematical calculation. The first one that occurred to Mark's mother was: 'I had to settle up with the milkman for three weeks. I get three pints a day, six days a week, at 15p a pint. I left him £8.10.' The next time she has to pay the newsagent or the milkman she will get Mark to help her.

What opportunities for helping with maths can you recognise in the following activities?

○ Getting ready in time for school?

○ Setting the table?

○ Allocating the breakfast cereals?

○ Sorting out pocket money and spending it?

○ Deciding which TV programme to watch?

○ Sharing sweets, buns, toys?

○ Going for a walk, ride?

Here are some suggestions we thought of.

Getting ready for school
Chatting about the *sequence* of events involved in getting ready (*first* I get washed, *then* I put my clothes on, next I go *downstairs*); becoming aware of time and telling the time ('You've get ten minutes left before school', 'It's time for school when the big finger is on 9').

Setting the table
1-to-1 matching (setting a place for each person gives children an idea of number values – 1 plate for 1 person, 6 plates for 6 people). It helps to establish the idea that 6 is 6 whether plates, forks, or dots on a domino. There is also scope for some calculations; there are 6 people, we have 4 plates, so we need 2 more.

Allocating cereals
This involves allocating *portions*, judging *amounts*, learning about weight and volume. A *large* packet of cornflakes is not as *heavy* as a *small* bag of sugar; making

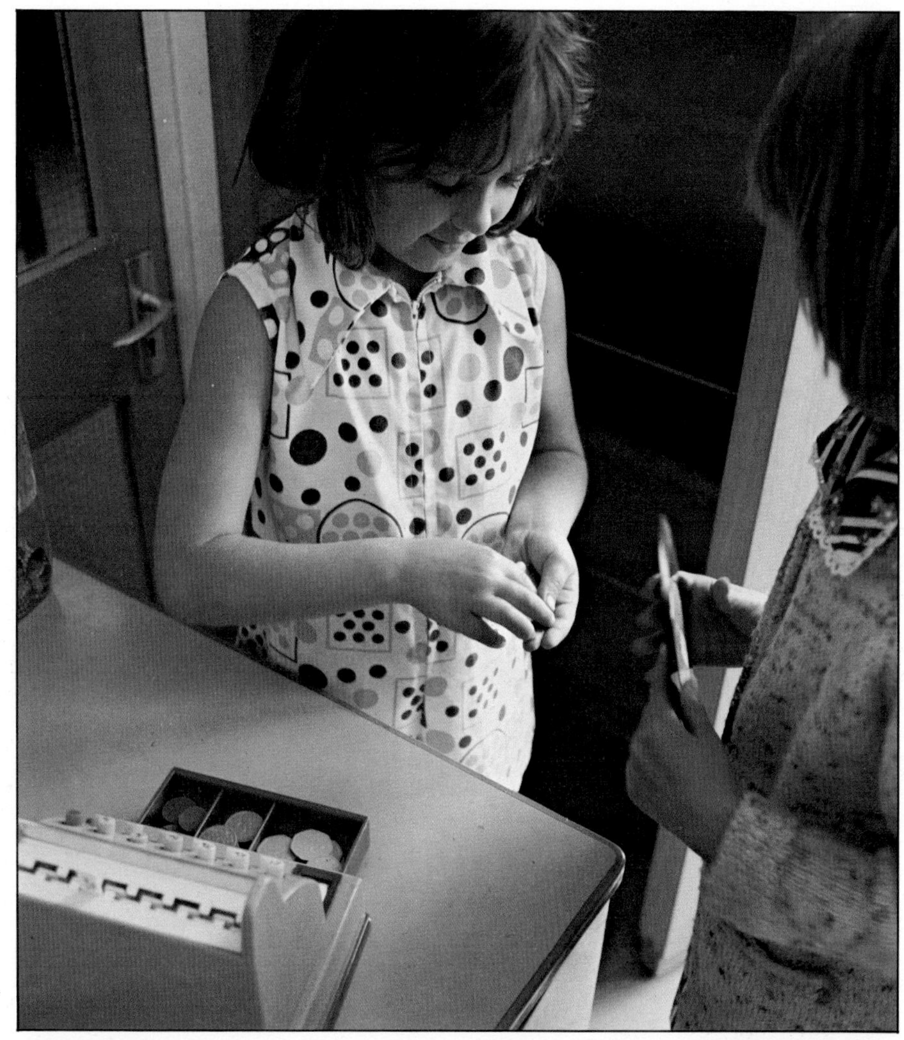

judgements of *enough, too much, too little, most* and *least.*

Sorting out money

Handling and discussing money gives experience with real money – the size, weight, and face value of coins; experience of counting money: comparing groups made up of different coins which have the same *value*, substituting coins for others, two one-penny pieces for one two-penny piece; deciding which things can be bought with the pocket money available and the amount of change which should be given.

TV programmes

Choosing TV programmes gives practice in reading the TV page as well; experience of time written as 7.45, 8.15; introduces am and pm; requires comparison of programme starting and ending times; requires understanding of the sequence of programmes; knowledge of how long a programme lasts may help to develop a concept of time – introduces understanding of *yesterday, tomorrow, next week, last week, next year*; introduces 'time language': *when, before, now, next, soon, later, second, minute, hour,* and so on.

Sharing

Sharing sweets or buns again gives opportunity for *matching* 1 to 1 and consolidating knowledge of *numbers*. There are opportunities for counting how many sweets there are and then giving them out on a 1 for you, 1 for me basis. In this way much is learnt about the multiples of numbers, (10 sweets – we got 5 each) or *odd* and *even* numbers (11 sweets – we get 5 each and 1 left over) or fractions if the 11th sweet is cut in *half*!

Sweets may be sorted into groups according to their colour or shape. Sorting and classifying of this sort requires logical thinking. Older children will see that 10 sweets can be arranged in two rows of 5 or five rows of 2:

○–○–○–○–○   ○ ○ ○ ○ ○
○–○–○–○–○   ○ ○ ○ ○ ○

This could lead on to understanding that 5 is $\frac{1}{2}$ of 10 or 2 is $\frac{1}{5}$ of ten.

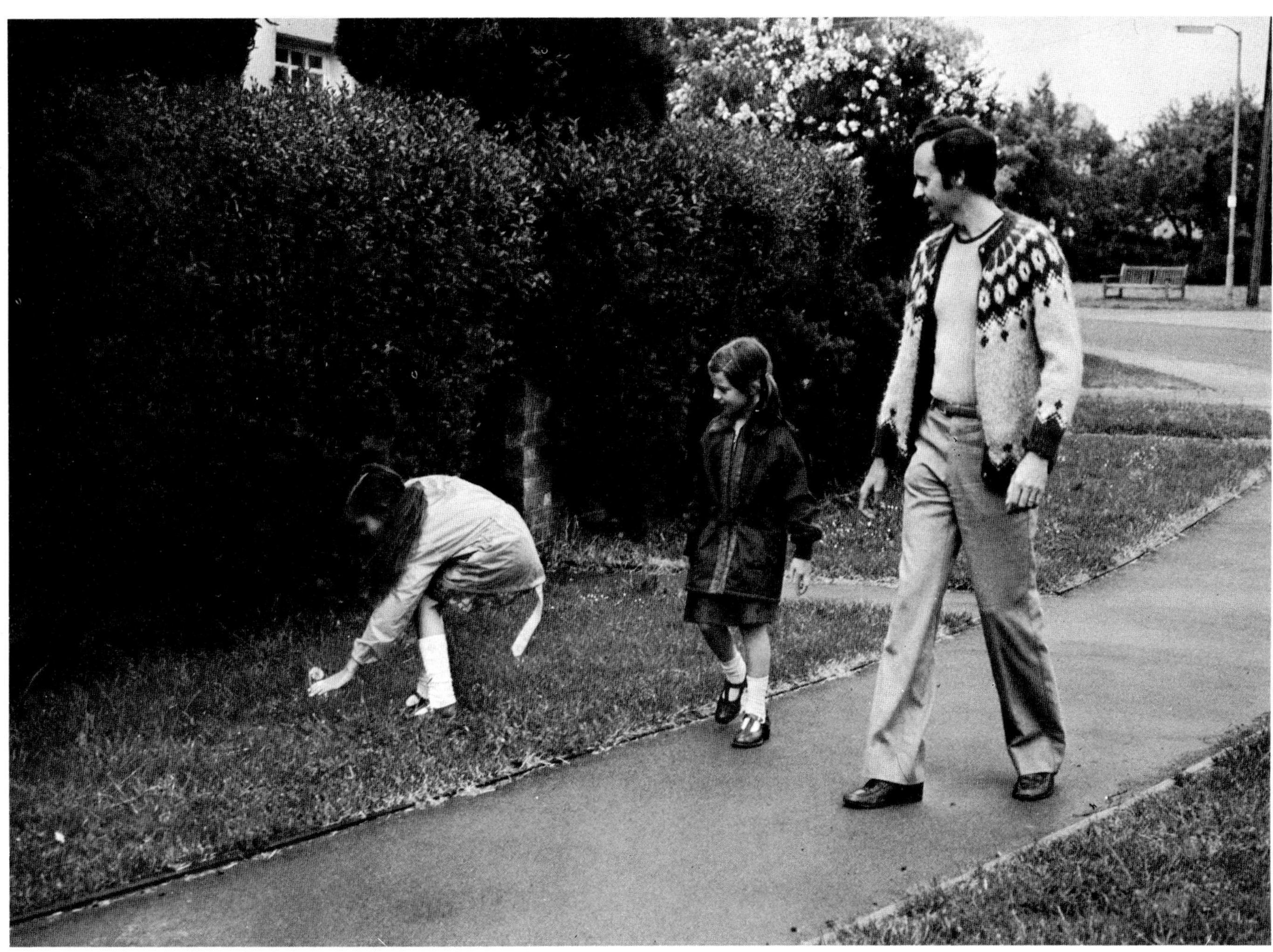

Going for a walk or ride

Travel of any sort involves consideration of *distances*. Discussions of questions like: 'How *far* is it to the sweet shop?' 'How many *miles* have we walked today?' give opportunities for developing concepts of distance which are sometimes related to time (on a car journey, for instance). The distance in relation to the *speed* at which you are travelling can be used to calculate the *time* the journey will take. Here you might talk about miles per hour, which could lead to discussions of different ways of measuring distances.

Perhaps you hadn't thought of experiences of this kind as maths before but all of these and many other everyday activities are the raw material from which children learn. Each child will get different things from similar experiences depending on their age, stage of development and past experience. For instance, at breakfast a five-year-old may gain a better understanding of 'less than', whilst his ten-year-old-brother will be getting acquainted with grammes.

Getting your child to develop positive ways of thinking about maths will not only help him solve mathematical problems but also to enjoy maths and to see its usefulness in real life.

You might also like to try playing these games with your children.

A shape game

Cut out a square of paper or cardboard and show it to your child as it appears in the first picture. If he knows the word 'square' he'll identify it as that. Now turn the card round as in the second picture: the shape now looks different. The important thing for the child to come to terms with is that the square is the same square, even though it may look different when it is on its side. A child of five will probably be able to name the shape in the first picture as 'square' but he will be nearer ten before realising that the shape in the second picture is the same one.

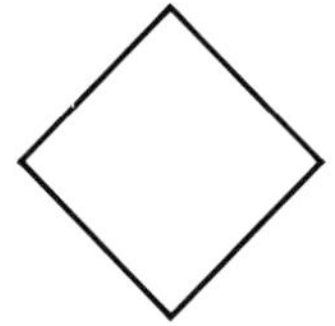

Picture 1 *Picture 2*

The same can be done with an equal sided triangle:

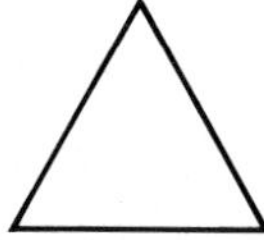

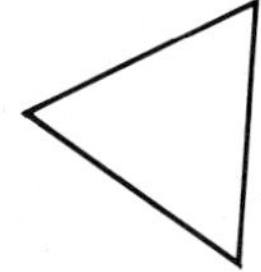

Picture 1 *Picture 2*

Children almost always identify the shape in the first picture as a triangle, but often have difficulty recognising it when it is tipped up. One way of explaining this is to ask the child what she is called when she's sitting down, then when she's standing up, then when she's running. Just as the child doesn't change her name when she moves around, so the shape doesn't either.

Number games
Here are a few samples of games that can help children understand numbers. Remember that games should be fun to play, so be careful not to force children into trying to play them. Let their natural curiosity draw them into the game.

1 This is a simple game involving some card and objects like toy motor cars, or animals or matchsticks. It helps children make the important association between numbers and objects.

Make a series of rectangular cards like the ones in the picture.

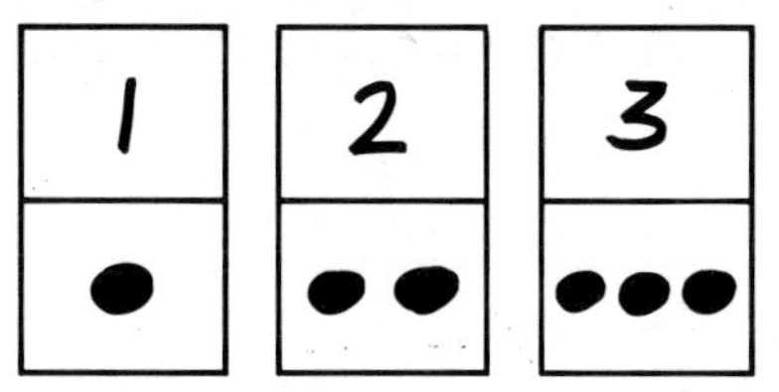

Ask your child to place the correct number of objects on each card as you lay it down. Later on you can cut the cards in two and only show him the top half. In this case he must recognise the number and link it with the correct number of objects without having the dots as a clue.

2 This game is called 'Blobs' and to play it you need to make sixteen cards with coloured blobs crayoned or stuck on them (see above right).

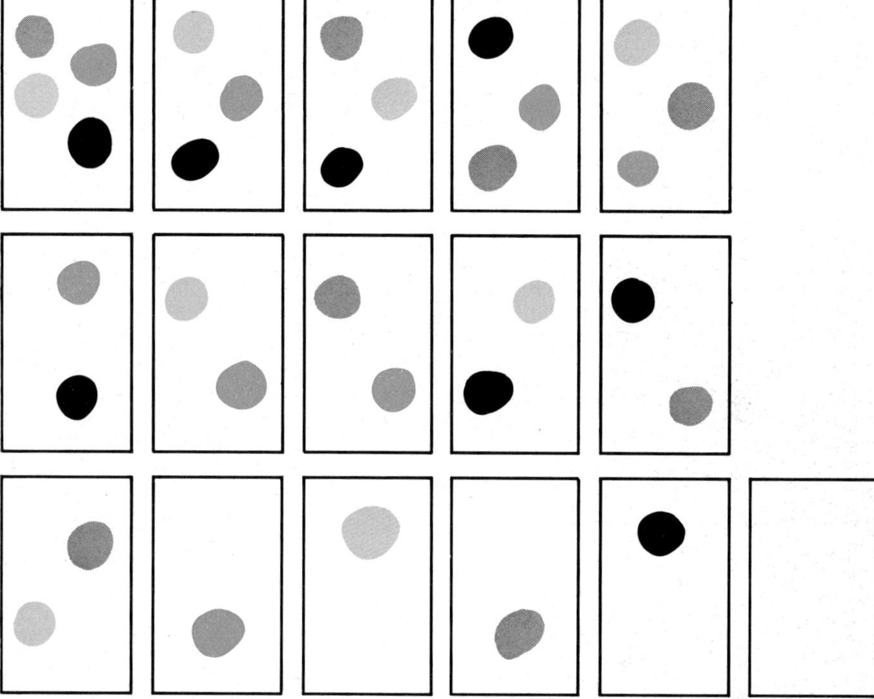

These cards show all the possible combinations of four different coloured blobs. This game helps the child to get used to dealing with numbers and 'groups of things in an abstract theoretical way.

Rules
Use two players. Each player gets an equal number of cards in his hand. The cards are kept face down and played off against each other one at a time. A card can take another card when it has the same coloured blobs on it *plus* some more blobs. Sometimes neither card will win, in which case the trick remains on the table and is collected as a bonus by the player who wins the next card. Here are two examples:

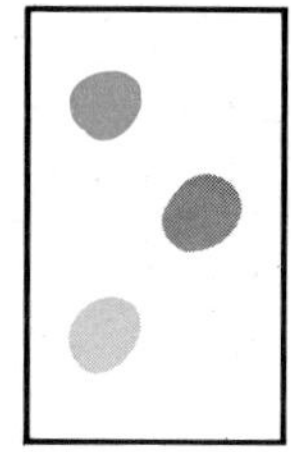

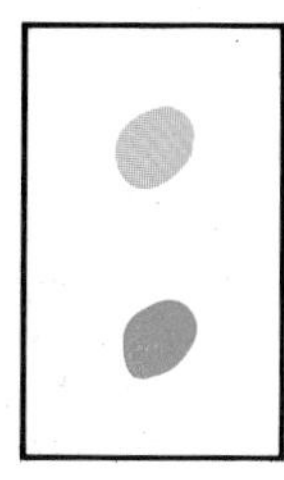

In the first (left) the card on the left wins. It has the same coloured blobs to match the card on the right – pink and red – and it has another blob – grey.

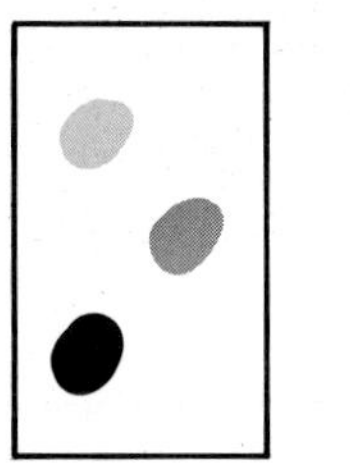

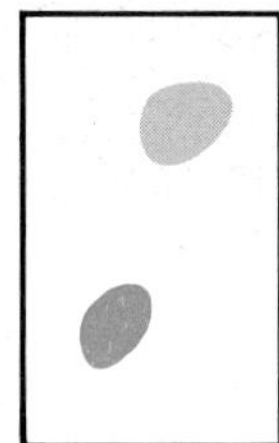

In the one above the card on the left has more blobs but does not win the trick. It doesn't include all the other card's blobs on it. In this case the cards are left on the table.

A more advanced version of this game is to allow players to select cards from their hand. Here children are involved in scanning their own hand to assess if they have a card that will beat their opponent's, and deciding which card to throw away if they can't win the trick.

Getting on with school

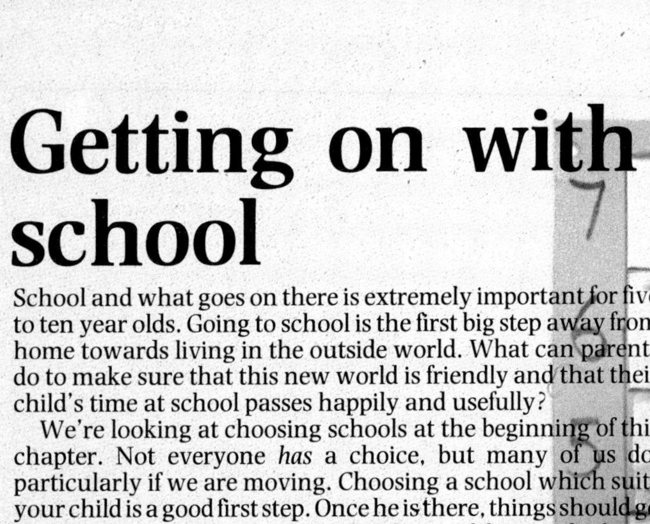

School and what goes on there is extremely important for five to ten year olds. Going to school is the first big step away from home towards living in the outside world. What can parents do to make sure that this new world is friendly and that their child's time at school passes happily and usefully?

We're looking at choosing schools at the beginning of this chapter. Not everyone *has* a choice, but many of us do, particularly if we are moving. Choosing a school which suits your child is a good first step. Once he is there, things should go well, but there are, unfortunately, plenty of things which can go wrong. We take a look at some problems connected with school, including the most common of all, not wanting to go. We also take a close look at bullying and what you might do to help your child cope with it.

All through your child's school career he will be making progress. How is it measured? How do parents get to know about it? What happens if he doesn't seem to be making progress? And are *you* helping or hindering him?

Supposing your child does have problems that have to do with school, where do you go to help get them solved? We give you some guidance to help you identify and approach the right person without delay.

When your child started school, did you ever feel that school was taking over and leaving nothing more for you to do? Parents and teachers *both* have an important part to play, and we discuss with you how you feel about putting your child into the school's keeping for several hours every day.

Do you find it hard to go into school to ask about something that worries you? The fewer barriers between home and school the better and we suggest ways to make it easier for you to talk to your child's teacher.

Finally, we talk about getting actively involved with your child's school: becoming a parent helper, or even a governor, helping on the PTA or just collecting bottletops.

6

A new school

What do you think a school should offer your child?

Going to a new school is a big event for a child, whether it's his first one or his third. You will, of course, want to help him to settle down there as much as possible. So, before he actually starts, you need to find out as much as you can about the kind of school it is. Then both of you will know what to expect.

You may be lucky and find that you have a choice of schools, but perhaps you feel uncertain about how you should set about choosing the best one for your child. Gathering and comparing information can be hard, especially if the school(s) you are looking at is very different from the one *you* went to.

Here are four checklists which should help you focus your ideas on what is important, for you, about a school. They will help you identify what you need to know, so that you can judge whether or not a school meets your requirements. If you are lucky enough to have a choice, you can use the lists to help you choose between schools.

Tick the questions that you feel are important in the first checklist. Then read the comments on each item before moving on to the next list.

Note down what information you have on each item you have ticked. If you don't have any, you need to find out. You can get factual information about schools by:

○ going into your local schools and asking. Nearly all schools have some sort of duplicated or printed handout: they should give you a copy. Or make an appointment to see the head teacher.

○ telephoning or writing to the local education office for your area (or the area to which you are moving). This will be listed in the telephone directory under the name of the local authority. So, if you live in Bucks, look up Bucks County Council. All the council departments will be listed in alphabetical order there. You should note the number given for the Divisional Education Office, under Education Services.

○ enquiring at the local town hall, information bureau, or Citizens' Advice Bureau.

○ asking other parents in the area – though you may not get a full picture and the information may be biased.

○ taking a look round the local school for yourself.

Checklist 1 Type of school

	Tick if important
Religious affiliation?	☐
Mixed or single sex?	☐
Day school/boarding school?	☐
Size of school?	☐
Size of classes?	☐
Infant school only (five to seven)?	☐
Junior school only (eight to eleven)?	☐
All-age primary school (five to eleven)?	☐
First school (five to eight)?	☐
Middle school (eight or nine to twelve plus)?	☐
Combined first and middle school?	☐
Children from just one zone/catchment area?	☐
School has a nursery class?	☐
School takes children who haven't had their fifth birthday yet (rising fives)?	☐
Children of different nationalities at the school?	☐
Open to handicapped children?	☐
School uniform?	☐

Type of school

The first three points in this list may determine the *width* of your choice of schools. If, for instance, you want to send your child to a Catholic school, but don't want to pay for his education, you may be restricted to one school, or, at the most, a choice of two schools; but if you are willing to pay for a single sex boarding school, there will be almost unlimited possibilities, and your choice may be decided by later elements in the lists.

The next eight points give you some idea of the *size* of the school, and the *age range* of the children who go there. You may find that a large school – perhaps a combined first and middle school – is going to have more and better facilities than a small school catering only for a small number of five to seven-year-olds.

Another advantage of having first and middle schools in the same group of buildings is that your child is not going to face many more changes when he goes up from first to middle school.

On the other hand, you may prefer a small school for your child because a small school, with comparatively few children in it, will be able to offer your child more attention.

If you are moving to a new area, and can choose between living in one county or another, you may well find that schools are organised differently in the two counties, with children changing schools at age eight in one and at seven in the other. If you have a preference in this matter, you will obviously choose the county that offers what you want.

The school's *catchment area*, or *zone* as it is sometimes called, may make a difference to your choice. Most local authorities allot places at primary schools by dividing their area into zones, and offering your child a place at the school in your zone. It may be that you live on the edge of two zones, or nearer to the school in the neighbouring zone than to the school in your own zone. In either case you don't *have* to send your child to the school that your local education authority has assigned him to. Check with the head of the school you prefer, and, if there is a vacancy, write to the local education authority and tell them of your choice. Zoning is for the convenience of the local authority; it is not a law that you *have* to send your child to the school they say he must attend.

The availability of a *nursery class* is of particular interest if you have other children under school age. Some schools have a nursery class where children aged between three and five can come – usually for half a day – for playgroup type activities.

Some schools take *'rising fives'* – that is, children who have not had their fifth birthday by the time the term begins, but will have had it by the time the next term starts. You may be lucky enough to live in an area where schools still accept children before they are five. The basic legal requirement under the Education Act is that schools take children at the beginning of the term *after* they are five. Many local education authorities have said they will not accept children before their fifth birthday, even if you happen to move from an area where your child *has* been allowed to start school. But you cannot force a school to accept your child till the beginning of the term after his fifth birthday.

You may think it is important that your child mixes with children who come from *different countries*; or you may feel that there are too many children of one nationality, or too many different languages are spoken by children in the school under consideration. You can check these points with the head teacher.

Handicapped children are sometimes warmly accepted at an ordinary primary school. It obviously depends on how handicapped they are, and in what way, and on how the school itself is built and organised. Many parents of handicapped children would like them to attend the local school with their friends. And many ordinary schools do have head teachers who feel that an effort should be made to take *all* children who want to attend. You may even find that special equipment, or money for special equipment, is available through your local education authority.

Private schools nearly always have a *uniform*, which may be compulsory. Some state primary and middle schools have a uniform, which may not always be compulsory. This is an important point to clarify if you are worried about the cost of the uniform, or are particularly keen on uniform because it saves other clothes or cuts down on children's jealousy of each other's things.

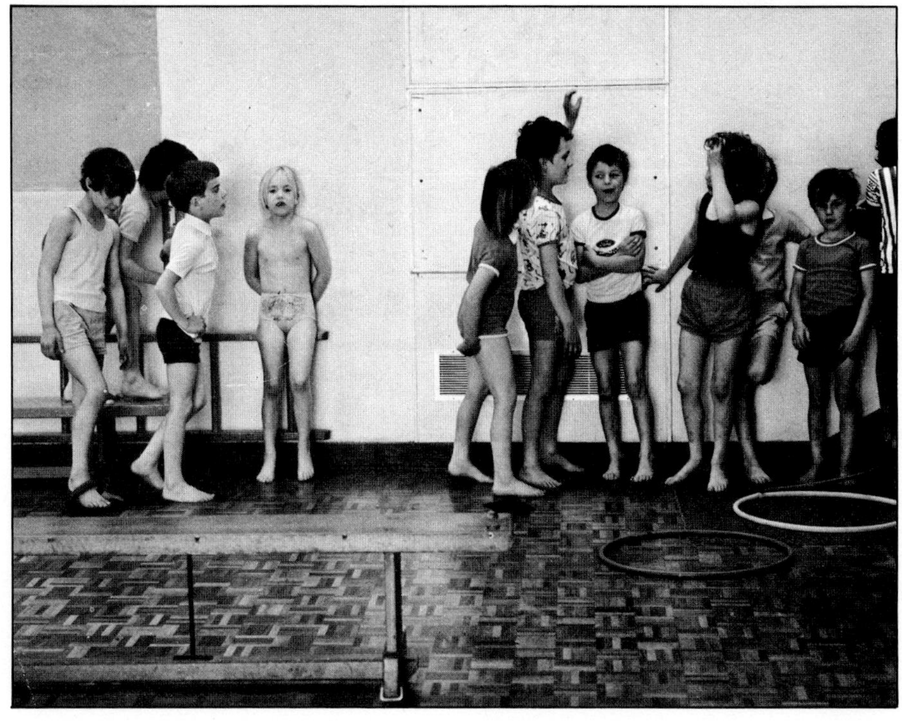

Checklist 2 Teaching

	Tick if important
Is there a high rate of staff turnover?	☐
Is there any form of family grouping (where children of different ages are taught in the same room)?	☐
Do any of the teachers specialise in particular subjects (maths, drama or craft work, for instance)?	☐
Are the classes streamed at all?	☐
Are there tests of any kind?	☐
What special help do fast and slow learners get?	☐
How is reading taught?	☐
How is maths taught?	☐
What type of project work is done?	☐
Is music taught?	☐
How is art taught, and what special facilities are there?	☐
Do boys and girls have the same opportunity to learn various subjects?	☐
If there are any differences between the opportunities for boys and girls, what are they?	☐

Teaching

When teachers come and go frequently in a school, it is hard on children, particularly if this happens in the middle of the school year. So it is wise to check on *teacher turnover*, if you can. This is particularly important when classes are organised in family groups. One of the big advantages of the family grouping system is that the child has the same teacher for a long time, so that they really get to know each other.

If the teacher changes too frequently then the children get all the disadvantages of this system without the advantages.

A *subject specialist* can make a valuable contribution to the teaching in a school. Children who are especially interested in a particular subject have the opportunity for more advanced work than they would normally get at this age. Ideally every primary and middle school should include a range of subject specialists amongst its teaching staff. In practice this can be hard to arrange, since some subjects are a lot more popular with teachers than others.

Many parents have strong feelings about *tests and streaming* so, if you are concerned, it is vital to check on the way the classes are organised. While children of this age are rarely divided up into different classes on the basis of tests and an assessment of their ability, you may often find that 'Kingfishers' or 'Mr Rivers' English Set', is the top group, and 'Swallows', or 'Mrs Turner's maths group' is the lowest ability group.

You may also want to find out how the school copes with *slow* and *extra fast learners*. You may well get a very general sort of answer to questions like this, such as, 'Oh, we give each child individual attention'. So, if you are particularly worried about these problems, you may need to ask for more detail. This may be embarrassing, but most schools welcome such inquiries.

Some schools call special meetings at which they explain to parents the new ways of learning *maths*, and actually provide a chance for parents to work through some typical maths books. If you think your child is going to be especially interested in *music or art*, then you could also ask about the teaching of these subjects; what instruments, such as chime bells, drums and cymbals, are available, and what crafts equipment, like pottery kilns, carpentry tools?

And sometimes it is possible for children to have individual teaching in instruments they want to learn; this is done either by teachers from their school or special teachers who work in several schools.

In primary and middle schools boys and girls nearly always learn the same subjects (apart from rugby if taught). But you may wonder whether, despite apparent equality, children are still being directed along traditional pathways in other, more subtle ways. Many schools still use reading books which reinforce traditional attitudes about boys' and girls' behaviour. If you would like your child to use one of the new reading schemes where boys and girls get an equal share of the action, find out what the school has available.

You may also find that boys are guided into doing 'male' projects (World Wars 1 and 2, football teams) and girls 'female' projects (historical costume, shopping comparisons). Check this out, if you are particularly keen to avoid it. You could ask the school whether they positively encourage boys and girls to do non-male and non-female projects.

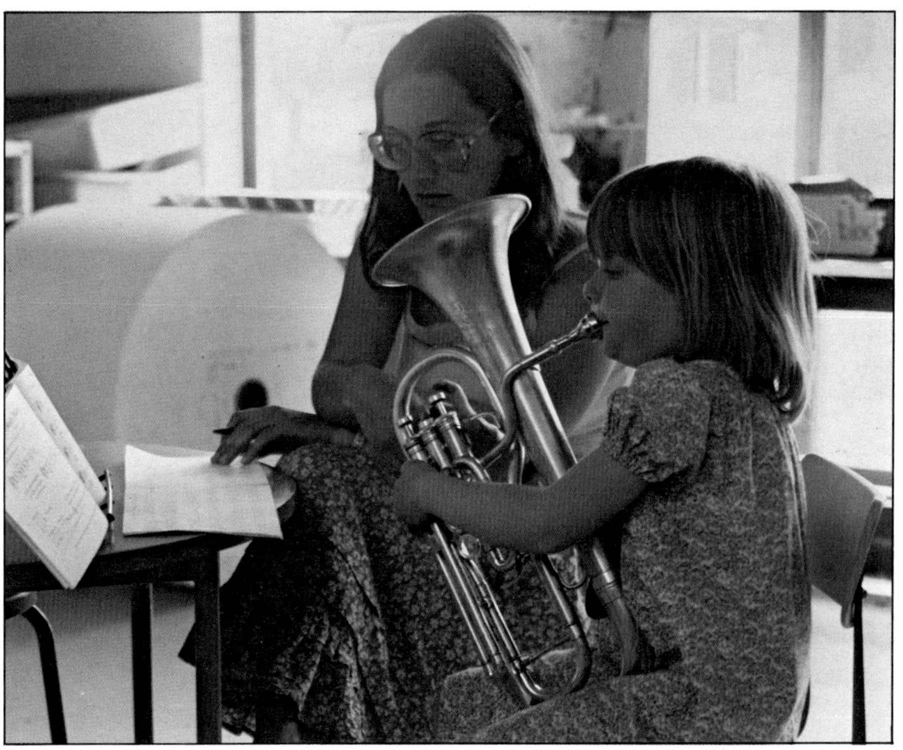

Checklist 3 The way the school works	Tick if important
Is there a set of school rules?	☐
What are the school's rules on discipline?	☐
Is homework given?	☐
Are parents encouraged to help in the school?	☐
Is there a Parent-Teacher Association (PTA)?	☐
Are there school reports? What form do they take?	☐
Are there regular school news-letters for parents, or a PTA newspaper?	☐
Do the children have much contact with the outside community?	☐
Are there open evenings/afternoons for parents to come and see children's work and talk to the teachers?	☐
What arrangements are made for children and parents to visit the school before the child starts?	☐
How old are the buildings?	☐
Are there playing fields and sports facilities?	☐
Are the school dinners popular? Are the children allowed to bring sandwiches?	☐
Is there a school library, and can children bring home books borrowed from it?	☐
Are there clubs in lunchtimes and after-hours for activities such as gymnastics, pottery, drama, sewing, orchestra, choir, etc?	☐
Are there animals in the school that the children have to look after?	☐

The way the school works

If possible, it is important to get some idea of the standard of the *discipline* at the school and how such discipline is enforced. Parents often worry because school standards differ from their own, and if the difference is very great, then the only answer may be to change schools. So almost all parents will want to get the question of *rules* – what they are and how they are enforced – sorted out to their own satisfaction. *Homework* is often given in middle schools; you may want to know how much and what the penalties are if it isn't done.

You will need to check what sort of *parent involvement* the schools really encourage before making your choice. You may think *PTAs* are vital, yet there are many first and middle schools which don't have them and don't believe they are necessary. Some PTAs are purely social and fund raising organisations; others involve themselves quite closely with the running of the school and publish a teacher/parent magazine. The head teacher will be able to tell you about the PTA, if it exists, and further questions can be answered by the chairman or secretary of the PTA.

Find out whether the school itself sends reports or newsletters to parents, if there is no PTA. This will help to give you some idea of how much the school has thought about the importance of good links with parents.

Many schools encourage contact with the *community* – recorder players and choirs are sent to entertain senior citizens, older children are encouraged to research local history by talking to elderly inhabitants of the town and work groups may be organised to paint underpasses, remove weeds or help out with mentally-handicapped children. You may like this sort of involvement, or you may consider that children should not use valuable school time for the kind of things you do with them anyway.

Nearly all schools have *open afternoons*, and *evenings*. If you work awkward hours, you should check that these are at times you can manage. You could also check on arrangements for visiting at other times; when you want to see your child's teacher or the head, must you make an appointment? Is there one day set aside for such visits? Some schools allow parents of children intending, or considering, coming to the school to bring them to visit before starting. Some let individual families come on their own. Others invite all the parents to bring their children on the same day.

If you are hoping for your child to eat dinner at school, it would be useful to know how popular the *school dinners* are. In some schools a choice is available, and meals may be so good that normally fussy children will stay and eat without complaints. In other areas, however, food may be cooked off the premises and simply get warmed up in your child's school. So it may not be acceptable to the majority of children. Some schools allow children to bring packed lunches and eat them in the lunch hour, however, and you may prefer to resort to this.

Running *clubs* in the lunch break and after school hours is extra work for teachers, but for many children with special interests, clubs are the best thing about school. If your child does have a special interest in drawing, say, or pottery you should check on whether there is a specialist club that caters for it. If there isn't one actually in the school, the teachers may be able to tell you of one nearby.

Pet animals are to be found in most primary and middle schools. Besides the lessons to be learnt from them (where did those baby gerbils suddenly come from?), children are encouraged to take the responsibility for cleaning out their cages, taking them home at holiday time, and so on. If you are unable or unwilling to have a pet at home and are worried about depriving your child, it may be important to you that there should be plenty at school.

Checklist 4 What you might check on a visit

	Tick if important
How far is it to the school from your home? How long does the journey take?	☐
Would your child have to cross a main road to get there?	☐
How do the teachers behave towards the children?	☐
Do the children seem to find it easy to speak to the teachers?	☐
Are the children busy and do they look as though they are enjoying their work?	☐
Is there a lot of children's work on the walls?	☐
Do the children have enough space to work and play?	☐
Are the children in each class all doing the same thing, or are they doing different work, either on their own or in groups?	☐
Is there a book corner in the classroom your child would be in? A dressing-up corner? Nature table?	☐
Do the equipment and books look reasonably new and up-to-date?	☐
Does the school look clean and pleasant? Do the lavatories smell? Are they indoors?	☐
How are the children supervised in the playgound? Does the supervisor walk about and take an interest in what is going on?	☐
Does your child like the look of the school and the teacher?	☐

What you might check on a visit

The first thing you should check is *how far* it is to the school. Even if you plan for your child to go on her own, or with an older brother or sister, it is important to know how long it takes, and find out what hazards they might encounter along the way.

The rest of the questions should help you to build up a picture of the school, what it is like to be there, and whether your child will fit in. There is nothing like a visit for getting the feel of a school, but many people feel confused when looking around and forget the points they meant to check. So take your checklists!

Making your choice

When you have worked your way through the four checklists, you should have a pattern of ticks that indicate requirements that are important to you and your child. What do you do if some points are much more important to you than others?

To sort out which are the most important features of school for you, you could use the following method.

Make a chart like ours (right). List your requirements (the features you would like in a school) down the left hand side of the page. Next, rate each of these requirements for importance, on a scale or 0–4. (0 = not very important, 4 = vital.) Put all the names of the schools you are interested in across the top of the chart. Now you can fill in how the schools measure up to each requirement. Again, rate each item for each school on a scale of 0–4. (0 = doesn't meet requirement, 4 = meets requirement very well.)

To find out which school scores highest, you multiply the ratings in the 'importance' column by the ratings in the school's column. For our chart, the school ratings are as follows.

Requirements	Ashfield Primary	Baytree Combined
Should not be more than fifteen minutes' walk from home	3 × 4 12	3 × 1 3
Bright, cheerful buildings	1 × 1 1	1 × 4 4
Staff turnover should be low	2 × 4 8	2 × 2 4
Should have a happy atmosphere	4 × 3 12	4 × 3 12
Totals	33	23

So Ashfield Primary comes out better in this particular case and this exercise helped the parent who did it.

You are probably going to have more requirements of a school than are included in this chart. But you can still use the same method to make your comparison.

Requirements	Importance	Rating	SCHOOLS: Ashfield Primary	Rating	Baytree Combined	Rating
Should not be more than fifteen minutes' walk from home	Not absolutely vital, but pretty important	3	About 3 minutes' walk – very near	4	About 15 minutes' walk – about the furthest possible walking distance	1
Bright, cheerful buildings	Perhaps not essential when I think about it	1	A very gloomy old place – though not bad inside the classrooms	1	Brand new buildings and fittings	4
Staff turnover should be low	Medium importance	2	A well-established school with very low staff turnover	4	New school, which hasn't been open long enough to judge	2
Should have a happy atmosphere	The most important feature of all	4	Fairly quiet, children seemed happy and were getting on well with their teachers; seemed on the formal side	3	Cheerful, young teachers; fairly noisy, noticed one or two children wandering around apparently aimlessly; very relaxed, modern ways of teaching	3

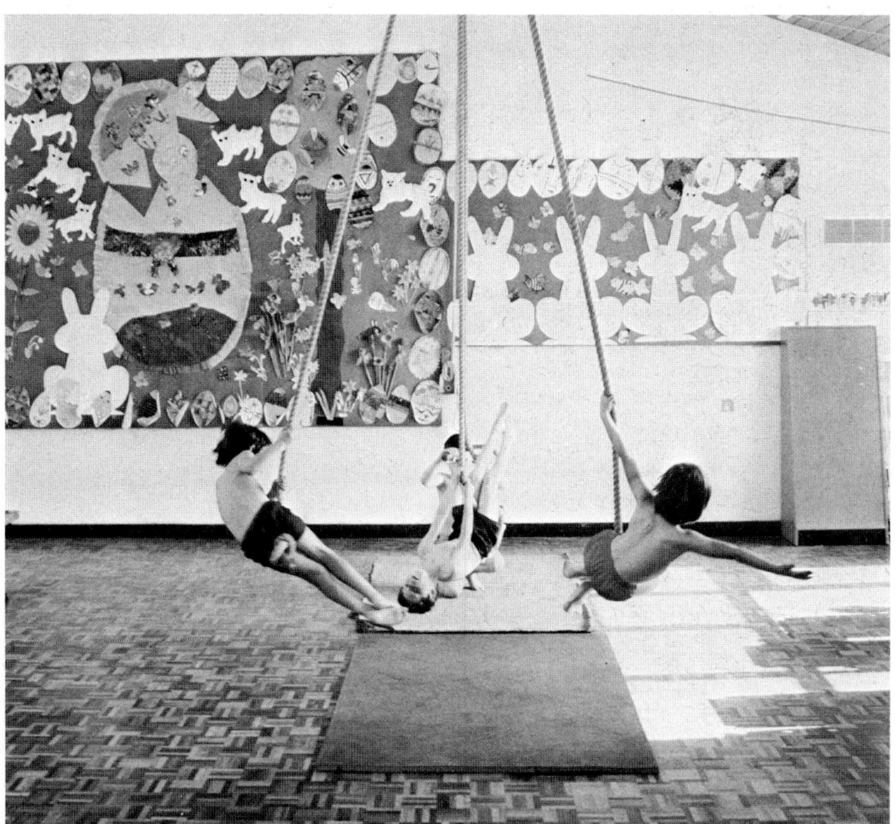

Fitting in

Look for any warning signs that your child isn't settled at school.

School occupies such an important place in the lives of five to ten-year-olds that many of the difficulties they face in life may be centred there. School demands certain sorts of behaviour from children: they have to fit into a large group, work and share with other children, keep still, keep quiet, do what they are told. The rules might not be strict but they are different from those at home.

Suddenly a child has moved from being an important person at home to being just one of a group in school. Home and school can be so different that children are often confused, and don't know how to behave.

So behaviour problems can often be caused because a child applies home behaviour in a school setting. The child may be using other conventions or rules and ignoring the school's, either because he doesn't know them, or because he has chosen to disregard them.

Behaviour problems can arise too, when a child has difficulty making friends or learning to get on with other people. Some children are very shy, others bully. In either case they haven't got the skills to get on easily with other children.

Some children have difficulties in breaking home ties. They find it hard to leave the family without distress. Or they dislike the school building, the teachers or the other children.

So behaviour problems are very different in type. But they can all be upsetting, to parents, teachers and children.

On the go all the time	□	□	□	□	□	Not active
Sleep/hunger erratic	□	□	□	□	□	Sleep/hunger predictable
Withdraws from new things	□	□	□	□	□	Rushes into new things
Unsettled in new situations	□	□	□	□	□	Adapts easily to new situations
Fusses and whines a lot	□	□	□	□	□	Easy-going
Tends to over-react by screaming and shouting	□	□	□	□	□	No very strong reactions, placid
Distractable even when interested	□	□	□	□	□	Doesn't bother what's going on around him
Loses concentration very quickly	□	□	□	□	□	Will stick at something a long time

Who will find it hardest?

Above right are a number of questions concerning the temperament of your child. Temperament is not good or bad, it is just part of our make up. But certain temperaments make it harder for children to deal with problems that others cope with easily. Look at the two statements at each end of the scale. Put a mark in the box where you think your child fits in on the scale.

Now join up your marks down the page and you have a pattern unique to your child. All children are individuals and few will have a straight line down one side of the chart or the other. But let's look at different temperament types.

'Easy' children tend to be those who are easy-going, have regular patterns, are flexible, mild in their reactions and adapt to new situations at school. They are usually well liked and enjoy life. These children don't often suffer with behaviour problems. But as they are not used to criticism, they may become sensitive to every cross or sharp word and may find it puzzling if behaviour expected at school varies greatly from behaviour expected at home.

'Difficult' children are unpredictable, often have irregular sleep patterns, don't like change and are not flexible. Their feelings are often negative and very intense. Children with this sort of temperament make strong demands on parents and teachers. Not surprisingly, they often do have behaviour problems at some time. Their particular difficulty is fitting in with the rules and expectations of family, teachers and the other children in their class, who will all find it difficult to get on with them. Children like this make others feel guilty and resentful; this creates yet more difficulties!

Children who take their time These children may be slow to adopt new ideas, and seem inflexible and negative. But given time, they will co-operate. Children of this sort may face difficulty in school if the teacher wants a quick response to something new. Parents know that such children will respond when they are ready, but teachers who are not used to them may find them withdrawn.

As parents you know your child best. It may be up to you to alert the teacher to the kind of temperament your child has and how he is best handled. You may know, for instance, that your child is generally placid, a steady worker who can normally be left to get on with things on his own. But for some reason he gets very silly whenever he is with the boy from up the road, who is also in his class. It is up to you to save the teacher time and trouble by letting her know that you think the two children are better kept separate when there is work to be done. Or your child may seem very shy and timid in new situations, but you know that she will settle down quickly as long as she sits with other little girls. She isn't used to boys yet.

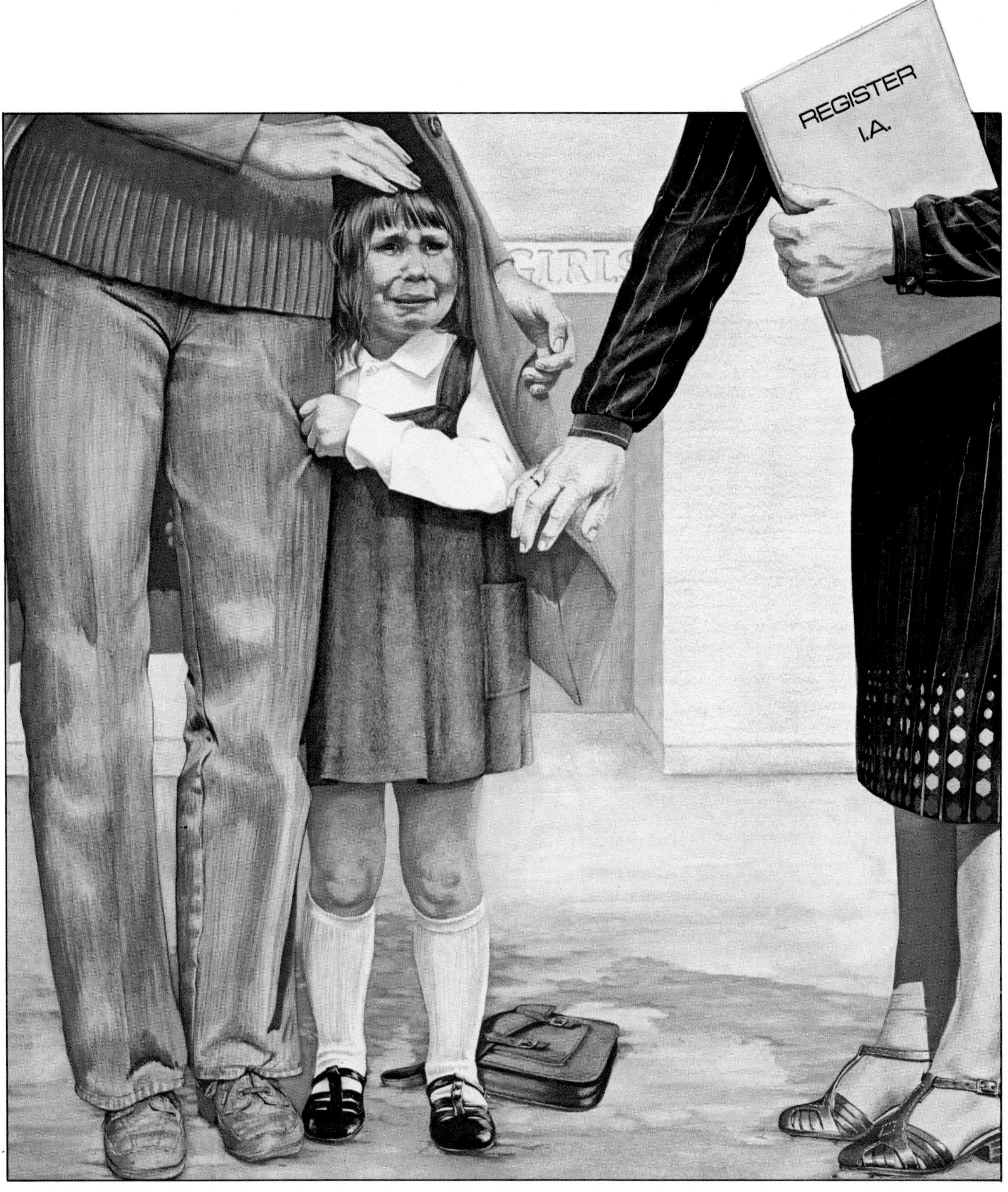
REGISTER
I.A.
GIRLS

What to do about problems

The handling of problems is as important as the problems themselves. 'Solutions' can create even more problems if you aren't careful. If, for example, Angela's mother tries to correct her daughter's lisp by making her repeat every word, Angela may become self-conscious and actually lisp more. If Nigel is stealing because he is unhappy and his mother punishes him severely, his misery and unhappiness may increase so much that he steals even more.

Parents need to understand what is behind the problem. Is it something straightforward that can be solved by a quick word with someone at the school? Is there something about home or school which is too much for the child to cope with? Is too much pressure being put on her somewhere? Is she having a lot of trouble fitting in with her class? Is there a physical problem for which you should take her to see the doctor? Or should you see the teacher for a talk? Or perhaps your child's problem is something that only time, and being at school for a while, will cure.

Not wanting to go to school

At some point in their school career, almost every child is reluctant to go to school. Feeling unwell is a frequent excuse – 'I've got pains all over,' 'My head aches,' 'I feel sick,' 'My legs won't work.' How can you tell if it's true? What should you do about it?

Here are three types of refusal to go to school.

○ **The constant refuser** There's something about school he doesn't like. It may well be a new teacher, some children who always bully him, or a new activity he can't cope with. Often it is the fear of leaving home; something awful might happen while he is away, or he worries that you will leave while he is not there.

○ **The occasional refuser** Every so often everything just gets too much.

○ **The panicked refuser** Something happened once that she couldn't cope with, and she is afraid it will happen again. For example, doing a colouring test wrong and getting told off; or dropping pants in a puddle in the lavatories.

What may help

Although it may be hard for the child to accept, time is a healer. Some things do just take getting used to, but it will help if you are sympathetic.

Talking and bringing it into the open may often be enough. The suggestions above may give you clues as to what the problem is and how you could tackle it. There are also practical measures, which you, your child or the school could try, if asked. For example, if he won't eat school meals he could start coming home for dinner; if he is overwhelmed by groups, you could encourage him to find a special friend for playtime; if he clings to you at the school gates, you could get someone else to take him to school, and have his teacher meet him there.

What doesn't help

○ Ignoring the problem. It's unlikely to go away, and may get worse. A once-off panic may turn in to a steady stream of refusals.

○ Simply allowing your child to stay off whenever he wants, without going into the problem further.

○ Sending a 'sicknote' saying he's got a cough or a temperature when he hasn't and you suspect the problem is something else. It would be fairer and more helpful to say 'he's upset', if that's what he is.

○ Making threats you won't carry out – like 'We'll have to send you away,' or 'I'll get a policeman after you.' These will only frighten the child further.

If he says he is ill...

You can check whether he really is ill by:

○ stressing the disadvantages of staying at home: 'You'll have to stay in bed *all* day, and keep very quiet – no television!'

○ watching for signs of health, like eating a hearty breakfast or running to the door when the postman comes.

○ taking temperatures, listening for coughs.

○ suggesting you'll phone the doctor.

○ sending him to school but relying on the teachers to let you know how he is once he has got there (and leaving details as to where you can be reached if they need to contact you later).

Other problems

On the chart (right) are some other problems children have with school. Check down this list to see whether your child has done any of these things. Across the top of the chart are some different suggestions for action. Tick the one you think applies for each problem.

Your reactions to these kinds of behaviour may range from annoyance to worry and downright distress.

Here are some simple solutions to these problems that you could try. If they don't work, or you feel that the cause is more complicated, you will, of course, need to make a much closer examination of the problem.

Your child . . .	See teacher to discuss	Change home timetable	Too much pressure on child – ease off at home and school	Take child to doctor	Explain to child he/ she will have to learn to cope	Discuss with child and offer explana-tions	Ignore
1 comes in from school frantically hungry and snatches forbidden handfuls of biscuits when you aren't looking?							
2 after school gets very babyish and sucks thumb or clutches teddy; uses silly baby language?							
3 throws a temper tantrum about something trivial as soon as he sees you outside the school, or on the way home?							
4 is very miserable and cries more than usual?							
5 goes to sleep as soon as she sits down to watch Playschool?							
6 follows you around the house, pestering and whinging?							
7 feels sick (may even be sick) every morning Monday to Friday but never at weekends?							
8 starts to wet the bed, which he has never done before?							
9 is outrageously noisy and rushes around frantically for some time after he has got home from school?							
10 lies awake during the evening and has difficulty in getting off to sleep at night?							
11 comes out in a strange rash and seems to have lots of allergies?							

1 **Comes in from school hungry** Could be that the child doesn't like the school dinners, or just finds it hard to eat much when there are so many other children about, who distract him. You might solve this problem by sending a packed lunch or, if you don't live too far away and are free during the day, having him home to lunch.

2 **After school gets very babyish** This is such a common reaction especially when starting school, that it can hardly be described as a problem, however odd it may seem to you. Usually improves quickly, as the child settles down at school, though he may resort to it again when problems come up at school or he changes classes. It can be really hard being grown up all the time at school, and it is his way of testing that he can still be your baby.

3 **Throws a temper tantrum** about something trivial. This can be extremely upsetting for a parent who is hoping that her child will be glad to see her after being away all day. Can also attract hostile glances from others, which doesn't help. Something has probably gone wrong at school and you should speak to your child's teacher. But it often happens that a child has been behaving extremely well at school, to get teacher's approval, and hasn't mentioned what is troubling him. It's only when he sees the familiar and trusted figure of his mother or father that all his aggressions and bad feelings come tumbling out.

4 **Cries more than usual** It's upsetting when a child dissolves into tears all the time, often over what seems like nothing. You should try to be sympathetic and listen to what your child is telling you. It often happens that she has had to fight back tears at school for fear of being laughed at, and this is the first opportunity she has of letting go.

5 **Goes to sleep** as soon as she sits down. The long school day is taking its toll! She needs more sleep than she is getting now, so move her bedtime back by an hour if you can.

6 **Follows you around, pestering** It's nice for your child to know that you are there, and that he can depend on you to listen to him, even if he has to share his teacher with thirty others. His behaviour should improve as time goes on and he learns that you haven't lost interest in him.

7 **Feels sick every morning** While it is worth checking with your doctor that there's nothing physically wrong with your child, there is not a great deal you can do about this problem. It should pass in time as the child finds out that school isn't too dreadful after all. It's important to allow as much time as possible for getting up, eating a good breakfast, getting ready for school and walking there. If sickness continues or only happens on certain days, you should check with your child's teacher that there isn't some person or lesson that is worrying her.

8 **Wets the bed** If this doesn't stop, you will need to talk to your child's teacher to find out if something is worrying him. You can also do the usual things, like cutting down on drinks last thing at night and making the child go to the lavatory last thing at night, before you go to bed.

9 **Is outrageously noisy** Another very common reaction, especially when a child is just starting school; it's hard to sit down for a lot of the day after you've been used to roaming around your house and garden as you wanted. If you decide you can't stand it any longer you could ask your child's teacher about gym clubs, football clubs, swimming clubs and other ways of letting off steam, otherwise you will have to direct him to the nearest park or open space.

10 **Has difficulty going to sleep** Children get so tense and over-excited about school, especially when they first go there, that they often have difficulty settling down at night, and then are even more tired in the morning. If you can spare the time, it is important to listen to what your child has to say about her day, and to get her relaxed and ready for bed. Even if your child has been getting herself to bed at night you could try closer supervision of her bath-and-going-to-bed routine, reassuring her that you are there and ready to listen.

11 **Comes out in a strange rash** This may be a simple allergy to something at school, which you can check with your doctor. But many children with a tendency to skin complaints come out in a rash at times of stress, such as starting or changing school. It is particularly hard if other children notice it and make nasty remarks about it, so try to cover it with long sleeves or trousers until it subsides. With any luck it will go away as the child settles down.

Parents and teachers

It isn't only children who have to adjust to school. Parents have to adjust too. Suddenly they are sharing the care of their children with someone else – a teacher.

Parents and teachers see children in different settings so they form different relationships with them. This list summarises the very different relationships of the parent with her child, and the teacher with the child.

Parents feel responsible:	Teachers feel responsible:
twenty-four hours a day	for fixed hours only
for everything a child is and does	for child's behaviour and performance in school only
for doing their best by their own children	for doing their best by a classroom of children

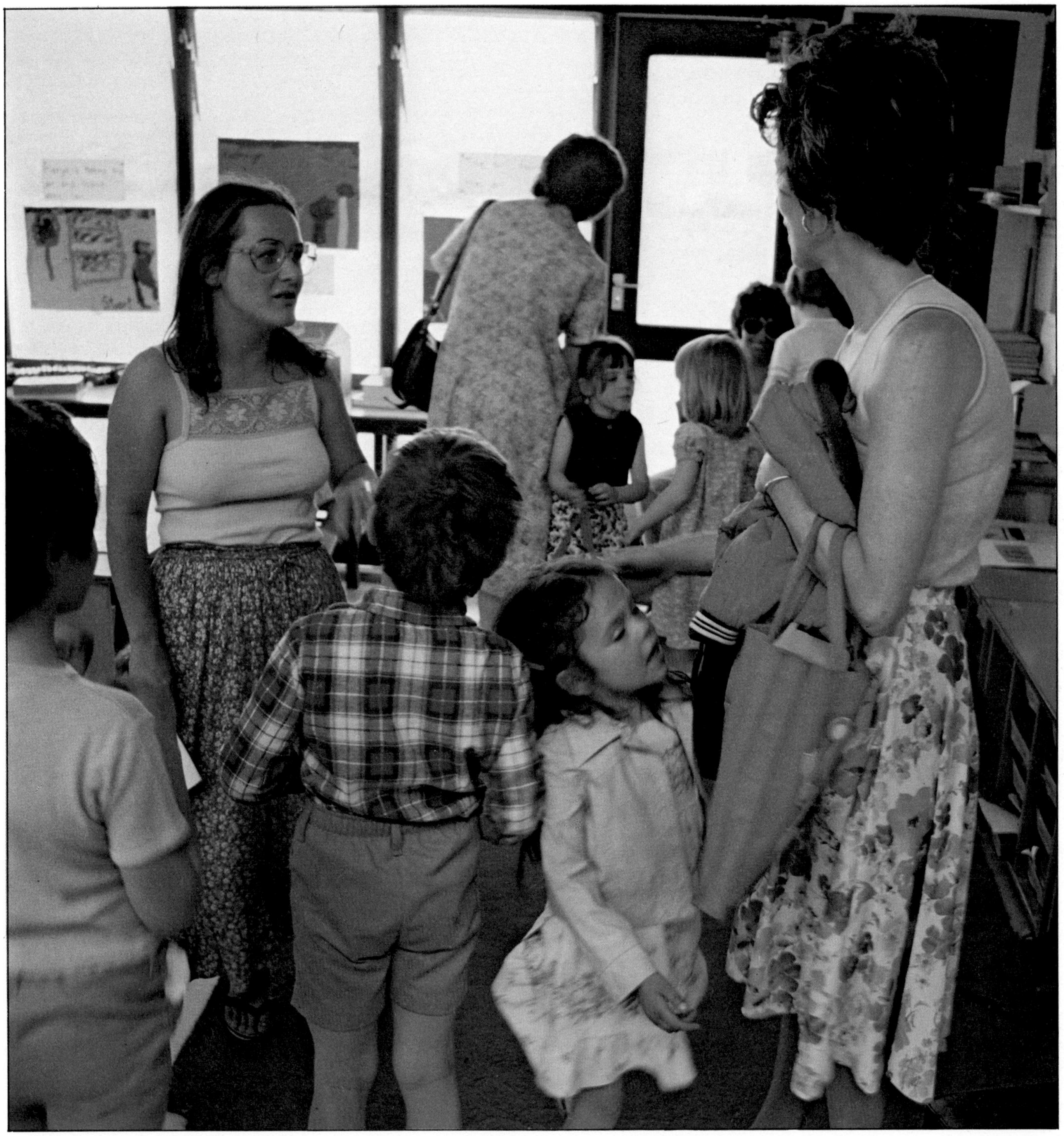

Parents' emotions are:	Teachers' emotions are:
strongly felt – whether stormy or tender	not as intimate, more distanced and formal
always there	there only until child moves into another class
rapidly changing – from anger to affection	more evenly balanced

Parents are:	Teachers are:
concerned first of all with the needs of their own child	concerned first of all with the needs of the group as a whole
tolerant of individual habits	trying to help children fit into a group
biased towards their own children	trying to be fair and impartial

Understanding each other

Children learn very quickly that the worlds of home and school are different. Behaviour in one is not always acceptable in the other. This can lead to misunderstandings when the two worlds meet.

For instance, children rarely throw tantrums at teachers. They soon learn that teachers expect children to control themselves. Parents are more tolerant of individual quirks and ways of expression. So children may throw a temper when both parent and teacher are present. They're bringing 'home' behaviour into public. The parent feels embarrassed and tries too hard to calm the child.

If the teacher has to take over, the mother feels she has failed. She leaves, and the temper stops. What is teacher's magic? Nothing. When the parent goes, so does 'home'. The child switches to 'public' behaviour for teacher. It leaves the parent feeling bad, and the teacher feeling good. Both misunderstand each other and miss the real point; the roles are different and the child knows it.

Learning to live with teacher

Both worlds are important to the child, and they work best if they work together. Sometimes it seems as though teacher can do no wrong and is the only adult who matters in the world, as far as your child is concerned.

This is a stage that passes. Learn to live with it. Teachers are a very important part of a child's life. A child's first class teacher is probably the first adult he has a close relationship with outside his family. This may lead you to experience some tension. For instance, you may fear you are being robbed of your own special position in your child's life.

Look at the occasions below. How would you react in each instance. Ring the letter that most closely matches your own. And then look at our ideas about what it is you are doing.

If your child . . .
Tells you something teacher says which you know you've told him, which of the following do you say?

a 'Teacher knows it all, doesn't she?'

b 'Mmm, that's interesting.'

c 'Haven't you heard that before?'

Asks if he can take something to show teacher, what do you say?

a 'She won't be interested in *that*'

b 'Yes, I'm sure she'd like to see it.'

c 'If you *really* want to.'

Comes home and tells you how Miss A got really angry with a friend, what do you say?

a 'That was horrid of her.'

b 'Well, maybe she had a reason. What do you think?'

c 'Well, your friend *is* very silly sometimes.'

Tells you that Miss C 'doesn't do it that way' when you're reading together, what do you say?

a 'Well, she's too good for me.'

b 'Tell me how she does do it, then.'

c 'Well, if I'm reading, we'll do it this way.'

The **'a'** answers put your child's teacher down. The **'b'** answers accept her and the **'c'** answers are neutral; they don't especially encourage or put her down. Your child will probably pick up your feelings from your answers.

You probably marked a mix. If your child is happy, don't spoil it. You can discuss Miss A without adoring her – as your child will come to do in time. Letting your child know you're fed up with her teacher can be unsettling. It doesn't make any of you feel better.

You and your child's teacher should be allies. You both want the best for your child. So let her know what your child says about school – it gives her an important insight into your child's home world. The more a teacher knows about the child's home world, the more sympathetic she can be towards the individual child at school.

Ask the teacher how your child behaves in class. Is she noisy and boisterous, or quiet and subdued? It will help you to understand your child's behaviour at home if you know what is going on at school. The more you both know the better.

Trouble with other children

Unless your child can stand up for herself, playtime can be hell.

Playgrounds are a natural place for children to show off developing personalities. Children of five do this in a very different way from children of ten.

Children of five to seven

○ are becoming more self-assured and confident.

○ often show off how independent they are.

○ are often boastful about what they can do.

○ need other children to play with and so they cooperate (but once they've had their turn they may want to go off to another game).

○ like competitive games where everyone is against everyone else and one person wins.

○ like to have a chance of being star turn, whatever's going on.

Children of seven to ten

○ cooperate more in games, and put 'the team' before themselves.

○ are less self-centred and more interested in the outside world.

○ want to be like other children of their own age and do the same things.

○ want to achieve things just to prove they can do them.

○ begin to accept 'leaders' and children with leadership qualities emerge.

All these traits have a chance to show themselves in the playground. Playgrounds are crowded and there are ways in which people in crowds act differently from when they are on their own. Children show 'crowd behaviour' in the same way that adults do.

Research has shown that:

○ they tend to be more emotional

○ they act less responsibly in a crowd than normally

○ they form themselves into sub-groups.

So don't be surprised if you hear reports of your child's behaviour in the playground which just don't fit with the child you know at home.

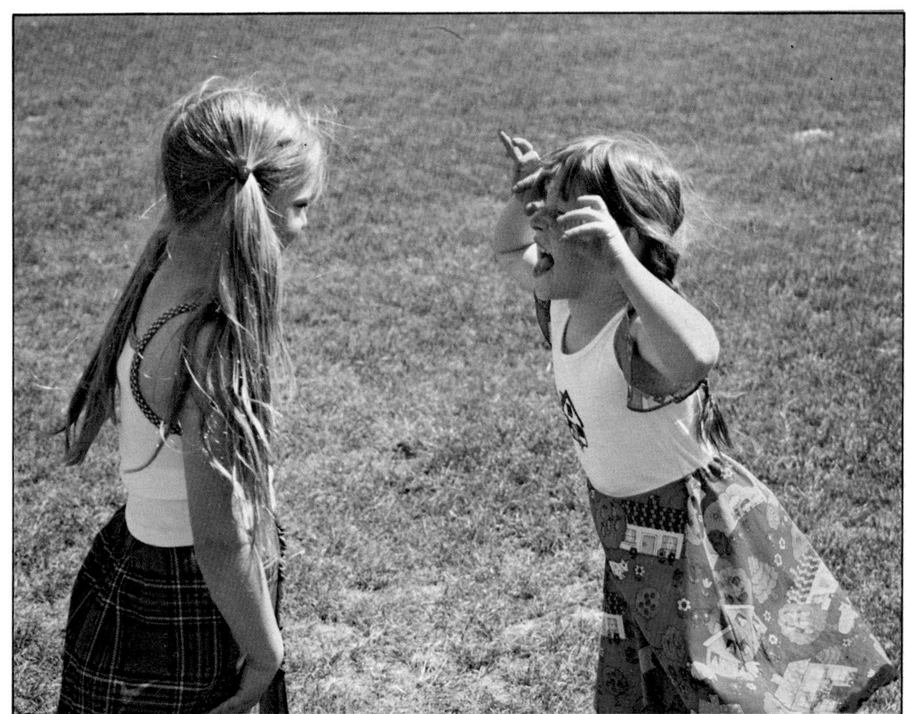

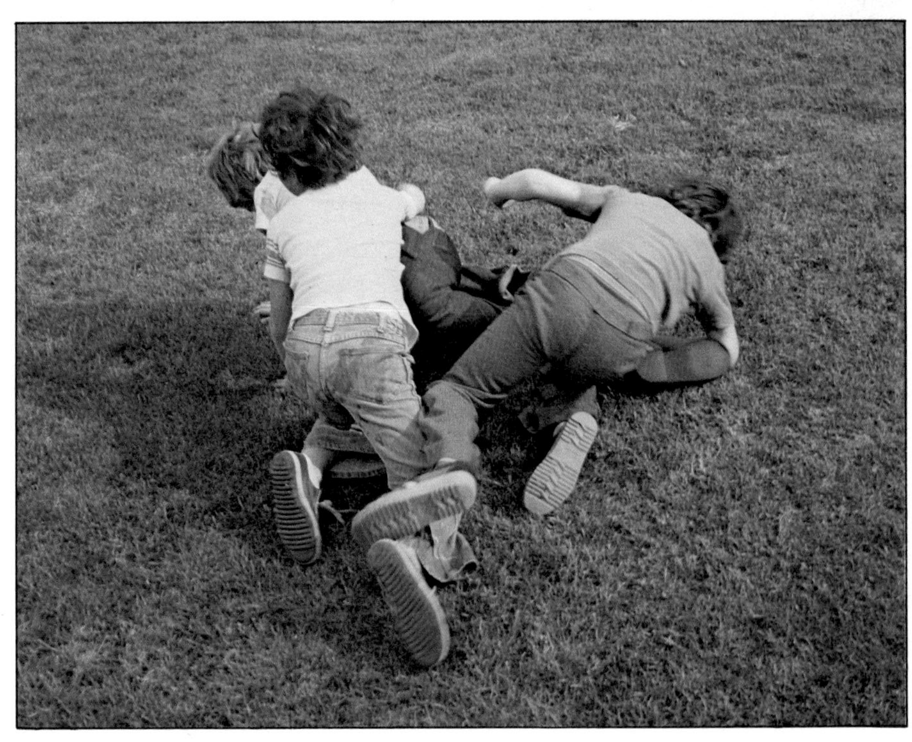

What do you think about children who:	Afraid of	Admire	Despise	Not bothered
A				
often say 'give me that'?	☐	☐	☐	☐
give dirty looks and stick tongues out at other children?	☐	☐	☐	☐
make up lies and get other children into trouble?	☐	☐	☐	☐
start a fight over nothing?	☐	☐	☐	☐
push and shove other children?	☐	☐	☐	☐
say mean things?	☐	☐	☐	☐
B				
fight well?	☐	☐	☐	☐
get what they want by fighting?	☐	☐	☐	☐
pester until they get what they want?	☐	☐	☐	☐
C				
say 'excuse me' even though they haven't done anything bad?	☐	☐	☐	☐
never get into a fight, even when picked on?	☐	☐	☐	☐
talk their way out of awkward situations?	☐	☐	☐	☐
Manage to distract children who want to fight with them?	☐	☐	☐	☐

Coping with fights

On the chart above are some questions to help you find out how children feel about their classmates and fighting. Use them in talking to your own child about what goes on between lessons and in the playground, and how he feels about other children's behaviour. Listen to what he says and then tick the appropriate columns.

A questions refer to children who are in the habit of being aggressive.

B questions refer to children whose aggressive behaviour has been successful.

C questions refer to children who avoid aggression at more or less any cost.

If you look back at the list you'll get some idea of the sort of behaviour your child admires. This may not, of course, be the same as his own behaviour. He may be a child who avoids aggression, but secretly wishes he was more of a success at getting his own way by fighting; or he might be a trouble-maker who would rather be naturally 'good'. How can you help your child to find the best way to cope with aggressive behaviour from other children?

Unfortunately one child may pick on another precisely because he knows his opponent doesn't know how to deal with aggression.

You could suggest that your child try to use some of the techniques he admires in others, always provided you admire, or at least tolerate them, as well. But if he gets bullied too often, you might want to draw on some of the ideas we are going to look at next.

Bullying

Bullying means taking advantage of someone else's weakness; knowing that they're afraid and upset and using it against them. Some children are brought up in a world of rough-and-tumble and when they become parents are naturally rough with their own children. This isn't really bullying because they don't do it out of malice – though quiet children might think they do.

Why some children are bullies

○ Perhaps for a child who finds it hard to make friends, frightening another child is less lonely than having no contact with anyone.

○ A child may be fighting back in some way against unhappiness at home. If she's always being put down there she may assume that this is an acceptable way for her to treat others. Or if she is jealous of a younger sister, she may take her feelings out on someone smaller at school.

○ A child may be under stress. His normal behaviour doesn't get him anywhere or solve his problems so he tries different tactics.

○ A child may feel inferior and have to try and prove he is better than his friends by bullying children who won't stand up to him.

Why some children are bullied

○ A child who is bullied has not learned how to defend himself.
○ A child may unconsciously encourage others to bully him, if that is the only attention he gets.
○ A child may be an innocent scapegoat; she might have arrived at school at a different time from everyone else, have a physical characteristic that is easy to pick on, or just look or be different from the other children.

Dealing with bullies

For the parent whose child complains of being bullied, it is necessary to find out exactly what is going on. You should check straight away with his teacher, to see whether she has noticed anything. You may also need to see the people who have been supervising the playground lately, to see what they have noticed. If the bullying has taken place *out* of school, but the children who did it go to the same school as your child, then you still need to speak to the teachers.

Clues

A consistent story from a child about being bullied is likely to be a true one. A change in a child's attitude to school may also back up the truth of his story. Suddenly he doesn't want to go to school at all. He wants to stay in at playtime. He wants his parents to start fetching him home from school again.

But he may refuse to say who the bully is. This doesn't mean he is lying. It means he is really frightened of him. Check with any friends or brothers at the same school whether they have noticed anyone treating him badly.

Once the truth of the story has been accepted, what then?
○ Make sure that the school has all the facts, and that they are going to do something about the bullying.
○ Give your child some guidance on how to behave so that bullying does not happen. For instance, tell him to keep within sight of the teacher in the playground. Or to keep within his own group of friends.
○ See the family of the child who is doing the bullying if this is possible without getting into a fight with them as well.

Helping your child

If your child goes on being bullied, not just by the original villain, but by his friends, or by other children who have noticed that your child is easy prey, it becomes even more important to help your child break out of this particular vicious circle, and learn to deal with bullying from others. Tell him that bullies get frightened too. He may not believe this at first but soon it will reassure him.

How do parents feel?

Some parents really don't mind too much about having their children bullied and some parents of bullies are quite proud of them. But many parents worry when their child comes home full of complaints of being hit or insulted. But he himself may have forgotten about the whole incident in half an hour; just telling you about what Tony Green did at afternoon break may be enough. If you rush off to see Tony Green's mother your child may be embarrassed and upset, and nervous about facing Tony Green the next day. On the other hand, Tony Green's behaviour may have become so outrageous that someone – probably the school – needs to put a curb on it. Try not to feel that it is *you* under attack. It's your child who is suffering and since you can't go to school with him and watch over his every move, it will be much more helpful if you can help him to handle the situation better on his own.

Name calling

There are other laws of the playground which are more subtle than bullying but perhaps as hurtful. Between the ages of five and ten children are developing their own ideas about the right way to behave and this shows in playground play. These rhymes and descriptions are part of a collection taken from many parts of the country. Look at them. Which ones do you remember from your own childhood? Ask your child about the words and rhymes used in her playground. Children are reluctant to talk about names that other children call them. This may be a way of drawing your child out.

Trouble-maker, trouble-maker
Fetch a pan and a cake we'll make of her.'

'Roses are red, violets are blue
Lemons are sour and so are you.'

'You're daft, you're potty, you're barmy,
You ought to join the army.
You got knocked out
With a brussel sprout.
You're daft, you're potty, you're barmy.'

'What's on the bread today? You with
I-N-G on the end.'

'You'd better watch that head of yours…
it's getting so big it will blow off
your shoulders one day.'

'Ask no questions and you'll be told no lies
Shut your mouth and you'll catch no flies.'

'Cowardy cowardy custard
Can't eat bread and mustard.'

Names children might get called
Crosspatch, randy baby, clever dick, know-all, bats, batty, crackers, dopey, goofey, cuckoo, bighead, peabrain, copy cat, swank-pot, toffee-nosed.

Other worries at school

While parents worry most about bullying and aggressive behaviour, there are other things that may upset or worry your child. Do any of these problems sound familiar?

Noise If children are always running about in class, your child might find the constant hum of conversation and the sound of feet walking to and fro and noisy equipment too much for him to concentrate.

Bad behaviour Because some children are badly behaved in the class, the rest of the class is included in the punishment; they are *all* kept in, or deprived of their story. The majority of children are well behaved at school, and the disruptive few can upset the obedient many.

Other children It is not just teacher's pet who is disliked by other children; children who get attention for other quite justifiable reasons, such as being handicapped, can be distracting. Often, such a fuss is made of a disabled child by other children and perhaps by the teachers that another child can be upset by it – and then feel guilty about feeling that way. Your child may also resent being bossed about by some slightly older child who has been appointed as monitor or captain.

Differences The other children in your child's class may say she's different because she is fat / thin / clever / stupid / posh / shabby. For one or more of these reasons she gets left out and is made to feel even more different from the others.

These are all problems associated with getting on with other people. While some of them could be solved by consultation with the class teacher (a quieter place to work, a word with a bossy monitor), most of them are part of the process of learning to get on with others, which all children have to go through. But being thought 'different' is a hard one, which many children never solve. If your child really is fat, spotty or clumsy, don't say, 'You'll grow out of it.' She is concerned with *now*. Suggest an easy diet or a spot lotion, so that at least she can feel that something is being done.

Making progress

How is he getting on? Do you know how to get help for problems at school?

When you are asked 'How is he getting on at school?', what do you immediately think of? The chances are, if your child has just started school, you will think about how he has settled in and how happy he is there. But, by the time he is seven, most parents are measuring progress in terms of what book he is on, whose group he is in, how well he is reading.

Children catch on quickly too – they soon know how to gauge how well they are doing. By ten, children know their 'place' in the class and often quite accurately – they may well be in ability groups. You often used to be able to tell where you were in a class by where you sat. But ideas change, and schools no longer encourage open competition. Class positions are not read out. But many parents, and some teachers, brought up to be aware of the top and bottom of the class still think in those terms. Their attitudes towards progress and the emphasis they put on it will affect the child.

Achievement and progress are important to every parent and child. Everyone wants to do well and denying the importance of achievement is unrealistic. Parents' attitudes towards such matters directly affect children because every child cares what parents think – they want to please. The right amount of encouragement will help a child develop and do well, but too much pressure can cause worry and tears and actually hold a child back. Do parents sometimes put the wrong sort of pressure on their children?

Great expectations?

Most people reckon that they do all they can to pass on the best of their aims and ideals to their children. But the child may get a different message entirely. He may end up doing almost the opposite of what the parents wanted. Do any of the statements sound like what you have said about your child?

'I'm very keen that my child should take full advantage of all her opportunities and do better than I did at school.'

'I'm really not bothered about how they do in school – no one in my family has ever done well there.'

'If he doesn't come top I do get worried as I know he can do it.'

'Really, all I worry about is whether they're happy or not. After all, they're only young once.'

'I think that if they do show talent, then you owe it to them to do the best you can and spend as much as you can afford on lessons and equipment.'

Parents who want more from their children than they achieved themselves can often unintentionally pressurise their children too much. Later on, pressure may backfire; the compliant, achieving child may reach the end of his tether and turn into a rebel – thus causing unhappiness all round. Children want to please but they want to be themselves too and this can mean something very different from what parents expect.

Parents who expect failure often encourage it and have children who fulfil their worst fears. Research shows that children who are expected to do well do better than those who are not expected to do well, regardless of their true ability. If parents fear educational success for some reason, then their children will not disappoint them.

'Nothing but the top is good enough' is a demand any child will find hard to meet. Telling children they are capable is one thing, expecting them to prove it all the time is quite another. Fear of failing may actually cause a child not to try at all. Or an unusually bad result may cause unhappiness completely out of proportion to its real importance.

'I just want you to be happy' allows a child to develop at his own pace – with modest encouragement. But if a parent is too relaxed about expectations and discipline, the child may be completely out of step with the school. A child has to learn to concentrate on a task and fit in with the rest of his class doing it.

Exceptional talents are quite rare but many parents seize on early signs of talent and work on them, to the exclusion of other, equally worthwhile gifts the child may possess. The child may come to hate the thing he is so extra good at, as it stops him joining in and giving time to other things that are fun.

Who is it all for?

The parents of the children in the following examples all have one thing in common: they think they are trying to do their best for their children. But is it really the children they are thinking about? Look at the questions and tick the answer you think is right.

Stephen, aged ten, wants to be a builder like his dad. But his dad says *'No, you can do better than that. You need qualifications these days.'* Stephen is puzzled because his dad didn't have any qualifications: he had started as a labourer on a building site and now he is a foreman. Stephen thinks that's fine, but his dad wants more for Stephen. He says he must work hard and pass a lot of exams.

What is Stephen's dad really telling Stephen?

You must do better than me. ☐

I want you to be like me. ☐

There is plenty of time to decide. ☐

Victoria, aged eight, has parents who are teachers. Imagine their surprise when Victoria, who still hasn't learned to read properly, says she hates books! They read to her, buy her books, play every imaginable game to help her learn. But Victoria is still far behind her classmates.

What message is Victoria getting?

We want you to like books and reading like the rest of the family. ☐

We don't mind as long as you're happy. ☐

You must try harder. ☐

Graham, aged nine, works very hard and does very well but his parents expect him to come top of the class. His father says, *'You've got a good brain, we expect you to use it.'* In a spelling test Graham got nine out of ten. His parents wanted to know why he got one wrong and told him he must do better next time.

What is his father saying?

Being top is most important to us. ☐

Do your best. ☐

Enjoy your school work. ☐

Theresa, aged eight, likes swimming and the instructor at the swimming pool said she has a strong stroke. That was all the encouragement her father needed to have her there every night practising. He saw her as a local junior champion in a couple of years, competing in national championships in five. Theresa likes swimming but she would like to do other things as well, like Brownies. But her father tells her not to waste the opportunity she has.

What is he saying?

I never had the chance I'm giving you. ☐

It is important to be good at something. ☐

Develop talents to the full. ☐

What are they really saying?

The mistake the parents here are making is in assuming that what *they* want is the same as what their own child wants.

Stephen's father is saying, 'do better than me' – and behind it is a wish for Stephen to have the success his father would have liked. In moderation those kind of sentiments are fine; every parent wants his child to do well. But they don't take account of the individuality of each child.

Victoria's parents were doing the same thing. They assume that Victoria, being their child, must enjoy the same things as they do. Victoria is reacting against this pressure to read by refusing to learn and, in doing so, asserts that she is an individual and not just like everyone else.

Graham and Theresa are both being pressured by parents' need for success and achievement through their children. Graham's parents want the cleverest, most able child and Theresa's father wants an exceptional child. They think they are helping their children but underneath they want it for themselves. They are using their children to achieve for them. It may be they had parents who didn't show that kind of interest and they want things to be different.

Does it do any harm?

Direction, guidance, pressure are all part of the same process. Parents are always involved in influencing their children's lives. It cannot be otherwise. Leaving a child to make all his own decisions is as harmful as not allowing him room to make any. So, as with everything else parents have to find the balance and avoid the pitfalls of extremes.

What progress?

It is natural to want to know what the teacher makes of your child: how he is doing, what he is good at or not. There are three ways of finding out.

Talking to the teacher is the most obvious and often the most satisfactory. Parents' evenings are a suitable time, but there may be a lot of other parents wanting time, too. Teachers tend to be diplomatic and will say very general things, unless they are especially worried about something. If you want to know particular things, then you will usually have to ask. If there is a real difficulty, then the school should contact you.

School reports come once a year, or maybe at the end of each term. There are also school records of your child's progress kept by the school, which you could ask to see if you are worried. Nothing in a school report should come as a *complete* surprise to a parent; if there is something totally unexpected, then you need to discuss it with the school.

Talk to your child and find out how he is getting on. Listen to him reading. Ask what he is doing in school, what project

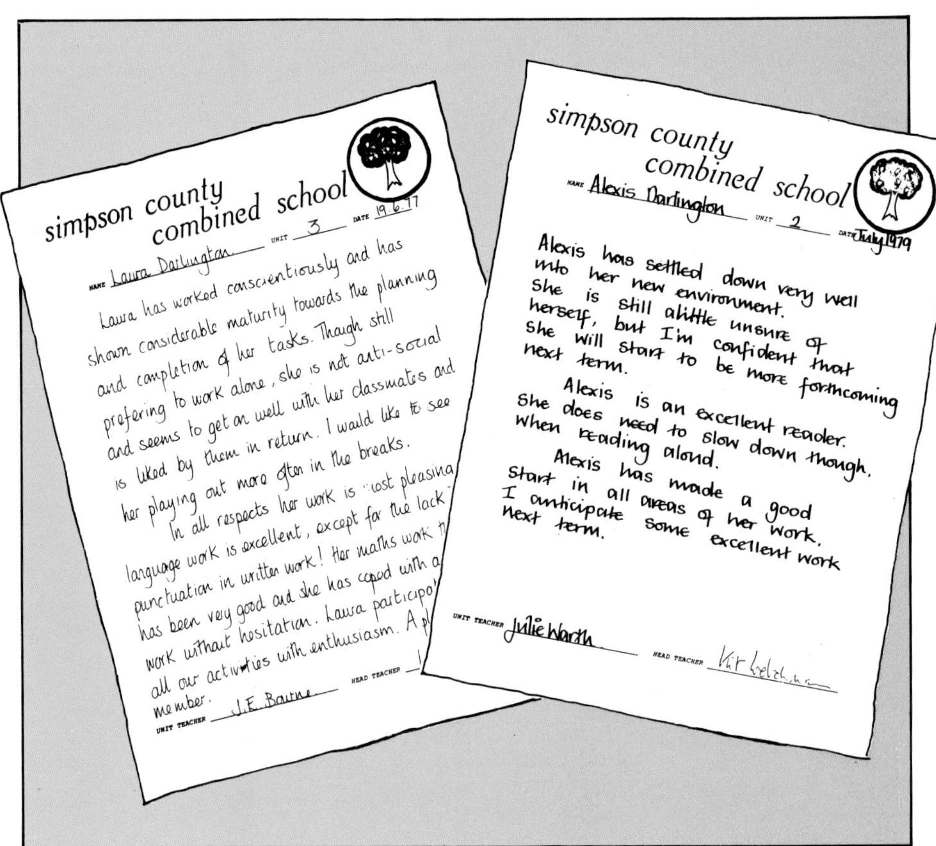

simpson county combined school

NAME Laura Darlington. UNIT 3 DATE 19.6.77

Laura has worked conscientiously and has shown considerable maturity towards the planning and completion of her tasks. Though still prefering to work alone, she is not anti-social and seems to get on well with her classmates and is liked by them in return. I would like to see her playing out more often in the breaks.

In all respects her work is most pleasing language work is excellent, except for the lack punctuation in written work! Her maths work has been very good and she has coped with a work without hesitation. Laura participa all our activities with enthusiasm. A pl member.

UNIT TEACHER J.E. Bourne HEAD TEACHER

simpson county combined school

NAME Alexis Darlington UNIT 2 DATE July 1979

Alexis has settled down very well into her new environment. She is still alittle unsure of herself, but I'm confident that she will start to be more forthcoming next term.

Alexis is an excellent reader. She does need to slow down though, when reading aloud.

Alexis has made a good start in all areas of her work. I anticipate some excellent work next term.

UNIT TEACHER Julie Warth HEAD TEACHER

work he is engaged in and what group he is in.

How is progress assessed?

All children in school are subject to different sorts of assessment. *Informal assessment* is going on continuously. Teachers are making judgements all the time about when to introduce new ideas and how each individual is getting on. Does he need more help? Could he do with more practice or is he ready to move on? Assessment is a positive, useful way of fitting the teaching to the child's needs.

Formal assessment in schools means a test carried out by the teacher, with individuals or a group. There are a number of different standardised tests used by teachers to find out more about how children are doing in maths, reading or spelling. The questions in these tests have been tried out on thousands of children. Results for your child can be compared with results for other children in his age group, and can give an accurate picture of how he compares. Some teachers give special tests to identify a child who is having difficulty, so as to be able to give her extra help.

Psychological testing

This is normally done by an educational psychologist, and parents will usually be told beforehand. The school asks for a psychological test when they are worried that a child is not learning satisfactorily or think that there may be some emotional block. All kinds of children, from very dull to very bright, may be asked to see an educational psychologist at some time.

Educational psychologists have all taught ordinary children as well as doing a specialised training in psychology. They work in schools and clinics and are concerned with learning and behaviour problems of school children. They should not be confused with psychiatrists who are medically trained doctors.

Psychological testing is a way of assessing a child using standardised intelligence tests and (possibly) personality tests to get an independent view of the child. The psychologist can say what level of intelligence a child has and in what specific areas of learning he has difficulty. He may also be able to suggest suitable teaching approaches that would help.

IQ tests, as intelligence tests are often called, may show how intelligent a child is without relying on things learnt at school. There are several tests available and the psychologist will pick the one he thinks most suitable.

Intelligence tests have several sections, testing different abilities. One of the features of the test is that it is very different from anything done at school every day. Children who have achieved almost nothing in school may score highly, and thus show that they do not lack intelligence. They may not be learning for other reasons, such as dislike of the classroom or fear of competition from other children.

But IQ tests are only used as a guidance for the psychologist. Their assessment is based on talks with the child and the parents too.

Other problems

Learning problems will be dealt with by the school; but parents and school usually need to co-operate to help solve behaviour problems, and problems involving other children.

Listed below are brief details of the jobs of half a dozen important people to be found at school. Ask your child about the same sort of people and teachers in *his* school and what he thinks they do.

Your child may be very clear about what the first three people do, but be less clear about the others. It's worth finding out whether he knows how the different people he meets every day could help him.

Description of person	Description of their job	How could they help me?
Head teacher	Responsible for the curriculum and internal organisation of the school; defines rules and decides what kind of discipline there should be	Can tell you about matters affecting the school as a whole, and should have a good idea of most things that are going on
Class teacher	In charge of class	Can discuss your child in particular, especially day-to-day problems which are worrying you
Dinner ladies	Serve out dinners and (sometimes) supervise at dinner time	Can tell you whether your child is eating dinner or not
School secretary	Answers phone, writes letters, takes dinner money	Can give you information about school holidays, trips, make an appointment with the head, etc
School caretaker	Looks after the building, heating, cleaning, etc	Can help you if anything is lost in the school grounds; when you need to get in to school after hours; or with any question to do with the school building
School welfare assistant	Looks after sick children, helps out generally	Can help or advise you on any health problem to do with your child

Other helpers

Besides the people listed on the chart, there are many other adults whom your child is likely to meet in school, mostly on an occasional basis, but sometimes regularly. She may not mention these people, either because she doesn't think you are interested, or because she's forgotten, or didn't think there was anything special about that person, or because she doesn't want to talk about the encounter for some reason. But some thirty different kinds of people might visit your child's school during the school year, and while some (like the fire officer) are concerned solely with the school, many are concerned with parents as well, and could help you to solve problems concerning school.

Some visitors come to look after your child's health (doctor, school nurse, dentist etc); others to entertain (musicians and actors, Father Christmas); and some to help with welfare problems (the education welfare officer) and behaviour problems at school (the educational psychologist). There will also be a miscellaneous collection of student teachers, parents helping with cookery, craft work, hearing reading, perhaps a representative of the school managers and inspectors, either Her Majesty's Inspector or a school adviser.

Here are some people you might want to contact.

The educational psychologist

We looked at part of this person's work in the last section. While the educational psychologist may be called on by your child's school if they consider this necessary, you are also able to make a direct approach if you have a problem that you don't want to take to school. Your doctor might also refer you and your child. The educational psychologist is usually based at your local child guidance clinic and you can make contact or leave a message for him there.

If you are desperately worried about something your child does – stealing, temper tantrums, bedwetting for example – and cannot solve the problem yourself, then you may want to approach the educational psychologist.

The education welfare officer

You can track the education welfare officer down through your local education office, through the school, through the social services department or even through your local Citizens Advice Bureau. While the education welfare officer often comes to schools in connection with truancy and absenteeism, you can also get help from her on welfare benefits – free school meals for instance.

School governors

When your child joins the school you should get a list of the school governors. Otherwise you can get a list from the local education office.

You might consult a school governor, particularly a parent-elected school governor, about general problems in the school. Perhaps you think that there is too much bullying, or that the playing field is unsuitable for the children to use. While school governors are not paid for the work they do, they take a strong interest in the school and ought to take an interest in your worries.

How many people help?

Although a problem might look very simple, and you might assume that only your child's teacher would be concerned, more people than you may realise may be involved in solving it. Opposite is a list of problems, and a number of people who might deal with it. Put a tick for each person that you think might be involved in each problem.

Who was involved?

1 If you have noticed that your child isn't hearing you all the time, or his teacher says he doesn't seem to be taking notice when he should, the teacher could ask the school welfare assistant to have him tested by the school nurse. You might also want to have him tested by your own doctor. He might be suffering from another form of deafness (ie, doesn't bother to listen to mother or teacher) or he might actually need treatment.

2 If your child is suspected of breaking into the school after hours, both her class teacher and the head teacher are going to be involved, as well as the caretaker. This may not be considered a serious crime at this age, but with frequent offenders and older children the police might be called in too.

3 Some children are particularly interested in subjects such as science and electronics which are not really covered at school. If the class teacher and the head consider that it would be a good idea for your child to have the opportunity to do extra work of this kind, they might call upon the school adviser that specialises in this particular subject.

4 You would need to check with the class teacher and with the school welfare assistant whether your child was *really* being sick at school, or just telling you to get extra attention. Dinner ladies and the school nurse might also cast some light on the subject. You might want to have him checked over by your own doctor if he really is being sick so often.

5 Dinner money has to be handed in to the class teacher or to the school secretary so you would need to inform these people first. If the money were lost in the school grounds, the caretaker might be able to help.

6 If your child's reading is a long way behind that of most other children in her class, the class teacher will probably call you in to discuss the problem with you, and the head might be involved. They may call on the remedial teacher, if there is one, and may suggest that she be assessed by the educational psychologist.

7 If you are worried about school children doing damage, you need to speak first to the head teacher. If the damage were to the school the caretaker would be involved and if the problems were very serious, the police might be called in. If you feel that vandalism is getting out of hand you could also approach the school governors and ask them to discuss the problem.

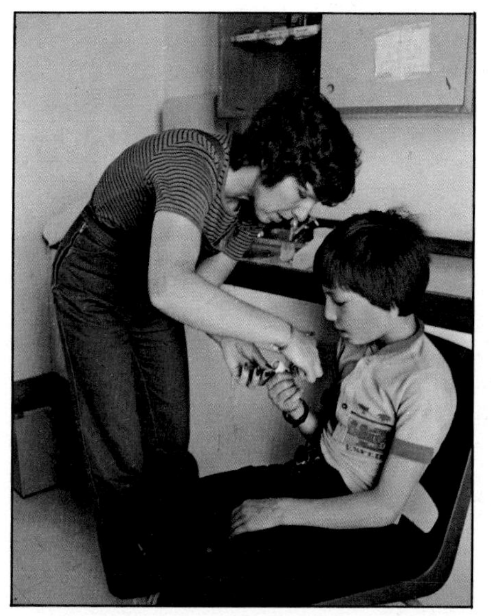

School problem	People												
	Head teacher	Class teacher	School secretary	Welfare assistant at school	Dinner ladies	Educational psychologist	School nurse	Your own doctor	School governor	School adviser	Caretaker	Police	Remedial teacher
1 Child seems to be deaf	☐	☐	☐	☐	☐	☐	☐	☐	☐	☐	☐	☐	☐
2 Child suspected of breaking in to school during evening	☐	☐	☐	☐	☐	☐	☐	☐	☐	☐	☐	☐	☐
3 Very bright child with interest in science, which cannot be met at middle school	☐	☐	☐	☐	☐	☐	☐	☐	☐	☐	☐	☐	☐
4 Child complains of being sick frequently at school	☐	☐	☐	☐	☐	☐	☐	☐	☐	☐	☐	☐	☐
5 Child has lost dinner money somewhere on school grounds	☐	☐	☐	☐	☐	☐	☐	☐	☐	☐	☐	☐	☐
6 Child's reading is well below that of the rest of her class	☐	☐	☐	☐	☐	☐	☐	☐	☐	☐	☐	☐	☐
7 Parents are worried about vandalism by school children	☐	☐	☐	☐	☐	☐	☐	☐	☐	☐	☐	☐	☐

Approaching the school

Both you and your child will benefit from close home/school links.

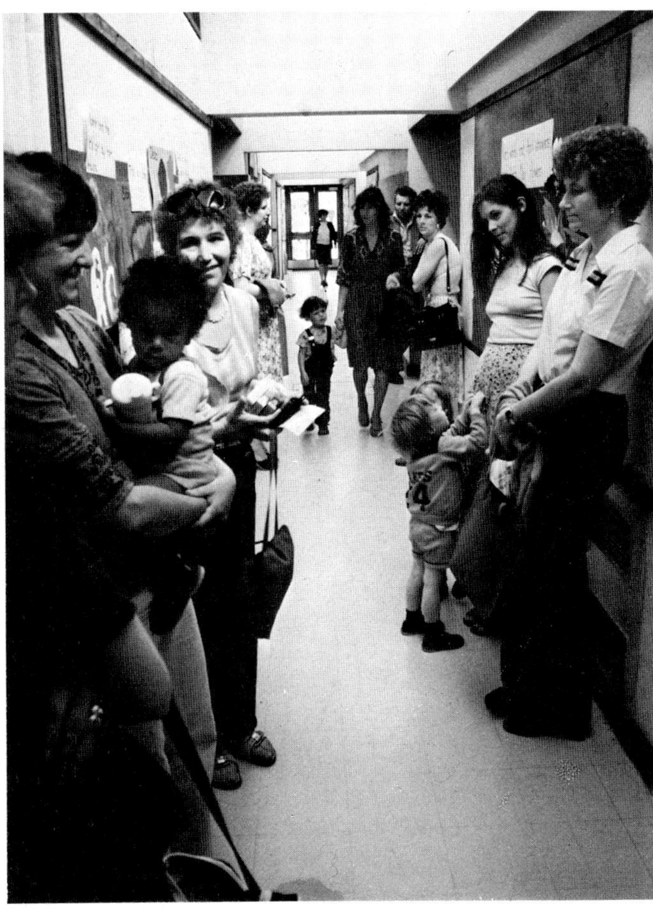

Good co-operation between home and school really does help children's progress in school. Parents and teachers want to get on with each other and yet it is not always that easy. What is more, not all schools are equally welcoming. When do you think you should approach the school?

- ○ If the children are ill?
- ○ If they are not attending for any reason?
- ○ If you are having problems at home?
- ○ If you are worried about his progress?
- ○ If he seems unhappy?

Why do parents stay away?

Often parents keep away because they themselves did not do well at school, and they are still nervous of teachers. They think of themselves as failures at school, and so they feel like naughty school children, rather than responsible parents, when they go there.

Another reason for not going into school is a fear of seeming over-protective and fussy! 'Up there, they just think I'm a pushy parent, and if I'd just leave Karen alone, she'd be fine. They make me feel like a real nuisance, sometimes, but I wouldn't go there if I wasn't really worried.'

Yet another reason why some parents find it hard to get to school is a genuine lack of time. Parents who go out to work find that visiting the school doesn't fit in easily. They make the effort to go once a year, to parents' evenings, but anything more may be difficult.

Another problem is that teachers often have difficulties when it comes to talking to parents. They may be very good with children but not so good at reassuring anxious parents. The parents then get put off going.

This is one example of how a parent and a teacher felt about a parents' evening.

Parent	Teacher
'I go along to Terry's class and there's this girl who's wet behind the ears just out of college and I feel nervous – I think she's going to laugh at me, so I don't say nothing.'	*'Parents can make me feel really small – it's as though they're thinking, "What do you know about children that makes you good enough to teach my kids." I hate parents' days.'*
Parents feel	**Teachers feel**
○ in awe of teacher	○ judged by parents
○ afraid to seem as though they're looking for favouritism	○ can't admit they don't know it all
○ powerless to affect what happens	○ threatened by parents' more intimate knowledge of their child
So they:	**So they:**
○ tend to talk about what really worries them only with other parents, not with the teacher	○ tend to keep parents at arms' length

It doesn't have to be this way, but it does mean putting both time and effort into the home/school relationship.

Is it worth it?

Look at the list (right) of advantages of good home/school links and the effort that needs to be made to achieve them. You can add to both from your own experience.

If these home/school links are made, there will be additional advantages for child *and* parent. The child will tend to do better at school work. The parents will find it easier to talk to the

Advantages of home/school links	Effort required
Child will feel happier at school knowing that parents think it's OK	Parent needs to make time to show an active interest in school work
Child will find that school problems are easier to bring home	Parent needs to make time to talk to child about school
Child will find school more understanding of his home background and special needs	Parent needs to take time to visit the school and talk to teachers

school about problems at home and will also feel more in control of their child's education.

The 'advantages' list is mostly advantages for the child, while the effort list is entirely effort the parent needs to put in. By thinking about the items in both lists, it may help to work out whether the time and effort spent on developing a good relationship with the school is worthwhile for you and your child.

Doing your own homework

Some parents feel shy when they go to talk to teachers. They can't get their questions out or they can't get the answers they really want. They are also frightened of looking foolish if they haven't got their facts right.

If these sorts of things worry you, it will help if you prepare what you want to say beforehand, as far as you are able. Obviously the whole interview could take an entirely unexpected turn, but if you have written down the most important points you want to raise, and have devoted some thought to how you are going to put them to the teacher, everything should go well.

If, for instance, your biggest worries are that your child hates games and dreads every PE lesson and that she is complaining that she is bored by the series of reading books she is on, then you could write down those two points, in case you get distracted by the teacher talking at great length about her craft work and where she is in maths.

Going in to school

If you can visit the school, this is probably best because it is a chance to get to know the school and teachers better. Going personally shows the school you are really interested and you get an immediate response to any questions or problems. Schools usually welcome parents of children in the five to ten age range.

If this is what you are going to do, then *choosing the right time* is important. Many schools have a time when they especially welcome parents into school. It may be at the beginning of the day or at the end. Find out by asking other parents, looking at the notices in the school for parents, or asking the teachers or the school secretary.

Telephoning the school

It is always worth making a special appointment to see the teacher if you have an important query, such as a problem or worry about the child, and you know you want time and privacy to discuss it. Teachers are grateful if they know beforehand, so they too can prepare for a discussion.

Telephoning also comes in useful for letting school know if your child is ill or has to have time off for the dentist or for quick inquiries about times and dates of outings.

Don't always expect to speak to teachers as in school time they are usually busy teaching. The school secretary can usually tell you about practical matters.

Writing a letter

This is a formal first approach but, if you feel nervous, can be a good way of starting. It is a way of making contact and lets the school know you are concerned. A note to the teacher may be the best way of saying you are worried about something or would like to meet.

When the school contacts you

You may fear the worst and think your child is in trouble and you will both be blamed. The result of feeling that way is that you go in ready to defend yourself and your child, feeling very angry and upset. These feelings can make it difficult to hear what is being said and even more difficult to have a constructive talk. You will, of course, feel nervous, wondering what it is all about and, if possible, you should take the child's other parent with you. But there may not be anything wrong at all. Schools are always looking for ways to help children more and it could be a question of suggesting an eye test or extra help for something he finds hard or a special class for something he is really good at. The reason for asking to see you is to get your help and opinion before making any decisions about your child.

Home link teachers

Many schools now have teachers with special responsibility for making links with parents. They may be called home/school liaison, or home link teachers and they will call to meet parents in their own homes at least once in the school year. Their time is limited, so use it usefully to discuss problems or ask questions that concern you.

Getting involved with the school

Your child's school needs you more than you may realise.

Different schools offer different opportunities for parents to find out more about and help with the school. Look at the ones we list in our chart. In the first column tick those that you have heard about at your child's school. Then, in the next column, tick the ones that you and/or your partner have been involved with in some way.

Ways to be involved with/ informed about the school	My child's school offers this	Partner and self involved with this
School events: fair, jumble sale etc. Entertainments put on by children	☐	☐
Open days: to see how school works	☐	☐
Parent evenings: to meet teachers	☐	☐
Parents helping out with cookery, reading, crafts, etc	☐	☐
Regular letters from school asking for help	☐	☐
Parent-Teacher Association (PTA)	☐	☐
Parents allowed to go into school when they want to consult with teachers	☐	☐
Becoming a parent school governor	☐	☐

If you have not been able to tick many of these activities, the chances are that your child's school does not encourage parents to be involved very much. How happy are you with this situation? Would you like the chance to be involved?

If you've ticked plenty of facilities but few ways in which you and your partner are involved then you are the sort of parent that your child's school is keen to encourage. Why are you uninvolved? Do you feel unhappy with the sorts of things the school asks parents to do? Do you think it makes little difference whether you are involved or not? Or are you just short of time?

Choosing what to do

Here are some ways parents can help at school.

○ By giving their time.

○ By using various skills.

○ By collecting things that the school needs.

What good does helping do? It shows a child that the parent is interested and involved in what he does. It helps the school and provides chances to do things socially that are enjoyable. It also helps build up knowledge about the school within the community.

Opposite is a list of some ways of joining in with the school and involving yourself, plus a number of considerations which may affect what you think about these activities. Tick the considerations which are important for you, for each activity. Of course, you may well be doing some of these things already. And if you're happy, fair enough. But if you're not entirely happy try going through the list to see if it helps you pinpoint what you are not satisfied about. It may be that there are other activities going on that you would find more interesting than the ones you are involved in.

Columns 1–4 show what you think the activity actually involves, in terms of time and organisation.

Columns 5–7 show which activities you are unlikely to join in with.

Columns 8–9 show how much importance you place on your own enjoyment of activities for the school.

Columns 10–11 show which activities you are likely to undertake because they benefit someone else.

If you haven't done any of these activities you may find your opinion will change when you do become involved. What seems like bossy organising from the outside may actually mean that things get done without anybody having to do more than their fair share.

School events
Most schools have open days, sports days, plays and jumble sales. You may not have much time to spare, lots of people don't. But these sorts of events don't happen very often. If you attend things like this you are helping the school and you will probably enjoy yourself as well. The audience at school events is part of that event and an important part at that.

Helping directly
If you do have some time and feel inclined to help, you are a valuable asset to the school. Some schools now have parent helpers and assign them to help with a different class from that of their own children. If you do this, you'll get close contact with and learn more about what goes on elsewhere in the school, which is useful.

The school should take some trouble to find out exactly how you could use your skills in school to the best advantage. This could mean helping with cooking or craft work, sorting out the school library, listening to children read (particularly interesting, as you learn more about the reading schemes in use) or pacing round a playground calculating how many strides it takes to cover certain distances. You could help on a regular basis, or you could come in occasionally for a special project – a talk about astronomy, say, or help with photography or a recording for the local radio station.

Some parents are good at setting up and organising parent groups, to represent the school to other people. Other parents are talented at working with children socially, getting up a club or running a play scheme after school. A school that encourages parental involvement will find ways of using all these sorts of skills.

Helping in school can also give you ideas for things that you can do with your child out of school too and an opportunity to try them out first.

Activities	1 Takes only a small amount of time	2 Takes a lot of time	3 It involves doing organising	4 It's fairly official	5 Takes too much time for me	6 It's too organised for me	7 It's too official for me	8 I find this interesting	9 It's enjoyable	10 I think it helps my child directly	11 I think it helps the school generally
Doing things for PTA (manning stalls, collecting jumble)	☐	☐	☐	☐	☐	☐	☐	☐	☐	☐	☐
Being on the committee of the PTA	☐	☐	☐	☐	☐	☐	☐	☐	☐	☐	☐
Being a parent helper	☐	☐	☐	☐	☐	☐	☐	☐	☐	☐	☐
Going to parents' social evenings	☐	☐	☐	☐	☐	☐	☐	☐	☐	☐	☐
Being a parent governor	☐	☐	☐	☐	☐	☐	☐	☐	☐	☐	☐
Running an out-of-school activity (chess club etc) for children	☐	☐	☐	☐	☐	☐	☐	☐	☐	☐	☐
Helping with raising money	☐	☐	☐	☐	☐	☐	☐	☐	☐	☐	☐
Collecting things for the school	☐	☐	☐	☐	☐	☐	☐	☐	☐	☐	☐
Helping to build things (swimming pool, animal centre) for the school	☐	☐	☐	☐	☐	☐	☐	☐	☐	☐	☐
Editing a school/home newsletter	☐	☐	☐	☐	☐	☐	☐	☐	☐	☐	☐
Taking parties of children to school activities in your car	☐	☐	☐	☐	☐	☐	☐	☐	☐	☐	☐

How do you feel about school?

Most parents have quite strong ideas about what schools are for. These ideas do shape what they are prepared to do at and for the school. But whether the school is encouraging or hostile also determines what they do. Here are some examples of how parents may get involved with schools.

Shaw Street School
Mary and David Jones are closely involved with school. David runs a judo club. Mary helps with the PTA, and they are only two of the many parents who are in and out of Shaw Street during the week.

Linda and Paul Hunt are both quiet and have never been involved much with the school. Lots of things are going on all the time, but they only go when they're invited, usually at open day and for the Christmas play.

Kensington Road School
Carole and Gerry Webb are keen to be involved with the school. However, the head refuses to have a PTA. Any discussions about the school Carole and Gerry have are with other parents, outside the school.

Christine and Derek Jenkins have only once been any further than the school gate. The school does not like parents in the school and they were even made to feel they were intruders at the school sports day.

If your child's school is like Kensington Road, you may feel you want to change things. How about a meeting with other like-minded parents and then arranging as a group for a meeting with the school?

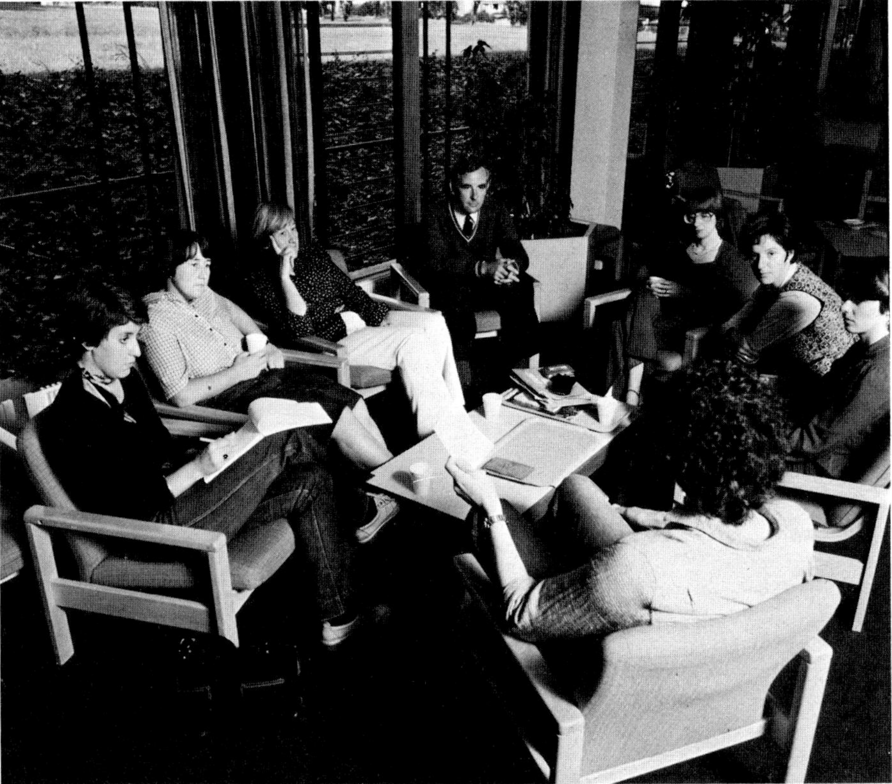

Parent-Teacher Associations (PTAs)

What do PTAs do? Well, it varies a great deal. The aim of most is to develop good relations between home and school. PTAs arrange meetings between parents and teachers to talk informally and they also hold social events of all kinds. They do a lot of fund-raising, usually for 'extras' for the school, but occasionally for vital things that are beyond the school's budget. They run school/parent newsletters, and will probably organise special discussion meetings if there are proposed cuts to the education service or when teachers are considering industrial action. If your school has a PTA it might be concerned with some or all of these things.

But not every school has a PTA. Some head teachers think PTAs mean interfering parents. But even some teachers who are keen on parents joining in also have objections. Here are some of the objections that have been voiced against PTAs.

○ PTAs are run by a small in-group of middle-class, articulate parents who don't represent the others very well . . . and so other, less confident parents are scared off.

○ Some head teachers only allow PTAs to act as a fund-raising body, but not to be really involved in the life of the school.

○ There is nothing a PTA could do that isn't already being done in the school.

○ The PTA might try to interfere with the running of the school.

If these are objections which *you* have been faced with, you could argue that PTAs work for the benefit of all the children at a school, not just for the children of the committee members. These committees are elected annually and it is possible for any parent to be nominated and elected. It is true that some head teachers like to keep the PTA's activities strictly limited to certain func-

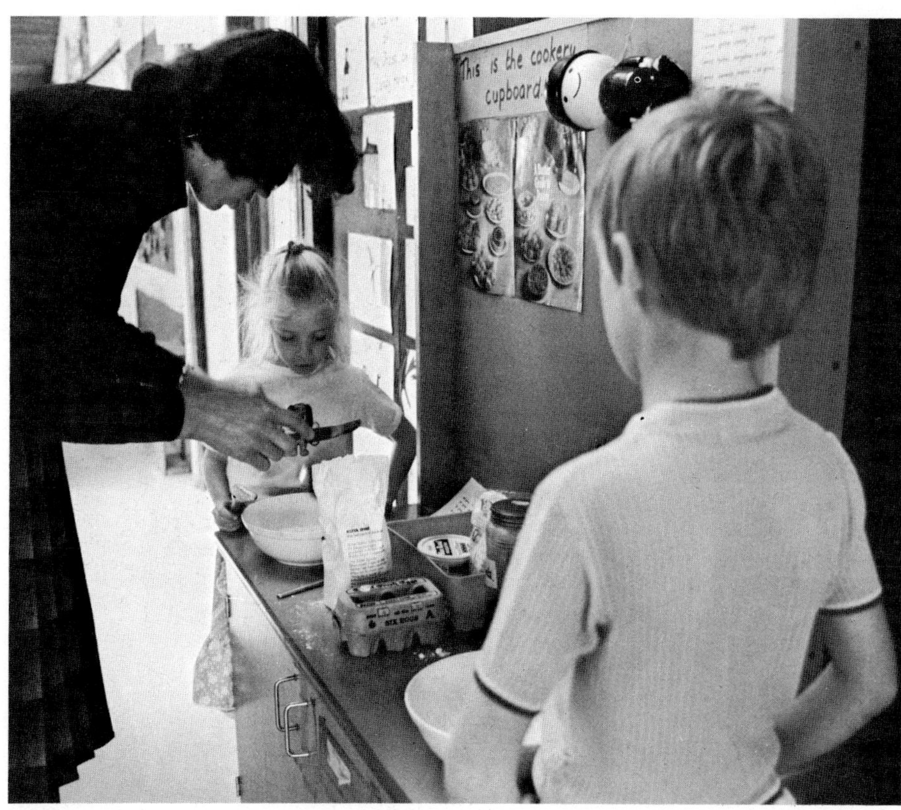

tions when they are first set up but, once they get to know the PTA committee, they usually respond to sensible suggestions and allow the PTA to take over more responsibility.

Most modern head teachers are in favour of PTAs. But a few heads take it as a personal criticism when parents ask for a PTA. In this case it can help if parents who have been involved in successful PTAs at other schools can show exactly how useful a PTA can be in doing uncontroversial things like fund-raising, which are nothing to do with teaching or running a school.

If the school says no?

So far we've looked at opportunities for parents to join in where schools are happy for them to do so. But what can you do if you are keen to help, and your school isn't interested in parents' involvement? It very much depends on how bold you are.

If you're bold You could go and ask the head teacher what he thinks about the matter. Find out exactly what his objections are to setting up a PTA or allowing parents to come in to hear children read. You will need a lot of patience and will need to be very determined. It helps if you know that several of the teachers are on your side. It's also worth enlisting the help of the school governors, local councillors and the local church if it is a church school. *However*, if the school isn't happy about parents being involved and you get nasty, you'll just go to prove the point that parents are awkward.

If you're not so bold You can chat to other parents – on the way home from school, at the local pub – places where you can have a useful talk without feeling overwhelmed by the school. If you have a serious worry about the lack of a PTA and other ways for parents to get involved, then the chances are that other people will be worrying too. Find out what their worries are.

As suggested earlier, you could perhaps have a meeting together and then approach the school with your ideas, as a group. Choose someone who *is* bold to act as your spokesman.

What do school governors and managers do?

Can you list five things which you think governors and managers have to do?

Not easy, is it? In fact, their responsibilities are laid down by law in documents called *articles of government* (for secondary schools) and *rules of management* (for primary schools). Each local education authority has such documents for all its schools and although these vary from one to another, the duties of governors and managers usually include:

○ general oversight of the conduct and curriculum of the school.

○ participation in the appointment, promotion and dismissal of staff.

○ deciding dates for the school terms and holidays.

○ overseeing finance and approval of budgets and estimates.

○ suspension of pupils.

To carry out their tasks effectively, governors and managers have to be in the know. They are there to represent the views of the community to the school and to help the school present itself well to the community, particularly to parents.

Membership of school governing bodies usually changes after the local elections. Remember that parents can elect their own representatives, so it is important you find out how, when and where the elections will take place. Go along and vote and, if you know of suitable parents, put their names forward as candidates. If you are really interested, why not get someone to nominate you as a governor?

If you are already a school governor or about to become one, you may like to know that the Open University has produced a short course to help train you for this role. Details of the course *(P810 Governing Schools)* are available from The Associate Student Central Office, The Open University, Walton Hall, Milton Keynes MK7 6AA.

Out and about

How does your child see the community that he lives in? Gradually, between the ages of five and ten your child builds up a working knowledge of his local community and the way that it fits together. To begin with he may only be concerned with things of immediate interest to him. But don't underestimate what he sees; they may not be things you would have noticed yourself but they do give you important clues as to the eyes with which he sees the world around him.

The environment is not just something he observes, though; he is involved with it too. As he gets older he'll probably start joining organisations and groups, choosing what he wants to do, trying things out. Such involvement has other spin-offs besides keeping him happily occupied. He will be learning new rules of behaviour and codes important for his safety. He will become more familiar with the ways of doing things that make moving about in the community both safe and enjoyable.

As a parent you will have a lot to do with this increasing involvement your child has with the community. As he gets older you probably won't be supervising as much but you will be able to provide him with a fund of ideas that he can act upon himself. The more you encourage him to think about what's going on around him, the more information he'll have to act on.

This chapter is about some of the starting points for your child's involvement with the community and how you can help him decide what he's going to do and how to go about it. It also suggests some ways that you can build on his own likes, dislikes and inclinations so that he begins to see that there are many things the community offers him – and many things he can offer to it.

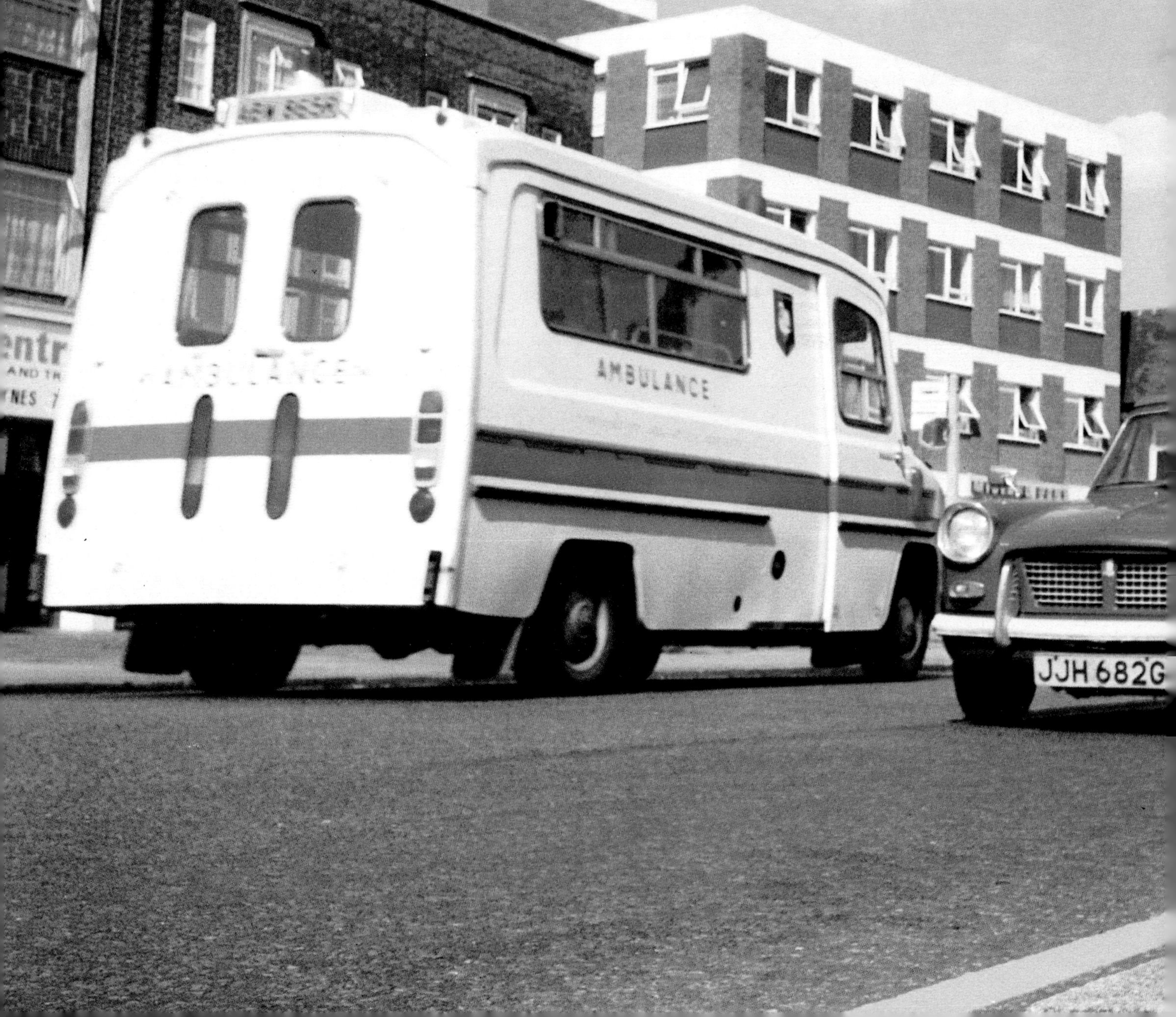

7

People . . .

There's so much for your child to learn about all the people he meets.

Everyone tends to put labels on other people. 'Joe is a milkman.' 'Paddy is my neighbour.' Labels are a way of reminding oneself of useful information about others. But sometimes labels can get in the way. Instead of helping, they stop people from seeing new and different sides of the 'labelled' person. You may be surprised to find that your milkman is the county chess champion, for instance. Your child may be equally surprised to find that her headmistress also has a family.

Your child probably uses labels already. What are they?

○ Start by making your own list of some of the people your children know. Try and include in it people from different areas of your child's life at home, in school, in the community – for instance, people in local shops or the doctor's surgery. The list can include people she may not know by name but sees often such as the milkman and the postman.

○ Show the list to your child and ask her to add to it people you have left out. She may need some help. Get her to think of people she's met in the past week, the past month, even the past year.

○ Cut the list up so that each name is on a different piece of paper.

○ Ask your child to make four piles of names. (If she has some difficulty in reading all the names you'll need to read them out to her so that she can put them into the right piles.)

People I see every day

People I see at least once a week

People I see once a month

People I only see every few months

○ Also ask your child to make several groups like this.

Children/grown ups

Male/female

Family/friends/others

People who have jobs/people who don't have jobs

People whose houses I know/people whose I don't

People whose names I know/whose names I don't know

○ When she has got used to the idea, play a game. Pick out a group of people and ask your child what they have in common. Here are some possible groups you could use.

People I know at school	Neighbours
Family	Women
Local shopkeepers	Children

○ Now change over and ask your child to make a pile of the names of people who have something in common. You then guess what it is and then she tells you what she had in mind.

This person is . . .

So far, mainly, you've asked your child to show you groups of people who have one thing in common (for instance they are all women). But for most of the people on your list your child will know several things about them.

So now write down on separate pieces of paper the various ways of grouping people that you've already talked about. Use either differently coloured paper, or a different coloured pen and then you won't mix them up with the papers that have people's names on.

Here are the labels that Carol and her mother used. You and your child may have used others.

This person is family	I know this person's name
This person is a friend	I don't know this person's name
This person is male	I know where this person lives
This person is female	I don't know where this person lives
This person is a child	I see this person most days
This person is an adult	I see this person once a month
This person is a neighbour	I see this person only a few times a year
This person has a job	
This person doesn't have a job	

Now ask your child to pick one person from her list of names and to select all the coloured labels that fit that person. Look at Carol's way of doing this. Her mother wrote these labels on a sheet of coloured paper and cut them up into separate pieces. Carol then placed them into two groups, one for her grandad and one for the newsagent.

Grandad Smith	Newsagent – Mr Perkins
This person is male	This person is male
This person is adult	This person is adult
This person is family	This person has a job
This person doesn't have a job	I see this person most days
I see this person most days	I don't know where this person lives
I know where this person lives	I know this person's name
I know this person's name	

After she'd done this Carol wanted to make up more labels, other things that she knew about her grandad and the newsagent. You will find out that your child is able to put together quite a lot of information about other people.

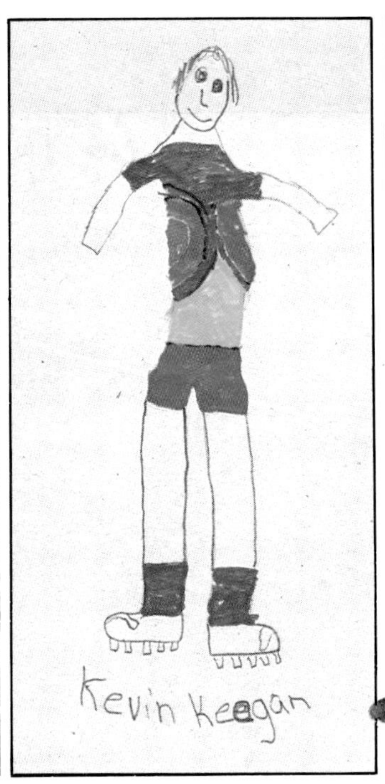

Appearance and character

You have looked at your child's view of the people around her. As she gets older the labels your child uses will change. They will be more about what people are actually *like* than simply what they do or where they live. The older children are, the more detailed the descriptions they're likely to give.

Aged 5/6	Aged 7/8	Aged 9/10
If your child mentions character she is likely to use simple words: 'She's a nice lady.' 'The teacher was cross'	Your child will probably include more character words mixed up with descriptions of other features: 'The rabbit is soft and furry.' 'That man looks sad'	Your child will probably have started talking about people's reasons for doing things as well as what they're like: 'Teacher was cross today because the weighing scales were broken'

Famous people

All this labelling doesn't just apply to people your child has met. She is also forming ideas about people she hasn't met . . . famous people, people whose jobs and lives are shown on television and in magazines and newspapers.

Try asking your child about some of these people.

The Queen
What is she like? What does she do? What does she eat? Where does she live? Does she get paid a lot?

The Prime Minister
What does the Prime Minister do? Where does she live? Does she get paid a lot?

The captain of a football team
Does he only work on Saturday afternoons? What does being captain mean?

The newsreader on television
Where does he find out about the news? Does he write it? How do people get to be newsreaders?

The Pope
Where does the Pope live? What does he do?

Who are these people?

When we meet or see someone new, we start forming ideas about them. Everyone forms opinions about people on first sight.

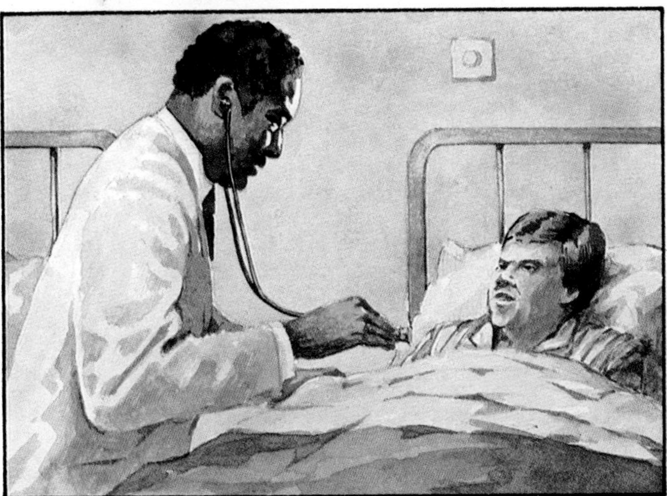

Look at these pictures with your child and ask her to tell you about the people in them. Remember that children of different ages will have very different descriptive powers. A five-year-old may give you a very different account from a ten-year-old. If you have more than one child in this age range, compare what they say about the pictures.

Some of the things your child might have mentioned about the various pictures are:

○ uniforms

○ the jobs that people do

○ people's ages

○ where people are

○ people's colour

○ the sort of things that people have with them

After you've got your child's initial reaction to the pictures, you might like to find out what she has to say about each of the things on this list. All these provide clues about people. They are all part of finding out about someone. But sometimes adults, once they have these clues, don't bother to find out anything else. They already have a firm idea that all people who wear uniform or all people of a certain colour behave in a certain way. They lose their sense of curiosity about people. Finding out can be fun, and for children it's an important part of their development.

Let's watch TV

Nearly everyone sees television, newspapers and magazines nowadays. A child doesn't have to wait to meet a nurse, a policeman or an Asian before forming her ideas about these people. So it's often inside your own home that your child will get a very strong impression of how other people live and what their outlook on life is. When you watch TV with your child you can find out a lot about her ideas.

A typical day's TV will show news about many different places: comedy programmes about a department store; a hospital; programmes about the police; detectives; a film set in Scotland. Pick out some television programmes that your child watches and watch it too.

Ask your child to describe to you what the people in these programmes do ... and then talk about any similar people she has seen in your town and what they do; for example, the police or the Scottish people she saw on her holidays and so on. Find out which programmes she thinks are most like real life and which she thinks are make-believe.

Your child is learning about other people all the time from many different sources. Getting to know and appreciate the qualities of other people is one of the busiest and most difficult activities of growing up. Children learn how to understand other people from a number of influences:

○ from other adults – their parents, their friends' parents, their teachers.

○ from their friends and classmates.

○ from their own experience.

They pick up very quickly on how you feel about the new neighbours, or how their friends rate a new pop star. The labels that you've been thinking about with your child help her to understand people more, but they are for convenience. They are a starting point. People who cannot alter their ideas and labels as they meet and get to know people are people who become prejudiced. And there's not much curiosity or pleasure in prejudice.

Sometimes the new people that she meets might seem familiar to her straight away – the friend she makes at Brownies who has the same interests. But other people might well be from a background that she hasn't come across before. She may be confused and struggle to find a way to understand. On the other hand, she may dismiss these differences by thinking the people are inferior or stupid.

Talk to her about anything she thinks odd about the new people she meets. One of the ways you could do this is to try and get her to work out what other people who didn't know her would think about her own life.

Look at this example.

Steve, nine, made friends with an Italian boy, Mario, and he was invited home one day. While the children all had fish fingers and chips for their tea, the adults, he told his mother afterwards, had some sort of meat pie with soggy green stuff in it, which smelt of very strong cheese and made Steve feel sick. He said it looked a real mess and would have put him right off if he'd had to eat it. The next day Steve sat down to a lunch of steak and kidney pie with mushy peas. His mother chose the occasion to ask him what a foreigner might think of mushy peas.

Everyone's behaviour is odd to some other people. However, as we get to know people we learn to live with their oddities and they with ours. The more tolerant a child learns to be, the less any oddities will worry him.

A new child in town

Ask your child what a boy or girl of the same age from another country would find odd if he or she came to live in your town, or even in your family. What would they need to do to fit in? What would they wear, what would they have to eat, what sort of people would they mix with, what jokes, games, songs would they need to like? What would they notice first?

The circle game

Now go back to your pieces of paper with people's names on. You have now thought about many other people as well – people your child doesn't know at all, people who present your child with problems of how to label them. How does it all fit together?

○ Find a large sheet of paper, a double sheet of newspaper or some old wallpaper. Draw a series of four circles one inside the other on the paper.

○ Together with your child write out on some more pieces of paper the names of the rest of the people you've talked about in this topic (mainly from the sections on 'Famous people', 'Who are these people?' and 'Let's watch TV').

○ Now ask your child to place all the pieces of paper on the large sheet, putting the people she knows best right in the middle circle, the people she's only heard of right on the outside and everyone else in between. Get her to arrange the labels so that the people who know each other are put close together on the large sheet of paper. While your child is doing this you could talk with her about what she knows about these various people.

Finding out about people

Your child gets information about a person by:

○ talking to him.

○ watching what he does and seeing what he looks like.

○ listening to what other people say about that person or reading about him.

Here's a chart that summarises the ways that your child will probably have collected her information about people she knows and people we have talked about in this topic.

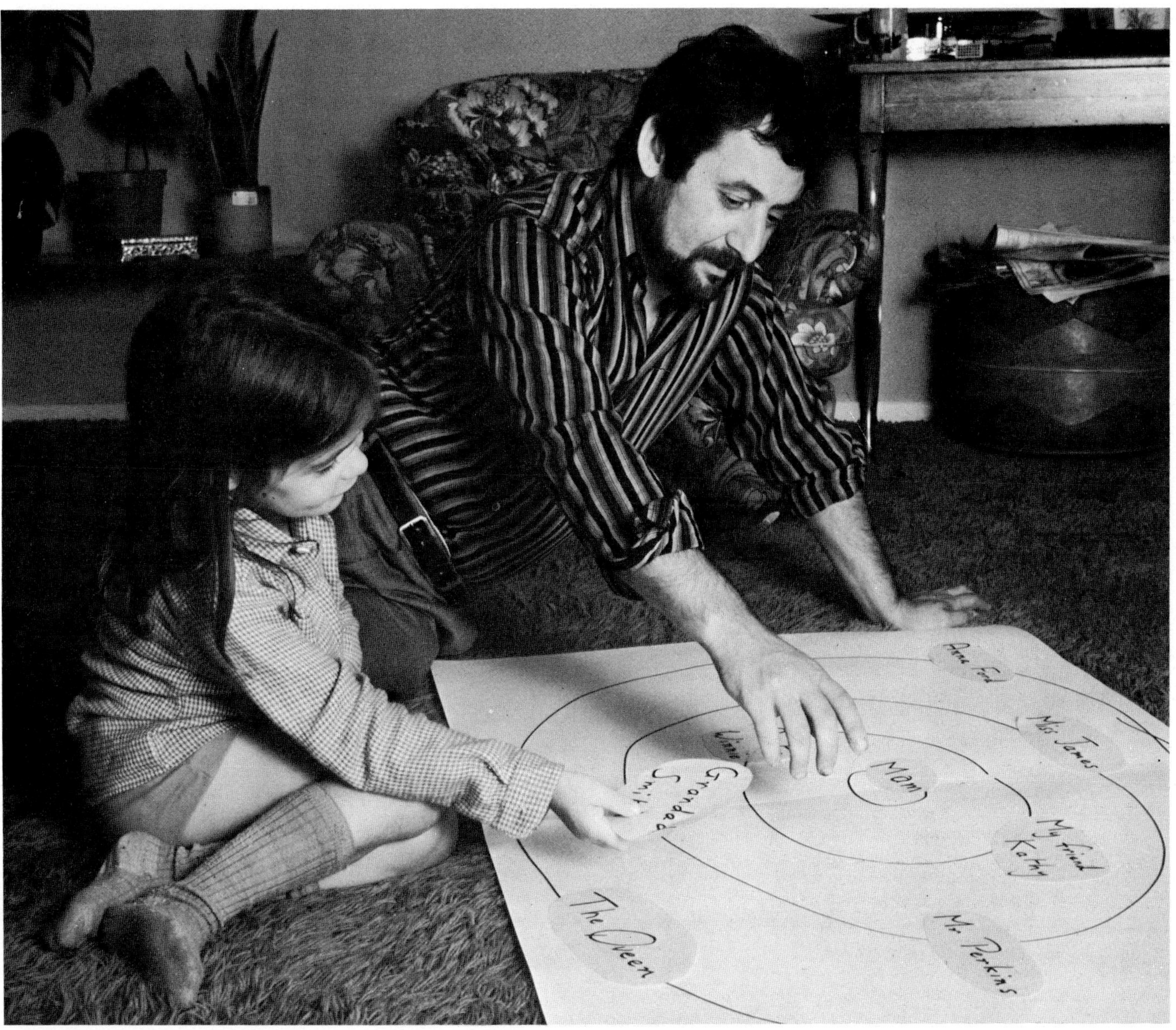

	Talking to him	Watching	Listening or reading
People I know	✓	✓	✓
Famous people		✓	✓
People on p. 193		✓	✓
People on TV		✓	✓

The more your child collects information from talking and watching and from listening to other people, the more easily she will be able to sort people out in her mind and make some predictions about how they will behave and how *she* should behave. There soon won't be many occasions when she meets someone she can't make head nor tail of.

Meeting people is part of growing and learning and changing. Finding out why people think, dress, act or look like they do is the first step towards understanding the world.

. . . Places

What do children notice in the world around them and what is most important to them?

Think about all the different places that your child goes to. Make a list of places in your area, places within a few miles of home and places further afield. Here's Mick Jenkins' list of places that his daughter Mandy, aged eight, goes to and knows something about.

Check your own list with your child and get him to include any other places that he has been to.

Now ask your child to draw a map, or picture-map, of your area showing the places he goes to. Ask him to draw in the routes he takes to get to various places and to fill in any other places he knows in your area. As children get older their knowledge of places grows but it's very patchy and you may have difficulty in recognising your own child's map, even of your own local areas.

○ Children draw places that are important to them.

○ They leave out things they don't know or care about.

1 **Places near home (Liverpool)**	2 **Places a few miles away**	3 **Places further afield**
Our street	Birkenhead (Auntie's)	Llandudno (summer holidays)
The next street	Runcorn (Granny's)	Lake District (school trip)
The town centre	Manchester (family friends)	Germany (Mandy was here when I was in the army)
School		
Bootle (Granny Jenkins)		
Sefton Park		
Church		
Church hall (Brownies)		

Mandy's journey

Children's ideas of an area are of course built up from the routes they take from one place to another. Here is a picture Mandy Jenkins did of her journey to school. You'll notice four main things in her drawing: the sweet shop, the church, the hill and the cars. These are the things that have made a strong impression on her during her journey to school.

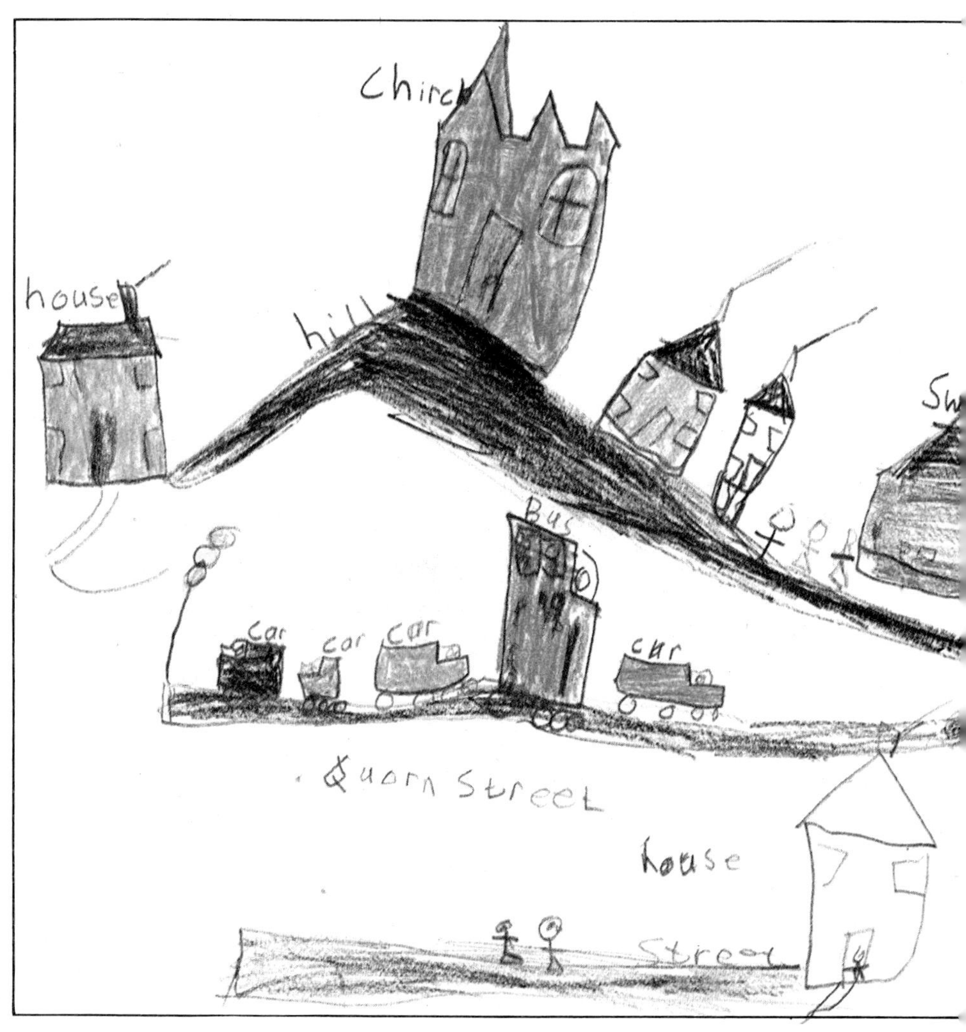

A walk round Liverpool

The things which make an impression on children are not always those that an adult would expect. And children can have very different views from each other too.

Here are two accounts of a walk around Liverpool; the first is written by David, the second by Paul.

'After assembly we got our coats and went out with our teachers. First we went on a coach, we were singing then when we got off the coach we saw a pub and we saw St George's hall we went to the cathedral. It had blue windows and all other colours. Then we went to the museum. When we came out we walked a bit then we went to the ferry we ate our food and saved some food. We walked up the hill and waited for the bus, we saw the bus by a building and got on it and went back to school.'

'After assembly we got our coats and hats and gloves and we went to the toilets and then we went on the coach with the school. We stopped by Abercromby Vaults pub and we went to the Metropolitan Cathedral. And we went inside and we saw beautiful stained glass windows and after that we went through the university and we went down London road and we crossed the roads. We went past St George's Hall and then we made our way to the museum and we saw some snakes and we saw some toads and some fishes and then we saw the town hall and then we saw the Liver building and then we went on the Ferry landing stage then we came back to school.'

David	Both mentioned	Paul
Singing	Pub	Toilets
Food	St George's Hall	Abercromby Vaults
Hill	(noticed at different	Cathedral
Bus	times)	Snakes, toads, fishes
Building	Ferry	University
	Museum	London Road
		Town Hall
		Liver building

Paul's picture of Liverpool Cathedral

David and Paul were from the same class in the same school, out on the same walk in Liverpool. They have expressed certain things in common. But each child has described quite a few different things as well. (See chart above.)

Get your own child to describe what he sees as you go on walks together. You can help him to make sense of the world around him but you also need to be sensitive to what he notices and what interests him.

The wider world

Now think about the other places you wrote down in your list, places a few miles away and places further afield.

In addition to the places you and he have already listed ask him to tell you of all the towns and cities that he can think of that are outside your immediate area. If he has some difficulty ask him to tell you:

○ a big town that he can think of.

○ a famous seaside town.

○ a town he thinks everyone will have heard of.

○ a place where there are mountains.

○ a place where there is a river.

Some children between the ages of seven and nine were asked to write down all the places they could think of. The seven-year-olds wrote down a list of places round their own towns. Other than these, they mentioned only the three largest towns in the country and a small town where there was at that time an industrial dispute that was being regularly covered on TV.

By the age of nine the children were beginning to add other places – other large towns in the country and lots of holiday resorts! Again it was the things that made a strong impression (such as holidays) that came into their minds.

So what shapes *your* child's knowledge of places? Is it football teams, grandparents, holiday resorts, places where disasters have happened? Probably some or all of these. Whatever it is, it's certainly a very personal view of geography!

Below is a list of reasons why your child might know various places. Go through the list that you've made together and find out whether they match the reasons why your own child knows about each place. Add to the list other reasons your child gives.

Relatives live here
It was in the news
Went there on holiday
Went here on a school trip
It was mentioned in an advert
Family has lived there
Football team is there
Learned about it at school
Someone told me about it

Knowing these various places and even having been to them doesn't mean your child has a very clear idea of where they are, or how they fit together. That is something which comes gradually.

You can find out just how local your child's knowledge of places is and how he sees them fitting together by asking him to draw a map of the world, and how where you live fits into it.

This map, illustrated on the right, by a Liverpool eight-year-old shows a certain amount of local knowledge but his ideas about the world as a whole are very patchy.

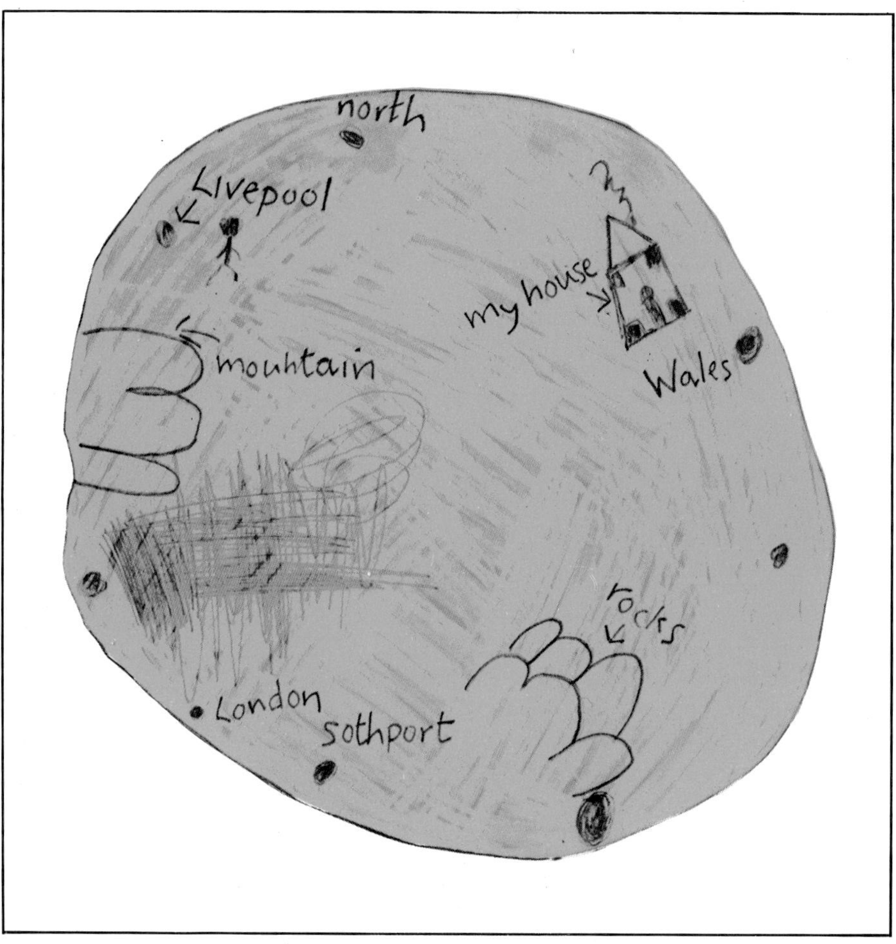

Using information

There are things about places that give us information, just as the appearance of people gives us information.

Here is a picture, on the facing page, from which it is possible to find out a good many things if you know what to look for. Look at this picture with your child and talk to him about it. You could ask him these questions, for instance.

○ Where is the bus going?

○ Where will it stop?

○ What kind of place is it?

○ Is it town or country?

○ How big is the place?

○ Is the place always as busy as it is in the picture?

○ What time of year is it?

○ What sort of shops are there?

○ What things would a person driving in a car pay attention to?

You will see as you look at the picture together there are lots of signs and clues.

○ **There are special signs**
They tell you to do things. They give people permission to do some things and tell them not to do other things. For instance there are quite a lot of road signs. And many signs in the middle of the town are for organising traffic. You wouldn't

see nearly as many of these together in one place in the country. Ask your child why we need signs like these.

○ **There are other signs**
These inform people, such as shop names, sale posters. Sometimes they are in words and sometimes they are symbols – the barber's pole.

○ **Then there are other clues**
They tell you things. The weather and the number of leaves on the trees can tell you about the time of year. The number of people, and what they are doing can tell you about the time of day.

When you look at other pictures with your child, look for these sorts of things and ask these sorts of questions.

But a picture catches only a moment in time. Stand with your child in a crowded street and then both of you try to pick out as many things as you can notice.

○ How many different kinds of people are there?

○ How many different sorts of buildings are there?

○ Look for damage to pavements, roads, lamp posts, etc.

○ Are there steps into the shops, could someone in a wheelchair use them?

○ Are the people hurrying or walking slowly?

○ Are the people using pedestrian crossings?

○ How many buses go past?

○ Look for places that need repairing.

Ask your child what sorts of things he'd look for in the street if he were:

1 A policeman.

2 A car driver.

3 A builder.

4 A handicapped person in a wheelchair.

Some places are highly important to your child. He links them with things he does and things he finds interesting. So talking to your child about places is one way that you can find out what's important to him.

Something different

It is hard for a child to cope with a lot of new things all at once. Here's how to help.

Between five and ten a whole world of new experiences is opening up to your child. There are new people to meet, new places to go, and new things to do. Going to school, joining a club, going to town on a bus are all new experiences that your child is learning how to cope with for herself.

It is not surprising that sometimes it becomes 'all too much' for children – very often when you think they're coping best. Being grown-up isn't something that is learned straight off; young children still need the security of a loving adult to step in when things get too difficult for them. Here is an example.

Melissa is seven and has pestered her mother to let her go to ballet classes for months. Her mother arranges for her to go to a class held at a nearby school, but not Melissa's own school. After the first lesson Melissa doesn't want to go any more.

By talking to Melissa her mother builds up a clearer picture of why the ballet lesson was such an overwhelming experience for her:

- the teacher was new to her.
- none of her own school friends were there.
- the lesson was strange to her and not as she had imagined it – they all stood in a row holding onto a bar along the wall and did exercises.
- the school building was unfamiliar.

There were so many new experiences involved in going to a ballet lesson that Melissa simply couldn't cope with them all at once.

Occasion	People	Place	Activity	Things used
Birthday party	relatives, friends	home	eating, games	food, toys
Shopping at supermarket	mum, shoppers, shop-assistants	town centre	buying	money, food
Going to church				
Going to dentist				
School open day				
Football match				
Maths lesson				
Day at the seaside				
Watching TV				
Playing marbles				

People, places, activities and things

For Melissa going to her first ballet lesson involved coping with new people – the teacher and the other children; a new place – a school she was unfamiliar with; a new activity – the ballet exercises; and new things – using the bar and so on. Looking at new experiences in terms of *people, places, activities,* and *things* might help you and your child to avoid situations where your child can't cope. Above is a chart listing a number of familiar occasions. Look at it with your child and together fill in the columns marked people, place, activity and things used. The first two examples are already filled in as a guide.

Some of these activities your child will be used to, such as watching TV or going shopping. But others are not so familiar. The first visit to the dentist can be very confusing and unpleasant. On some occasions it may be just the people or the place that is new. On others it may be everything that is new all at once.

What's new?

Dividing occasions up into the people, the places, the activities and the things used can help you decide whether a new occasion is likely to be too much for your child. In the example of Melissa's first ballet lesson the people, the place, the activity, and the equipment used were all unfamiliar to her. Yet she is perfectly capable of going to the local shop on her own to buy a pint of milk. In this case she knows the shopkeeper, the shop is familiar, and she knows how to ask for the milk. The only unfamiliar part is paying for the milk and being given the change.

Now think of a number of activities or occasions that involve your child. Choose one that takes place at home, one from school and one that occurs in the community. Then think about the people involved, the place where the event occurs, the activity they do and the things they use.

Make charts for each of your occasions, like the ones over the page shown for Robert. For each element of the event, tick whether it is not familiar, quite familiar or very familiar to your child.

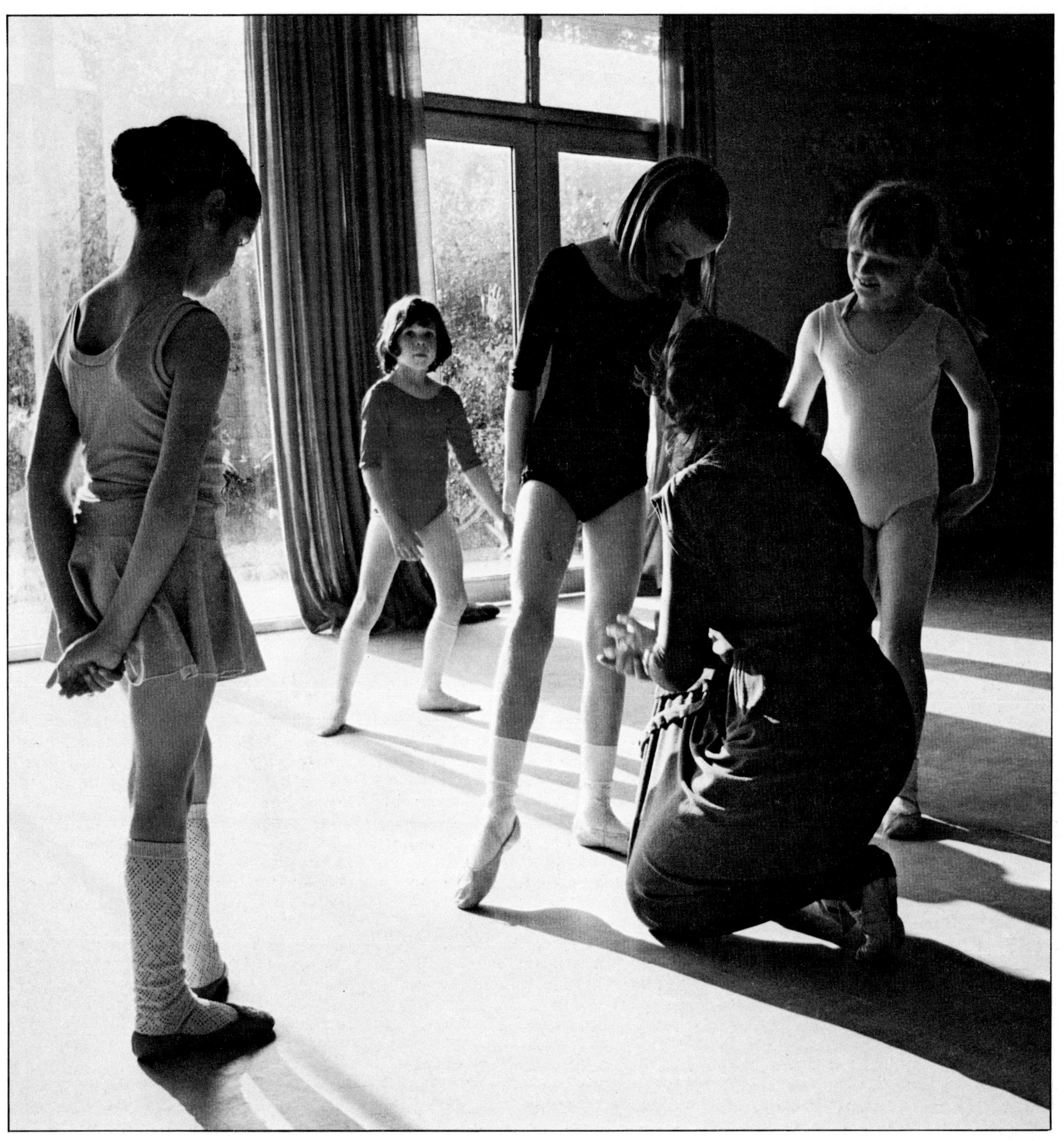

Robert's charts

Occasion: School gym lesson

	not familiar	familiar	very familiar
people	☐	☐	☑
place	☐	☐	☑
activity	☑	☐	☐
things used	☑	☐	☐

Occasion: Going swimming

	not familiar	familiar	very familiar
people	☐	☑	☐
place	☐	☑	☐
activity	☐	☐	☑
things used	☐	☐	☑

We have filled in ticks for Robert. His first gym lesson is a mix of familiar and unfamiliar things. He knows the people because they are his classmates and he knows the teacher. He also knows the place – it's the main hall where they have assembly every day. But he has never been on a trampoline before and some of the other equipment he has never seen elsewhere. Trying to vault over a box is a new experience for him.

But he has been to the swimming baths lots of times. He knows how to swim and he is familiar with the swimming baths themselves. Each week there are different children at training sessions but he knows some of them well enough to talk to.

Any occasion, then, consists of elements that are more or less familiar to your child. The more familiar it is the more easily she will take it in her stride; the less familiar it is, the more prepared you need to be to help her if she can't cope. Doing new things is riskier than doing familiar things, but it can also be more rewarding – it gives her a chance to learn how to cope with new skills, new roles, new materials.

Activities done at home can be just as new and adventurous as activities done at school or out in the community. Look at the list in the left hand column of this chart and put a tick in one of the columns marked along the top to show where your child is most likely to come across each experience. You may find some of these experiences are spread through the three areas of home, school and community.

Experiences	Place: Home	Place: School	Place: Community
People			
1 Will have a chance to be involved with children the same age	☐	☐	☐
2 Will have a chance to be involved with people of a variety of ages	☐	☐	☐
3 Will be with the same people a lot of the time	☐	☐	☐
4 Will have the chance to join an organised group	☐	☐	☐
5 Will have the chance to spend much time with friends	☐	☐	☐
Activities			
1 Will be able to choose what she wants to do	☐	☐	☐
2 Will be able to develop skills by working with her hands	☐	☐	☐
3 Will be able to develop physical skills	☐	☐	☐
4 Will be able to develop language, reading and number skills	☐	☐	☐
5 Will be obliged to do a particular activity at a particular time	☐	☐	☐
6 Will be able to decide for herself how long to spend on an activity	☐	☐	☐

If this is the case you can see that each of these areas provides a wealth of learning opportunities for children. As a parent you can help your child by allowing her to tackle as many new experiences as possible, but at the same time watching out for the times when it may suddenly become 'all too much'. With a few adjustments, you should soon get over that stage, and your child will be coping with a wider range of activities.

Things used			
1 Will be able to have her own things	☐	☐	☐
2 Will need to share things	☐	☐	☐
3 Will need to take good care of things	☐	☐	☐

Outdoor risks and hazards

You can't protect your child from all dangers.
But you can teach him how to cope.

Between the ages of five and ten, your child is meeting new situations and learning to cope with new experiences at an astonishingly fast rate. Here are some of the things that he is probably now learning to do on his own.

○ Catch a bus on a route he knows.

○ Walk through a town centre or shopping precinct by himself.

○ Go swimming in the public baths.

○ Wait in a public place until collected.

○ Walk along main roads and cross them.

○ Use pedestrian crossings.

○ Find and use short cuts to places he knows.

What worries you?

When your child does go out without you you may get anxious. For part of the time that he is out of sight he'll be in the care of other adults who know him. But not always. What worries you when he's out of your sight?

Here are some situations in which children may find themselves. Read them through and underline the things that you feel would worry you if your child were involved.

Jane Jones, 8, and her friend Lizzie, 8, go to the swimming baths every Thursday evening. They leave Jane's house at 6.00 pm and catch a bus to the town centre. They walk through the shopping precinct to the swimming baths and go to a public session of the baths for one hour. They then wait outside the baths for Lizzie's mother to pick them up between 7.45 and 8.00 pm and take them home by car.

Philip Davies, 7, goes to and from school by himself. He walks through the estate, along the main road and across the pedestrian crossing. Then he takes a short cut over the playing fields to the school.

Freddie Wilkinson, 7, comes out of school and walks through the town centre to a high rise estate and stays there in a fifth floor flat with a child minder until 6.00 pm. On three nights a week his father picks him up in the car; on the other two nights he walks back into town where his fourteen-year-old big brother meets him and they catch a bus home.

What did you underline? A lot will depend on what you personally find worrying, and on what you know about your own child and the area you live in. For instance, Philip Davies's mother may be quite happy for him to go to school by himself because she has taken him along that route herself several times and talked to him about the possible danger spots. She also thinks the area is fairly safe for a small boy out on his own.

Here is a list of things that some parents have admitted to worrying about. Some *are* extreme but if you've ever had the same sort of feelings add your own particular fears. The list is divided into four sections, each being one particular type of worry.

A hostile world?

○ I keep thinking that the brakes on an articulated lorry will fail and it will career into him.

○ When that school gym fell down I immediately thought about the prefab where she goes to Brownies.

○ The paving slabs are so uneven and if he fell over one he might fall into the street.

People who can't be trusted?

○ Those swimming baths are so crowded I have nightmares thinking maybe the attendant isn't watching.

○ There's so many awful people about and she's so trusting. I'm sure she's going to be taken away by a stranger one day.

○ What if the nurse accidentally uses the wrong injection?

Children who can't be trusted?

○ He's really good on the roads normally but as soon as the ice-cream van arrives, I

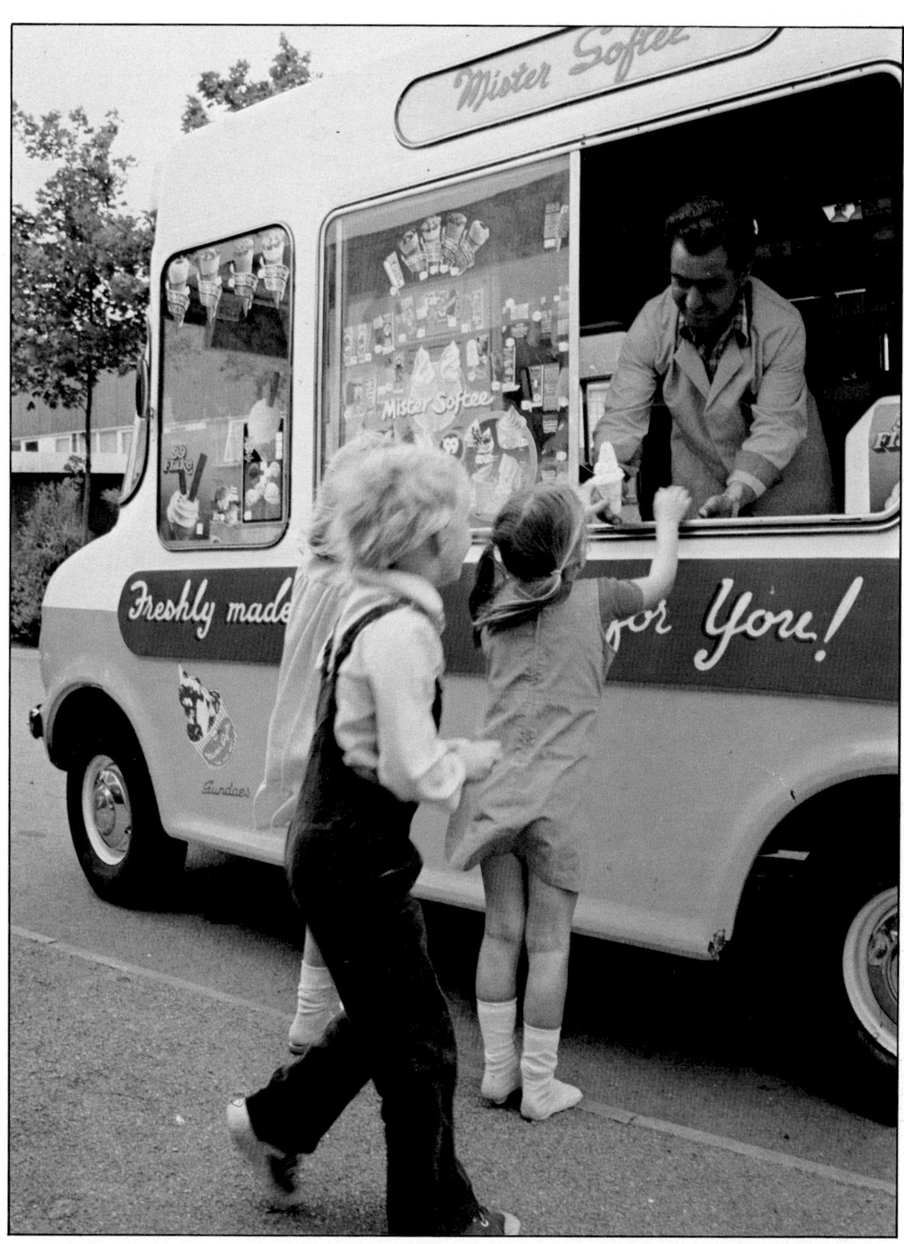

keep thinking he's bound to forget and rush into the road.
○ I suspect he fools around when he's walking along the canal.
○ She can go into town all right but if she lost her bus fare – she'd be stuck there and frankly I don't think she'd have the sense to know what to do.

Your child who is naughty?

○ She stole something from the newsagents once. I feel like searching her pockets now when she comes in.
○ They might throw a brick through the window of a deserted house.
○ I hear her friends shout names after people in the street and I'm frightened she might do so too.

Many people have these sorts of fears. Some of them you can do something about. But others you just can't prevent unless you wrap your child in cotton wool and protect him completely. And if you do that he doesn't learn to cope. Then you will never gain any confidence about your child going out without you.

How do parents get such worries?

They know that awful things do happen to children. They read in the newspapers and see dreadful things on television.

They see what goes on around them. They know about dangerous crossroads in their areas, and of local gangs of children roaming around doing destructive things.

They know their own child. They see that he does act irresponsibly at times. They are aware that he does break rules.

If your worry is something that you can't do anything about, keep it as *your* problem, don't give it to your child. An anxious worried parent will let his child know that the world is a dangerous place and the child will worry too. A relaxed parent will convey confidence to his child.

Rules for out and about

Now look at some real situations where you make rules for your child to follow. We have provided a list to help you but choose your own as well.

Going on the bus

Going to the park

Going to visit friends by foot

Going to school

Meeting someone in town

Walking round town

Playing out of doors

Going out in the street on a bicycle

Going out on rollerskates

Playing in the street

Going to the newsagents

Now make a chart like the one shown here and fill it in, as Jenny has done, but for your own situation and with your own rules. You could do it twice. Once for something your child does regularly, once for something he'll soon do for the first time on his own.

The chart has four columns.

○ Things you tell your child to do.

○ Reasons why you included each rule or instruction.

○ Explanations that you give him.

○ Things to help your child carry out your instructions.

Occasion: *Sean going to Auntie Audrey's on the bus by himself*

Things I told him	Why I included that rule	Explanations (if given)	Things he needed in order to do what I told him
Gave him the exact fare each way			A pocket to put the bus fare in
Told him the exact time of the buses: 3.45 there and 5.45 out	So there was no chance of him having to hang around	So he didn't have to wait long at either end	A watch so that he would know the time
Told him the number and destination of the bus			To read OK. He can do this
Told him to go only downstairs	The stairs can be difficult to get down while the bus is moving	Same	
Told him not to talk to anyone on the bus	Strangers sometimes want to harm little children	Same	
Told him not to get on or off the bus while it was moving	It's dangerous and he could fall over	Same	
Told him what to do if the bus was late or if he missed it	Don't like him hanging around. I think it's dangerous because he might get frightened by somebody	Said come back home or go back to Auntie Audrey's – save having to wait in the cold	
Told him to ask the bus conductor to put him off the bus	If the bus conductor has his attention drawn to Sean I reckon he's much safer	Said that even if the bus was crowded Sean and the bus conductor between them would be sure he got off at the right stop	

Try a little experiment

Now let your child actually carry out the instructions and rules you've made up for a new occasion. Then look at your chart again. When he does this new thing for the second and third time, will you:

○ mention all the same rules?

○ give the same explanations?

You may need to repeat rules that haven't been fully understood the first time, or to mention some different rules on the second and third occasion – perhaps things you hadn't anticipated. If you find you mention fewer rules you're probably feeling more relaxed. There are some things he can cope with.

Adding more rules for the sake of your own feelings of worry do not necessarily make for greater safety. If your child is following your rules conscientiously and you still feel unhappy work out whose the problem is – yours or his?

Safety first

Children gradually learn to keep themselves safe. But you can do a lot to help them. Here are three suggestions.

1 Remove the dangerous things from around your child.

2 Give him rules, together with explanations as to why he should avoid them.

3 Give him firm rules about safety and danger but without explanation.

The first places the burden of protection on to you entirely. Your child doesn't have to learn to cope because you cope for him. But then what happens in an emergency?

The second helps your child to learn to cope for himself. Rules backed by explanations are powerful. Explanations give meaning to children for the rules they have to follow.

The third may help your child learn to cope – but rules without adequate explanations are frequently the first to be disobeyed.

Explaining is important

There are situations where you make rules for your child. And for these rules you have reasons. When you talk about the rules you give to your child you can help him make sense of them. Check back on your own charts and look at Jenny's chart again. How much do the explanations you give your child and the reasons you have for them fit together? Jenny's fit together quite closely – except that she doesn't tell Paul what really worries her if he has to wait around for the bus. He just thinks he is going to get cold and have to wait a long time.

A child who can cope with danger is far better protected in the long run than one whose parents take all the responsibility for protection. But you have to find the right balance. If you over-stress dangers you may not be believed or you may cause a lot of worry. If you pass things off as unimportant that's how your child will see them.

Test out what your child has understood by your explanations for rules and what they apply to.

○ Draw a rough map of your local area. Draw on it things that you have made rules about.

○ And then talk to your child about why she thinks the rule exists.

○ Or ask her to draw you pictures of things in the area that are dangerous and to tell you why.

This list of rules has been made by Maria for her daughter Violetta. Look at the difference between Maria's thoughts about safety and Violetta's understanding of the rules.

Maria	Violetta
Park Apparatus dangerous	**Park** Tore my trousers there on the slide. Mummy told me I mustn't spoil my clothes so I can't go on the slide again
Woods Dangerous/ lonely	**Woods** They are on the other side of main road. And I mustn't cross the main road myself
Bus stop Other side of main road. There are strangers around here and she might go off with them	**Bus stop** It's the other side of the main road
School Cross at crossing; lollipop man safe	**School** Cross at the crossing. The lollipop man helps me

Violetta only understood that the woods and the bus stop were forbidden because of the main road. This was the explanation she'd been given. And it didn't fit entirely with her mother's worries about dangers. The same thing happened over the park. If Violetta was to be in the park in her oldest clothes, what would she make of the rule about going on the slide?

Do you explain dangers to your child in terms he can understand? Here are a number of things you might say to your child about the various hazards that he could face. Tick which of the statements you would be most likely to use.

Road safety

A You can only cross a road when it's clear. ☐

B Cars going quite slowly still take time to brake and stop, even when they may have seen you. ☐

C Pedestrian crossings are the only safe place to cross and even then you must *always* take care. ☐

Fire and matches

A Fire and matches can burn you so it's important to keep away from them. ☐

B Fire and matches can send out sparks and burn things quite a long way away. ☐

C Matches should always be struck away from you so the flame doesn't get anywhere near you. ☐

Strange animals

A Some animals are frightened of strangers, even of children, and may bite you so it's best not to go up to them. ☐

B You can tell a friendly dog by its wagging tail and the noise it makes; growling means keep away. ☐

C Animals are best left alone unless you know them, or the owner says you can stroke them. ☐

Talking to strangers

A You never talk to strangers or go anywhere without me because I want to know exactly where you are. ☐

B People have been known to attack children; often they offer them gifts or say they have a message from Mummy or Daddy. You must never go anywhere with someone you don't know. ☐

C Some people can frighten and even hurt children by wanting them to go with them. They offer sweets and other treats to children. That's why you must always say no and not talk to people you don't know. ☐

Of course the age of your child will have a lot to do with the sorts of explanations he can understand. And you may have thought some of the answers given wouldn't be suitable for your own child (**A**s were thought generally to be suitable for 5–6 year olds. **B**s for 9–10 year olds and **C**s for a child anywhere in this age range).

The sort of instruction you use is bound to depend on what's going on at the time. Just as your child is about to step off the pavement in front of a bus is not the best time for a detailed explanation of road safety rules. You'd probably use an answer along the lines of **A**. When there's more time it would be worth remembering the incident and giving a more thoughtful answer, as in **B** and **C**.

Road safety

As everyone knows many children are killed and injured on the roads. Roads can't be avoided so children must learn to use roads safely. Explanations can take place anywhere–at home or while you're actually out and about in traffic. Talk out loud as you cross the road. Get your child to 'take' you safely across the road. This is good practice for him and if you get him to explain why he is doing what he's doing to you, you can check he knows how to cope.

As he grows older there'll be more to talk about. He'll want to learn more about bikes. Back your explanations up with demonstrations. For instance try a game of testing on the bike to see how long it takes for the brakes to work.

Matches and fires

Children are fascinated by fire. Of course it is dangerous and a child needs to be

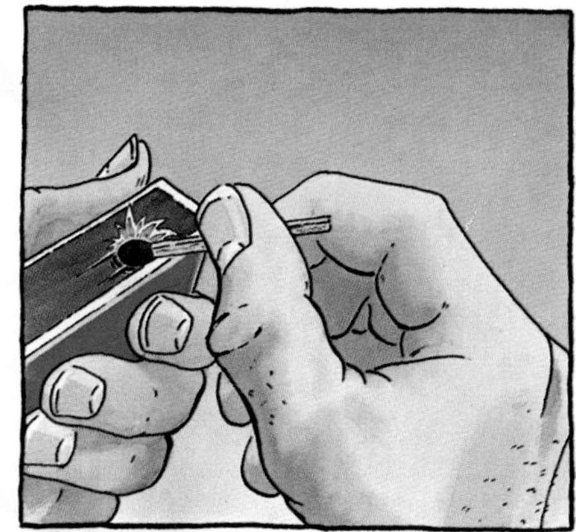

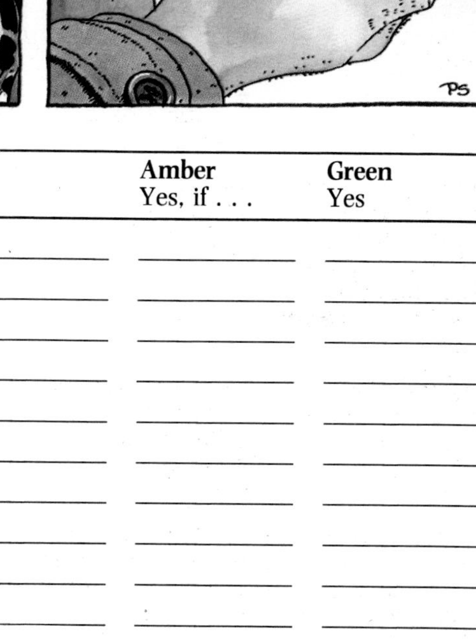

aware of danger. But he also needs to learn confidence. Show him how to put a match or little fire out by smothering it or pouring on water. Talk to him about the precautions you take when dealing with fire. 'This pan has been on the stove and will be hot, so I'll use a cloth to pick it up with.'

Strange animals

Many children who like animals will rush up to strange cats and dogs and expect them to be as friendly as their own pets. But even animals who are friendly at home will snap at children they aren't used to, especially if the child makes more noise than they are used to. Even the friendliest dog will tire of being patted all the time. Ask your child if he would like it himself.

Talking to strangers

This is a real fear of all parents. You can take one very practical step, to avoid misunderstandings later. Tell your child you would *never* send him a message via a stranger so, if a stranger ever says that mummy asked him to come, don't believe him. You can also explain that not all people are good.

Your own attitude towards strangers is also telling. A cool detached polite attitude will give clues to your child that with strangers you keep your distance.

Rules are like traffic lights

Red You say 'No' and explain why.

Amber You point out that there is danger but that if great care is taken, then the activity may be carried out.

Green You say 'Yes you can do this'.

By himself	**Red** No	**Amber** Yes, if . . .	**Green** Yes
Going to the park			
Going on the bus			
Going in to town			
Going out on a bicycle			
Playing in the street			
Going to school			
Playing indoors			
Going to visit friends			
Going to an organised activity			
Going to the local shops			
Doing a paper round			
Helping the milkman			

Look at the list and write down the age of your child at which each 'traffic light' applied. Add any of your own.

If you've got more than one child in this age range you might like to look at how the rules vary from child to child. Children do vary in how they can cope with rules. There's no one right time when to change or relax the rules. So you won't find all children taking more responsibility at exactly the same age. If you have a chance to talk to the parents of other five to ten-year-olds about their rules you'll probably find a great variety.

The difference in rules doesn't always reflect what a child can or can't do for himself. For instance, you may find your rules are quite relaxed about your own child going to school by himself. The school is only two hundred yards away from your home and you can practically see him go through the school gates. But a friend on the other side of town might well have much stricter rules. The school her child goes to is half a mile away, over a main road and through a shopping centre.

Adventures and trouble

Where do you draw the line between natural high spirits and thoughtless or deliberate misdeeds?

If your eight-year-old stole a packet of sweets from a shop you would probably be worried, angry and upset. But he may only do it once. It doesn't mean he's destined to become a burglar and spend a good part of his life behind bars. If a child throws a brick through the window of a deserted house, it doesn't mean he's going to grow up a vandal.

There's a narrow margin between high spirits and getting into trouble. High spirits can be entirely innocent. And any child may do something just for fun that an adult thinks is gravely serious. What is the difference between having adventures and getting into trouble?

Is it serious?

Look at this list of activities and tick which you think is most serious/quite serious/not very serious. Then cover your own answers and ask your partner to do the same. Finally talk to your child about the activities and ask him which he thinks are most serious/quite serious/not very serious.

All of these things would be viewed as 'wrong' by most parents. Yet any child, however well brought up, is capable of some of these. Of course parents do make allowances for occasional lapses of behaviour but they would be worried if their child was regularly doing things marked as most or quite serious.

	Self			Partner			Child		
	Most serious	Quite serious	Not very serious	Most serious	Quite serious	Not very serious	Most serious	Quite serious	Not very serious
Cheating in a school exam	☐	☐	☐	☐	☐	☐	☐	☐	☐
Posting rubbish through letter boxes	☐	☐	☐	☐	☐	☐	☐	☐	☐
Taking money from mother's purse	☐	☐	☐	☐	☐	☐	☐	☐	☐
Knocking on doors and running away	☐	☐	☐	☐	☐	☐	☐	☐	☐
Placing objects on railway lines	☐	☐	☐	☐	☐	☐	☐	☐	☐
Letting down the tyres of a parked car	☐	☐	☐	☐	☐	☐	☐	☐	☐
Stealing sweets from a local supermarket	☐	☐	☐	☐	☐	☐	☐	☐	☐
Urinating in a public telephone box	☐	☐	☐	☐	☐	☐	☐	☐	☐
Deliberate cruelty to animals	☐	☐	☐	☐	☐	☐	☐	☐	☐
Spraying slogans on walls of local buildings with aerosols	☐	☐	☐	☐	☐	☐	☐	☐	☐
Shouting rude things at people in the street	☐	☐	☐	☐	☐	☐	☐	☐	☐

But people will differ as to the degree of seriousness they attach to any of these offences. It's quite likely that in a group of parents no two would have exactly the same list. You probably found your list was different from your partner's list. Talk to your partner about the cases you saw differently. You may have found that your child's views were a lot different from both yours and your partner's.

Cruelty to either people or animals is considered by some parents to be worse than damage to property. Some parents – perhaps some fathers in particular – will expect (and secretly want) more mischief from their sons than their daughters. After all, 'boys will be boys'.

Other parents wouldn't mind if their child tried to cheat the school exam system, if they hadn't liked the school system themselves. Everyone has different standards. And that includes your child too.

Playing victim

But can he appreciate what it would be like to be the victim? Go through the list (left) with your child and talk about who would suffer and what that person would feel like. Ask him to imagine having such things done to himself or his own things.

Now ask what punishment he thinks adults (you) would deal out if he had done each of these things. At the younger end of the five-to-ten age group your child will be less concerned with the intention behind the behaviour than the actual damage done. He'll think it's more serious to break a window than to try to burn the tail off the cat. As he gets older you may find he thinks the most serious punishment should be reserved for behaviour which is cruel to other people.

Encouraging the right attitude

You want your children to be aware of, and sensitive to, other people's feelings and to feel some responsibility for the environment around them. To help them understand, develop the idea of 'victims'.

○ If the subject of stealing comes up one day, get your child to imagine being the victim. Describe a shopkeeper who is very kind and likes his customers. Explain how he has to buy all the things he sells in his toy or sweet shop. Children keep coming along and stealing things from his shop. He loses a lot of money and becomes poor. Ask your child what he would do if he were the shopkeeper.

○ Talk to your child about what it means to hurt and harm people. He will probably think only of physical pain. Ask him about things that 'hurt' or upset him, like being teased, made fun of or left out.

○ Tell him about an old lady (like his grandmother or other elderly person he is fond of) who was upset when some boys emptied her dustbin on her doorstep. Tell him how difficult it is for old people to bend and pick things up. Ask him what he would do if he saw some other children doing this.

When trouble happens

In law, a child in this age group is not considered socially responsible for his actions. The parents are. And this is why you feel worried.

Now think about what you would actually do if your child did anything seriously wrong. Whatever way parents choose to deal with their children's deviant behaviour they will have similar aims in mind:

○ to make it clear that he has done something they consider wrong.

○ to deter the child from doing it again.

What can you do?

Here are some common approaches.

Physical punishment
May hurt but probably won't have the effect of deterring your child too much. Out of sight, out of mind.

Withdraw privileges
Stop him from doing some of the things he enjoys. This can be the most powerful weapon of all.

Bring in other authority figures
This certainly takes care of the times he is supervised but he still has to spend some time on his own.

Impose more and stricter rules
Go back a few squares – maybe not as far as 'no' but make sure that you are still giving responsibility to your child for keeping rules. Tighten up on supervision.

Apologising
It is important for him to say sorry to the person he has wronged but remember to go with him. Do not expect him at this age to be able to face another adult alone in this sort of situation.

Giving back
If you learn your child has taken something that does not belong to him, then go with him to return it. A word of explanation from you ('My little boy took these sweets by mistake and wants to return them to you') said with a 'knowing look', will let the shopkeeper know what you are doing and also allow your child to save face.

Repairing damage
Damage caused can often be put right. A child who has chalked slogans on someone else's wall can be made to scrub them off. Even if he is not successful at getting everything off he is unlikely to want to do it again. If other children were involved, get them to help too.

Whatever you do, it is your attitude that counts. You want to make wrongdoing unattractive to your child. But you don't want to make him pay so hard that he does more naughty things just to spite you. Try to make him feel that he is learning to exercise choice for himself. 'I won't break Mrs Jones' windows because then I'll have to apologise and pay for new glass out of my pocket money and I don't want to have to do that.'

Since you know your own child best you will devise the punishment which fits his crime. But it's worth considering whether the method you have always used is still the most effective. If not, then change it!

Mum, can I join a club?

Thinking of letting your child join some local activity? Read this first!

No doubt there are various sorts of opportunities for children in your local area. Some of them will appeal to your child. Some certainly won't! Look at what's available, then see if any of the activities match your child's interests. The first thing to do is think of people who might know.

You can start by putting down a name for each of the groups listed below.

- ○ Friends and acquaintances who have some contact with things that go on. ____________
- ○ Friends of your own children who attend things that go on. ____________
- ○ People in official positions whose jobs mean that they know what goes on. ____________
- ○ People who know things that go on because they run them. ____________

To begin with you may only have one name on your list. However you should be able to fill in more names after asking your first contact. Remember also that your own child is likely to know a number of activities that go on.

If you've had difficulty filling in the names of people in official positions or elsewhere who may help, try:

- ○ teachers at school
- ○ health visitor
- ○ librarian
- ○ vicar
- ○ next-door neighbours
- ○ local shopkeepers

There are other sources of information that you probably have some access to. For instance, local newspapers that announce local events and activities, local radio and television that sometimes do the same, newsagents' advertisements, newsletters from school, car stickers and announcements that come through the letter box.

In addition there will usually be posters and leaflets available at places where regular events take place. So fill in some places where you know that activities take place.

____

____

____

If you've had difficulty thinking of places in your local area, see if this list helps.

- ○ Church
- ○ Church hall
- ○ Local community centre
- ○ Local school
- ○ Swimming baths
- ○ Recreation centre
- ○ Local football field
- ○ Council offices
- ○ Village hall
- ○ Library
- ○ Doctor's surgery

You may think, especially if you live in a small town, that if there were any activity on offer which your child could join in, you'd know about it anyway. Don't be too sure! Jess, who collected most of the information for this topic, commented: 'The information was quite difficult to obtain to start with. I found there wasn't much publicity. But I asked around and started to hear lots of things by word of mouth. Once I'd made contacts, loads of information was readily available.'

Will it work out?

Once you have found out about an activity that sounds promising, you'll need to find out whether it is suitable for five to tens, whether it will cost anything and whether you can fit it in with the family routines.

Place, time, costs

Here are some questions to ask yourself. For each activity you consider, weigh up overall the advantages and disadvantages of place, time and costs.

Place	Your answers
Is it near enough for my child to get there by himself on foot or by bike?	
Do I have the time to put aside to take him there?	
Could anyone else take him there?	

Time	Your answers
Is it held on a day convenient for my child?	
Is it held on a convenient day for the family routine?	
Is it held at a convenient time for my child?	
Is it held at a convenient time for the family routine?	
Does it go on for a length of time my child can cope with?	

Costs	Your answers
Can I afford the session costs?	
Can I afford exam fees?	
Can I afford the uniform/find second-hand uniform?	
Can I afford bus fares/petrol costs or make arrangements for shared travel costs?	
Can I afford to contribute to fund-raising if it's necessary?	

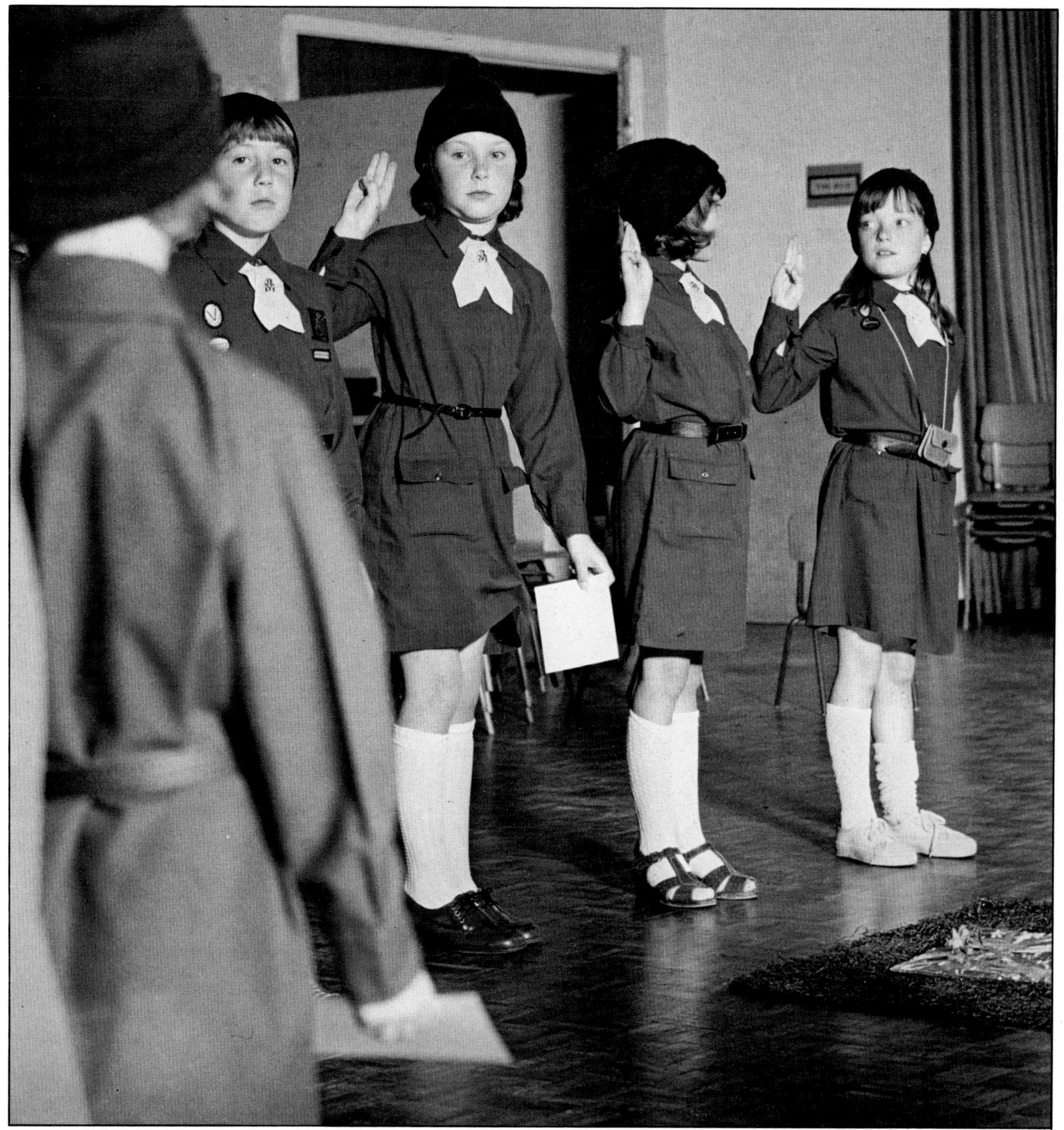

Some of these questions require you to think about the other members of the family and how they are affected. But, in addition there is the question of how much parents are expected to help with the activity and whether you've got the time to do it.

It's fairly straightforward to work out just how convenient, or possible, places and times are. But the costs are more complicated and it may be worth your while to do a fairly detailed break-down of just how much each activity would cost you.

The following charts show some of the information that one mother, Jess, collected and how she used it. Look at them and make similar charts of your own.

The range of activities that Jess discovered was all to be found in a Midland village which is about four miles away from the nearest town. The population is about 3,000.

Having worked out the cost, next Jess put all of the information together, putting a tick if the place or time was basically convenient and a cross if it was

	Judo Club	Library	Youth club	Play scheme	Cubs	Woodcraft folk	Gym club	Junior trampoline	Swimming club	Sunday school	Boys and girls brigade	Dancing class
Each week												
Fees												
Bus fare												
Petrol costs	25p				10p	40p					10p	35p
Totals over year												
Fees												
Bus fare							£2.25*	£3.00*	£3.30*			
Petrol costs	£12.50	£2.00			£5.00	£20.00					£5.00	£17.50
Once off costs												
(fill in which you'd choose)												
Uniform – new												
Second-hand one	£5.00				£5.00						£5.00	
Equipment												
Bought												
Hired (over year)												£5.00
Exams												
Over year	£2.00											£5.00
Other												
Badges						40p	40p	40p	40p			
TOTAL	£19.75	£2.00	–	–	£10.10	£20.80	£2.65	£3.40	£3.70	–	£10.10	£27.85

**for 8 sessions a year* NB *These costs are based on 1980 prices* inconvenient. In addition she put the overall cost per year of each activity. This provided her with a good idea of the practical considerations involved with each activity.

	Place	Time	Costs
Judo club	☑	☑	19.75
Library	☑	☑	2.00
Youth club	☑	☑	
Play scheme	☑	☑	
Cubs	☑	☑	10.10
Woodcraft folk	☑	☑	20.80
Gym club	☑	☒	2.65
Junior trampoline	☑	☑	3.40
Swimming club	☑	☒	3.70
Sunday school	☒	☑	
Boys & girls brigade	☒	☒	10.10
Dancing class	☑	☒	27.85

By now you too should have a good idea of the practicalities. But how do you work out which activity your child will like?

What is available?

Some groups exist mainly for social reasons, for children to get together and enjoy themselves (youth clubs, play schemes).

Some groups exist mainly for children to learn something or acquire new skills (sports, music).

Some groups exist for children to get together and enjoy themselves but learn something at the same time (Brownies, Woodcraft Folk).

Joining in an activity in the community provides children with a chance to build on their experience. But it does need to be something that they enjoy or it's not worth doing.

Everything has its advantages and disadvantages and you may find that your child is prepared to brave some things he dislikes because of other special things he likes a lot.

If you think your child is too shy to mix happily and easily, it may be best to suggest an activity where he is there to learn and only incidentally meeting other children. Of course, once he starts, he'll get used to mixing without realising it. You may be surprised to find how much he likes it when he has settled down.

Which activity?

You've already worked out the opportunities that are actually available to your child – activities that he can get to, you can afford, at times that are convenient. Now you need to work out how appropriate they are for your child.

Below you'll see a chart to help you find out which aspects of the different types of activities your child might enjoy. Talk to your child about the ideas in it and fill it in together.

My child enjoys	Not much	Doesn't mind	A lot
Entertainment, having fun with other children	☐	☐	☐
Mixing with both sexes	☐	☐	☐
Mixing only with his or her own sex	☐	☐	☐
Letting off steam	☐	☐	☐
Acquiring new skills	☐	☐	☐
Competition	☐	☐	☐
Doing things for exams	☐	☐	☐
Getting rewards for doing something really well	☐	☐	☐
Dressing up, wearing uniform	☐	☐	☐
Travelling and being away from home occasionally	☐	☐	☐

This is Jess's chart for her son Martyn

	Not much	Doesn't mind	A lot
Entertainment, having fun with other children	☐	☑	☐
Mixing with both sexes	☐	☑	☐
Mixing only with his own sex	☐	☐	☑
Letting off steam	☐	☐	☑
Acquiring new skills	☐	☐	☑
Competition	☐	☐	☑
Doing things for exams	☐	☐	☑
Getting rewards for doing something well	☐	☐	☑
Dressing up, wearing uniform	☑	☐	☐
Travelling and being away from home occasionally	☑	☐	☐

Martyn is very keen on getting rewards, winning and letting off steam, preferably with other boys of his own age. He is not too keen on wearing a uniform, nor on being away from home for long periods.

	Judo	Library	Youth club	Play scheme	Cubs	Junior tramp-oline	Wood-craft folk	Gym club	Swim-ming	Church youth club	Sunday school	Boys & girls brigade	Danc-ing class
Membership													
Is for both sexes	☑	☑	☑	☑	☐	☑	☑	☑	☑	☑	☑	☐	☑
Is for one sex	☐	☐	☐	☐	☑	☐	☐	☐	☐	☐	☐	☑	☐
Social													
Involves letting off steam	☑	☐	☑	☑	☐	☐	☑	☐	☐	☑	☐	☐	☐
Involves entertainment, having fun with other children	☐	☐	☑	☑	☑	☐	☑	☐	☐	☑	☑	☑	☐
Skills													
Involves acquiring new skills	☑	☐	☐	☐	☐	☑	☑	☑	☑	☐	☑	☐	☑
Competition	☑	☐	☐	☐	☑	☐	☑	☐	☐	☐	☐	☐	☑
Doing things for exams	☑	☐	☐	☐	☑	☐	☐	☐	☐	☐	☐	☐	☑
Getting rewards for doing something well	☐	☐	☐	☐	☑	☑	☑	☑	☑	☐	☐	☑	☐
Obligations													
Dressing up – wearing uniform	☒	☐	☐	☐	☒	☒	☐	☒	☒	☐	☐	☒	☒
Travelling – being away from home occasionally	☒	☐	☐	☐	☒	☐	☒	☐	☐	☐	☐	☐	☒

Now check which of the things you've marked are to be found in the groups and activities you've discovered.

○ Make a chart like the one we show above for Jess's son Martyn. Along the top list the range of activities you've found in your area and which you think are promising for your child.

○ Then put a tick for each feature involved that your child likes or doesn't mind and a cross for each one he doesn't like.

You can check through your list in several ways.

Reading downwards

○ Activities where there are more ticks than crosses are hopefuls.

○ The more marks you've put in on any activity (whether crosses or ticks) – the more variety there is in that activity.

Reading across

○ Ticks spread through 'social' and 'skills' means that your child should have quite a variety of choice.

○ Ticks heavily in favour of 'social' or 'skills' show you which sort of activity your child would be happier with. In fact if your child's interests are almost entirely confined to 'skills' you might want to consider his going to individual lessons where the skill really is the central feature and there are far fewer social elements.

Rules
Different organisations have different rules and different ways of going about things. It's worth checking up on them because they may well be a deciding fact when you and your child come to discuss what he'd like to do. Describing the rules and organisation of the activity may bring home to him what it's all about. Jess's table on the right shows some of the sorts of rules she found and her comments on them.

Some suggestions
Here are a few stories about parents and children and activities. They may give you some further ideas if you find it isn't too easy deciding what your child should do.

Lloyd filled in the charts with his dad. Everything pointed to the fact that Cubs would be an enjoyable activity for him to take up. But his older brother Winston already attended the only local Cub pack. And Lloyd said people were always saying his brother was better at things. He wanted to do something on his own.

Activity	Rules and special features	My comments
Judo club	Cleanliness. Short nails, hair. No jewellery. Skills only to be used in self-defence against a man	I approve entirely. Martyn would never be so clean for my sake! I'm also happy about the danger side
Library	Parents sign applications. Parents responsible for damaged, lost books	Fair enough. I'd actually make Martyn pay for the lost book
Youth club	At a special school. Children can go if they can't find anything else. Parental consent	I like the idea of all sorts of children getting together
Play scheme	Goes on during the school holidays	I'd be quite happy for Martyn to go to this as well
Cubs	Cubs have to abide by laws. Service to community/bob-a-job vetted to make sure it's safe	I like the idea of control of bob-a-job
Junior trampoline	No exams but little tests	
Woodcraft folk	Expected to wear suitable clothes. No exams	I like the emphasis on organised activities. Even though it's noisy, the leaders have control over the children
Gym club	Expected to wear suitable clothes. No exams	I like the organisers saying about suitable clothes. Its not me that's nagging then!
Swimming club	Put into appropriate class for degree of skill	They are very careful about safety. Classes well divided up
Sunday school	Join in late on in church service. A monthly breakfast in church	I wonder if Martyn would feel out of it since we don't go to church
Boys & girls brigade	All members have to belong to a church or Sunday school, but a wide range of activities	He'd have to go to Sunday school as well to do this
Dancing class	Suitable clothing. Can take exams if want	Travel etc required and extra time to do exams

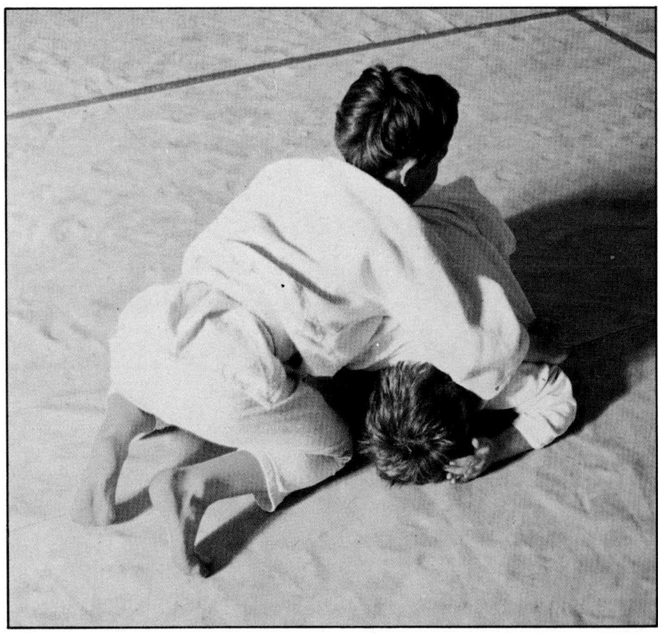

Possible solutions? His dad could check back on chart for nearest equivalent to Cubs. or see if there's any way Lloyd can conveniently get to the Cub pack in the next village.

Mary, who was very quiet, just refused point blank to do anything unless her friend Amanda would do it as well.

Possible solutions? Her parents could talk with Amanda's parents and find activities they would both like to do.

Paul had three smaller sisters under six and said he wanted to do something that wasn't sissy.

Possible solutions? His parent could pick solely those activities limited to boys. Or look at activities which concentrate on skills and learning, rather than people.

Here are two parents' accounts of their children's experience of joining in. Damian and Helen are two very different children. In their chosen activities they both found a number of things to appeal to them.

Woodcraft folk

Damian is nine, and the middle one of three children. He is a member of the Elfin group of the local Woodcraft Folk which he attends with his younger brother. His older sister, who is eleven, is a Pioneer (a Woodcraft Folk group for older children).

Damian's mother says that she first heard of the Woodcraft Folk from friends whose children had been members for some years. The 'non-religious' character of the group was what first appealed to her ('no church parades'), and she was also keen on the outdoor activities – hikes, frequent camps and woodcraft lore.

Now that Damian has been going for about a year, she finds that the group suits him well, and allows him to work off some of his high spirits in the rough and tumble of the games. She has observed that, despite the apparent chaos, the leaders manage to control the children well.

Damian's mother also approves of the 'circle of friendship' which begins and ends the Woodcraft Folk meetings, and of their creed, promising friendship to others. She likes the international aspects of their camps, though pointing out that conditions at camp can be extremely spartan. Her children need to be fairly outgoing to enjoy the Woodcraft Folk, since the rough games might be too much for the more timid. 'But my lot enjoy them!'

Damian says: 'I wanted to join because my sister Lorna went – it sounded like quite a good thing. Though I didn't know I had to take 10p, and forgot it the first time! When you go the first thing you do is say the creed, and promise to be a loyal member of the world family. You can do work for a badge – for Badge 1 you have to be able to tell the time, tie a bow, and know the creed off by heart, that sort of thing. The camps I went to were very wet – but we hiked all over the Malvern hills. I liked going away to camp and getting away from the parents – and when they came on parents' day, they brought chocolate cake, which was OK. I liked the midnight feast at camp, too. I like the meetings – especially the games and skidding around the place. It's better than watching 'Tomorrow's World', anyway.

'You're able to join Woodcraft Folk when you're only six, younger than the Cubs, and I like Woodcraft Folk better. There's more about friendship. What else do we do at Woodcraft Folk? Well, there's News, like my tooth fell out, or our house collapsed, and we get told things about jumble sales – they have loads of those. And sometimes we get to stay up really late when parents are late coming to fetch us!'

Brownies

Like Damian, Helen is nine years old and the middle one of three children. She is a Brownie, and has been one for a year. Neither her older nor younger sister goes to Brownies with her.

Helen's mother recalls that she let Helen join the Brownies because one of her few friends (Helen is not very popular with her class mates) was already a Brownie, and Helen was keen to join her. It was also something that her older sister *hadn't* done and was a chance for Helen to strike out on her own for a change. Helen's mother hadn't been a Brownie in her youth, and had only a vague idea what happened at meetings, but knew that Brownies were encouraged to help people.

When Helen's mother went along to the Brownies to see Helen enrolled, she was pleased to hear Brown Owl telling the Brownies that they should be making themselves useful at home and, indeed, the group seemed to be having a civilising influence on Helen, which was badly needed, she reckoned.

Helen does have some difficulty in keeping the various bits of her Brownie uniform together – and her mother was taken aback by the initial cost of the uniform, since there were no second-hand ones available at that time.

However, Helen does make some effort to look tidy for Brownies, even polishing her own shoes, as Brown Owl makes a point of commenting on especially well-turned out Brownies. Helen enjoys dancing round the giant toadstool as part of the Brownie ritual though her mother is not too keen on this or the strong religious bias.

Helen says: 'I wanted to join because Tanya said it was great fun – so I asked mummy and she said I could. What do I like best? I liked the show we did, when we dressed up as gipsies. I think that's good because you learn to act well and not be nervous in front of an audience.

'At the meetings, first of all, you play games, then you sit down and talk about things, like what a success the Brownie show was, and so on. Then you learn a song, or a game, or work for badges. The sort of badges you do are like the hostess badge, where you have to invite someone, and be invited for tea, make a cup of tea, that sort of thing.

'There are other badges like horse riding, booklover and taking care of animals. I'd like to do those. What don't I like about Brownies? Nothing, really, I like it all. And I especially liked the Brownie annual I got for Christmas, it's super fun.'

Look back over these accounts and check this list of the things that were important reasons for the children liking their chosen activities.

Damian	Helen
Didn't mind doing something that his sister did	Wanted to do something away from her sisters
Was high spirited and enjoyed the rough and tumble of the group	Enjoyed learning things for badges
Enjoyed learning things for badges	Enjoyed making an effort at being organised for the Brownies
Enjoyed going to camp away from parents	Enjoyed going to something with her best friend
Enjoyed the emphasis on friendship and other children	Enjoyed dressing up

Some of the activities they enjoyed were new to them, so their parents couldn't judge beforehand how they would get on. But other elements, such as your child wanting to be with friends or mixing easily with the opposite sex, can be checked beforehand and considered carefully when finally deciding on an activity. Then there is far less chance of the whole project coming to grief!

The community comes to you!

One of the advantages of joining in various local activities is to make a child feel that he does belong to a wider group than just family or school.

But communities are not just local areas, they are groups of people who have interests in common. If it is not possible for your child to go out to an activity, there are still ways he can 'join in' without leaving home.

Look at the information that local newspapers offer. One week buy a selection of your local newspapers and look at the ways they provide interest and involvement for your child. Here's one local selection.

Walsall Herald
Children of five upwards can join Uncle Tom's Brigade.

○ There is no fee but each member receives a badge.

○ The children's page each week has an article to interest children, eg, the history of pantomime or something about the latest children's film.

○ Frequently there is an article which tells of the achievement of one particular child in a local activity.

○ Each week there is a competition with 25p postal orders awarded for the best efforts.

The Cannock Post
Children between five and fifteen can join Uncle Tom's Brigade.

○ No fee. If a telephone number is included in the application, the paper arranges for a photographer to take a picture of the child which then appears on the children's page.

○ The paper features an article of interest to children.

○ There is a competition in which children are asked questions about the article and a small prize is awarded for the best answers.

Sunday Mercury
There's a double page spread of cartoons, jokes, competitions and articles for children in this paper. Children can submit jokes and get 50p for good ones.

Wolverhampton Argus
This paper has a special service for children of up to fourteen. Once a week there is an advertisement section by children for children. There's a token fee of 5p (goes to charity) and the only conditions are that:

○ the child must be able to write his own advert.

○ no advertisement exceeds a set length.

○ the advert must be signed by a parent.

The column appears on Saturdays and each week over a hundred advertisements are sent.

Newspaper snippets in one week also publicised the following things.

○ Active puppet group in Lichfield.

○ Junior stamp fair in Walsall.

○ Christmas fairs – all over the place.

○ Exhibition of international children books in the central library at Walsall.

○ Cubs – sponsored eat-in – as many fish fingers as possible. Record to beat 130 centimetres of fish fingers.

○ Advertisements for talented dancers 7–10 to be in TV dancing teams for children's programmes.

Getting involved

Do you make use of the community you live in? This chapter is about your involvement as a parent in the community – how to make use of the facilities already available and how to set up new ones where the need arises. Local government provides a bewildering array of professionals who are there to help with your own and your children's various problems and concerns. The most difficult decision for many parents is which of them to turn to first. So we take a look at the professional services available to you and your child and at how to use them effectively.

But very often the kind of support you really need for your child is simply not available. If you're a working parent, day care in the holidays and after school are particularly important, but in many areas there is no official provision. In this chapter we look at how to find out what is available and how to set up your own child care schemes if none exist already.

Luckily, children seem to be able to play almost anywhere and with anything. But with a bit of imagination you can make your own house and back yard into a more exciting and absorbing place for them to play in. This chapter provides some ideas on how it's done.

Finally, we explore how self-help schemes of imaginative kinds can benefit both parents and children, and give some examples of schemes that have already been successful. After that, it's all up to you.

A large play scheme along the lines of the Grand Avenue holiday play scheme would need a grant from the local authority. Permission to use a school or local community centre would have to be granted. Then you would need to arrange the publicity and meetings and also take out insurance. Work would have to start some months before the holidays – because getting local authority funding and permission to use a school or community centre takes time. All in all, it would require a lot of hard work and organisational skills.

A small play scheme along the lines of Little Lane holiday play scheme would not require a lot of early planning. The parents involved would need to provide their own play materials and be able to entertain children as a group. They would have more control over the running of the scheme and could organise it for the times that suited them best.

Do you need a play scheme?
Think about how *you* felt during the last summer holidays and fill in on the chart what you really hated about them and what you really liked about them.

I hated the holidays because:	I liked the holidays because:

This is what Jean Oliver wrote.

I hated the holidays because:	I liked the holidays because:
I was frightened to leave the children playing alone for two minutes in case they ran out in front of a bus	*Enjoyed having more time just to play with the children*
I found myself exhausted at the end of the day with them	*I enjoyed not having to get up so early in the morning to get them to school on time*
I lost my temper more often than I meant to with them	
I found it difficult to get all the household jobs done with the kids under my feet	

If your 'likes' list is larger than your 'hates' list you are either very easy-going or you use some form of local play facility already. If, like Jean, your hates list is a lot larger than your likes list an investigation of local play schemes might be a good idea. Now consider these additional benefits.

○ Joining a play scheme might help you and your children enjoy the holidays.
○ It might help you make new friends with other parents.
○ It might put you in contact with people who can tell you about other interesting things that are going on elsewhere.

PLAYCENTRE

Jobs to do

People who get involved in organising play schemes don't all have the same skills. Nobody expects that. Different people contribute different things to successful groups.

Here are the experiences of three friends who all became involved with a holiday play scheme. They describe what happened when it first began, and what was happening after three weeks.

At the first meeting	After three weeks
Janet	
Thought the play scheme was a good idea, but only came along to the meeting because my friend Daphne over the road was going. Didn't say anything and stayed in the background	Find that I spend most days at the play scheme now. Usually make sandwiches for lunch first thing and then spend the whole day there. Between us we usually organise the games and join in ourselves. Other parents come when they can but the really regular attenders are the ones who tend to be in the thick of it all
Pat	
I did quite a lot of groundwork, looking for some where to have the scheme, investigating insurance and so on. But I was very relieved when other parents volunteered to take over the bulk of the day-to-day work. I passed on a load of pamphlets on play schemes from the National Playingfields Association and other organisations	The play scheme is running well. Janet and Daphne who are the mainstays know they can call on me if there are any problems. So far it's worked well and the kids are having a great time. Already people are beginning to mention lessons learned ready for setting up next year's project. And I'm noting them all down in a diary
Dave	
Felt very enthusiastic about the play scheme. It could take a great weight off my mind, knowing that the children are not only being looked after but also are doing things they really enjoy. Feel a bit guilty because I can't help much	I really made a nuisance of myself at the office collecting jumble for the sale and odds and ends – bottle tops, glue, string for the children to make things with. I try to do something special on my half day, like a trip to the baths, to give some of the other parents a rest

These are three different parents with different resources and dispositions – all of them playing a part in the play scheme. In what way do different sorts of people fit into a play scheme group? You can discuss this matter with other interested parents and see who is prepared to do what. Look at this list together and fill in names accordingly.

		Happy	Wouldn't mind	Unhappy
1	Going to see officials			
2	Writing to officials			
3	Writing to newspapers/ publicity posters			
4	Standing up and talking in front of a group			
5	Keeping people in the group informed			
6	Sticking stamps, distributing leaflets			
7	Smoothing over arguments			
8	Asking around, talking to people to get support			
9	Organising fund-raising			
10	Helping with things like jumble sales			
11	Finding out information the group might find useful			

		Happy	Wouldn't mind	Unhappy
12	Being willing to talk about problems to do with the group			
13	Being a contact person that other people can get in touch with			
14	Using your house for group meetings			
15	Spending a lot of time with the children			
16	Dreaming up things for the children to do			
17	Ordering stock			
18	Keeping accounts			

If you can turn your hand to several of the things on the list, you'll be a boon to any group. Remember, though, someone who is prepared to turn their hand to anything frequently ends up by doing a lot of the work!

If you filled in:	You are:
1, 2, 3, 4, 9	an organiser. You are prepared to stand up and take the limelight. You are able to take on problems
5, 7, 8, 11, 12, 13	a communicator. You are one of those people who are good at keeping a good line of communication within the group; you know people need to know what's going on; you know difficulties occur but can be smoothed out
6, 10, 14, 17, 18	a backroom boy. One of those invaluable, but sometimes rare people who are prepared to do the day-to-day unglamorous work. Backroom work is crucial
15 and 16	an entertainer, and you are aware that this is the point of the group. Not everyone who helps to set up a playscheme is good at this level of activity

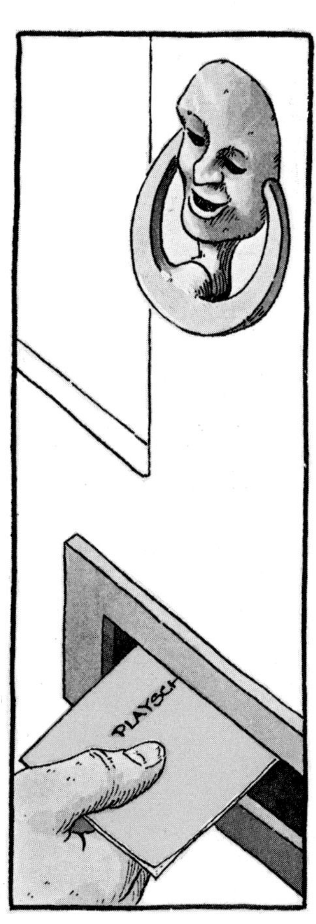

All of these skills are useful for a group. When starting a play scheme you'll need to bear in mind that lots of different talents are required.

What next?

This section provides an action guide on how to set up a large and a small play scheme.

A 'Grand Avenue' play scheme

The first step is to prepare for a public meeting where interested people in your area can meet to discuss the whole idea. You'll want to have all the information you can get about possible funding to put before the meeting, so:

○ find out if there is a 'play association' or 'play council' in your area. These are made up of representatives from all the local play projects. If you have a play council visit it. They may even have a representative on the local council and they will give you help and advice about how to get some funding for your play scheme.

○ visit your local youth office. They tend mainly to deal with youth clubs but they should be able to help you with advice about play schemes. Explain in full your ideas about a holiday play scheme. Sometimes it helps if you write your ideas down on paper before you visit any officials.

○ go to the Town Hall. Make an appointment to visit the appropriate council department with two or three other local parents. You may be lucky enough to have a play officer in your area – but if not try the Parks and Recreation Department. If they do offer you money you should make sure there are no inconvenient strings attached.

Now you are ready to arrange the public meeting. Posters and leaflets are two of the best methods of getting word about your meeting around the area. Posters displayed in prominent positions in your local shops and pubs will attract quite a lot of attention. Try car stickers too. This can be followed up by house-to-house distribution of leaflets before the meeting.

The public meeting

At your initial meeting it is worth discussing the following points.

1 The best dates and times for your play scheme.

2 How many children the play scheme can cater for.

3 The age range of the children. You need to be definite about this. It will depend on the number of adults working on the play scheme, the facilities that are available and the range of activities offered.

4 Premises for the play scheme. Your options here might be a playground, youth club, school, church hall, sports hall, village or community centre.

5 How much it is likely to cost.

6 How many people are prepared to help out with the scheme. Make a list of names. This can always be added to as the scheme develops and more people hear about it and want to join in. Remember your list can also include people with very limited time but a specific skill to offer. For instance, perhaps you can persuade some local drivers to take children on a day trip to the seaside.

7 Delegate people to deal with the following tasks and ask them to report their progress at subsequent meetings. Arrange a date to meet again.

Premises

Someone should go to all the possible sites and check each one.

○ Is it safe from traffic?

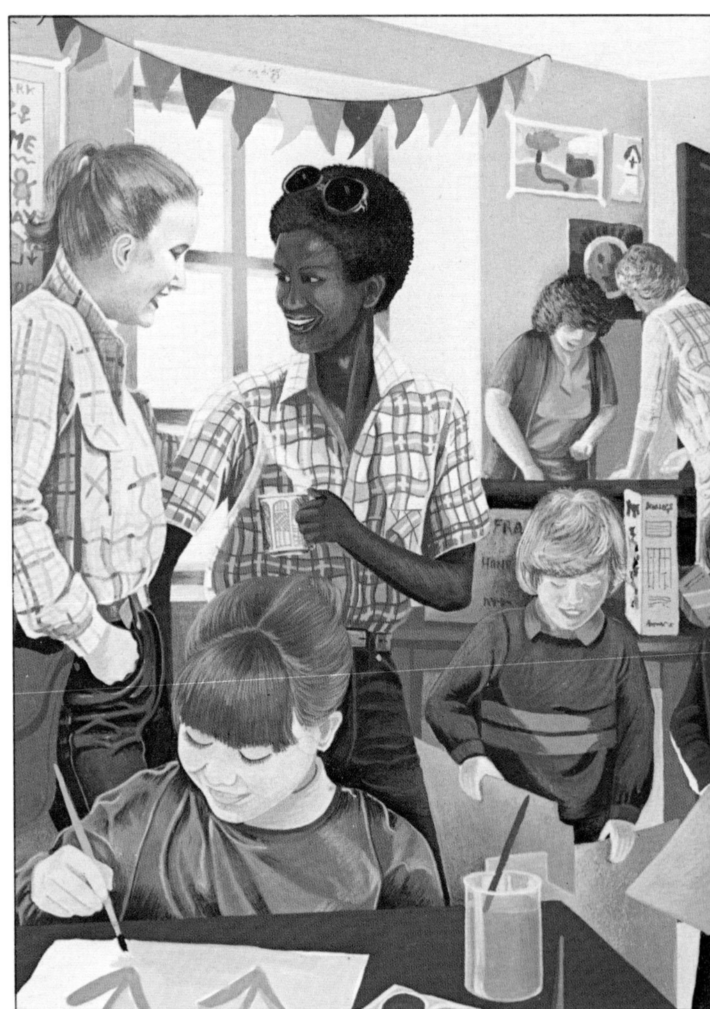

○ How far is the nearest bus from the site?
○ Is the site flexible/suitable for a large number of children?
○ Are there facilities for cooking and catering?
○ Is there a telephone?

Publicity
At an early meeting you should arrange how you are going to organise the publicity for the play scheme and put someone in charge. Colourful posters and leaflets are probably the best methods. You could also try and get a play bus to visit the area. It would draw lots of parents and children and could be used as part of a publicity drive for more permanent play facilities.

Insurance
Play associations will arrange this, but if this isn't possible delegate someone to investigate possibilities. Any reputable insurance broker will be able to advise you about this.

Finances
When the scheme gets off the ground, appoint a treasurer who can keep tabs on where all the money's going.

If you get a grant from the local authority it may not be enough to cover all the costs of the play scheme. You may need to hold jumble sales and raffles; also try approaching local employers for handouts either of cash or materials. Try begging letters to local dignitaries – the Lord Mayor, your local MP, etc.

First aid
This must always be available on your play scheme, or when you take a group out on a trip. Accidents can happen and it's always best to be prepared. Keep a note of the local doctor's number and the nearest casualty department. For swimming trips you need a qualified lifesaver on hand. Public baths should always have one on duty.

Programme
Make up a programme of daily activities for the play scheme. You should have some standby events in case of bad weather.

A 'Little Lane' play scheme

There's no need to arrange much advance publicity or call a special meeting for a small scheme. Discuss the idea over a cup of coffee with the neighbours. If you don't know anyone in the area put an advert in the local newsagents or in the local paper.

Over coffee ...

1 Decide which dates and times suit you best. Arrange a rough timetable of who will take charge of the children on which days.

2 Think through standby plans for at least five wet days – games, trips to the swimming baths, cinema, etc.

3 Assemble a list of the sports equipment you have between you and start collecting play materials, paints, brushes, paper, fabric scraps, clay and plasticine, wood, cereal boxes, yoghurt pots, etc.

4 Remember to ask the children what *they* think they'd like to do in the holidays!

Records
Whichever scheme you choose, when it gets going (or even before), it's well worth keeping a diary of what happens. Record it in words and photos. This will:

○ act as a trigger for your memory next year, or enable you to provide help for future organisers.

○ give you material to show to people who might donate money towards a more ambitious play scheme.

Planning to play

Help your children find interesting places to play in your house and garden

Children are very imaginative when it comes to play. But you can help by providing them with interesting places to play in and a wide variety of stimulating play materials.

It's not a matter of weighing in and organising, but making an opportunity that your child can use for himself to create his own world, with or without his friends.

Children do use places imaginatively in play and you can help them in this by making sure that parts of your home and garden or backyard can be used flexibly. Other people in the family use these places too, so, remember, it is a matter of compromise.

Planning for play in your home

Plan a children's play room. In most houses this will need to be a bedroom arranged so that what goes on is the children's affair, and as free as possible from outside interference.

Remember:

- there is more space in a room than most people think.
- make sure that something that takes up a lot of room really has to be there.
- if your children share a room there are still opportunities for giving each his own corner. The important thing is for a child to have some space which is all his own.
- children have their own ideas. Allow them some real initiative. Don't over-plan. For instance, let them choose their own wallpaper within your price range. It is their room.
- be adaptable. As children grow, their needs change. The way a five-year-old will want to use his space will be different from that of a ten-year-old.

Nooks and crannies

Think how your children use your house. Talk to them about it. Play a game.

If this house were a ship then the bridge would be ... my bedroom.

If this house were a castle then the drawbridge would be ...

If this house were a rocket ...

If this house were a mountain ...

You will see that, to your child, the various parts of your house can be used imaginatively for many different games. So look at the possibilities that exist in nooks and crannies, the room under the stairs, under the kitchen table, the garage. You may wonder how under-the-stairs can be so attractive to your child, but it is. See if you can find somewhere in your home that will make a good den.

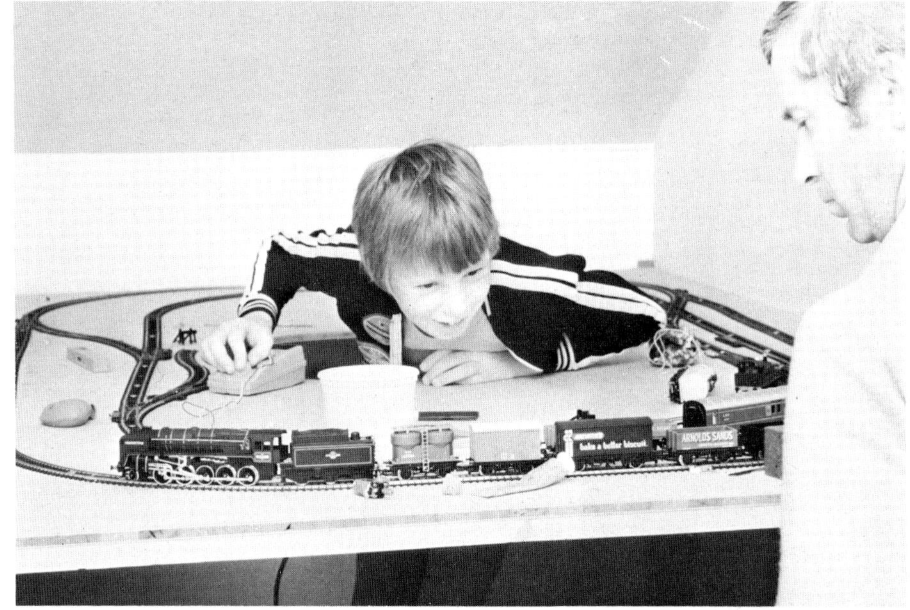

Planning for play in the garden

Outside your home your children frequent a large variety of places. Parents don't approve of all of them by any means. So it might be worth making your garden more attractive, if you have one.

Before you start thinking about your garden or backyard, try and find out what kind of things your child enjoys outside in the wider world.

Here is a list of places children might choose to go and play. Talk to your child about the sorts of things he'd choose to do in each of these places and what he likes about them.

Street, wild area, building site, park, school premises, playground, around garages and outhouses.

Make a list of what your child says about each. Here are a few questions you could ask.

○ Are there lots of things to do here?

○ Is it very noisy? Do you like noisy places?

○ Is there lots of colour and movement?

○ Are there plenty of people around?

○ Would you like to be by yourself here?

○ What sorts of games would you play?

○ Is it a place where you can get very messy?

○ Is it an exciting place?

From the things your child says there are probably a few attractions that you could create in your own garden or backyard.

Laying plans

Even the smallest gardens can, with a bit of careful planning, provide some valuable playspace for children. Draw a plan of your garden. Mark out the areas taken up by plants, paving and lawn. Decide where the children's own special garden space can be sited, where a sand pit could be installed, which part of the lawn could accommodate a swing, a slide or a climbing frame. Larger gardens offer a wider range of possibilities – remember 'play' need not mean equipment. An area of garden left rough, a fish pond, an old tree stump, stepping stones between the flower beds, a solidly built staggered wall, the corner of the shed not used for storing things – all these things bring interest into the garden and need not necessarily conflict with the other needs and uses. Here is a sample garden plan.

The garden or the backyard isn't exactly the outside world but it can be an exciting place.

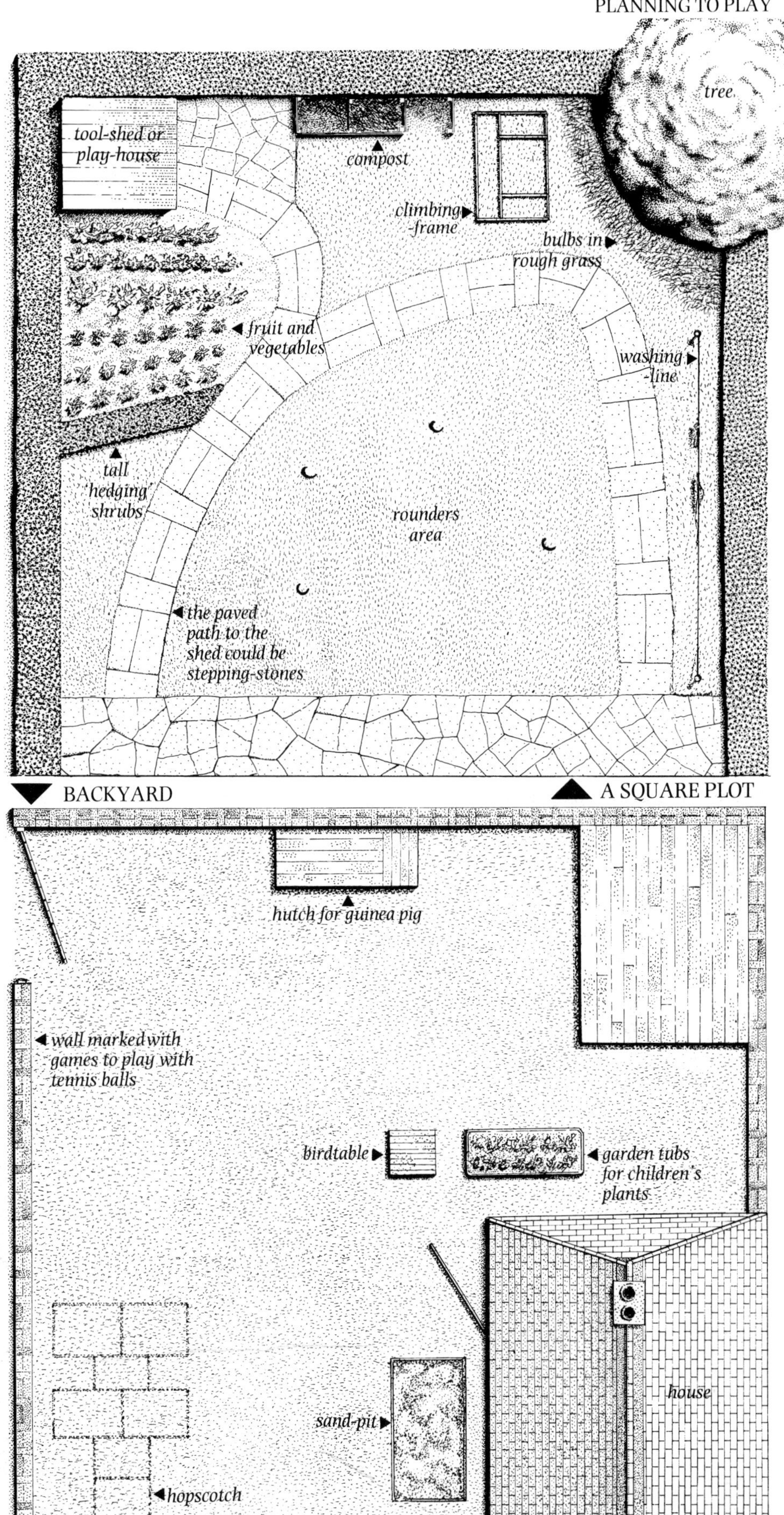

Branching out

Your children are starting to do things on their own, both at home and out in the community.

Activity	Mother	Father	Child 1	Child 2	Child 3	Child 4
	☐	☐	☐	☐	☐	☐
	☐	☐	☐	☐	☐	☐
	☐	☐	☐	☐	☐	☐
	☐	☐	☐	☐	☐	☐
	☐	☐	☐	☐	☐	☐

Activity	Jenny	Dave	Tracey	Frank	Michaela
Pre-school playgroup	☑	☐	☐	☐	☑
Brownies	☐	☐	☑	☐	☐
Cubs	☐	☐	☐	☑	☐
Swimming	☐	☑	☑	☑	☐
Football match	☐	☑	☐	☑	☐
Park	☐	☑	☐	☐	☑
Pottery	☑	☐	☐	☐	☐
Cinema	☑	☑	☐	☐	☐
Darts	☐	☑	☐	☐	☐
Pub	☑	☑	☐	☐	☐
Residents association	☑	☑	☐	☐	☐
Zoo	☑	☑	☑	☑	☑
TOTAL 12	6	8	3	4	3

It's always good to encourage independence but there may be times when the whole family can enjoy – and benefit from – activities done all together; or times when the same activity, done with different people, can seem like a whole new game.

Think about the activities that you and your family regularly take part in outside the home. Some of them you'll probably do separately, some together. Keep a diary for a few days of what various people do and then go back and fill in the chart on the left. Down the side write in the various activities your family do. In the columns tick which people do which activities.

Even if the same activity happens several times in one week mark down each occasion so that you have a full week's diary of your family's activity in the community.

Here is the Dawson's chart for Jenny, Dave and their three children Tracy, 9, Frank, 7, and Michaela, 4.

Look at your own chart. See how many activities are undertaken by one family member only, how many involve a parent and child, parents or children only or the family as a whole. The only thing the Dawsons did all together in the week was go to the zoo. And everyone except Michaela does an activity that's all their own.

Family circles

Try making a family circle. Count up the events your family takes part in and divide your circle into the same number of segments.

○ Colour in red the occasions people attend by themselves.

○ Colour in blue the occasions where parent and child are together.

○ Colour in green the occasions where parents are together.

○ Colour in purple the occasions where children are together.

○ Colour in brown the occasions where the whole family is together.

To help you, we have shown the circles drawn by the Dawsons, the Carters and the Andersons.

The Dawsons have a fair spread of colours; they do a lot of community activities, together and apart.

The Carters are very different. They don't do many things in the community and, when they do, these tend to be planned outings for everyone.

The Andersons are different again. They do lots of things but they do them separately. The only time the whole family gets together is to go shopping.

Different families do have different styles and each style has advantages. Here are some of them. (See overleaf.)

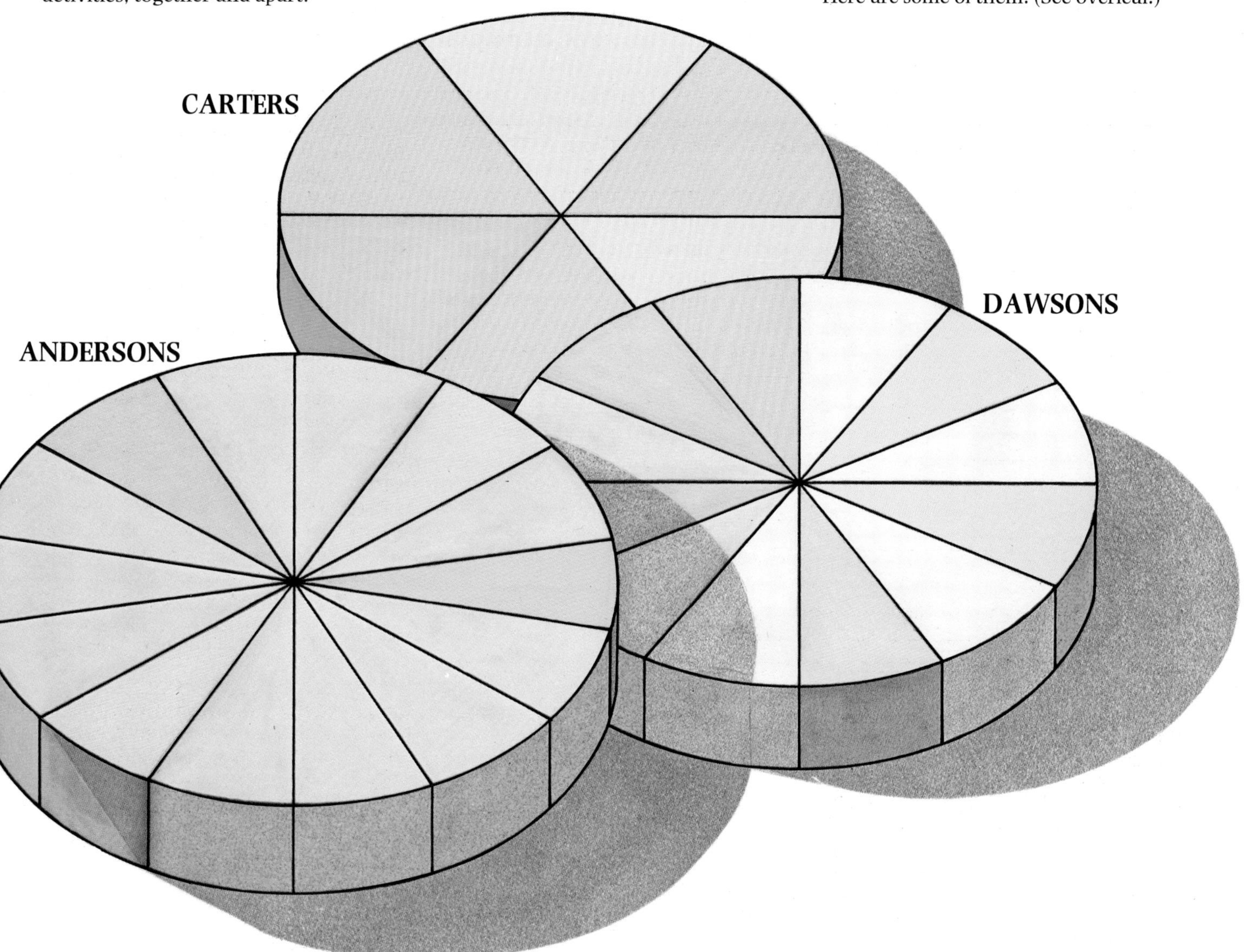

ANDERSONS

Chess	Judo
Mothers union	Football
Church	Library
Dressmaking	Car maintenance
Woodcraft	Dancing class

- Pub

- Cinema
- Swimming

- Saturday shopping

CARTERS

- Swimming
- Cubs

- Club

- Playing golf in the park
- Outing to the seaside
- Cinema

DAWSONS

Brownies	Pottery
Cubs	Darts

Football	Park
Swimming	Play-School

- Cinema

- Pub
- Residents Association

- Zoo

RED **Going it alone**	BLUE **Parent and child**	GREEN **Parents only**	PURPLE **Children only**	BROWN **Whole family**
People in family act independently of each other	Child can get the whole attention of one parent	Parents can express themselves apart from their children	Older children have a chance to act responsibly	Chance to experience community together
An individual can get on with his own interests	Parent can keep an eye on child	Can show children that parents have a social life of their own	Makes younger children feel more grown up	Creates common interests
Child has a chance to stand on own two feet	Parent can enjoy child's increasing involvement in community		Children of different ages can be together	

You might decide, when looking at your chart, that you'd like to try some things differently. Jenny and Dave Dawson did.

Jenny: We looked at our circle and thought the best candidates for a change were swimming, football, the park and the cinema.

Dave: We thought about Jenny taking Tracey and Frank swimming instead of me and then we thought, no, we'll have a whole family outing, seeing as we'd only got one on our list!

Jenny: So, off we went. It was a scream. Michaela had never been before and Tracey and Frank had great fun showing off to her: and they were showing me how much progress they'd made.

Dave: Needless to say Michaela was more taken by the hot chocolate machine than anything else and the fact that she got to stay up really late – 8 o'clock.

Jenny: Then Dave took Tracey to the football match too, and she's getting to the pop star age so she had a wonderful time admiring the striker.

Dave: And she was very taken with the crowd. She'd never been in a really big crowd before.

Jenny: Well, we'd really got off on the idea by now and so we sent all the kids to a nearby park by themselves. I think Tracey overdid it a bit, she wouldn't let go of Michaela's hand at all. Michaela said after that Dave and I were much more fun to go with!

Try it yourself. And make a point of finding out what people in the family think. A familiar event done with different people can seem entirely new.

Play – a year of ideas

The changing seasons, with their own fruits and vegetables and flowers, provide variety for play. And special days on the calendar may be celebrated by special events which your child will enjoy.

This calendar is designed to give you some ideas. Depending on whether you live in the country or town, or near the seaside or mountains, your own calendar might be different.

Check out local events on special occasions – the summer holiday fairs, the carnival, egg rolling at Easter, skating or sliding when the weather is freezing. Make up your own calendar of things for your children and their friends to do.

	To collect	To make	To grow	To cook	To go
January	decorative junk for collage	collage	mustard and cress on flannel	pastry people	tobogganing on plastic bags or trays
February	matchboxes	matchbox models	jam jar runner beans	pancakes	looking for catkins
March	signs of spring	Easter eggs	indoor garden	French toast	to the museum
April	ideas for street games	tie/dye printing	plants from pips	hot-cross buns	to see the lambs
May	garden pool materials	garden pool	(sow) sunflower seeds	maypole cake	to the zoo
June	junk for musical instruments	musical instruments	bedding plants in pots or garden	chocolate krispies	to the paddling pool
July	pebbles	pebble jewelry, painted stones	window box	pop corn	to a garden party
August	sea shells	shell models	flower arranging	cheese scones	to the carnival, fruit picking
September	conkers	bird table	plant indoor bulbs	hot chestnuts	to the harvest festival
October	autumn leaves	pumpkin lanterns, pictures from leaves	plant outdoor bulbs	toffee apples	on an autumn picnic
November	fir cones	bonfire and Guy Fawkes	indoor plants	hot dogs	to look for dried flowers and grass
December	holly and mistletoe	Christmas decorations	cacti	mince pies	the Xmas fayre, carol singing

Self-help schemes

Do you enjoy working with people to get things done?

Have you ever moved to a new area where you don't know the neighbours and suddenly realise there is nobody to call on if you fall ill or just need someone to keep an eye on the children for ten minutes?

Have you ever felt helpless when an official said 'no' to a request you thought was perfectly reasonable?

Do you find that talking about your worries to other people who share similar difficulties helps you to cope?

If you said 'yes' to any of those you will certainly get something out of joining a parent self-help group if you don't belong to one already. Parent self-help groups can be large and well organised – like Gingerbread, the organisation for single parents; or they can be small and informal – three or four parents who take it in turns to pick their children up from school.

Parents are fortunate that their children immediately give them something in common with other parents – it's a subject they all enjoy talking about. Meeting other parents at school open days, while picking them up from school, at the playground or out shopping, all provide opportunities for getting to know them better.

The most obvious way of helping each other is to share looking after the children. Setting up a holiday play scheme, or taking turns to look after each others' children for a few hours after school or in the holidays can help to take a lot of pressure off busy parents.

The same principle can be used to make shopping easier and cheaper, by taking turns to bulk buy for a group of people.

Or you could decide to exert group pressure to try and change the policy of local government over services that aren't up to scratch.

Here are some examples of real self-help groups in action. They may give you some ideas.

The chart (right) lists some of the benefits that can come from working together in self-help groups to achieve a shared objective. We have looked through the different schemes and ticked the benefits we think apply. The space at the bottom of the chart is to help you assess the benefits of a self-help scheme you are already involved in, or one you would like to start.

Share-a-garden scheme

Allotment gardening is flourishing as more people realise the benefits of fresh, cheap, home-grown vegetables, and the satisfaction of growing them yourself. The only problem is that the demand for allotment land always seems to exceed the supply. One solution is a Garden Loan Scheme.

A listener to one of Radio Solent's 'phone-ins' suggested that people without a garden who wanted one should borrow one from an elderly or disabled person who couldn't cope with a garden on their own. Mrs Fennemore of Bournemouth took up the idea and formed a register of local people who wanted a garden, and those who were offering a garden. To publicise the scheme she sent an information letter to the editors of the local newspapers, and the response from readers was immediate. With the co-operation of the Parks Department, gardeners applying for allotments were told of the scheme and many were able to 'borrow' a garden near their homes as a result.

Rebuilding a school playground

Parents from a primary school in Croydon decided their children's school playground needed a face-lift. They discussed ideas at a meeting of the Parent-Teachers Association and a group of parents plus one teacher was formed to organise the work. First, a list of possible designs for the playground was drawn up. The children's ideas were included right from the beginning and the teachers helped by basing classroom project work on the playgound scheme. The children filled in questionnaires, made drawings, made up songs, and brought in plants for the playground garden. A programme of work was drawn up and the playground was built by a team of volunteers during the school summer holidays.

Anti-dampness campaign

The group was formed by tenants in a complex of 1200 prefabricated concrete flats, built between 1969 and 1973 in the Gorbals area of Glasgow. Dampness had begun to appear about eight weeks after the flats were occupied and the problem got steadily worse, causing staining, fungus and smell. The authority argued it was only condensation and therefore a tenant problem which could be solved by properly heating and ventilating the flats. The tenants disagreed and the argument persisted for nearly three years.

Eventually the tenants got together and started a campaign. They organised a plan of action involving public meetings, letter writing, public demonstrations and coverage in the newspapers, on radio and television. After a long struggle the tenants did win their right to compensation, and they got a rebate of one-third of the rent paid since they moved in. They are glad they stuck to their guns, despite all the nuisance.

Childminding circle

Four parents with children attending the same primary school got together to help look after their children after school. They took it in turns to pick up the children from school, keep an eye on them for two or three hours and give them tea.

The children liked it because they enjoyed playing together, and the parents liked it because it gave them a welcome early evening break for a couple of evenings a week.

One of the parents was a single working father who welcomed the re-assurance of knowing his child would be looked after when school finished, but was unable to take his turn during weekdays. He made his contribution by taking the children on trips at the weekends – to parks, football matches, swimming baths and so on – which the mothers found a valuable help.

These schemes need to be flexible to be most effective. They work best if everyone concerned is willing to contribute.

Children benefit

Children learn a lot from your involvement in self-help groups. The children in the groups described did.

The children whose parents were rebuilding a school playground were closely involved with their parents and teachers in a joint project. They were finding out how to work closely with other people, and sharing in the satisfaction of a successful and practical group effort.

The childminding circle gives children a glimpse of how other parents do things – from opening a tin of beans to getting them all to be quiet. It gives the children a wider experience of different people and places that will help them to develop their own understanding of the world. And, of course, it's fun to play with other children and share different toys. Variety is always appealing.

The anti-dampness campaign and the share-a-garden scheme are self-help groups that don't directly involve children. But children learn to develop their own grown-up behaviour from watching the adults around them – and most of all they learn from what their own parents do.

Children can pick up very quickly that co-operation is a good way of tackling problems; that grouping together with people in a similar position to yourself can be very effective; and that it can be fun.

In fact before you know it, they'll probably have formed a toy-sharing scheme of their own.

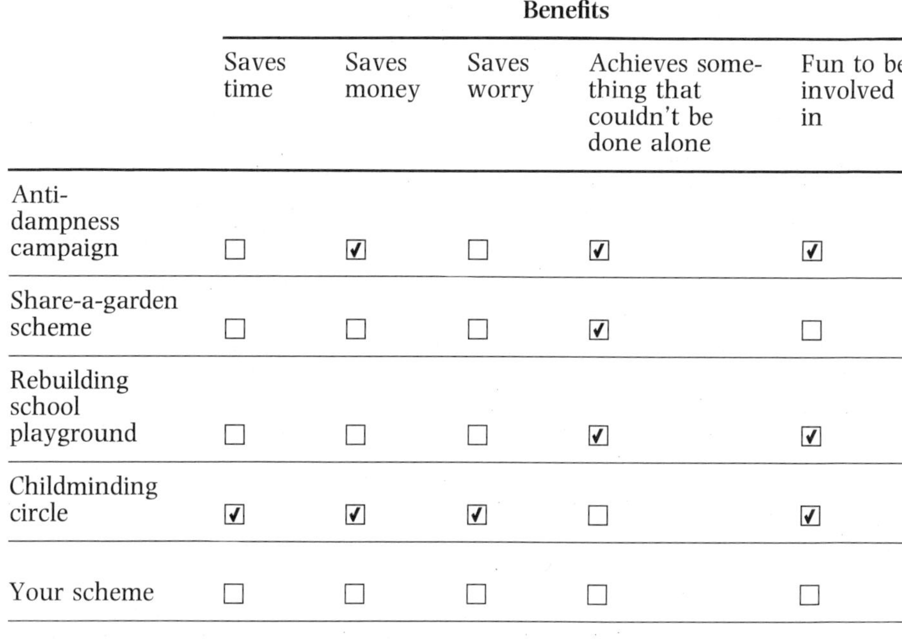

	Benefits				
	Saves time	Saves money	Saves worry	Achieves something that couldn't be done alone	Fun to be involved in
Anti-dampness campaign	☐	☑	☐	☑	☑
Share-a-garden scheme	☐	☐	☐	☑	☐
Rebuilding school playground	☐	☐	☐	☑	☑
Childminding circle	☑	☑	☑	☐	☑
Your scheme	☐	☐	☐	☐	☐

Conclusion

Now that you have worked right through to the end of this book, we hope you will agree with us that the ages between five and ten are exciting not only for children but for you, their parents, too.

It is the time when children are exploring their world and becoming interested in the people who inhabit it with them. It is a time when you can share with them the joys of finding out and set them off on many roads of discovery.

In fact, your role as parent takes on tremendous importance during this time. You are no longer just a person who is there to supply affection, security and regular food, vital though those functions are and will remain. You are your child's first guide into the exciting unknown and the more opportunities you create for him to learn about people and places and the ways of the world, the stronger and more secure your child will grow.

It is during this time too that you must accept for the first time that other people are going to play an important part in the direction of your child's life – chiefly, teachers at school. It can be a hard wrench to let go of your very special position, but, of course, in reality, you never really do. You are the stable, ever-loving element of your child's life, whatever happens outside and however immersed he seems to be in the activities and people that engage him elsewhere.

Yet, by seeming to let go and give him his head, encouraging him to involve himself in projects at school and, with or without you, in projects in the community, you'll be strengthening, not weakening, your family bonds.

As T. S. Eliot said, home is where one starts from. But it is also where a child comes back to, if it's an easy, warm and giving place.

List of organisations

Chapters 1 and 2

Health Education Council, 78 New Oxford Street, London, WC1 1AH.

Scottish Health Education Group, Woodburn House, Canaan Lane, Edinburgh, EM10 4SG.

Toy Libraries Association (TLA), Seabrook House, Wyllots Manor, Darkes Lane, Potters Bar, Herts.

Chapters 3 and 4

Countrywide Holidays Association (CHA), Birch Heys, Cromwell Range, Manchester, M14 6HU.

Gingerbread, 35 Wellington Street, London, WC2. 39 Hope Street, Glasgow, G3 7DW.

Justice for Children, 35 Wellington Street, London , WC2E 7BN.

National Childminding Association, 236A London Road, Bromley, Kent, BR1 1PQ.

National Children's Centre (NCC), Longroyd Bridge, Huddersfield, West Yorkshire.

National Children's Home, 83 Highbury Park, London, N1 1UD.

National Coordinating Committee of Self-Help Groups for Parents Under Stress, Public Relations Officer: Mrs Jane Moss, 10 Pakenham Road, Edgbaston, Birmingham.

National Council for One Parent Families (formerly the National Council for the Unmarried Mother and her Child), 255 Kentish Town Road, London, NW5 WLX.

National Society for the Prevention of Cruelty to Children (NSPCC), 1–3 Riding House Street, London, W1P 8AA.

Save the Children Fund, 157 Clapham Road, London, SW9.

Chapters 5 and 6

Advisory Centre for Education (ACE) Ltd, 18 Victoria Park Square, Bethnal Green, London, E2 9PB.

Campaign Against Sexism and Sexual Oppression in Education (CASSOE), 7 Pickwick Court, London, SE9.

Campaign for the Advancement of State Education (CASE), David Pearson (Secretary), 1 Windermere Avenue, Wembley, Middlesex, HA9 8SH.

Centre for Information and Advice on Educational Disadvantage, 11 Anson Road, Manchester, M14 5BY.

Commission for Racial Equality, Elliott House, 10–12 Allington Street, London, SW1E 5EH.

Education Otherwise, 18 Eyham Road, London W12.

Federation of Children's Book Groups, 22 Beacon Road, Horton Bank Top, Bradford BD6 3DE, W. Yorks.

National Association of Governors and Managers, Mrs B. Bullivant, 81 Rustlings Road, Sheffield, S11 7AB.

National Association for Multi-Racial Education, c/o Ms. Madeleine Blakely, 23 Doles Lane, Findern, Derby, DE6 6AX.

National Confederation of Parent Teacher Associations, 1 White Avenue, Northfleet, Gravesend, Kent, DA11 9DS.

Scottish Community Education Centre, 4 Queensferry Street, Edinburgh, EH2 4PA.

Scottish Parent Teacher Council, 4 Queensferry Street, Edinburgh, EH2 4PA.

Service Children's Education Authority, Court Road, Eltham, London, SE9 5NR.

Society of Teachers Opposed to Physical Punishment (STOPP), 10 Lennox Gardens, Croydon, Surrey, CR0 4HR.

Worldwide Education Service (PNEU), Murray House, Vandon Street, London, SW1.

Chapters 7 and 8

Boys Brigade, Brigade House, Parsons Green, London, SW6 4TH.

British Association for Settlements and Social Action Centres (BASSAC), 7 Exton Street, London, SE1 8UE.

Community Projects Foundation, 60 Highbury Grove, London, N5 2AG.

Community Service Volunteers (CSV), 237 Pentonville Road, London, N1 9NJ.

Fair Play for Children, 248 Kentish Town Road, London, NW5.

Girls Brigade, Brigade House, Parsons Green, London, SW6 4TN.

Girl Guides Association, 17–19 Buckingham Palace Road, London, SW1W 0PT.

Grapevine, BBC TV, London, W12 8QT.

Handicapped Adventure Playground Association (HAPA), Fulham Place, Bishops Avenue, London, SW6.

National Committee on Fixed Equipment Playgrounds, 248 Kentish Town Road, London, NW5.

National Playbus Association (NPA), Secretary, Jane Martin, 48 Blagove Lane, Wokingham, Berks.

National Playing Fields Association (NPFA), 25 Ovington Square, London, SW3 1LQ.

Scout Association, Baden Powell House, Queen's Gate, London, SW7 5JS.

Services to Community Action and Tenants (SCAT), 31 Clerkenwell Close, London, EC1R 0AT.

St John Ambulance Brigade, 1 Grosvenor Crescent, London, SW1.

Woodcraft Folk, 13 Ritherdon Road, London, SW17 8QE.

Youth Hostels Association (YHA), 14 Southampton Street, London, WC2.

General

Capital Kidsline (London), Telephone 01-222 8070.

Children's Rights Workshop, 4 Aldebert Terrace, London, SW8.

Child Poverty Action Group, 1 Macklin Street, London, WC2B 5NH.

MIND (National Association for Mental Health), 22 Harley Street, London, W1.

National Association for Gifted Children (NAGC), 1 South Audley Street, London, W1.

National Association for the Welfare of Children in Hospitals (NAWCH), 7 Exton Street, London, SE1.

National Children's Bureau, 8 Wakley Street, London, EC1V 7QE.

National Deaf Children's Society, 45 Hereford Road, London, W2 5AH.

National Society for Mentally Handicapped Children (MENCAP), Pembridge Hall, 17 Pembridge Square, London, WC2 4EP.

Royal Society for the Prevention of Accidents (RoSPA), 1 Grosvenor Street, London, SW1.

Voluntary Council for Handicapped Children, National Children's Bureau, 8 Wakley Street, London, EC1V 7QE.

Further reading

Chapters 1 and 2

de Bono, E (1972) Children Solve Problems, Penguin Books Ltd.

Bower, T (1977) The Perceptual World of the Child, Fontana.

Diagram Group (1979) Child's Body: A Parent's Manual, Corgi.

Goodnow, J (1977) Children's Drawing, Fontana.

Janov, A (1977) The Feeling Child, Sphere Books.

Jolly, H (1978) Book of Child Care, Sphere Books.

Martin, N (1976) Understanding Children Talking, Penguin Books Ltd.

Newson, J & E (1976) Seven Years Old in the Home Environment, George Allen and Unwin Ltd.

Opie, I & Opie, P (1969) Children's Games in Street and Playgound, Oxford University Press.

(1977) Lore and Language of Schoolchildren, Paladin.

Rutter, M (1975) Helping Troubled Children, Penguin Books Ltd.

For your child:

Althea (1973) Going to the Doctor.
(1974) Visiting the Dentist.
(1975) A Baby in the Family.
(1977) I Go to Hospital.
(1978) Having an Eye Test.
Dinosaur Publications.

Andry, A and Schepp, S (1968) How Babies are Made, Time Life Books.

Elgin, K (1970) The Human Body series, Franklin Watts, includes books on the brain, the eye, the ear, skeleton, digestive and reproductive systems.

Knudsen, P (1975) How A Baby is Made, Pan Books.

Rockwell, H (1974) My Doctor.
(1975) My Dentist.
Hamish Hamilton.

Showers, P (1964) Find out by Touching.
(1967) Follow your Nose.
(1967) Your Skin and Mine.
(1974) Sleep is for Everyone.
A & C Black Ltd.

Wilson, R (1978) How the Body works, Ward Lock.

Chapters 3 and 4

Fletcher, R (1969) Family and Marriage in Britain, Penguin Books Ltd.

Kempe, R and Kempe, H (1978) Child Abuse, Fontana.

Kempe, H and Helfer, R (1972) Helping the Battered Child and His Family, Lippincott.

Renvoize, J (1970) Web of Violence, A Study of Family Violence, Routledge, Kegan Paul.

(1975) Children in Danger: Causes and Prevention of Baby Battering, Penguin Books Ltd.

For your child:

Lindgren, A (1976) Pippi Longstocking.
(1976) Pippi goes Abroad.
(1977) Pippi in the South Seas.
Puffin.

Thorvall, K (1977) Instead of a Dad, Kestrel Books.

Bawden, N (1972) The Runaway Summer, Puffin.

Chapters 5 and 6

Burgess, T (1973) Home and School, Penguin Books Ltd.

Croall, J (1978) The Parents' Day School Book, Penguin Books Ltd.

Hartley, K and Newby, M (1980) How to Help a Child at Home, Home and School Council, 17 Jacksons Lane, Billericay, Essex.

Holt, J (1969) How Children Fail. (1970) How Children Learn. Penguin Books Ltd.

Mackay, D and Simio, J (1976) Help Your Child to Read and Write, Penguin Books Ltd.

Nickols, R (1974) Helping Your Child to Read. (1978) Helping Your Child to Spell. University of Reading, Centre for the Teaching of Reading.

O'Connor, M (1977) Your Child's Primary School, Pan Books.

Pluckrose, H (1979) Children in their Primary Schools, Penguin Books Ltd.

Stone, J and Taylor, F (1976) Parents' Schoolbook, Penguin Books Ltd.

Chapters 7 and 8

Lambert, J and Pearson, J (1974) Adventure Playgounds, Penguin Books Ltd.

Law, F (1977) Things to Make from Junk. (1977) Things to Make from Card. (1978) How to Make Print Patterns. (1978) How to Make Puppets and Dolls. William Collins, and Co. Ltd.

Matterson, E (1970) Play with a Purpose for Under Sevens, Penguin Books Ltd.

Orlick, T (1980) The Co-operative Sports and Games Book, Writers and Readers Publishing Co-operative.

General

Carr, J (1980) Helping your Handicapped Child, Penguin Books Ltd.

Dinham, B and Norton, M (1977) The Directory of Social Change, Volume 1: Education and Play, Wildwood House.

Family Welfare Assoc. (Annually) Charities Digest, Family Welfare Association Ltd, and The Butterworth Group Ltd.

(Annually) Guide to the Social Sciences, Macdonald and Evans for the Family Welfare Association Ltd.

Holt, J (1975) Escape from Childhood: Needs and Rights of Children, Penguin Books Ltd.

Jackson, B (1980) Living with Children, Sphere Books.

MacMorland, B (1977) An ABC of Services and Information for Disabled People, third edition, London Disablement Income Group Charitable Trust Ltd.

Mollan, C (1979) Children First: A Source Book for Parents and Other Professionals, Arlen House, The Women's Press Ltd. (Deals with Ireland).

National Council of Social Services (1978) Voluntary Social Services: a Directory of Organisations, Bedford Square Press of the National Council of Social Services.

National Foundation for Educational Research (1975) Helping the Handicapped Child
I In the Family: M. Jobling.
II At School: R. Gulliford.
III In Day and Residential Care: J. Parfit.
N.F.E.R. Publishing Co.

Norton, M (1977) The Directory of Social Change, Volume 2: Community Wildwood House.

Pugh, G and Russell, P (1977) Shared Care: Support Services for Handicapped Children, National Children's Bureau.

Stone, J and Taylor, F (1977) A Handbook for Parents with a Handicapped Child, Arrow Books Ltd.

Illustrators

Ian Beck	pages 34, 190
Kate Canning	page 223
Ken Cox	pages 5, 28, 47, 103, 104, 105
Robin Harris	page 116
John Ireland	pages 101, 176
Aziz Khan	page 239
Sally Launder	pages 23, 39, 41, 95, 121, 123
Vivienne Monument	pages 236–7, 245
Graham Philpot	pages 46, 79, 128, 143
Ingram Pinn	pages 111, 193, 242
Paul Stickland	pages 58, 209, 235
Tristram Woolston	pages 21, 86, 136, 199, 241
Joe Wright	pages 18, 22, 26–7, 29, 66–7, 87, 171, 174–5
Kathy Wyatt	pages 106, 118–9, 132, 133, 165

Photographs

All photographs by David Sheppard, except the following:

page 67 Mary Evans Picture Library, pages 69 and 70 Zefa (London), page 126 GLC Photograph Library, pages 134, 136, 146, 147 John Melville, page 231 Inter-Action Trust Ltd, page 159 (inset) BBC Open University Productions (photographer David Amy), cover by Clive Boursnell.

Acknowledgements

While preparing this course, *Childhood 5–10*, the course team has drawn on a wide range of current research in the child development field. In particular, we should like to acknowledge our debt to the work of

John and Elizabeth Newson
Peter and Iona Opie
Jean Piaget
Rhona and Robert Rapaport
Jessie Reid
Jerome L. Singer

The course team would also like to say thank you to all the parents and children who have helped with the development of this course, especially the Community Education Project in Coventry. We should also like to thank all our friends in the Pre-school Playgroups Association.

The conversation on page 132 is from 'Communication Skills in Early Childhood' by Joan Tough (Schools Council Project 1976), reproduced with permission of Ward Lock Educational Ltd.

The poem on page 139 is from the Hill-Billy album number 1 'It Ain't Gonna Rain No More' by Francis Day Hunter.

The exercise on page 143 is adapted from 'Nelson's Spelling' by Denis and Helen Balance (1977), reproduced with permission of Thomas Nelson and Sons Ltd.

The words and numbers section on page 149 is from 'First Problems' by K. A. Hesse, published by the Longman Group Ltd, 1964.

The game on page 155 is from 'Let's Play Maths' by Michael Holt and Zoltan Dienes (1972), reproduced with permission of A. P. Watt and Son.